THE NATION AS A LOCAL METAPHOR

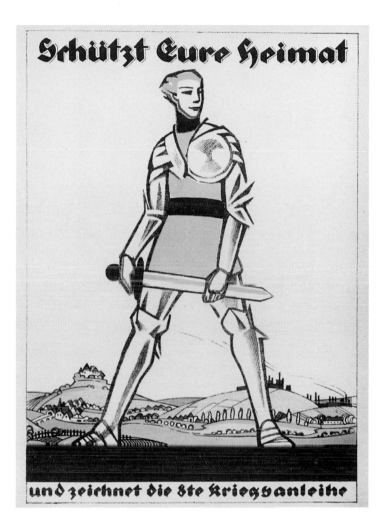

den Feinden zum Trutz / der Heimat zum Schutz

Ungeschwächte Waffen
Reichster Erntekranz
In der Heimat schaffen
Aller Augen Glanz.
Jeden muß der Ruf erreichen:
Du sollst

Kriegsanleihe
zeichnen!

Druck von W.Eisfeller, Köln.

ALON CONFINO

The Nation as a Local *M*etaphor

Württemberg, Imperial Germany,

and National Memory,

1871–1918

The University of North Carolina Press   Chapel Hill and London

© 1997 The University of North Carolina Press

All rights reserved

Designed by April Leidig-Higgins

Set in Minion by Keystone Typesetting

Manufactured in the United States of America

The paper in this book meets the guidelines for permanence and
durability of the Committee on Production Guidelines for Book Longevity
of the Council on Library Resources.

Library of Congress Cataloging-in-Publication Data

Confino, Alon.

The nation as a local metaphor : Württemberg, imperial Germany, and

national memory, 1871–1918 / by Alon Confino.

p. cm.   Includes bibliographical references and index.

ISBN 0-8078-2359-7 (cloth: alk. paper). — ISBN 0-8078-4665-1 (pbk.: alk. paper)

1. Nationalism—Germany—Württemberg. 2. National characteristics, German.

3. Württemberg (Germany)—Politics and government. 4. Germany—Politics

and government—1871–1918. I. Title.

DD801.W765C66   1997   96-52039

320.54′0943′47—dc21   CIP

01 00 99 98 97   5 4 3 2 1

Per Francesca

Contents

Illustrations

A map of Württemberg and the German Empire appears on page 18.

Preface

*I*n 1988 I began research on the ways Germans constructed a sense of nationhood after the unification in 1871. The world was then, in a sense, simpler. The East was in the east, the West to its west. Separating them was the Berlin Wall that divided Europe and the German nation. No one, at least no one that I know of, predicted any revolutionary changes in Europe's geopolitics any time soon. The question of German national identity in a postunification era belonged, I believed, to the study of the past.

And so, as I was sifting through material describing the post-1871 conflicts about German national identity—about the desirable national flag, anthem, and holiday, about the ways to invent a new past for Germans who in fact shared little of it—the 1989 revolutions swept Eastern Europe, and before long East and West Germany were unified. On the public agenda was now the character of the new Germany: how to construct a unifying past for two societies that lived apart for forty years and had to come to terms with either Nazi or Communist dictatorships, or both? Suddenly, the question of German national identity in a postunification era belonged to the present. Typically, in June and July 1990, *Die Zeit*, the distinguished German newspaper, ran articles devoted to "Symbols for the new Germany" and "How should the new Germany be called? Which anthem should it have? And which national holiday?" My object of study and people's experience outside the archive seemed to overlap in one of these rare and unexpected turns of history.

The events of 1989 took me by surprise, though an absorbing one at that. I saw some tenets of my historical thinking realized into everyday reality, when history was made by the unpredictable and unintended consequences produced by human actions and beliefs. The year 1989 resembled a revenge of history against those who attempt to confine it within a procrustean bed of single, overarching explanation; for history is also what people unexpectedly accomplish while some scholars and laypersons formulate another theory about the way it works.

This is a book about the ways in which Germans internalized the nation and made it an everyday mental property between 1871 and 1918. Modern German nationhood is an intense historical topic for scholars and the public alike because, as we know, of what came to be seen as the Ur-events in modern German history, the Third Reich and the Holocaust. Thus the historian of modern Germany must shape his or her historical understanding and narrative particularly aware of the moral and political consequences of his or her interpretation. At the same time, being conscious of how one writes and thinks about history, I informed my study on a clear yet crucial principle: Germans in imperial Germany did not know what lay in the post-1918 future. The poetic words of Alexander Herzen best reflect my way of thinking: "If humanity marched straight toward some result, there would be no history, only logic. . . . If history followed a set libretto it would lose all interest, become unnecessary, boring, ludicrous. . . . history is all improvisation, all will, all extempore—there are no frontiers, no itineraries."

Although this book focuses on Germany, my real interest was, in a sense, not so much Germany per se, but the larger problem of how and why people in the modern world become so attached to their sense of national belonging. The case of Germany served as an example to illustrate, I hope, a larger argument. My aim has been to explore nationhood with neither condemnation nor adulation. Some people—I actually know one of them, an Italian friend—profess to have no national convictions. But in our world, these persons are exotic species. For most people, the sense of national belonging commands enormous political authority and emotional profoundness. I am not interested in the manipulative and aggressive uses of nationalism in domestic and foreign policy, or in nationalism as an ideological legitimacy to terrorize other people. Rather, I explore the ways people turn national: how they devised a common denominator between their intimate local place and the abstract national world, thus transforming the nation into an everyday life experience.

I would like to thank the institutions and foundations that generously supported my study. A fellowship from the Deutsches Akademisches Auslands Dienst enabled me to conduct the research in Germany in 1988–90. My research was also assisted by a grant from the American Council of Learned Societies and the Social Science Research Council. I completed my dissertation thanks to the generous Chancellor Fellowship, John L. Simpson Fellowship at the Institute of International Studies, and Hans Rosenberg Fellowship for European Studies awarded to me by the University of California at Berkeley. I was then lucky enough to get a chance to refine this study in my own Heimat thanks to postdoctoral fellowships by the Israel Academy of Sciences and by the Institute for German History at Tel Aviv University, which conducted in 1992–93 a seminar, "Rethinking Nationalism," çochaired by Israel Gershoni and Shulamit Volkov.

I am deeply grateful to the staff of the Hauptstaatsarchiv Stuttgart and especially of the Württembergische Landesbibliothek. I could not have possibly completed my work without the assistance of librarians Marianne Janssen-Bülow, Ute Saccardi, and Doris Plankl.

It is a great pleasure for me to thank those who contributed to the making of this book over the years. I am deeply grateful, first, to Gerald Feldman, who, as my advisor at the University of California at Berkeley, followed, supported, and contributed to this project from its inception. In Germany, I was introduced to the world of Swabia by Dieter Langewiesche from the University of Tübingen. My thanks are also due to Victoria Bonnell for her generosity and intelligence. Eric Midelfort read an earlier draft of the manuscript, and fortunately did not spare me his characteristic wit and critical spirit. In Italy, where I wrote part of the book, I greatly benefited, most often over dinner in a Roman piazza, from the insights of Monica Martinat and the sagacity of Giovanni Levi. Their friendship I cherish. At the history department at the University of Virginia I found an extraordinarily congenial and stimulating environment. I am especially grateful to Melvyn Leffler, a real Mensch in a world where this quality is rare, and to Peter Onuf, who encouraged the completion of this book in more ways than he can imagine.

Many colleagues and friends showed toward me extraordinary generosity and shared with me their constructive comments and critical advice. In particular I would like to thank Celia Applegate, Edward Ayers, Saul Friedlander, Margot Fröschle, the late Amos Funkenstein, Larry Eugene Jones, Bettina and Peter Kuske, Benjamin Lapp, Vernon Lidtke, Allan Megill, Ajay Skaria, and Reginald Zelnik. For their time and insight, thanks to Lewis Bateman, Ron Maner, and the rest of the staff at the University of North Carolina Press.

With my father, Michael, I have shared a passion for history over many a conversation. Without his wisdom of things historical this book would be the poorer.

My sons, Paolo and David, were born while I was completing this book. They have impetuously conquered my mind, time, and space, and I have surrendered willingly.

The book is dedicated to Francesca Fiorani, who has enriched my world the most.

The essence of a nation is that all individuals have many
things in common, and also that they have forgotten
many things.—Ernest Renan, *What Is a Nation?* (1882)

CHAPTER ONE

Thinking about German Nationhood,

1871–1918

THINKING THE NATION

*I*n the past decade the most influential way of making sense of the sense of national belonging has been to regard the nation as a cultural artifact, as a product of invention and social engineering.[1] This "cultural turn" in the study of nationalism displaced the modernization theory, prevalent during the 1960s and 1970s, that argued that nationhood was a necessary concomitant of modernity, a form of belief produced by the cultural, economic, and technological transformation into and of modernity.[2] But in spite of the now flourishing interest in nationalism, the sense of national belonging remains a puzzling problem. This is due, in part, to the paucity of studies exploring the ways in which theories of nationalism have worked in practice in distinct countries. Perhaps more important is the failure of theory to encompass the malleability of nationhood. Scholars have usually emphasized one aspect of nationalism, such as economy and industrialization (Karl Deutsch, Ernest Gellner), ethnicity (Anthony Smith), or invention of the past (Eric Hobsbawm).[3] But nationhood defies these definitions. Although they are part of it, none fully embraces its ambiguous and often contradictory meanings. The multifariousness of nationhood is indeed striking: while it represents attachment to a defined territory, the *inter*national spread of nationalism appears to be its essence; while it is a new historical phenomenon, it is believed to be ancient; while it is part of modernity, it obsessively looks back to the past; while it yearns for the past, it simultaneously rejects the past by seeking to construct an improved version of it; while it represents the uniform nation, it tolerates a host of identities within the nation.

In order to understand the multifaceted character of nationhood and how it works, we should take note, I believe, of two features. The first is the process by which people internalize the nation. The modernization theory has been unsuccessful in providing an answer because by viewing nationhood as an inevitable product of modernization it has made national identity an inescapable progression from traditional to modern identity, whereas in reality nationhood is an irregular and uneven process in which people simultaneously embrace and repudiate the past. Scholars of the new cultural approaches to nationalism have not been more helpful. Although Eugen Weber, employing Deutsch's approach, has shown us in his study *Peasants into Frenchmen* how people pull themselves from local affairs into national affairs, we still lack a similar study that incorporates the new cultural and anthropological approaches to nationalism, delineating how people internalize the abstract world of the nation to create an imagined community.[4]

Indeed, the state of the research can be illuminated by the following example. Since 1983 Anderson's fascinating notion of the nation as an imagined community has become a household term in the way we conceive nationalism; but we still await a study that explores the process—social, political, and cultural—by which people come to imagine a distinct nation. Nationhood is a metaphor for social relations among millions of people:[5] we need a method that can tell us about the way people devise a common denominator between their intimate, immediate, and real local place and the distant, abstract, and not-less-real national world. Such a method must also be a remedy to the artificial dichotomy between nationalism from above and from below by exploring nationhood as a process by which people from all walks of life redefine concepts of space, time, and kin.

The second feature of national identity is its ability to represent the nation without excluding a host of other identities. Because it rejects other nations, national identity has often been regarded by scholars and laypersons as exclusive. The striking potential of nationhood to integrate diverse and frequently hostile groups within the nation is forgotten too easily. The full force of this fact becomes clear when we consider nationalism not as an ideology, like liberalism, fascism, or communism, but as a religion.[6] Nationalism, like religion, is a common denominator that defies gender, regional, social, and political divisions, relegating these categories to secondary position. Both are capable of representing the oneness of something, God or the nation, and simultaneously the particularity of other identities; their representation is more than the sum of the identities that coexist in them. We need a method of analyzing national society and culture that embraces both nationhood and other identities that exist in the nation.[7]

How, then, are we to look at nationhood?

I should like to consider this question by looking first at interpretations of the construction of national belonging in Germany. My aim here is neither to review the historiography of German nationalism nor to discuss the origins and disastrous consequences of the German national idea. Rather, I should like to discuss the implicit and explicit assumptions about the making of German national belonging advanced by three leading interpretations of modern German history: the modernization approach; its particular German offshoot, the *Sonderweg* interpretation; and post-*Sonderweg* historiography.

The modernization approach suggested that German nationhood was a creation of the social and economic transformation from a traditional to a modern, industrial state.[8] Challenging an earlier view, presented in the works of Hans Kohn and others, that saw nationalism as the history of an idea, this approach viewed German unification in the 1860s as the outcome of the growing economic unification since the *Zollverein*, the customs union among German states founded in 1834, and of Prussia's superior economic development and social organization.[9] The modernization approach substantially broadened our knowledge about the forces that produce national belonging: how social and economic changes pulled Germans from local to national institutions and worldviews, and how roads, schools, and military conscription developed in them a sense of community. But this approach explored the diffusion of national belonging, not its meaning. By giving a social and economic explanation, it ignored the fact that national belonging is essentially a problem of culture. And by viewing nationalism as an inevitable product of modernization, it also viewed national belonging as an immutable fixed process from traditional into modern identity, while in fact the process was full of fluctuation where people simultaneously repudiated and reclaimed past ways of life and thought.

The *Sonderweg* view centered on the notion of the peculiarity of German history, interpreted as diverging from the history of other Western countries in its inability to produce a liberal democracy. It determined a particular reading of national belonging. Setting out to explain why Nazism developed in Germany, the *Sonderweg* thesis applied modernization models of nation building to German history and suggested that aberrant German nationhood was the creation of a discrepancy in German society between modern economic development and the persistence of traditional and antidemocratic social, political, and cultural structures.[10] "Normal" nationhood, by extension, was the reflection of a simultaneous process of nation building: industrialization in the economic field, democracy in the political system, liberalism as an ideology, and the hegemony of the bourgeoisie in state and society. Compared with this yardstick of historical development, Germans' national sense of belonging was "wrong," as was the German historical development that failed to accomplish a bourgeois revolution and a democratic regime. In German society, viewed by the *Sonderweg* proponents as a closely knit entity, national feeling largely originated from the ruling elites, predominantly the Junkers, and their dominant culture. The elites manipulated national sentiments and imposed them on other segments of society through imperialism abroad and hatred of "enemies of the empire" (*Reichsfeinde*) at home, in particular Catholics and socialists.[11] The meaning of German nationalism thus became a means to divert attention from a repressive regime.

The *Sonderweg* thesis appears to be an exemplary case of the dangers of imposing an explanatory ideal-type model on the vicissitudes and contingencies of historical and human affairs; it has been less successful in exploring the changing development of German national feeling than in measuring its alleged deficiencies against "normal" development. As a consequence, the *Sonderweg* approach focused on what German nationhood was not, instead of on what it was. Perhaps more important, this perspective has treated national belonging not as a way of construing national life, but as a coercive instrument to hold power. We need to resort to a great deal of guesswork from the practice of manipulative nationalism to the reality of national identity. By interpreting national feeling as the mere product of manipulation, the *Sonderweg* thesis obscured the fundamental difference between nationhood and aggressive nationalism, for aggressive nationalism may or may not be part of nationhood, but is not equivalent to it. Moreover, the *Sonderweg* thesis has not emphasized enough the interaction between social groups that is essential to every concept of society and culture. It interpreted German national belonging as having been produced by the ruling elites in an orderly fashion and then imposed on society, while in reality it was an unpredictable process where many social groups interacted. As a result, in spite of its contribution to German historiography in various fields of research, the *Sonderweg* thesis has not bequeathed to us models for understanding the diversity of German culture and society.

The *Sonderweg* generated a historiographical reaction in the early 1980s from historians who have questioned the peculiarity of German history.[12] Unlike the *Sonderweg* historians, who were committed to social science history, the critics of the *Sonderweg* have constituted, in terms of methodology, a heterogeneous group influenced by social history, historical anthropology, and literary criticism. Post-*Sonderweg* historiography has not articulated a comprehensive interpretation of modern German history, but it has provided some illuminating new directions for understanding the German Empire. Critics have reversed the *Sonderweg* thesis's depiction of German society by emphasizing history from the bottom up, conceiving German society as a multitude of social, political, confessional, and gender groups. This approach has substantially broadened our knowledge of groups that were traditionally neglected in the historiography, such as the family, peasants, and women.[13] The comprehensive study of single social groups has received a methodological support by *Alltagsgeschichte* that traces the social and cultural everyday life experience of a defined group.[14] One result of post-*Sonderweg* historiography, therefore, has been a view of a German society fragmented into separate enclaves because critics of the *Sonderweg* have been less interested in looking at German society as a whole than in exploring the subjective experience of its component parts. As a result, no comprehensive view has emerged of the social and cultural factors that created among diverse and opposed groups a feeling of belonging together as Germans; topics about cultural common denominators in German society have been left unresearched.

The three approaches have bequeathed a number of problems to the study of national belonging in the German Empire. The modernization and the *Sonderweg* approaches shifted the meaning of Germans' national belonging away from what actually happened in the empire. The first focused on the origins of national belonging, the second on its outcome, Nazism, thus making the actual experience of its construction insignificant. In consequence, we know very little about how Germans actually internalized the nation. The *Sonderweg* and the post-*Sonderweg* historiographies have not provided an analysis of German society and culture that embraces both nationhood and other identities that existed in the nation. The *Sonderweg* approach regarded German society as a whole, as a global entity, and German identity as dominated by Prussia and the Junkers, thus largely failing to look at the various modes and types of relationships between the component parts of German society and culture, between the multitude of social, regional, and confessional identities in German nationhood. Post-*Sonderweg* historiography looked at the component parts, but did not provide a view of German society and identity as a whole. Both interpretations failed to convey the exceptional characteristic of national identity, that is, its successful attempt to represent both the nation and the peculiarity of other identities.

How, then, are we to look at German nationhood in particular and at nationhood in general? I suggest viewing it from the perspective of collective memory, as a product of collective negotiation and exchange between the many memories that existed in the nation. It is a developmental approach to the history of German nationhood, emphasizing the contingencies in its construction. By stressing the interaction between national memory and other memories, this approach explores nationhood through the metaphor of whole and parts, taking cognizance of German identity and German society as a global entity where peculiar component parts interacted.

The notion of collective memory has been used in the past decade, with uneven degrees of success and sophistication, to explore how a social group, be it a family, a class, or a nation, constructs a past through a process of invention and appropriation and what it means to the relationship of power within society. The notion of memory has been a latecomer in historical studies.[15] Historians were preceded by psychoanalysts (Sigmund Freud), philosophers (Henri Bergson), and writers (such as Marcel Proust), who, unlike historians, regarded memory as a faculty of the individual mind; by anthropologists, who found memory a more suitable concept than history to understanding illiterate societies (Jack Goody); and by sociologists (Maurice Halbwachs and Roger Bastide).[16] The first to have used the concept systematically was Halbwachs, whose fundamental contribution was to establish the connection between a social group and collective memory. In a series of studies Halbwachs argued that every memory is carried by a specific social group limited in space and time.[17]

Of course, social groups cannot remember, for this is only a faculty of the individual.[18] And certainly, people cannot remember events in which they did not take part. Yet you do not need to have stormed the Bastille in order to celebrate 14 July as a symbol of national identity. One's memory, like one's most intimate dreams, originates from the symbols, landscape, and past that are shared by a given society. Since the making and the reception of memories, personal and collective, are embedded in a specific cultural, social, and political context, we can explore how people construct a past in which they did not take part individually, but which they share with other members of their group as a formative sense of cultural knowledge, tradition, and singularity.

Building on the new and increasing body of literature, I find collective memory useful for elucidating the two features of nationhood I mentioned earlier.[19] It allows us, first, to explore the relationships between national belonging and the host of identities that exist in the nation. The nation is a conglomeration of opposing and at times contradictory memories (such as national and regional, Catholic and Protestant, bourgeois and working class) that—in spite of their confrontations—add up into something that is bigger than the sum of its parts. The concept of collective memory allows us to explore how opposing memories construct a national memory, and how national memory and other memories exist in tension but without breaking. When they do break, sometimes nations break up. In Germany, as we shall see, local memories were strong after the unification in 1871, and stood in the way of creating a unifying national memory. This study explores the negotiations between local memory and national memory and how the multitude of local memories in Germany constructed a local-national memory.[20] In this respect,

I am not so much interested in Württemberg local memory or German national memory per se, but in their meeting point—where antagonism and friction reconciled in the end through a process of remembrance and forgetfulness in the Heimat idea as an image of the German locality, region, and nation.[21]

Here I would like to underline a point that, I believe, has too often been overlooked in the study of collective memory, and which is meaningful for this study. One of the essential and significant points made in recent studies has been to emphasize the conflicts that are inherent in the construction of memory. Memory is a subjective experience of a social group that essentially sustains a relationship of power. Simply stated, it is who wants whom to remember what, and why.[22] This has been a leading theme, perhaps *the* leading theme, in the growing body of literature about memory. Because memory attempts to sustain a relationship of power, the construction of memory emerges as a contested process, as a social, cultural, and political conflict to define the "correct" image of the past. This theme is no doubt illuminating to our understanding of the functions and meanings of collective memory. But it seems to me only partially illuminating. Conflicts are certainly embedded in the meanings of collective memory. But this only begs the question: how then, *in spite* of the conflicts, does a nation hold together? What were the common denominators that united Germans across social, religious, and, most significant for this study, regional differences? Without ignoring the conflicts generated by the production, reception, and representation of collective memory, this study seeks to illuminate what I call the common denominators of variousness among regional Germans.

Collective memory is also useful, secondly, to explore how people internalize the nation. I use collective memory as a tool to explore the everyday level of perceptions of the past: how an image of the past endures in material objects of everyday life.[23] What was the lasting image of the nation in the mind of Germans in everyday life during the long, peaceful, "normal" period of 1871 to 1914 and then during the turbulent First World War?[24] My aim is to show how the everyday plane of the mental internalized and represented the abstract notion of nation. Let me illustrate this by giving the example of Heimat iconography. Heimatlers produced a visual image of the nation that represented interchangeably the locality, the region, and the nation. This image was a fundamental vehicle for internalizing the impersonal nation by placing it within the familiar local world. Arousing sentiments of patriotism, sacrifice, and sacredness that nations often evoke, the image was a unifying symbol of the First World War campaign for war loans (*Kriegsanleihe*). At the same time, it also became part of the mundane life of entertainment, vacations, and tourism. Heimat images appeared on posters, postcards, newspapers, journals, publications of Heimat associations, school textbooks, Heimat books, and Heimat museums. Significantly, the worldliness and everyday use of the Heimat image reached a peak when it was adopted by associations for the promotion of tourism (*Fremdenverkehrsvereine*): Heimat images became a necessary part of travel guides, and Heimat posters were placed in German train stations, pubs, restaurants, tourist sites, and other public places. The Heimat image brought the nation to mind anytime and anywhere, without special celebratory events, as the humble sources of Heimat iconography and the pedestrian occasions in which it appeared show.

Eventually, Germans internalized the nation and made it an everyday mental property: they carried its image in their heads. I use collective memory to explore how Germans visualized the homeland in the imagination. Halbwachs elaborated the relations between landscape and memory in *The Legendary Topography of the Gospels in the Holy Land*, a study of the changing sacred topography of Palestine in the imagery of Christian communities in the West.[25] Although the link between landscape and memory appears fundamental, it has not been systematically taken up by scholars.[26] In spite of the growing research on nationalism, we actually know very little about how people visualize their homelands. In other fields scholars took to studying the image of a different kind of holy and not so holy homelands in the minds of Christians—heaven and purgatory—depicting how Christians visualized, in words and images, life after death in God's sacred territories.[27] We should think of national memory also as an iconographic process. How do people construct a collective image of this modern sacred territory, the national territory? More specific to our topic, how did Germans construct a collective image of the nation?

To answer this question I suggest expanding the notion of national memory to embrace also the notion of imagined community, so that memory can tell us not only what people remembered of the past, but also how they internalized an impersonal world by putting it in familiar and intelligible categories. Anderson described a similar process: the nation "is imagined because the members of even the smallest nation will never know most of their fellow members . . . yet in the minds of each lives the image of their communion," or, we may say, the image of their national memory.[28] By combining the notions of national memory and imagined community we can understand how people visualize the impersonal nation: how Germans created an iconographic stereotypization of Germans and German landscapes that united local and national memories.[29]

The recent upsurge in the study of collective memory has produced illuminating results, and also some confusion. "Social memory" and "cultural memory" are often used terms in the literature, but, inasmuch as they wish to emphasize that memory is socially and culturally situated, the adjectives "social" and "cultural" are redundant. Everything is. Michael Kammen in his encyclopedic study of American memory distinguished between collective memory as "usually a code phrase for what is remembered by the dominant civic culture" and popular memory as "usually referring to ordinary folks." This distinction is anything but helpful because ordinary folks also possess collective memory.[30] Scholars have used the term collective memory to denote very different things. Take Holocaust memory, for example. Here the concept has been used to explore, first, the memory of survivors who actually experienced the Holocaust. In addition, the concept came to denote the memory of the Holocaust by successive generations in books, images, and cinema. And it has been used to describe the perceptions of historians and intellectuals about the Holocaust, notably in the *Historikerstreit*, the West German Historians' Dispute in the mid-1980s about the historicization of the Third Reich and the uniqueness of the Holocaust.[31] Methodologically, the use of collective memory has been very loose, and it often functioned as an embellishment or a catchall term for the traditionally distinguished "perceptions of the past." In the Historians' Dispute in particular, "memory" was used with abandon. But in spite of these problems collective memory has been extremely useful as a tool to think about how people construct pasts, and doubtless part of its success has been its open-endedness, namely that it is applicable to historical situations and human conditions in diverse societies and periods.[32]

I use collective memory in this study as a tool to get at a component of the historical mentality of Germans in the past, namely that which concerned local-national memory. I view memory as a symbolic representation of tradition and of the past embedded in the context of social action. Differently put, the study of collective memory explores the experiential history of people's perceptions of the past where social action and symbolic representation commingle. The notion of collective memory is interesting and useful in that it can tell us not only about how the past is represented in a single museum or commemoration but about the role of the past in the life of a social group. In the study of collective memory we should look not only at the representation of the past, but also at its rejection and reception. Every society sets up imagined pasts. But to make a difference in a society, it is not enough for a certain past to be selected. It must steer emotions, motivate people to act, be received; in short, it must become a sociocultural mode of action. Why is it that some pasts triumph while others fail? Why do people prefer one invented past over another? The answers to these questions lead us to formulate hypotheses and perhaps draw conclusions about historical mentality. I attempt to answer these questions about the symbolic representations of the German nation in Sedan Day and in the Heimat idea, and to explain why Germans rejected the former while accepting the latter. In other words, attempting to go beyond the study of the image of the past and of who wished whom to remember what and why, I attempt to illuminate *how* local-national memory in Germany between 1871 and 1918 was transformed, and *why*.

The relation between history and memory is fundamental to every study of memory. This relation has been discussed by Maurice Halbwachs and Pierre Nora as forms of historically situated social practice. Their basic argument has been that memory belonged to a premodern society where tradition was strong and memory was a social practice, whereas the discipline of history, emerging in the nineteenth century, belonged to modern society where tradition declined and relations to the past were cut off by the "acceleration of history."[33] Halbwachs sharply distinguished between history as a scientific rendition of the past and memory as a malleable one.[34] For Nora, history and memory were united before the development of scientific history in the nineteenth century and have been split since. Consequently, he distinguished between a premodern memory as a social practice, a milieu of memory, and a modern memory as voluntary and deliberate.[35]

Almost no historian would subscribe today to Halbwachs's view of history as a scientific discipline and to the consequent sharp division between history and memory. Collective memory both differs from and converges with history. Memory is a malleable understanding of the past that is different from history because its construction is not bounded by a set of limiting disciplinary rules. Invented pasts are characterized by features that historians attempt to avoid in their studies: anachronism, topocentricity, presentism. Of course, history is also a malleable understanding of the past but it is governed, with varying degrees of success and problems, by rules of evidence and verification. Memory and history converge because the historian conceives of his or her story within the general image of the past shared by society, within a collective historical mentality. The historian's task is to reveal the connections between memory and history without obscuring their differences.

The relations between history and memory have received considerable attention in recent years. Yet no less important is the argument made by Halbwachs and Nora, which assigned memory and history to specific historical periods. The idea that we live in an age of manufactured history that has displaced memory as a social practice seems to me a reflection of either an excessive belief in the power of scientific history (Halbwachs) or a nostalgic view of putative authentic relations in premodern society between people and their past (Nora). Behind Nora's distinction of premodern memory as a social practice and modern memory as deliberate is a rather sentimental view of premodern society as a world of unmediated relations to the past. I agree that modern memory is fundamentally different from premodern memory because its essence, I believe, lies in expansion and proliferation as mass media produce and commercialize an ever growing number of collective memories and turn the past into a commodity for mass consumption. But this does not prevent a group of people in modern society from creating a milieu of memory based on social practice. I will attempt to show how bourgeois Germans in the

Second Empire created a social milieu of Heimat memory and how this memory was both different from and similar to the popular national history of the time represented by Heinrich von Treitschke.

In German historiography, the concept of collective memory has been largely limited to studying the ways the Third Reich has been remembered, with two consequent results. On the one hand, a fast-growing literature has substantially contributed to our understanding of the Holocaust and of the reception of the Nazi past in the former West Germany.[36] On the other hand, the historical memory of other subjects by other Germans in other times has been largely disregarded in historical studies.[37] We have neither a comprehensive project on German national memory similar to Pierre Nora's of France, nor monographs on discrete topics. This study is an attempt in this direction, and traces the fabrication of a mythical local-national memory, the "invention of tradition" in Eric Hobsbawm's splendid phrase, new as the nation-state, yet believed by Germans to exist from time immemorial.[38] Shortly before he died, Norbert Elias spelled out the foundation of his book *The Germans*: "in the case of the West Germans, any consideration of the national habitus trespasses into a taboo zone. The hypersensitivity towards anything that recalls National Socialist doctrine results in the problem of a 'national character' being largely shrouded in silence."[39] In the light of these remarks I believe we should introduce to German historiography the notion of collective memory as a historical research tool and as a theme of research in German history as a whole. What, then, was the matrix of German memory in the new nation-state?

GERMAN NATIONAL MEMORY, 1871

Germany's modern national memory began in 1871. Before 1871 there was a history of the Germans and German history, but no history of Germany; only thereafter did German history proceed as a single development. As James Sheehan has aptly said, before 1871 " 'Germany' did not exist. . . . there was no clear and readily acceptable answer to the question of Germany's political, social, and cultural identity. German history, therefore, [was] not the single story of a fixed entity . . . [but] many different histories that coexisted."[40] The unification of 1871, therefore, joining the German nation, German society, and a German state within a single territory, redefined the spatial and historical dimensions of the nation and the ways Germans remembered their pasts. To be sure, Germans had national recollections before 1871, but the foundation of the nation-state conditioned a reevaluation of old memories as never before. To suppose otherwise is to view German history and German national memory as predetermined; but, on the contrary, before the Prussian-Austrian War in 1866 the exclusion of Austrian history, the hegemony of Prussian history, and the superiority of Protestant to Catholic memories, to mention only a few notable examples, were not inevitable for German nationhood.[41]

At the same time, in spite of the unification of the nation-state, German nationhood continued to exist as a patchwork of regions and states, a mosaic of divergent historical and cultural heritages sanctioned by the nation-state's federal system. While the regional states lost their sovereignty, they maintained their preunification structure including a head of state, symbols, a Landtag (regional parliament), a government, a bureaucracy, and peculiar laws. Of course, slowly in the 1870s and more effectively from the 1880s, institutions were developed on the Reich level that introduced standardization throughout the empire. One can think of the standardization of currency, weights, and measures put into effect in 1873, or of the more complex and gradual system-atization of law and the court system. But in general, standardization in important fields such as education, social policy, economic policy, national symbols, and also courts and jurisdiction proceeded little by little; the constitution of 1871 left policy in these and other matters largely to the choice of the states.[42] Perhaps the most revealing element of this Matryoshka-doll principle of German nationhood was the multitude of political systems in the empire. In Germany, as in the United States, the empire had one political system, while every region kept its own traditional one. As a consequence, the empire had an authoritarian political system based on free male suffrage and a Reichstag that had little real power to influence the government and the emperor; Prussia had a conservative and antidemocratic three-class suffrage system designed to keep the Junkers in power; and Württemberg enjoyed a more liberal and democratic political system. These incompatible political systems and cultures coexisted. The high level of regional fragmentation reflected the diversity of regional identities and their autonomy with respect to national identity.[43]

Among the many peculiarities that have recently been attributed to German history, this was a genuinely distinctive feature—for no European people set up a nation-state as a conglomeration of regional *states*.[44] Regional diversity, of course, has been a common feature in the European nation-states, and over-lapping regional and national allegiances were not at all unusual. An obvious case was Italy, unified between 1860 and 1870 from as many regions as Germany, which had to cope with a tremendous level of regional fragmentation between North and South. But even nineteenth-century Britain, which is often viewed as enjoying a progressive integration, knew a similar phenomenon. Victorians strongly perceived national diversity between North and South in England, between London and the provinces, and between the distinct national identities of Scotland, Wales, and England.[45] In Germany, however, regional diversity was institutionalized in regional states. Maintaining such a level of regional variegation and autonomy within the nation was more than simply acknowledging regional differences, which were also acknowledged in countries that did not have the German form of nationhood. It was rather a reflection of the essence of the nation as a whole composed of regional identities, and, by extension, of the locality and the region as the cradle of German nationhood.[46]

The notion of collective memory enables us to reinterpret the unification of 1871 and the regional fragmentation of Germany within the context of consciousness of national belonging. What Ferdinando Martini, secretary of education, declared during the patriotic outburst following the humiliating Italian defeat at Adua in 1896—"We have made Italy: now we must make Italians"— applied after 1871 to regional Germans: they had made Germany, now they had to make Germans from the multitude of regional identities, Germans who would be attached to the region as well as to the nation-state, not ceasing to be local patriots but acknowledging the supremacy of national patriotism.[47]

In spite of a shared national feeling, Germans of diverse regions disagreed over fundamental issues of national identity. Preunification regional memories needed to be transformed in order to fit the new requirements of the nation-state. In the civil war of 1866, for example, only five years before the unification, Germans killed each other over the future formation of the nation. Prussia's victory imposed the *Kleindeutschland* solution (Smaller Germany: the unification of Germany under the hegemony of Protestant Prussia and the exclusion of Catholic Austria from German affairs) against the opposition of Austria and the small German states. To share a common past, Germans needed to modify, perhaps even obliterate, this memory. Prussians needed to forget the victory, citizens of the small German states to forget the defeat, and all to forget Austria. Moreover, the memory of the lost sovereignty of the regional state stood in potential contradiction to the sovereignty of the nation. All Germans needed to reconcile regional memories and the new national one: particularists who hung on to the memory of the independent region and supporters of the empire who looked for a modus vivendi between region and nation. To be German after 1871, therefore, meant to have a national history that was a single development composed of a multitude of regional histories. The Bismarckian nation-state demanded a monopoly of national loyalty, but without demolishing regional identities. The problem was, how to construct a national memory that would reconcile the peculiarities of the region and the totality of the nation?

WÜRTTEMBERG, 1871

A study of German national memory that takes as a point of departure the region is thus a methodological choice determined by German historical reality. In light of these considerations, I chose to undertake a regional study of the

South German state of Württemberg and to explore how Württembergers turned German, or, more precisely, how Württembergers, who were already some kind of Germans before 1871, turned into a different kind of Germans by reconstructing their regional and national memories. Württembergers did not completely change after 1871, but they did not remain the same either: they lost some of their old regional peculiarities and integrated them into a new German belonging. It should be underlined that in principle any region in Germany is as fruitful a topic of study as Württemberg, for Germans in every region needed to refashion their memories.

I view the construction of national memory from regional memories as a contested process that was articulated along two binary oppositions—center/ periphery and uniformity/diversity. The center/periphery opposition gave a new meaning to Goethe and Schiller's famous quandary formulated in 1796 at the dawn of nationalism in Europe and Germany: "Germany? But where is it? I do not know how to find the country." It provided a certain answer to the origins of the nation: were they to be found in Berlin or Stuttgart, in Prussia or Württemberg, or perhaps in the small local places of *l'Allemagne profonde*? The opposition uniformity/diversity provided a certain answer to the appropriate relations between the heterogeneity of the regions and the aspired homogeneity of the nation. This study traces the answers given by Württembergers, and how they drew a common denominator between their immediate local world and the abstract national one.

The modern history of Württemberg began, like the history of modern Europe, with the French Revolution and its aftermath.[48] Under Napoleon's pressure, the Duchy of Württemberg, ruled by Frederick II, joined France in 1805 in the campaign against Austria and Russia. After the military victory Württemberg was generously rewarded by Napoleon, who created from the Southwestern German states the Confederation of the Rhine as a counterweight to the power of Prussia and Austria in Germany: Württemberg gained territory, especially at the expense of Austria, and was elevated into a kingdom. While Frederick, now the king of Württemberg, and Napoleon maintained close relations (they called each other *mon frère*), Württembergers contributed to the defeat of Prussia in 1806–7 and fought in the German Wars of Liberation, in particular the Battle of Nations in 1813, against their fellow Germans.[49] The Napoleonic Wars resulted in prestige and power for the Württemberg state, but also revealed the tortuous and multifaceted relations in the nineteenth century between Württemberg identity and German national identity. The debate over the proper way to connect these two identities was, in a sense, the story of Württemberg's identity from 1805 to 1871.

Württemberg extended between Switzerland, the Swabian Jura (*Schwäbischer Alb*) and Lake Constance in the south, the Black Forest and Baden in the west and northwest, and Bavaria in the east and northeast. The Swabians, the people of Württemberg, prided themselves on having one of the most distinguished and significant histories among German regions.[50] The cradle of five important imperial and royal lineages—the Hohenstaufen, the Guelphs, the Zollern, the Habsburg, and the Zähring—Swabia was a territory replete with German history. After 1871 the Swabians especially liked to emphasize that the Prussian royal house, the Hohenzollern, which was called Zollern before the name was changed in the mid-sixteenth century, originated in Swabia. Swabians held in high esteem their contributions to German culture, which included the poets Friedrich Schiller, Ludwig Uhland, Gustav Schwab, Eduard Mörike, Ferdinand Freiligrath, Friedrich Karl von Gerok, and Friedrich Hölderlin, the Heimat writer Bertold Auerbach, the activist for Germany's economic integration Friedrich List, and G. W. F. Hegel.

During the Reformation large parts of Württemberg turned Protestant, in particular the traditional heart of the region, the areas of Stuttgart, Heilbronn, Tübingen, and Calw, also called *Alt Württemberg*, or old Württemberg. Not all Württembergers, however, were Protestants; some remained proudly Catholic while maintaining their Swabian identity (Schwäbisch Gmünd comes immediately to mind), and although they lived in a state dominated by Protestants, from the king downward, relations between Catholics and Protestants were relatively peaceful. In addition, the territories gained during the Napoleonic Wars were mostly inhabited by Catholics in Oberschwaben, who as newcomers remained somewhat on the margins of the Württemberg state.[51] Similar to the empire, the ratio in Württemberg between Protestants and Catholics was 2:1. This datum strengthens the choice of Württemberg as a topic of regional study of German national memory. Christian interconfessional relations were one of the fundamental issues in German society, and a study of a region that included both confessional communities is essential to understand German identity. Catholics in Württemberg, as in other German states, looked in the nineteenth century to Catholic Austria as a cultural, religious, and political point of reference, in particular once the possibility of a German unification under the leadership of Protestant Prussia became more real.

The debate in Württemberg on the proper way to place local identity within German identity was significant to German national memory because it emphasized particularism and anti-Prussianism, especially in the 1860s when a Prussian solution to the German Question appeared in the making. King William I, who reigned between 1816 and 1864, was known to have said in the beginning of the 1860s, "Better be an ally of France than the vassal of Prussia."[52] King Karl I, who reigned until 1891, shared this idea, and one of his first acts was to change the uniforms of the army, making them look virtually identical to the uniforms of the Austrian army.[53] In the context of the Prussian-Austrian dispute over Schleswig-Holstein, this act was a clear sign of the king's political preference. The government, the state bureaucracy, particularists, and

Württemberg and the German Empire, 1871–1918

German Nationhood, 1871–1918

EAST PRUSSIA

A

RUSSIA

Neckarsulm   Öhringen
                            Crailsheim
        Heilbronn   Hall

    Marbach   WÜRTTEMBERG
                                Ellwangen

                                Aalen
                    Cannstatt   Gmünd
    Stuttgart   Esslingen   Neresheim
Calw   Göppingen

            Kirchheim   Heidenheim
        Herrenberg
Nagold   Tübingen   Nürtingen
    Horb   Reutlingen

        HOHENZOLLERN   Ulm
Sulz

                    Ehingen
    Rottweil
                Riedlingen
                        Biberach
                Saulgau

Tuttlingen   Waldsee

                        Leutkirch

            Ravensburg
                Tettnang   Isny
                        Wangen

Catholics shared *Großdeutsch* (Larger Germany) sentiments, that is, support of Austria and of the independence of the small German states and opposed *Kleindeutschland*, that is, a Germany without Austria under the hegemony of Protestant Prussia.

Members of the politically active bourgeoisie in Württemberg were organized in the liberal and democratic parties.[54] After a short period of cooperation in the late 1850s, based on agreements over domestic political issues, the liberals and democrats split over the national issue. In 1864 the democrats founded the Volkspartei, whose policy was expressed clearly by its leader, Carl Mayer: "Today the national question appears in the foreground. Whenever the national principle and the issue of freedom come into conflict, our [party] will be on the side of freedom."[55] The democrats opposed the *Kleindeutschland* idea and propagated the Third Way to solve the German Question, a federation of the South German states as a counterweight to Austria and Prussia. The liberals, who founded in 1866 the Deutsche Partei that was connected to the German National Liberal Party, supported an immediate unification under Prussia's leadership. The deep-seated particularist feelings in Württemberg in the 1860s aggregated in the party not only liberals, but also other groups that supported the *Kleindeutsch* idea, such as Pietists.

The Gordian knot of the German Question was cut in the summer of 1866 in Königgrätz. Württemberg, like the rest of the small German states, fought on the side of Austria against Prussia, and lost the war. After the German civil war, the exclusion of Austria from Germany and the foundation of the North German Federation headed by Prussia exacerbated anti-Prussian sentiments. The Volkspartei became the leading political force in the land, while the political support of the Deutsche Partei was described by Julius Hölder, a liberal leader, as "horrifying."[56] The democrats and the *Großdeutsche Klub*, a group of Catholic and conservative opponents of Prussia, campaigned against the defense treaty between Württemberg and Prussia signed in August 1866 and against the renewal of the Customs Union (*Zollverein*) demanded by Prussia. The Deutsche Partei, in contrast, supported both agreements. As a political and national answer to the North German Federation, democrats proposed a South German Federation with Austria and the solution of the German Question in an alliance between the independent South German and North German Federations. In spite of this opposition, the government and Landtag approved the agreements with Prussia because after 1866 Württemberg's political options were limited. The year 1868, however, gave two important occasions to measure the public mood about national unification. In the election for the Customs Union parliament at the beginning of the year, democrats and *Großdeutsche* won all seats, except six seats that went to government candidates, while the Deutsche Partei was unable to put through even one candidate.

In the Landtag election in December of the same year the democrats and *Großdeutsche* won a landslide, taking 40 seats to 14 of the Deutsche Partei.

The war against France in 1870–71 changed the course of German history, and also of Württemberg history. Whereas in 1866 opponents of *Kleindeutschland* blamed the war on Prussia, in 1871 all, including democrats and *Großdeutsche*, were convinced that France bore the responsibility for the conflict. Even the democrats were reluctant to see France occupying their land. National enthusiasm grew under the impact of the military victories. A Landtag election was called in December 1870, after the battle of Sedan in September 1870 and before the declaration of the empire in January 1871, to approve national unification.[57] The Deutsche Partei campaigned under the slogan: "Are you in favor of entering the North German Federation?" The response was yes, and the Deutsche Partei increased its seats from 14 to 30, while the democrats dropped from 40 to 17 seats. By voting for German national unification, however, Württembergers did not abandon their individual identity, but expressed a German national feeling that was impossible to negate in 1870–71. Their problem of how to reconcile local and national identities was not resolved in the Landtag election in 1870; rather it only began.

In spite of the novelty of 1871, it seemed that *plus ça change plus c'est la même chose*. Württemberg entered the German Empire retaining its royal house, king, Landtag, and constitution. Württemberg kept its regional symbols, and its coins portrayed the profile of King Karl, not of Emperor William I, since coins in the empire portrayed the regional sovereign. According to the agreement with Bismarck, Württemberg had its own stamps, and independent postal and railway services. The empire was especially absent on the local level. The school system and school textbooks remained unchanged, and the empire had only limited legislative power in Württemberg. Even the Prussian-German army after 1871 was not a perfect means of national integration, as one might have expected from the institution whose role in Prussian society was to educate the nation. The Württemberg army was incorporated into the Prussian-German army as the XIII Württemberg Army Division, a separate unit that kept intact its old structure and personnel. To be sure, according to the empire's constitution the command of the German army rested with the Prussian king in war and peace, and Prussian personnel and methods increasingly enjoyed influence in the XIII Württemberg Army Division, but the Württemberg army still maintained a significant autonomy. Württemberg retained its war minister, underlining the uniqueness of its military tradition within the nation. Most important, the consequence of building a distinct Württemberg unit within the German army was that soldiers from Württemberg did not mix with soldiers from other German regions as happened, for example, in the French and Russian armies.[58]

Moreover, Württemberg's policy after 1871 was to cooperate with Bismarck but at the same time to safeguard—assiduously and steadfastly, but within the political limits of the new empire—any encroachment upon its institutions and independence. To the liberals' disappointment, the king and the royal court remained opponents of the unification and of Prussia.[59] Consequently, the king entrusted the direction of Württemberg's policy to Prime Minister Baron Hermann von Mittnacht, a *Großdeutscher*.[60] The nomination of Mittnacht was significant not only because it showed the particularistic sentiments in Württemberg, but also because he was a Catholic. While Prussia and other German states in the empire waged in the 1870s and 1880s the *Kulturkampf*—the campaign orchestrated by Bismarck and the German liberals against the Catholic Church and political Catholicism—Württemberg remained, in the words of Karl Bachem, the historian of the Catholic Center Party, "an oasis of peace."[61] A number of reasons contributed to this peculiarity. Protestants in Württemberg never felt threatened by Catholics because of the strong Protestant identity of Old Württemberg and of the tight control of the state over the Catholic population. In addition, the *Kulturkampf* was viewed by democrats, particularists, and Catholics as a Prussian affair, a result of Prussian authoritarianism and liberals' anti-Catholicism that contradicted the democratic tradition of Württemberg. Finally, many Protestants in Württemberg, such as the democrats, shared with Catholics *Großdeutsch* political ideas, making the national issue, not the religious one, the main dividing line in Württemberg society. *Großdeutsch* and anti-Prussian Protestants and Catholics allied to prevent liberals from fomenting the *Kulturkampf*, for many a symbol of the new Germany, of Bismarck, of Prussia, and of religious intolerance.

Three major attitudes to the German Empire coexisted in Württemberg after the unification. *Großdeutscher*, conservatives, and loyalists of the royal house, represented in the Landespartei (the party of Mittnacht, the Catholics, and a large part of the state administration), accepted the nation-state as a fait accompli: without enthusiasm, but recognizing that cooperation with Bismarck was the only way to safeguard Württemberg's peculiarity. Democrats, after a period of inactivity following the shock of the unification, assumed the role of a vocal and radical opposition to Prussia and the empire's authoritarian system. Finally, in a society impregnated with particularism, the liberals and other supporters of the empire took upon themselves to be the agents of the nation-state in local life.

Württemberg, 1871, is the point of departure of this study. Evidently, the heritage Württemberg brought into imperial Germany was a difficult one to reconcile with Prussia and *Kleindeutschland*. Württemberg society itself was deeply divided over the national issue, and remained so after 1871. Otto Elben, a most influential man in Württemberg, a leader of the Deutsche Partei, a member of the Landtag and the Reichstag, and the editor of the *Schwäbische*

Kronik, the most important newspaper in Württemberg, jubilantly described his sentiments after Württemberg's entry into the empire: "A happy German is writing you: we are Germans, entering into the solid Federation of our brothers."[62] Württembergers were Germans, but what kind of Germans was still to be determined.

PART ONE

Germany and Württemberg:
An Uncomfortable Coexistence in Sedan Day

The Nation in the Locality

On 2 September 1873, at eight-thirty in the morning, some 700 people gathered in the marketplace at Langenau to celebrate Sedan Day. The ceremony included greetings by the mayor of this community of about 3,655 inhabitants, followed by a prayer, patriotic songs, and the unveiling of the Veterans Association's flag. After a ceremonious lunch a procession took off through the town streets led by the schoolchildren with their teachers, followed by thirty-eight young ladies—some dressed in white with black-white-red scarves and some in "our rustic national costume"—clergymen, members of the town assembly and associations, visiting veterans associations, and citizens.[1] This impressive participation was not uncommon in the 1870s and 1880s when Württembergers celebrated on Sedan Day, as one teacher in Stuttgart explained to his students, "the refoundation of the German Empire . . . so that now we know the correct answer to the question 'Was ist des Deutschen Vaterland?' " (meaning: how far does it extend?).[2] He referred, of course, to Moritz Arndt's famous song of the 1813–15 Wars of Liberation against Napoleon: "What is the German fatherland? / Is it Prussia, is it Swabia? / . . . / O no! No! No! / . . . / Entire Germany should it be!"[3]

There was nothing peculiar about Germans celebrating a national holiday after the unification in 1871; nation-states commonly set up a national holiday to forge national identity. What demands explanation is why twenty-four years later, in 1897, a restaurant in Heilbronn (population 33,000) was considered large enough to contain the local celebrants of Sedan Day.[4] It is not because German national feelings had diminished or disappeared. In the following pages I explore the celebration of Sedan Day as a vehicle to understand the spasmodic and contested process by which provincial Germans attempted to construct notions of nationhood and localness during the 1870s and 1880s. The liberal bourgeoisie, the originators of the holiday in Württemberg, forged in

Sedan Day a national identity that reflected their values and aspirations. As supporters of the *Kleindeutsch* solution to the German Question before 1871, they felt vindicated after the creation of the nation-state and devised the holiday as a way to speak for the nation. But Catholics, socialists, particularists, and democrats opposed and boycotted the holiday. Democrats, especially, were successful in delegitimizing the liberals and their holiday by evoking local identity: "We have people in Württemberg who ceased to be Württembergers, but instead became totally Prussian. These people support wholeheartedly the Sedan Day celebrations."[5]

This judgment, made in 1873, was a strong condemnation in particularistic Württemberg. Why did Sedan Say initially succeed and ultimately fail? Why did it encounter fierce opposition? And how did the liberals represent the nation in the celebrations? Was it as an integrated community of all the Germans, or as an exclusive community that projected an image of a disunited nation? The celebrants of Sedan Day gave to German history and German identity a controversial interpretation, and thus, because of the holiday, different ideas, wishes, and apprehensions within German society collided over the construction of a post-1871 national community.

Although there has recently been a growing interest in the study of German national celebrations and their relations to political culture and collective identity, the celebrations of Sedan Day have remained marginal in the historiography of the German Empire.[6] Hermann Hesse recalled Sedan Day in his Swabian hometown Calw as "splendidly celebrated."[7] But most historians have either condemned the holiday as dull and insignificant or deplored it as a proof of Prussian-stifling official culture, or, most commonly, disregarded it altogether.[8] The general picture of Sedan Day that emerges from recent literature is that the holiday "had been organized from above in a conservative manner, had stressed discipline, and gradually excluded popular participation."[9] It was "ordered and initiated by the political establishment with the sole purpose of consolidating and glorifying the power of the regime."[10] Therefore, according to this view, it comes as no surprise that public ceremonies of Sedan Day were centered around the military,[11] and were "glittering but empty spectacles of imperial pomp and power."[12]

This discouraging historiography conveys indifference. Participants were indifferent, spectators were indifferent, and, maybe most of all, historians have been indifferent. So was Hesse fantasizing? Or does the paucity of research on Sedan Day raise serious doubts about the current historiography? The problem of the Sedan Day historiography is that it has told us *wie es eigentlich nicht gewesen ist*, instead of telling us how the national holiday shaped and reflected Germans' conceptions of their history and values. The historiography considered Sedan Day as a functional model, and has transformed the success or failure of the holiday as an integrative force into a yardstick for evaluating its meaning. As a consequence, since the holiday failed it was also viewed as meaningless; but what meaning it had even if it failed—and it did—we don't know. The functional model has emphasized two moments in the holiday's lifetime—birth and death—and has thus made the actual experience of the celebrations inconsequential. At the one end of the holiday's lifetime, historians have looked at the intentions and projects of the originators in 1871–73. On the other end of the holiday's lifetime, they have assessed the effects of the holiday's failure in the 1890s on the integration of German society.[13] But we know virtually nothing about the ways Germans celebrated and opposed the celebrations of Sedan Day beyond general characterizations of the celebrations as not being dynamic, inspirational, and spontaneous.[14] As a result, we have a holiday with no celebrants and no celebrations.

Another problem with the historiography of Sedan Day is the prevalent assumption that Prussia was the German Empire and the German Empire was Prussia, thus centering the research about the holiday in Berlin, and most frequently at the capital's drill ground where the emperor reviewed the parade. An implicit assumption that national belonging in Germany emanated from Prussia runs through the Sedan Day historiography. Historians who looked for the importance of Sedan Day in Berlin, in Reichstag debates, or in decisions of political and religious leaders quickly concluded that the holiday was much ado about nothing. But the meaning of the holiday was decided by German provincials, not by the emperor who refused, as we shall shortly see, to sanction the celebration officially.

Moreover, these relations between center and periphery are connected to one more weakness of the historiography of Sedan Day, namely the relation between the holiday's intentions and its content. The intentions of the holiday's organizers (believed to be the establishment) have been too often taken as the actual experience of the participants. But a decision to celebrate taken in Berlin does not inform us about the meaning of the holiday actually celebrated in Württemberg and about problems of national integration that existed, often regardless of policies from above, in small German communities.

Sedan Day stood out among holidays in the German Empire because of its dynamic relationship between celebration and the production of new perception. The emperor's birthday celebration in Württemberg, for example, was celebrated at an evening banquet of speeches that never attracted many participants and did not provide an elaborate mix of form and content to communicate a representation of Germany.[15] It was an occasion for bourgeois sociability but never developed into a popular festival. The celebrations of the gymnastic associations (*Turnverein*) and the singing societies (*Liederkranz*) were by definition not national because they comprised specific groups and excluded most of German society; the associations could not claim to represent the nation as a whole. Sedan Day was different. No other national celebration in the German

Empire was celebrated annually for such a long period (1873–1914). The celebrations, occurring on a fixed date with a symbolic and a historic meaning, recreated the emotions and the excitement of the most powerful event in contemporary German history. The celebrants of Sedan Day, moreover, proclaimed it *the* national holiday that celebrated the foundation of the nation-state. No other holiday enjoyed this status. Other national celebrations, by gymnastic associations or singing societies, for instance, had been celebrated before 1871, and were therefore quite independent of the nation-state. Sedan Day, however, was tied with the unification and with the nation-state, and had no meaning outside it. So, for better or worse, contemporaries identified Sedan Day with the new era that began in 1871.

THE ABDICATION OF THE STATE

Given the common view of the primacy of the empire in the making of Sedan Day, it is necessary first to consider the role of the empire in the origination of the holiday. The national holiday of imperial Germany was born between January 1871, when Leipzig's *Kirchliche Gemeindeblatt* issued the first call to commemorate annually the foundation of the nation-state, and 2 September 1872, the first celebrations of Sedan Day. The first important stimulus for a national holiday was an address to the emperor by the Association of German Liberal Protestants (Deutscher Liberaler Protestantenverein), published in the *Karlsruher Zeitung* on 11 March 1871. The eighty-eight signatories—a group of bourgeois professors, publishers, civil servants, newspaper editors, and leading members of church councils who came mostly from Berlin and Heidelberg— requested the emperor to support the idea of celebrating "annually the refoundation of the German Empire in a general national and religious holiday."[16] The new national holiday, according to the bourgeois patriots, should pass on "the memory of the . . . victory, the fallen heroes . . . and the unification of all the Germans, accomplished after a long [inner] discord."[17] Similar calls for a national holiday were heard throughout Germany by, for instance, the *Kirchliche Gemeindeblatt* in Leipzig in January 1871 and the *Neue Evangelische Kirchenzeitung* from Berlin (organ of the Deutscher Zweig der Evangelischen Allianz) in February of the same year.[18] Promoters of the national holiday argued that it should epitomize the new conditions of the nation after the unification, namely the supremacy of the national will over particularism and the preeminence of the new history of the empire over the old history of the states. March 1871 passed in expectation of the emperor's response.

On 4 April 1871, the emperor announced that a national holiday would not be officially sanctioned. He did express his satisfaction with the idea of celebrating the victory of 1870–71, but the initiative, he added, should spring spontaneously from the people, as already happened in 1814 after Moritz Arndt's call to celebrate the Battle of Nations. The emperor's position was essentially noncommittal: he suggested that a celebration occur, but refused any official responsibility or participation. His decision should not be seen as totally surprising because the German Empire was a compromise, as one historian put it, "between modern nationalism and traditional dynasticism. . . . [It] stood halfway between a Prussian dynastic and a modern nation-state."[19] Bismarck refused to sanction several basic national symbols because they implied a transference of legitimacy from the dynasties to the people. Thus Germany lacked a national flag until 1892, a national hymn until after World War I, and a national holiday.

Nevertheless, as if to confirm the hybrid character of the nation-state, the empire in the Bismarck era shaped national identity through other symbolic means, such as in architecture (the Reichstag, built between 1884 and 1894), in museums, and in the universities.[20] The mixed policies after 1871 about national symbols continued a tradition of the regional German states in the nineteenth century that reacted to the national movement as a potentially subversive popular movement. In the case of Sedan Day, the emperor, in spite of the unification, reacted in a sense more like the king of Prussia than the emperor of the Germans.

The refusal of the empire to celebrate officially was not a deadly blow to the holiday because bourgeois civil associations of the national movement were traditionally instrumental in promoting national monuments and celebrations. The associations carried the national movement before 1871 when the celebrations were at times in open defiance of the German states, as in Hambach in 1832. After 1871 the message changed, but the invention of national symbols continued. Despite official reticence, the bourgeois Germans celebrated Sedan Day, waiving the black-white-red flag as the national flag. The emperor, for his part, reviewed the military parade in Berlin every 2 September, and commemorated the military victory over France, but not on the national holiday that he refused to sanction. Moreover, bourgeois civil associations played an important role in the construction of national monuments. The *Deutscher Kriegerbund*, for instance, a mass organization that included 214 branches and 27,500 members when it was founded in 1873 and 1 million members in 1900, initiated the construction of the *Niederwald* monument for Emperor William I, built between 1874 and 1885.[21] In Dortmund, local citizens, supported by the city's authorities and the regional Landtag, also initiated the monument for Emperor William I in Porta Westfalica.[22] For bourgeois Germans, then, the official participation of the empire's authorities in a national holiday was desirable but obviously not required. In fact, as we shall see, the absence of the empire opened a space for the bourgeoisie to shape national identity in their own image.

An excellent illustration of the empire's hands-off policy in regard to national symbols, and the consequent increase of initiatives from civil society, is the lobbying of Grand Duke Frederick of Baden for a national holiday. Following the emperor's announcement of April 1871, a host of civil organizations and associations began promoting the case for a national holiday. The date that received growing support as the most suitable was 2 September, but Grand Duke Frederick saw this date as inappropriate. Translating words into actions, in August 1872 he proposed as a national holiday 18 January, the date of the declaration of the German Empire in Versailles in 1871, "the symbol of German unification."[23] The grand duke was especially dismayed by the absence of an official guiding hand, a situation that led to a confusing proliferation of suggested suitable dates. He proposed, therefore, to pass a motion in the Bundesrat "in order to prevent that the present private initiatives for the establishment of a German national holiday will lead to further contention and disagreement."[24] But as Baden's Prime Minister Julius Jolly reminded the grand duke, the policy set by the emperor ruled out official intervention. A motion in the Bundesrat was therefore out of the question and "private initiatives" remained the only way to bring forth a national holiday.

Although his campaign for an official national holiday failed, the grand duke continued to lobby for 18 January as the date of the national holiday. But here, too, he was rebuffed by Prussia. The matter was discussed between Berlin and Karlsruhe, and on 23 January 1873 Baden's ambassador in Berlin, von Türckheim, sent home Prussia's definitive answer: Prussia opposed the idea of 18 January because "it is an old Prussian remembrance day, which Prussian identity [das spezifische Preußentum] would reluctantly see disappear in a German national holiday."[25] Von Türckheim was referring most probably to 18 January 1701, when the elector Frederick III of Brandenburg gave himself a new royal title to become Frederick I, king of Prussia. The foundation of the modern Prussian state stood in the way of celebrating the foundation of the German nation-state. Since the Prussian authorities of the empire held to a view of the nation as a network of dynastic communities, and since they regarded a supradynastic national holiday with apprehension, a national holiday had to emanate from a different section in German society.

Neither the nonintervention policy of the empire about a national holiday nor the failed intervention of Grand Duke Frederick dimmed the enthusiasm of supporters of the empire. Their activity centered around a Prussian Protestant pastor, Friedrich von Bodelschwingh, who was since 1864 a minister in Dellwig, Westphalia. On the occasion of the birthday of the emperor, Bodelschwingh published an article in the Westfälischer Hausfreund on 19 March 1871 that called for a national holiday.[26] He further encouraged Germans to set up a national holiday in a lecture entitled "The German Popular Festival," delivered on 27 June 1871 in the Rheinisch-Westfälischer Provinzialausschuss für Innere

Mission to an audience of about 130 ministers, professors, teachers, and high civil servants. Newspapers throughout the country published the lecture (or excerpts) and three thousand copies were distributed nationwide on 19 July 1871 by the Provinzialausschuss. After the nationwide campaign of July 1871 the holiday started to spread in Germany, sotto voce in 1872 and with a crescendo thereafter.

In Württemberg, the pattern of official passivity and public initiative in the creation of Sedan Day recurred. The liberals promoted Sedan Day through meetings, newspaper articles, and petitions to city councils, but Karl I and the government refused to participate. The king never made a secret of his negative feelings about the unification and, by extension, about Sedan Day. Before the first celebrations in Württemberg, in August 1872, he refused to respond to a petition to support the holiday.[27] A directive of the Ministry of the Interior in 1874, when the holiday was first successfully celebrated in Württemberg, ordered that flags fly over government ministries and offices of public service be shut down, with the exception of urgent cases.[28] This modest role by the state was significant in one respect, namely that it allowed civil servants who supported Sedan Day to participate in the daytime celebrations. But I found no evidence that this policy continued in the following years. A more significant indication of the king's attitude toward the holiday is found in a letter from September 1874. He restated the reserved position of the Württemberg state that "refrains from participating in a civil holiday . . . and avoids participation of the state authorities [in any eventual celebration]."[29] The king, like the emperor, was motivated by particularistic sentiments, though his sentiments were directed of course against Prussia.

Sedan Day in Württemberg, as elsewhere in Germany, began unsuccessfully on 2 September 1872. The main reason for the failed start was the refusal by Stuttgart and Berlin to commit the state officially to the national holiday, and the ensuing confusion this decision created. After the emperor's response of April 1871 many in Germany still expected that an imperial body would invest the holiday with legal and official legitimization. When no such body came forward, it cleared the way for every community in Germany to embrace or to reject the national holiday at will.

The case of the celebration manqué in Stuttgart in 1872 was typical. Supporters of Sedan Day petitioned twice to the city council in the summer of 1872 in favor of a celebration. The city council discussed the matter a number of times and declared its approval in principle. However, the council observed, it appeared opportune to wait for the definitive decision by the rest of Germany and especially by the Reichstag about the date of the celebration because "it is first of all the task of the empire's authorities to direct the holiday."[30] Stuttgart's city council waited in 1872 until after 2 September, but no official response arrived from Berlin. As a result, no celebration took place at all. The vacuum left by the empire's authorities was filled in the following years by the city council and local associations.[31]

In 1873, the future of the holiday was contingent on the behavior of local and provincial Germany. How different was the reality of Sedan Day from the historiographical argument that the imperial authorities controlled the holiday! On the national and local level the state refrained from directing, planning, and supervising the holiday. Also bourgeois civil associations and others in civil society did not centrally control it. The initiatives of the Provinzialausschuss, Bodelschwingh, liberals, and newspapers did not produce a body to coordinate and organize the holiday nationwide. What Bodelschwingh, and all other promoters of Sedan Day, did was to suggest guidelines for the holiday and give the necessary stimulus to transform an idea into reality. But Sedan Day was left at that. Every community was left to decide whether and how to celebrate. The history of Sedan Day reflected the regional diversity of German nationhood and its impact on national memory after 1871, for if the holiday was to be celebrated at all it was only thanks to grass-roots commitment.

In the absence of official coercion to participate, and of civil central organization, the Sedan Day celebrations transformed every locality in Germany into a microcosm of the debate about new national life after 1871. Even the weekly newspaper of little Nürtingen, 4,815 inhabitants in 1871, conveyed faithfully the feeling of urgency over the celebrations of Sedan Day and over the participation of each community. Never before in German history was a national holiday so opportune, wrote the weekly. "[But] in South Germany . . . , where, as it is well known, one has always to be different, Sedan Day is not generally celebrated as in North Germany. Unfortunately, here in Württemberg neither a church ceremony nor school celebrations have been organized. To celebrate the holiday, therefore, it is all the more the duty of the single communities."[32] The holiday became an ongoing plebiscite about the content and form of the national community after 1871.

WÜRTTEMBERG: WHO CELEBRATED THE HOLIDAY, WHERE, AND WHAT DID IT MEAN?

The originators of Sedan Day on the national level were the liberal Protestant bourgeoisie who experienced the German unification not simply as a political event but as the crowning of the inherent mission of German history. As the right-wing liberal Heinrich von Sybel stated after the unification in a letter to Hermann Baumgarten on 27 January 1871: "How have we deserved the grace of God in being allowed to experience such great and mighty things. . . . What has been for 20 years the content of all [our] desires and aspirations, has been fulfilled now in such an infinitely magnificent way!"[33] Liberals in Germany, who were commonly university-educated bourgeoisie, believed in a society as a community of free, rational citizens. An important tenet of their worldview was the idea of the strong, centralized national state as the protector and accelerator of social, economic, cultural, and political progress. After 1871, the National Liberal Party became Bismarck's main political ally and contributed to shaping during the Liberal Era (1871–79) the nation-state according to some of liberalism's most cherished values. Liberals saw many of their objectives realized in the founding of the national bank, the creation of a single national market, the unification of weights, measures, and currency, the reforms in the penal code, the national press law, and the freedom of movement for individuals. Moreover, the liberals viewed the *Kulturkampf*, the campaign by Bismarck and the German liberals against political Catholicism in the 1870s and 1880s, as a step in the realization of their broader program. While liberals were not in principle antireligious, they considered Catholicism as backward, superstitious, and antimodern, and wished to break the power of the clergy over believers, especially in education.[34] And the liberals opposed what they viewed as the extranational identification of Catholics with the pope in Rome.

The creation of Sedan Day should be seen as an additional element in the liberals' wish to reshape German society after 1871: what the national bank was for economic reforms and the *Kulturkampf* for church-state relations, Sedan Day was for national identity. It provided a symbolic representation for the shared beliefs of liberals: *Kleindeutschland*, nationalism, Protestantism, Bismarck. The holiday reflected, in a sense, changes between 1848 and 1871 in the essential qualifications to lay claim to speak for the nation. In 1848 several political programs for the German Question were viable. These included particularism, *Großdeutsch* and *Kleindeutsch* ideas, the third way of South Germany as a counterbalance to Prussia and Austria, and even republicanism in democratic circles. The course of German history from 1866 to 1871 limited the numbers of legitimate and practical solutions to the German Question, while support of the *Kleindeutsch* nation-state under Prussia's hegemony became an increasingly important qualification for those claiming to represent national identity.

As a result, liberals emerged in a good position to influence the shaping of national identity because they unquestionably accepted nationalism as an ideology, and the Second Empire as the political solution for Germany. The unification of 1871 was the fulfillment of all possible aspirations, as von Sybel wrote, and it was in this spirit that liberals originated Sedan Day. Other groups in German society after 1871 either rejected the full legitimacy of nationalism (the international working-class movement, as well as the emperor and other loyalists to the regional royal houses) or raised reservations about the *Kleindeutsch* solution (Catholics, democrats, particularists, and *Großdeutsche*). Catholics, democrats, and socialists, unlike liberals, viewed the events of 1871 with various degrees of foreboding and found themselves on the sidelines of the new nation-state because of religious, political, or social reasons. The process of integrating them into the nation was slow and at times painful (witness the *Kulturkampf* and the Anti-Socialist Law, the restrictive political measures against German socialists between 1878 and 1890).

In Württemberg, to return to local reality, Sedan Day originated from the Protestant liberal-bourgeois notables. The liberals organized the celebrations in local holiday committees that comprised everywhere the crème de la crème of communal politics, culture, and society. In Stuttgart in 1876 the committee boasted the best names in the country: three members of the Reichstag, two members of the Landtag, seven members of the city council, two school rectors, chairmen of the city's various associations (like the Gymnastic Association and the Veterans Association), four professors, and one general.[35] In Tübingen the university rector magnificus, one of the most distinguished academic positions in all the German speaking countries, advocated the cause of Sedan Day before the town council so that the holiday would be recognized officially and supported financially while other university professors participated on the organizing board.[36] Other places, which could not recruit such luminaries, entrusted the preparations to the museum society (*Museumsgesellschaft*), a local club of notables that had nothing to do with museums and exhibitions, but was an important locus of influence and status in the community. Such was the case, for example, in Nürtingen, Giengen an der Brenz, and Kirchheim unter Teck.[37] Sedan Day was described accurately and critically by *Der Beobachter* (The observer), the newspaper of the democratic Volkspartei, as the celebration of the "distinguished and most distinguished" elements of the community.[38]

The notables vigorously used their influential position in the community's church, school, and town hall to invest the new Germany with legitimacy. Ministers promoted the holiday relentlessly: in Crailsheim the two local clergymen convinced the community to organize a celebration with the official participation of the municipal council; in Ulm they helped prepare the holiday; and in Reichenbach the minister nailed on the doors of the town hall a detailed program for 2 September, elaborating the religious and national reasons for the holiday.[39] To the length and breadth of Protestant Württemberg, ministers held services on Sedan Day. Schoolteachers instilled the message of the holiday in pupils, and, as we shall see shortly, the school festivities became one of the highlights of the holiday. Public officials (*Beamten*) also lent the holiday their considerable prestige through their participation in, and organization of, the celebrations.[40]

The notables shared two important attributes: they supported the empire and they were leaders of the community who commanded status, prestige, and political influence. But within the group there were marked differences of social status and political power. Notables in the capital Stuttgart, who often were affiliated with the royal court, and in university, religious, and economic centers such as Tübingen and Heilbronn, enjoyed higher prestige and wealth than notables in small communities.[41] Teachers, whether in Stuttgart's distinguished Karlsgymnasium, or in Giengen an der Brenz's local school (population 2,560), exerted considerable influence in the community and were likely to participate in the organization of the holiday. But between them they did not share the same social status, the Karlsgymnasium being one of the elite high schools in Württemberg reserved for children of the best upper-class families. Notables in Stuttgart and the big towns constituted the intellectual and economic haute bourgeoisie (*Bildungsbürgertum* and *Wirtschaftsbürgertum*), university professors, gymnasium teachers, lawyers, rich merchants and entrepreneurs, high civil servants, and university-educated ministers. In small localities that often did not exceed several thousand inhabitants, notables tended to come from the petite bourgeoisie (*Kleinbürgertum*): the local teacher, minister, and merchant, and at times also the butcher and pharmacist.[42] These local notables were often people of limited education and wealth who in most likelihood never left their district or region. The point here is not to have in mind a uniform image of the notables as, say, the opulent and well-bred Buddenbrooks. The national holiday of the mighty German Empire was normally not a glamorous celebration by rich, refined personalities in the sophisticated atmosphere of a metropolis. Sedan Day in Württemberg was a holiday celebrated mostly in provincial localities by provincial people.

The kind of haute bourgeoisie who celebrated Sedan Day was exemplified by the career of Gottlob Egelhaaf, a liberal and a member of the Deutsche Partei. Egelhaaf was a high school teacher in Heilbronn in the 1870s and 1880s who enjoyed a wide reputation in Württemberg. His series of Württemberg history books were popular among students, and were used as local-history books in the homes of educated bourgeois families. After closely losing a competition to become a professor in Tubingen, he held from 1895 to 1919 the distinguished and powerful position of rector at the Karlsgymnasium in Stuttgart. Active in the cultural life of Württemberg, Egelhaaf was in 1891 a founding member of the Württemberg Committee for Local History, a typical haut bourgeois notables' association. Like many of his peers, Egelhaaf was deeply interested in and involved in politics. As one of the leaders of the Deutsche Partei, he participated in several election campaigns as candidate for the Landtag, which he won, and the Reichstag, which he lost. A renowned scholar, educator, and politician, Egelhaaf moved in the circles of power.[43] Few notables in Württemberg emulated Egelhaaf's brilliant career. Being a local notable was obviously a relative matter.[44]

While notables were the backbone of the holiday, they were by no means the sole celebrants. In Stuttgart and the big towns where social divisions were more clearly delineated, and notables included the best names in the land, the men and women of the liberal haute bourgeoisie kept the holiday largely to themselves. But in small and medium-sized Protestant localities, Sedan Day developed from the mid-1870s to the second half of the 1880s into a popular event that included, in addition to local notables, peasants, artisans, and women. One way to draw people from different social groups together, as we shall shortly see, was to deliver the new national message of Sedan Day through traditional local festivities, as when the popular Children's Festival (Kinderfest) was shifted to 2 September.

Another way was via local voluntary associations: the ex-servicemen's association, the veterans association, the singing society, the fire brigade association (*Feuerwehrverein*), the gymnastic association, the trade association (*Gewerbeverein*), and others.[45] German towns and cities contained a dense and interconnected network of voluntary associations that were the focal point of social and political influence, and had, since the end of the eighteenth century, taken control of the emerging public sphere.[46] The liberal notables attempted to secure the support of associations for the celebration, a tactic that sometimes backfired when opponents split an association over such an issue.[47] But when an association endorsed the holiday it created a sense of social and political togetherness that encouraged fellow travelers and some who were politically indifferent to join in. Moreover, towns usually had one major club to which recruitment was strictly controlled that was the center of local associations and set the tone for proper behavior in the community. In many localities the museum society played the role of the leading association.[48] The position of the society in the forefront of the holiday's supporters was, therefore, a powerful statement that led other associations to follow suit. Because most communities in the 1870s were small, for the 2,560 inhabitants of Giengen an der Brenz, the 4,815 of Nürtingen, or for the 5,863 of Kirchheim, the active stance of the museum society could not have gone unheeded.

Overall, three groups of celebrants participated in the holiday. Occasional participants, Protestants with no ideological affiliation to the liberal worldview, attended specific events that were celebrated in conjunction with the holiday, such as the unveiling of a monument or the Children's Festival. A more committed group of petit bourgeois Protestants, who shared the liberals' national ideals, was recruited by local notables. Most significant, the Protestant liberal-bourgeois notables originated, organized, and carried the holiday from 1873 to the end.[49] The history of the holiday in Württemberg was inextricably tied with these notables and, as long as they maintained a commitment to celebrating Sedan Day, the holiday survived.

The preceding discussion provides a necessary corrective to a misleading historical view: that of the holiday as being celebrated only in Berlin and rejected by the public. In fact, the gist of Sedan Day appears to have been as a holiday that represented the nation in a setting of localism, enjoying a popular and committed following. It was mostly celebrated in small and medium-sized communities that were only beginning to make their way into the communication and transportation network of the modern world, and that, in the 1870s and 1880s, often were not connected even to the regional railway system. Most of their inhabitants never left the surrounding area. The local newspaper, if one existed, was mainly a vehicle for advertising and publishing official announcements by local authorities and included very little news from the region and nation, let alone the world. News still spread fastest by traditional means, by milkwomen, for example. An important argument in Untertürkheim against a plan to restructure the role of milkwomen was their social role as disseminators of news.[50] The marketplace was the best location to keep up-to-date on what was going on. In Ulm news about the bad weather that hit the hinterland was brought by peasants who came to sell their merchandise.[51]

It would be a mistake, however, to attribute the strong sense of localism, and often provincialism, only to the life-style of inhabitants of small localities. An announcement in the *Beobachter* in 1871 read as following: "Lost! A red-leather purse with small change and a golden chain was lost from Tübingerstraße to Gopheinstraße. Return for reward: Marienstraße 46, 1st floor, Stuttgart."[52] That someone placed such an add was a measure of a world that had still been governed, though progressively less, by closely knit and personable social relations in the family, neighborhood, and workplace levels that made it conceivable for the person from Marienstraße 46, 1st floor, to believe in the return of a purse even in a city of 111,486 inhabitants, as was Stuttgart in 1871. Furthermore, even refined, haut bourgeois notables felt at home in the Swabian homeland in such a way that made them ill at ease elsewhere in the nation. Even a man like Julius Hölder, a haut bourgeois liberal notable if ever there was one, a leader of the Deutsche Partei, a member of the Landtag and the Reichstag, the speaker of the Landtag from 1875 and secretary of the interior from 1881, felt lonely and isolated during the Reichstag sessions in Berlin. Missing the social and political network of close friends and colleagues, the acquaintanceship with whom went in most cases back to the 1840s and 1850s, Hölder organized in Berlin "Württemberg evenings" that gathered members of the Reichstag and civil servants from Württemberg, people who could speak Schwäbisch and knew how to appreciate the gourmet taste of *Spätzle*. These evenings compensated for what he described in his diary as the lack of "intimate exchange of ideas" in Berlin.[53]

Hölder combined the patriotism characteristic of the German liberals with the provincialism characteristic of Württemberg society. Like him, the celebrants of Sedan Day linked in the holiday the closely knit and, at times, limiting conditions of local existence with a belief in the nation, the unification, and Bismarck. In short, through the holiday they represented the nation in the locality and brought it into the locality.[54]

THE CELEBRATION: BEQUEATHING LOCAL AND
NATIONAL MEMORIES

How did people celebrate Sedan Day? On 2 September 1889 young Hermann Hesse made his way back to his hometown Calw after spending the summer vacation with relatives in Stuttgart. His grandfather wrote: "Today is Sedan Day, about which Hermann Hesse deeply reflects as he returns home."[55] Hesse himself described the Sedan Day festivities in 1895 in the following words: "2 September was splendidly celebrated. . . . Beautiful procession, obsequies by the war veterans at the church yard, etc. In the afternoon we celebrated, as usual in the holiday, on the Brühl [a hill near the town] enjoying fruitcakes, cider, and wine. Everyone was extremely merry, savoring music, gymnastics performances, etc. Thirty young ladies dressed in white participated in the procession, among them also Adele [Hesse's sister]."[56]

To give the spirit, colors, and noises of the holiday, let us describe the celebrations in Calw, population 4,662 in 1880, that so delighted the famous writer. The opening act of Sedan Day was the procession, a showy display of the holiday's message and participants and the axis of the daytime celebrations. The pupils assembled at eight o'clock at the school courtyard, where the teachers held a lecture about the day's significance for Germany. Thereafter the congregation marched to the marketplace, where at 9:30 the main morning procession moved onward to the church—pupils, teachers, members of the associations, and clergymen. Pupils of both genders from all educational institutions in town participated: the youngest ahead, then came the girls, dressed in white, their heads crowned with wreaths, and flowers in their hands, and last the boys, with colorful flags and gymnastics iron poles. After the church service, where the throngs sang "Lieb Vaterland magst ruhig sein" (Beloved fatherland may you stay tranquil), the participants marched back to the marketplace for additional music and singing. At midday church bells in and around the city tolled honoring the holiday.

After the lunch break, the celebrants took off again to the sound of drums, music, and salvo of a saluting gun on the day's main procession to the Brühl, where a festival for the children was to take place. In addition to the schoolchildren the procession included the Veterans Association, the Singing Society, the Choir Society, and the Gymnastic Association, all represented with their flags and ensigns. Finally, there were the local police, city and state civil servants, and many citizens. Festivities continued in full swing on the Brühl until the evening, when Calwers returned home after a day that combined fun with patriotism.[57]

What was the meaning of this celebration? Clearly, the liberals commemorated "the memory of the political rebirth of the nation," as judge Dr. Elsäßer, the keynote speaker in the 1885 Stuttgart banquet, put it.[58] The holiday was a festival of the unification, the most important turning point in contemporary German history. This is beyond question. But why did the liberals choose this symbolic representation to celebrate the nation and what did it mean? When we look for an explicit explanation the sources on Sedan Day, which are so rich on other matters, are silent. There is no evidence to indicate that other forms of celebrations were suggested or that a debate developed among the liberals on the proper symbolic representation of the nation in the holiday. It is most improbable that the *Schwäbische Kronik*, which reported on the holiday with great detail, would not have covered and participated in such a debate had one taken place. We may interpret this silence as a sign of boredom, but this view is not borne by the ample evidence about the enthusiastic, self-conscious role played by the liberals in Sedan Day. The silence of the sources is significant in itself, therefore. It seems more plausible that liberals never questioned this form of celebration.

In order to understand the symbolic meaning of the celebration in Calw, we must place the holiday within the larger context of national celebrations in nineteenth-century Germany. In what ways was Sedan Day different from or similar to pre-1871 representations of the nation in national holidays? Did the liberals consciously depart from the symbolism of pre-1871 national holidays so as to match, on the symbolic level, the newness of the nation-state as a historical and experiential event?

In fact, Sedan Day in Calw could just as well have depicted any national celebration in Germany in the nineteenth century, for there was very little new in either the program or most of the symbols. Throughout the nineteenth century national celebrations in Germany followed a "matrix of German national holidays."[59] The matrix was introduced in the commemoration on 18–19 October 1814 of the liberation of Germany from Napoleon at the Battle of Nations, and repeated later in Wartburg (1817), Hambach (1832), and the Schiller festivals (1857) and in the numerous celebrations of the gymnastic associations, sharpshooters associations, and singing societies.[60] The procession maintained its central role and it was common for a procession to start a celebration. Evening banquets with songs and speeches, excursions to natural or historic sites, and joint celebration of a national holiday with the local Children's Festival were common. Collective symbols included wreaths, planting oaks or linden trees, and children dressed in white representing the religiously and morally pure nation. Local variations existed and changes were introduced over time when celebrants added symbols that corresponded to their experience:

the national festivals in the 1848–49 German Revolution featured a marching group of men-in-arms symbolizing the self-defending nation,[61] while the celebration of Sedan Day, as we shall shortly see, included war monuments for the fallen soldiers in 1870–71. Similar symbols changed their meanings over time: monuments for the fallen soldiers in the Napoleonic Wars symbolized for Germans the anticipated nation-state, while war monuments of the unification war symbolized in Sedan Day the fulfilled national promise. These were changes in degree, not in kind. As a whole, Germans shared a common tradition of national celebration. Describing the national celebrations in 1848–49, Jonathan Sperber argued that "as a result of this earlier experience [national celebrations since 1814], the festive discourse of the nation was a familiar one, shared by all classes of mid-nineteenth century."[62] As the Calw celebration shows, this evaluation is true for the period of Sedan Day as well.

It is significant that Sedan Day and national celebrations before 1871 shared similarities in organization, social composition, and relations with the German states. Before 1871 the initiative to celebrate came from local notables and associations as the authorities of the German states stood by passively. Combining nationalism and middle-class sociability, local associations organized the celebrations and mobilized the public.[63] In like fashion, Sedan Day was ignored by the empire. It was the local notables who organized and supported the celebration with the help of local associations, which encouraged popular participation. The holiday continued a pre-1871 mode of creating national symbols that was local, popular, and organized from below.

What, then, was the meaning of the celebration that continued a festive tradition rather than creating a new one? By adopting the common tradition of celebration as a representation of the nation-state, the celebrants of Sedan Day placed the new nation within German traditions—the tradition of local festivals and the tradition of the celebrations by the German national movement. This was a way to internalize the new nation-state through an old and familiar form of symbolic representation and it was also a way to appropriate the authority of the traditional national celebrations in the service of Sedan Day. By doing this, the celebrants placed the locality in the context of Germany and emphasized the nation without obliterating the locality. The program of the Sedan Day celebration was a conscious attempt to integrate the spatial and historical continuum of the locality with the time-bounded, historical event of the German unification. It aspired to unite the historically commemorated event with the immemorial past of the locality. Places that represented the ancientness, tradition, and character of a town—church, town hall, cemetery— became part of the new celebrations. Celebrants literally walked from one symbolic site to another in order to create a tangible continuity between the old town and the new holiday, that is, the empire.

To understand the symbolic meaning of the celebration one must consider the two basic ways to convey meaning in the holiday. The first is the use of the holiday's rhetoric as a means of convincing the public as well as a way to strengthen the speaker's beliefs.[64] Usually, the prescribed form of conducting such a ceremony entails the passive participation of an audience. The second way to transmit meaning consisted of the actions and activities that people were engaged in during the celebrations. The behavior of people became the message. The symbolic meaning was a combination of the people's choice of space, time, and location.

The main ceremony of Sedan Day that connected the community directly with the war of 1870–71 was the commemoration of fallen soldiers at the foot of war monuments. Although ceremonies at war monuments had been part of national celebrations before 1871, and monuments were not new as national symbols, in Sedan Day they created a space to place the national unification in a local setting.[65] Many communities set the unveiling ceremony deliberately on Sedan Day. In Marbach, in 1875, after the procession to the church, the celebrants unveiled a memorial tablet for a fallen local citizen. In Isny a simple stone with the names of the fallen was unveiled in the cemetery. And in Riedlingen the town's minister unveiled the monument in the cemetery, which was followed by a speech given by the chairman of the Ex-Servicemen Association and songs by the Choir Society. Then the participants, led by the school-children, marched through the town.[66]

The ceremony at the war memorial bound local experience to German national history. The Reutlingen war memorial successfully captured this spirit by symbolically placing the fallen sons of the locality within a larger national context. It commemorated fallen soldiers according to provenance: the names of local soldiers were engraved on the north and south sides of the memorial; Württemberg soldiers who died in Reutlingen's hospital were engraved on the west side; and fallen North Germans on the east side.[67] One discovered the full meaning of the monument by circling it and considering the combined effort of local, regional, and North German soldiers. The monument was unveiled on 2 September 1872, a year before the first Sedan Day celebrations in Württemberg, and became thereafter an integral part of the holiday's program.[68]

Local veterans, who personified the memory of the unification, conferred it to the young generation in numerous speeches near the monument.[69] No war memorial ceremony ever took place without their participation as they became the custodians of the history of the war. They connected the historic unification with everyday life, especially in communities where no war memorial existed. A veteran in Dörzbach, accompanied by the members of the newly formed Veterans Association, got married on 2 September 1873, thus linking the personal and the national.[70]

Another element in the holiday's program that bound local and national history was statues. One fundamental change in the physiognomy of European urban space in the last decades of the nineteenth century was the appearance of a great number of monuments and statues.[71] It was a way for the ruling groups to affirm their dominant position by shaping the public sphere according to their image. In Germany, symbols of German culture and of the German Empire dominated the urban landscape: statues of Wolfgang Goethe and Friedrich Schiller, of Emperor William I and Bismarck, and many others. By incorporating the new statues, the liberals adapted the holiday to the changing local architecture and honored the heroes of the unification with a special ceremony. Unveiling a monument on Sedan Day augmented its significance as well as that of the holiday. The main event in Heilbronn's 1893 festival was the unveiling of Emperor William I's monument.[72] In Isny, fifteen years after the ceremony for the modest war memorial, a new impressive war and victory memorial was unveiled on Sedan Day 1890.[73]

Above all, celebrating Sedan Day near a local statue was a way for the community to honor itself and its achievements and to establish a continuity between local history and German national history. This was especially evident for towns that could boast a monument dedicated to a famous native citizen who contributed in some way to the rebirth of the nation. Such a monument aggrandized the importance of a locality and its people in German history. Tuttlingen, the town of Max Schneckenburger, the author of the popular song "Watch on the Rhine," was a case in point. Schneckenburger was born in 1819 in the small village of Thalheim, raised in nearby Tuttlingen, and died in 1849 in Burgdorf near Bern, Switzerland, where he was buried. After the unification, the inhabitants of both Thalheim and Tuttlingen wished to attach Schneckenburger's fame to their community by erecting a statue. Disagreement arose over which community had a more justified claim to Schneckenburger's legacy. As the district's capital, Tuttlingen enjoyed a political and financial edge over Thalheim's pedigree. Thalheimers, where most of Schneckenburger's relatives lived, argued for a system that counted the number of relatives as an objective measure to determine the issue, while Tuttlingers argued implicitly that Thalheim was too provincial as the seat of an important German monument. In the end, the leaders of the two communities reached a compromise whereby the bones of Schneckenburger were brought over from Switzerland and reburied in Thalheim in 1886 and a statue was unveiled in Tuttlingen in 1892.[74]

Both projects received big publicity across Germany and put small Thalheim and Tuttlingen on the national map. The emperor and his wife donated 500 and 300 marks respectively to the statue's fund.[75] Between 12,000 and 15,000 foreigners arrived in Tuttlingen, population 10,000, for the unveiling ceremony.[76] Most important, the patriotic mood and national values received a local touch, expressed by the keynote speaker in 1886, who viewed Schneck-enburger as "a simple German man from our land and this area."[77]

After 1892, the statue in Tuttlingen became the center of Sedan Day celebra-tions. The monument and the square around it formed a most suitable scene and space. A three-meter crowned Germania ready to pull her sword from the sheath dominated the area, standing atop a three-and-a-half meter pedestal. The large grounds, surrounded by plants and trees and beautified by two fountains and two oaks, one each for Bismarck and Moltke, were located a bowshot from the Danube.[78] The highlight of the celebration in 1895 was a grandiose procession of the schoolchildren, all the associations in town, mem-bers of the town assembly, reserve officers, city and state civil servants, and citizens, who went first to the church and then onward to the monument. There, after a ceremony, the crowd naturally sang the "Watch on the Rhine," accompanied by an orchestra.[79] By identifying with a local hero, the ceremony transmitted an image of a nation that for many was still an abstract entity. The memory of past national exploits mingled with recent local memories, thus giving the community an opportunity to celebrate itself in a holiday that emphasized the nation.

As a whole, the Sedan Day festival took symbolic control of the public sphere in the name of the nation. Imagine the effect on the small town of Calw, with its 4,662 inhabitants, of the schoolchildren, various association members, the local police, city and state civil servants, and many citizens crisscrossing the town for an entire day. The celebrants marched in the most significant and crowded places in the community: the school, the marketplace, the church, and the Brühl. They further took symbolic possession of the community by accompanying sounds of bells, drums, trumpets, and saluting guns, and deco rations of wreaths, flags, iron poles, and associations' ensigns. It was virtually impossible to shut one's eyes and turn a deaf ear to the sights and sounds of the day.

Continuing the tradition of nocturnal celebrations on nineteenth-century national holidays, the festival conquered also the nighttime public space.[80] It began on the evening of 1 September when bonfires were lit on hills around towns to signal the opening of the holiday. The idea was to distinguish sym-bolically the twenty-four hours between the evening of 1 September and 2 Sep tember from the everyday life. Torchlight parades were often held.[81] A more elaborate performance was staged in Neckargröningen. The school youth as-sembled with drums, trumpets, and flags for a nocturnal procession to the lawn near the Neckar River. There the youth staged scenes from the summer of 1870: King William of Prussia, resting peacefully in Ems, receives a petition from an old lady and talks to a veteran; in the meantime Napoleon III and Lulu are having a wild amorous adventure in Paris; the war trumpets blow and the youth, divided into red and blue armies, face each other; the battle of Sedan ensues, with wounded everywhere; Napoleon and his family are taken prisoners, and are led away by the victorious, singing Germans. The riverbanks were crowded with spectators.[82]

The picture that emerges from the festival is that celebrants, rejecting the creation of a new symbolic representation in the wake of the unification, based the holiday on the traditions of local and national celebration and thus placed the locality within the nation. Celebrants, in a sense, understood the nation in terms of the locality. This was especially evident in the school celebrations, in which children related to the abstract concept of nation through the immediate local world in which they lived.

THE PEDAGOGICAL HOLIDAY:
NATIONAL WINE IN LOCAL BOTTLES

In a way, the memory bequeathed in Sedan Day concerned not only the past and the present; the past was over, and the present temporary. In contrast, the control of the future opened unlimited possibilities. Here was a vital purpose of Sedan Day: to transmit the values of the holiday—*Kleindeutschland* patriotism, the empire, emperor, Bismarck—to future generations. Celebrants therefore directed their efforts to the children and the youth whose identity and personality were still in a sense a tabula rasa. The *Schwäbische Kronik* went so far as to view the holiday as a national initiation rite for the youngsters.[83] The holiday was thus a national pedagogical project aimed at impregnating the spirit of Germany according to Sedan Day.[84]

The first point to note about the youngsters' participation in the holiday is their full and total mobilization. All levels and types of educational institutions in the land took part in the celebrations: teachers' training colleges, gymnasiums, high schools, nonclassical secondary schools, lower-grade secondary schools for boys and for girls, elementary schools, other schools and institutions for girls, and boarding schools.[85] Even kindergartens participated.[86] This overwhelming picture was in accordance with the massive support teachers and educational figures gave the holiday. Even Catholic pupils at times participated in the school festivities through lectures and singing,[87] though in general Catholic youngsters stayed away from the holiday.[88]

The ceremonies in the schools were a continuous and unrelenting propagation of the *Kleindeutsch* nation-state by means of solemn speeches and lectures. The similarities between Emperor Frederick Barbarossa (the Red Beard) and Emperor William I, alias William Barbablanca (the White Beard) and their quality as heroes of German history were a recurrent theme, as well as the importance of Prussian history to non-Prussian Germans and the place of Frederick the Great as a linking chain between the two emperors.[89] The traditional enmity between Germany and France was continuously illuminated: in a Catholic school in Stuttgart, for example, the teacher lectured about the nagging question, "How much was France the traditional enemy of Germany?"[90] Others recounted the disgrace of the German people before 1871 as a result of their lack of political unity.[91] And naturally the history of the war was told again and again. One imaginative teacher drew a big map of Metz with colored chalks to illustrate the battle around the city on 14–18 August 1870, and then repeated the operation for the battle of Sedan.[92] In Eßlingen a veteran of the unification war enchanted pupils with stories about his patriotic adventures.[93]

The holiday's program did not simply relegate youngsters to the status of passive spectators. The youngsters were active participants in the school and outdoor celebrations. Outstanding pupils were selected to present papers before the class or the entire school. The topics were already familiar: one pupil talked about "national pride, its justification and dangers," delineating past decay and present regeneration in German history; another presented the political and literary relationship between France and Germany in 1570, 1670, and 1870. Another still talked about the connection between the new overseas success of German politics and the ancient dominating position of the Hanseatic towns.[94] Prussia's role in German history was an obligatory motif, with presentations about the "regeneration" of the Prussian state after the defeat of Jena and its significance for the unification. Other presentations compared the parallel cases of Frederick Barbarossa and Heinrich VI with that of Emperor William I and his son Emperor Frederick.[95] The "liberated" territories, Alsace-Lorraine, were another popular topic: for example, "The role of Metz in the political history of Germany," and "Strasbourg in the literary history of Germany."[96] Württemberg's history, which made only a modest part of the school festivities, was presented in lectures like "The merit of our great king in the German unification."[97]

Not only lectures kept the pupils active. Staging famous plays that were suitable to the occasion was very popular. Schiller's *Wallenstein's Camp*, about the famous general during the Thirty Years' War, was a common choice. In Stuttgart's Karlsgymnasium the gymnastic hall was transformed into a theater and decorations and set designs recreated the seventeenth century. The city's Singing Society provided appropriate costumes and cooperated with the school's Singing Society. Rehearsals started weeks before the holiday, and the show, given before pupils and parents, was an enormous success. Its meaning, according to the explanation provided to the spectators, was to show Germany during a period of its deepest disgrace in contrast to the present when Germany enjoyed political unity and an army to defend itself.[98]

Sedan Day was a pedagogic project: it imprinted on the impressionable personalities of the children the values of the new nation-state. In this respect, the importance of the holiday went beyond 2 September. It provided an opportunity for teachers to introduce a corrective to Württemberg school textbooks that, in spite of the unification, remained largely unchanged between the 1860s and the 1890s.[99] The textbooks ignored the empire, except for the addition of a section about the unification war, and underplayed the role of Prussia in the new nation-state.[100] The school celebrations, in contrast, emphasized the new empire, Prussian history, and only to a lesser extent Württemberg. Consequently, Sedan Day became one of the main occasions in school to instill in the youth of Württemberg the spirit of *Kleindeutschland* and the new empire.

The best way for children and adults to perceive the nation through the local texture was the celebration of the Children's Festival, or Kinderfest, together with the holiday. The advantage of this joint celebration was that a traditional, local festival was imbued with new and national messages, uniting tradition and novelty as well as the locality and the nation. Sedan Day was not the first national celebration in Germany to appropriate the Children's Festival, though it used the festival exceptionally well.

The Children's Festival in Württemberg was a version of the old May Day celebration of spring or autumn and had been celebrated since before the Thirty Years' War.[101] It was an important event for the community with a table d'hôte, a special program for the children, and a big ball in the evening. It was not unusual to move the festival to a date of a big religious or local holiday.[102] Thus in many localities the celebrants of Sedan Day, after an approval by the town council, set the communal festival on 2 September.

The effect of the combination of local traditions with a new national holiday was immediate. The joint celebration turned out to be a tremendous success in Württemberg.[103] A report from Schwaigern, a small locality of 2,059 inhabitants in 1871, indicates that even mothers participated in Sedan Day after it was united with the Children's Festival, and that the popularity of the holiday soared.[104] In Ehingen (population 3,547) the celebration of Sedan Day in 1876 failed because bad weather postponed the Children's Festival; a year later, Sedan Day was moved to 3 September to ensure a united celebration.[105]

The joint celebration was a determining factor in the pedagogical project of Sedan Day. The holiday's supporters found an ingenious way to instill the values of Sedan Day in the community in an indirect and therefore more effective way. The initial motives of many participants in the joint celebration may have been far from national; they came to celebrate a local feast, and only secondarily, if at all, Germany's victory and unification. But in so doing they were exposed to the ideas of Sedan Day. The program of the joint celebration combined local traditions and national innovations: old customs like games and plays for the children, and refreshments donated by the town council, mingled with the new values of the nation displayed in speeches, flags, patriotic singing, laying wreaths, and solemn attire. In the end, the joint celebration was an appropriation of the community's own historical memory in the service of the new national holiday. The traditional, local, and popular festival legitimized the holiday and endowed it with authenticity.

In Stuttgart and large towns such old customs as the Children's Festival died away as modernity advanced. But even without calling it a Children's Festival, schools maintained the core of the traditional festival by making an excursion to the country on Sedan Day, far from the noisy, hectic city. Hesse described the fun on the Brühl. Children in Stuttgart's elementary schools and kindergartens went for an outing that included songs, games, and patriotic speeches.[106] Youth groups were taken on longer excursions. The Realgymnasium in Stuttgart had a tradition of visiting a place in Württemberg that was connected to Germany's unification; favorite sites were castles, archaeological ruins, and beautiful natural locations.[107] This mode of celebration was a continuation of an old custom in an urban setting. Taking a walk to a medieval castle was a pleasurable way to raise the youth's consciousness about national history. (Note how far back in the past the history of the unification began.)

Sedan Day celebrated the nation, but localism had its own grip on the holiday; it changed the holiday as much as it was changed by it. The celebration of the Children's Festival and Sedan Day underlined the importance of localism to the success of the holiday. This reality was far from the idea that Berlin controlled the national holiday. The joint celebration enhanced the holiday's popularity and resulted in its spread to remote Protestant villages in Württemberg. It was popular in small rural communities with as few as 1,000 to 3,000 inhabitants, where traditional ways of life persisted despite the forces of modernity. The importance of localism was also demonstrated in the preference given at times to local over national considerations. In Sulz the holiday fit local conditions when the celebration was moved to the end of August because the annual market day was at the beginning of September.[108] Sedan Day could be adapted to local experience, needs, and aspirations; in doing so, the holiday changed its form but at the same time maintained its national educational goals.

Localism gave rise to reactions toward the holiday that eloquently showed people's feelings and motivations. Although most of the celebrants did not leave written records of their thoughts, their behavior, gestures, and mischievousness were telling in themselves. People found original ways to express their happiness about, and the solemnity of, the occasion. In small Bartenstein in 1874 the German flag was unfurled on top of the church tower at the exact time the French army waived the white flag in Sedan in 1870. In Göppingen a huge bonfire was set on the Hohenstaufen, where many people assembled at the foot of the mountain to watch the spectacle, while the Singing Society pleasantly sang patriotic songs in the darkness. Celebrants in Hoheneck opened the day with a salvo of an 1870–71 French gun. And in Tuttlingen five veterans of the Napoleonic Wars participated in the procession to symbolize the unyielding will for unification.[109]

The picture that emerges in this chapter provides the necessary corrective to the historical view of Sedan Day as determined by militarism and official culture. In history the sources govern: there is no evidence to corroborate the view that celebrants expressed in their behavior and language the prevalence of either military ideas as a constituent element of social organization or a bourgeois mentality of subservience to the authoritarian state. Quite the contrary, the holiday showed the autonomy of local initiatives in constructing a national identity in imperial Germany, for the liberal bourgeoisie in Württemberg originated Sedan Day in spite of the lukewarm attitude of the emperor and Bismarck to the idea of a national holiday. To be sure, this study presents the experience of the holiday in one region. We need further studies of Sedan Day in Germany to reach general conclusions.

When we abandon the myth that the holiday's significance lay in militarism and subservience to the state, we can appreciate the success and meaning of Sedan Day in the 1870s and 1880s as based on perceiving the nation through the lens of common tradition of celebration and on placing new national values in a local context. The holiday, in a sense, helped people comprehend the novelty of the nation-state by using a familiar symbolic representation. People internalized the nation-state by transforming it into a local experience. In essence, by using traditional symbolic representation, Sedan Day gave the abstract German nation a tangible "look."

The traditional symbolism of national holidays produced a shared national image between Protestant notables and common folks and helped to spread the holiday to the countryside. This shared image did not imply, however, that celebrants shared similar motivations and perceptions of the nation. Some people in small localities showed great patriotic enthusiasm. Others may have joined the holiday in order to celebrate the Children's Festival; we don't know whether the holiday changed these people's perception of the nation. But we do know that they joined the national holiday in the first place because of the local aspect of the holiday and the traditional practice of celebration.

The festival of Sedan Day directs our attention to the importance of the 1870s and 1880s in inventing a national tradition in Germany. Most of the research on the invention of national tradition through festivals and monuments in the German Empire has centered on Wilhelmine Germany. Eric Hobsbawm's argument that "the invention of tradition of the German Empire is . . . primarily associated with the era of William II" is correct only insofar as we consider the role of the empire and the Hohenzollerns in inventing new traditions.[110] William II no doubt opened a new era in the empire's shaping of national identity by actively supporting monuments and celebrations. He was often personally involved in such projects, as when he directed the construction of the *Siegesallee* in Berlin in the 1890s, a boulevard adorned with monuments of the unification's heroes.[111] Nevertheless, when we shift our focus from the empire to civil society, it is obvious that Germans did not wait for William II to begin inventing national traditions; the liberal bourgeoisie reacted to the symbolic passivity of the emperor and Bismarck by originating Sedan Day. Moreover, a *Siegesallee* in Berlin in the 1870s and 1880s would, in any case, not have succeeded in rendering an experiential image of the nation for Württembergers. The significance of Sedan Day was that it was, in a sense, the anti-*Siegesallee* representation of the nation, namely an image of the nation that could be effectively represented, understood, and acted out in the locality.

While Sedan Day was not a holiday originated and imposed from above by the empire, it nonetheless originated at the local level by an elite, the liberal bourgeoisie, conscious of its patriotic role in the region and the nation. Since symbolic representations of national identity are, as is well known, sites of political and ideological conflicts we should turn now to explore the politics of national identity as expressed in the holiday.

CHAPTER THREE

Sedan Day:
A Memory for All the Germans?

W as Sedan Day a holiday for all the Germans? This was a vital question for the national holiday that aspired to stand for post-1871 Germany. Since Sedan Day was originated by liberals, we should in fact ask, Was Sedan Day ever intended by its originators to be a holiday for all the Germans? The crux of the issue is, How did liberals articulate a concept of the nation in the celebrations: as an integrative and inclusive community, or as a restricted and exclusive one? Did they attempt to co-opt—or at least to *appear* to have co-opted—different views of the nation by celebrating an open and integrative holiday, and thus project national solidarity and harmony? Or did they celebrate an exclusive holiday, thereby projecting a disunited and conflict-ridden community? To answer these questions we must first place Sedan Day within the political and social developments in Württemberg.

SOCIETY, POLITICS, AND THE HOLIDAY

The creation of Sedan Day in the immediate years after 1871 was a result of the liberals' shared feeling of optimism about the opportunity to forge a new national society. The *Schwäbische Kronik* commented on the 1871 Reichstag elections in which the National Liberal Party won 12 seats out of the 17 Württemberg representatives and 64 percent of the votes: "The result of our Reichstag elections gives shining, highly gratifying evidence of the fortunate transformation that has taken place in our people's political ideas and frame of mind. With one exception, all the Reichstag representatives have national sentiments and no Volkspartei (VP) candidate was elected. The split of the last election for the Customs Union parliament has been remedied. This dark period lies forever behind us without aftereffects, without trace."[1] This sentiment reflected the political reversal of fortune of the Württemberg liberals in 1871.[2]

In the 1860s, as we have seen, opponents of the unification under Prussia's hegemony, the *Großdeutsch* Landespartei and the leftist Volkspartei, dominated the political scene, while the Deutsche Partei (DP), founded in 1866 by the pro-Prussian and pro-unification liberals and moderate conservatives, faired poorly in local politics. In the 1868 Customs Union parliament elections, the liberals failed to win a seat and had to watch the victory of the democrats and *Großdeutsche*. In the 1868 Landtag elections democrats and *Großdeutsche* won 40 seats to only 14 of the DP. The political situation changed when the Deutsche Partei, riding on a wave of patriotism, won the Landtag elections in December 1870, increasing its seats to 30 while the VP declined to 17. The main political issue at the elections was the imminent unification and its supporters, headed by the Deutsche Partei, decisively won.[3]

Following the unification, the liberals in Württemberg constructed a group identity by cultivating the differences between their national stance and the *Großdeutsch* sentiments of democrats, Catholics, particularists, and even the king, all of whom the liberals viewed as supporters of the pre-1871 defunct political order. They used this strategy in part to counter particularistic tendencies and in part to set themselves apart as the "true" representatives of the empire and the nation on the local level. The liberals claimed the mantle of patriotism so assiduously that they once succeeded even in portraying Bismarck as insufficiently patriotic. Following a vacancy of a Reichstag seat in Württemberg in the summer of 1872, Bismarck suggested that the Prussian ambassador in Stuttgart, von Rosenberg, work "in the interest of our policies in the empire" for the election of Baron Friedrich Gottlob Karl von Varnbüler. Although as Württemberg prime minister before 1870 Varnbüler did not support the Prussian solution to the German Question, Bismarck proposed the candidacy of Varnbüler in order to reinforce a policy of reconciliation with the states that fought Prussia in 1866. When von Rosenberg contacted the leaders of the DP, they opposed the idea because of Varnbüler's policies before 1871, although in 1872 his program was similar to the DP's. In the end, the DP presented its candidate, who lost the elections to Varnbüler. Bismarck, perplexed by the behavior of the DP, commented that in Württemberg one can be either national or antinational, "while the nuances increasingly fade."[4] In fact, the liberals, emphasizing their patriotism by downplaying the national loyalty of others, used a tactic that should have been familiar to Bismarck.

The liberals' political self-confidence and general optimism following the unification serve to explain the immediate post-1871 background of the production of Sedan Day. Beyond this, the production of national identity in the holiday between 1873 and the 1890s, the period when the holiday had attracted significant crowds and been celebrated most meaningfully, reflected three long-term trends in Württemberg society and politics.

The first trend was unmistakable: the holiday coincided with the considerable political influence of the liberal-bourgeois notables between the unification and 1895. The political success of the liberals did not stop when the wave of patriotism expectedly subsided after 1871. The victory in the Landtag elections in 1870 was followed by electoral successes in 1876, when the DP won 57 percent of the votes, in 1882, when the party again won 57 percent, and in 1889, when it drew 64 percent of the votes. Once the party lost in the 1895 Landtag elections, sinking to a relatively miserable 24 percent, it never again regained in imperial Germany its dominant role in local politics.[5]

In the period of its electoral success the DP became a *Regierungspartei*, a party of government, in the administrations of Prime Minister Hermann von Mittnacht (1870–1900), who led a political system that combined a strong prime minister with constitutionalism. Mittnacht was the key political figure in Württemberg after the unification. The Social Democratic *Schwäbische Tagwacht* observed that "what Bismarck was for two decades in the empire, Mittnacht was for three decades in Württemberg. Mittnacht was 'the government.'"[6] In 1877, for example, he held the position of prime minister and was responsible for foreign affairs, transportation, justice, and relations with the royal house, and served as a member of the Landtag. In spite of his disproportionate political influence, Mittnacht sought the cooperation of the Landtag, which he used to strengthen his position opposite the king and Berlin on specific political issues. The party composition of the Landtag was suitable for cooperation. Mittnacht, a *Großdeutscher*, who after 1871 conducted a German policy that combined political pragmatism with a touch of particularism, could rely on the support of his party, the Landespartei, and the DP, which wanted to expand Württemberg's integration into the empire.[7] The party benefited from this cooperation. Julius Hölder, the party leader, became speaker of the Landtag in 1875 and secretary of the interior in 1881. The party stepped up to realize its political program by supporting reforms in the judiciary, administration, and Landtag.[8]

Given the impressive electoral victories of the DP until 1895, the question to ask is, How could the *Kleindeutsch* liberals attain political success in a Württemberg society that maintained, even after 1871, *Großdeutsch* sentiments? The unification, to begin with, dealt a severe political and ideological blow to the liberals' main rivals, the democrats. In the early years of the empire, the shock of Prussia's victory was so deep that VP activities and grass-roots participation ceased almost completely. Only *Der Beobachter*, the organ of the Volkspartei, maintained a loud and clear democratic voice in Württemberg. Since the unification was now an accomplished and irreversible deed, many VP voters shunned the ballot box or chose to express in their vote immediate local interests that could best be delivered by the government's parties. Thus in the 1876 Landtag elections, the first in imperial Germany, the VP won only 4 seats, a number which rose slightly to 8 in 1882 and 12 in 1889.[9]

More generally, the political success of the liberals until 1895 should be seen in the context of the German *Honoratiorenpolitik*, a political system controlled by notables where people often expressed in their vote ties of patronage instead of social, political, and economic identities and interests. Before the rise of mass- and interest-group politics in the 1890s participation in Landtag elections was still relatively low, hovering around 65 percent, and only a limited number of people were politically active. These were mostly the notables, a closely knit group of acquaintances who met before elections, often in a local restaurant, to decide on a candidate who frequently ran unopposed. Liberal notables influenced local politics by virtue of their status as leaders of the community and by virtue of their position in the state and local administrations. The DP included many highly ranked officials and judges in addition to many officials on the communal level. Among the DP representatives in the Landtag from 1868 to 1882, 50.5 percent were either administrative, judicial, or local officials.[10] This gave the DP an important advantage in elections that were habitually strongly influenced by the government in favor of its parties.[11] By contrast, the VP was mainly a party of the petite bourgeoisie and only 21.6 percent of its Landtag representatives between 1868 and 1882 were officials, all on the communal level.[12] The symbiosis of liberal notables and state officials explains why the DP, whose support for the empire was a minority position in largely *Großdeutsch* Württemberg, succeeded in local elections. So, while some voters were obviously liberal, many others cast their vote because of direct influence by local and regional officials.[13]

The second trend evident in the production of Sedan Day by the liberals was that the main division in Württemberg politics from 1871 to 1895 was national, not religious or social.[14] The holiday pitted *Kleindeutsche* against *Großdeutsche*, pro-Prussians against anti-Prussians, and, only secondarily, Catholics against Protestants or rich against poor. While liberals used, as we shall soon see, *Kulturkampf* rhetoric in the holiday, the essence of Sedan Day was never a religious conflict between Catholics and Protestants because the *Kulturkampf* never took hold in Württemberg, and the democrats, who were mostly Protestants, joined Catholics in their opposition to the holiday and the *Kulturkampf*.

The party composition of the Landtag reflected the national division of Württemberg politics. The Landtag included 93 members, of whom 70 were elected in secret, universal manhood suffrage, while 23 members were non-elected notables, or *Privilegierten*, from the clergy, universities, and nobility. In spite of the unification, the Landtag remained unchanged from the 1860s to 1895 and consisted of three political groups. The *Großdeutsch* Landespartei, comprising most of the *Privilegierten*, gathered Protestant and Catholic conservatives under the leadership of Mittnacht. The democratic left of the VP and like-minded Catholics opposed the government, as well as the unification of Germany under Prussia's hegemony and, in the first years after 1871, the empire. And the DP viewed its reason for existing as supporting the pro-Prussian German empire. Two important national parties did not participate in Württemberg local politics: the Catholic Center Party and the Social Democratic Party (SPD). The Center Party in Württemberg was founded only in 1890 in part because the Württemberg state did not conduct an official *Kulturkampf* against Catholics.[15] Catholics voted for the *Großdeutsch* parties, the Landespartei, and, to a lesser extent, the VP. The SPD, for its part, was weak in Württemberg, whose industrialization remained tenuous. Württemberg had only one big city, Stuttgart, and was still a region of small and medium-sized communities. As a result, the first Social Democrat entered the Landtag only in 1895 and the Reichstag in 1898.[16]

In the three-corner universe of Württemberg political parties—the DP, the VP, and the Landespartei—the DP stood out as the only political group that wholeheartedly supported the empire before and after the unification. There were two advantages to the DP's splendid isolation as the party of the national stance. One advantage was symbolic: the DP claimed to speak for the nation and it was in this spirit that it supported Sedan Day. The second advantage was political since the party, being the only political representative of the national voice in Württemberg, did not have to compete with other parties for the votes of German nationalists in Württemberg. When this electoral advantage is coupled with the consequences of notable politics—namely, the powerful positions in state and local administrations and the possibility of influencing elections—then the extended influence of liberal notables on local politics becomes clear.

The advantages of the liberals in local politics become even clearer when we compare Landtag elections to the Reichstag national elections in Württemberg. Main features of notable politics were evident also in Reichstag elections (low turnout, for example). Nevertheless, one important difference was that the participating parties in Württemberg Reichstag elections included the Center Party and the SPD. Reichstag elections divided Württemberg society, as they did for German society, along national but also along religious and class lines. Under these circumstances the liberals did not do nearly as well as in Landtag elections. Starting in 1874 the Center Party consistently won four Reichstag seats in the Catholic areas in Württemberg. The VP ran strong in a number of elections, particularly in 1881 when seven of its candidates were elected. The difference between Landtag and Reichstag elections was also one of political style. The acrimonious campaign and rhetoric in Reichstag elections were not simulated in Landtag elections. In Reichstag elections, more than in local politics, Württembergers expressed their ideology, religious beliefs, and economic interests, and when they did so, the national stance of the DP appeared not as popular as one might think by looking at Landtag elections results.

Paradoxically, therefore, the liberals, who in Sedan Day set out to construct a national identity to suit the new nation-state, owed their local political influence to the fact that Württemberg's political system reflected the traditional preunification national divisions and that it did not conform after 1871 to the national party political structure. The liberals could maintain their influence only as long as the pre-1871 notable politics and party structure remained intact.

The third trend manifest in the holiday was that Sedan Day was celebrated by a liberal minority in a society that shared deep feelings of particularism. In the 1870s, when the memory of the independent Württemberg state was still fresh, particularism was often raw and uncompromising. J. Haußmann, a leader of the VP in Württemberg, greeted a meeting of the Deutsche Volkspartei in the early years of the empire with the following words: "In spirit we are one / In the empire, though / When it will crumble / Home happily we'll go."[17] The liberals were often the target of scathing remarks and their national stance was seen as un-Württembergian. So while the liberals called themselves proudly "national," many in Württemberg called them "Prussian." The view that the liberals relinquished their local identity was even seen as un-German. None other than Karl I expressed this sentiment in 1872: the liberals by "renouncing their own fatherland [Württemberg], can be of help neither to the empire nor to Prussia, for one who is not loyal to his Heimat is unreliable, wishing only upheaval and revolution."[18] In the 1880s and 1890s, although the idea of a return to an independent Württemberg disappeared, particularism remained strong in the form of anti-Prussianism. In 1886 Karl I instructed the Prussian ambassador to Stuttgart that the conduct expected from the new Prussian commander of the Württemberg army was to respect the identity of the land and its people "since we are Swabians and we want to remain Swabians."[19]

The celebration of Sedan Day can only be understood against the backdrop of notable politics, along with the political success of liberals in local elections, the symbiosis between liberal notables and state officials, the continuation of the preunification party allegiances, and the sentiments of particularism. The liberals, of course, were not villains who wished to Prussianize Württemberg. They felt themselves to be Württembergers and indeed seemed to Germans outside Württemberg remarkably *schwäbisch* and even particularistic, only showing the level of particularism among democrats and the king.[20] In the context of Württemberg society impregnated with misgivings about the empire, however, they assumed the role of national educators. The purpose of Sedan Day, according to Stuttgart city councillor Dr. Göz, the keynote speaker in the 1878 banquet, was "to tie the fatherland together with the feelings, emotions and thoughts of the coming generations, to whom the fatherland should be indispensable . . . like the air we breath." We celebrate Sedan Day, he continued, "to instill the ideas of the great German fatherland in the flesh, blood, and soul of the German people."[21] But whose "ideas"? And who constituted "the German people"?

EXCLUSION AND THE APPROPRIATION
OF THE NATION

That liberals never intended to make Sedan Day a holiday for all the Germans was clear from the beginning. In 1872, the democratic *Beobachter* wrote that liberals celebrate under the slogan "He who is a German celebrates Sedan Day."[22] The principal of the girls school Olgastift in Stuttgart identified those who apparently were not German enough for the liberals: "The enemies of the empire—atheism, particularism [read: democrats], Ultramontanism [Catholics], and Social Democracy."[23] Sedan Day was a vehicle for liberal notables to reaffirm their leading position in local society and thus try to appropriate the role of the sole interpreters of national history and national identity. In doing so, on the one hand, they voiced their own ideas of Germany and of German history in a way that made these ideas incontestable, and on the other hand, they sought to subdue rather than to co-opt differing views and to exclude rather than include other Germans. The holiday was an instrument of power through which the liberals attempted to formulate and to codify through exclusion and absence a national identity that, they hoped, would ensure their monopoly on the way to order and to interpret national life.

Exclusion had many faces and many methods. The liberals excluded Catholics by supporting in the celebrations the *Kulturkampf*. Anti-Catholic feelings led people at evening banquets to sing the traditional combative hymn of the Protestants "Ein' feste Burg ist unser Gott" (A mighty fortress is our god).[24] Catholics were equated with the archenemy France; similarly, Stuttgart city councillor Reiniger, after describing how Bismarck led Germany to victory in Sedan, stated that "The chancellor, who refuses to go to Canossa, protects us also against another enemy of the empire."[25] Liberals justified the exclusion of Catholics from the celebrations by arguing that Catholics denied the nation a boundless devotion and maintained a supranational loyalty to the pope in Rome.[26] The toast to Bismarck at the evening banquets was a popular occasion to attack Catholics, as in Stuttgart in 1875: "At the battle of Sedan stood the man [Bismarck] who since then took charge of the *Kulturkampf*. The *Kulturkampf* is a historical challenge, and it is therefore the duty of all of us to guarantee [its success]."[27] In fact, the *Kulturkampf* excluded Catholics even when liberals did not mention it in the holiday: it was enough that the liberals in Germany led the *Kulturkampf* for Catholics to avoid the celebration.

A different, but no less effective, way of exclusion was practiced in Tübingen. Engineer Haller, a democrat, showed up at the evening banquet. In the hall a member of the Holiday Committee, Walcker, approached Haller shouting, "Don't you understand that your presence here is a scandal." Walcker accused Haller of coming to the banquet to spy for the democratic Volkspartei and tried to throw him out. Other celebrants joined Walcker's attacks, and only the police rescued poor Haller from the public's rage.[28]

In the case of democrat Haller, exclusion from the celebration was effected through physical force after he had arrived at the banquet. A better way was to prevent nonliberals from showing up in the first place. The liberals sorted out the participants in the early stages of the holiday planning by exercising an exclusive control over the organization and the personnel of Sedan Day. The clubs and local committees of the DP organized the holiday all over Württemberg.[29] Its people participated in the holiday committees. And it was the local branch of the party that requested the town council to contribute modest financial or material aid to the celebration.[30] Not surprisingly, contemporaries in Württemberg associated the holiday with the DP; it "belonged" to the party. When *Der Beobachter* ran a satire about how to organize a celebration of Sedan Day, the newspaper titled it "A Meeting of the Deutsche Partei in Dingskirchen on the Evening Preceding Holy Sedan Day."[31] For democrats, Catholics, and socialists the identification of the holiday with the DP was reason enough to shun the celebrations.

For the liberals, the policy of exclusion had one big advantage: it shaped their national identity as the only true patriots. The keynote speaker at the evening banquet in Tübingen in 1885 denounced the "antinational" enemies of Sedan Day—"the Ultramontane Party, the Deutsch-Freisinnige Partei, and the . . . Democrats"—and in the same breath praised the celebrants of Sedan Day, the "national parties, here in Württemberg the Deutsche Partei."[32] The liberals used the policy of exclusion to establish certain national qualifications that set them apart from other groups in Württemberg. The first and indispensable qualification was a belief in the 1871 solution of the German Question, the *Kleindeutsch* nation-state under Prussia's hegemony, contra *Großdeutsche*, democrats, and socialists. They added anti-Catholicism, in the spirit of the *Kulturkampf*, and admiration for the emperor and Bismarck, who was revered not only as a statesman but also as a politician. The toast for Bismarck in evening banquets included intense attacks against Catholics, socialists, and democrats. The true German, therefore, according to the liberals, and the common Sedan Day celebrant was thus an ardent supporter of the empire, an anti-Catholic, antiparticularist, and antisocialist, an admirer of the emperor and Bismarck, and a Protestant.

The liberals also used the policy of exclusion to marry their idea of national identity to their social identity as bourgeois notables. In small communities, where the holiday developed into a local festival, they shared the celebrations with Protestant popular classes. But in Stuttgart and large towns, where social divisions were more clearly drawn, the social distinction of the liberal haute bourgeoisie was evident. The democrats were on the mark when they described Sedan Day in Tübingen as the holiday of the "most distinguished," although not necessarily when they called its message derogatorily "Eggheads talk" [*Professoren Reden*].[33] A small entrance fee was at times a requirement to participate in the holiday. Celebrants of the Stuttgart banquet in 1874 had to donate a small amount for a war invalids fund.[34] In Tübingen, in 1893, the holiday's main attraction—a concert by the band of the local battalion at the drill ground—charged 20 pfennigs entrance fee, and 10 pfennigs for members of military associations or visitors.[35] In both cities the fee was cheap, but the participation in the holiday was not free. Perhaps more effective, the evening banquet imposed the need for manners, decorum, and attire that were wholly unaffordable and intimidating to most people. The banquet was an occasion for the liberals to introduce, indeed to codify, a form of respectability that commingled their liberal worldview, their idea of national identity, and their social status.[36] Celebrating in splendid isolation, the liberals attempted to distinguish their position in society by claiming that their status and prestige in local life made them the most suitable group to shape national history and identity.

The policy of exclusion offers a key to understanding the meaning of the holiday. It underscores the centrality of the liberals to the process of forging a national identity in Württemberg after 1871. Given the various degrees of reservations and hostility of Catholics, democrats, *Großdeutsche*, and socialists, the liberals emerged as the only group that seriously wished, and could attempt, to construct a national identity. They derived their legitimacy from claiming to have supported the empire in a way that no other group in Württemberg society and politics did. The liberals translated in the holiday their ideological position, reinforced by their social status and political influence among like-minded and politically indifferent Protestants, into symbolic action. And the most sustained and original effort to define the new nation was by creating a national narrative rewriting German history.

By founding Sedan Day the liberals strove to make sense of German history; to explain it was to own it. To interpret the past—better, to domesticate it—for their own purpose was a way to take symbolic possession of the present. The liberals thus set out to rewrite German history from its origins to the present. Their narrative followed the grand storyline of German history but was limited neither by evidence nor by rules of control and verification. For them evidence was optional and invention was self-conscious; they were limited only by the scope of their imagination, for their story was a fable, a legend, and a propaganda.

The national narrative was a regular part of Sedan Day's speeches in banquets, churches, and schools. The newspapers *Schwäbische Kronik* and *Tübinger Chronik* published large numbers of speeches in full. Between the 1870s and 1890s the national narrative hardly changed, and I use illustrative examples from different years. Speeches of the national narrative were the main part of evening banquets and at times they lasted hours. Whether adults or children at school, listeners always expected the narrative to be interesting, dramatic, and entertaining, and speakers performed accordingly.

My mode of proceeding is to explore how events and periods were remembered, or modified, repressed, or completely forgotten. To unravel the essential conceptions of the narrative I will look at the semantic inventory of its rhetoric, at particular words that conveyed the underlying assumptions of the story. And just as collective memory was part of the structure of collective forgetfulness, what could and could not be said in the rhetoric was woven together.

According to the liberal bourgeoisie, before 1871 German history was a long and painful story of humiliation as the European nations conquered and annexed German territories and fought their wars on German soil.[37] France in particular, whether headed by Cardinal de Richelieu, Louis XIV, revolutionaries, or Napoleon, sought to subdue Germany.[38] The words used in the national narrative to characterize the German nation in this period expressed a profound disunion among Germans:[39]

Zersplitterung	fragmentation	*Uneinigkeit*	disagreement
Zerrissenheit	inner strife	*Zwietracht*	discord
zerklueftet	fissured	*zerfahren*	burst asunder
gespaltet	divided	*zerfallen*	disintegrated
Zwist	contentiousness	*zerrütten*	disorganized

The reason for Germany's troubles was Germans' particularism, for everywhere in Germany reigned the "jealousy of the regional states that went their separate ways pursuing different destinations."[40] While other nations united, Germans had "separate formations, particular military systems, distinct monetary and transportation systems."[41]

A second reason for Germany's national hardship, so the story went, was the German apolitical character: Germans before 1871 were "the people of dreamers—rich, no doubt, in philosophers and poets, rich in intellect, science, and art, but incapable of holding a powerful position among the nations."[42] The liberals referred to the characterization of Germans as the people of *Dichter und Denker*, poets and philosophers, a recognition of their extraordinary contribution to European culture. They appreciated the literary and artistic achievements of the German intelligentsia, but resented the predominance in German history of the intelligentsia over the politicians, and of culture over politics.[43] German national history had been in need of actions, not words, as Professor Dietz, the main speaker in Stuttgart's evening banquet in 1895, explained: "We were called the people of poets and philosophers, and this is certainly true, for the German lives only too willingly in ideal worlds that make him forget the real ones. He remembers humanity, and meanwhile forgets the fatherland. . . . That is why, as our history shows, German national life and aspiration were always neglected."[44]

Germans' lack of political consciousness was told in a variety of ways. In the period of Frederick the Great, "political greatness was ruined by an aesthetic generation. Over young Werther's grief of love flowed many tears, over the inner disruption of the fatherland only a few were shed."[45] Later, at the beginning of the nineteenth century, "Napoleon had to overtake Germany's quiet world with demonic vehemence in order to teach the Germans that the ultimate destiny of a nation is determined not by the amiable realm of poetic pleasure, but by the tempestuous realm of politics."[46] Shapeless territorially and powerless politically, Germany lacked a defined identity; the nation was a formless entity, a mere "geographical idea," a phrase doubtless referring to Metternich's remark at the Congress of Vienna that the idea of Germany and of a German people was an abstraction.[47]

The new era that began in 1871 was a reverse image of the trials and tribulations experienced before. Antonymous vocabulary was used to describe the nation-state as a constitution of a tightly knit whole. The key words that transmitted the ideas and sentiments of the new period portrayed a work of construction. The nation was represented as "a structure" (*Bau*) and a "new building" (*das neue Gebäude*), whose "foundation stone" (*Grundstein*) was the battle of Sedan.[48] For the first time in history, national boundaries defined the German homeland, giving it a specific "form" and "shape" (*Form, Gestalt*), words frequently used to describe the nation-state.[49] Like a change in a state of aggregation, the nation transformed from a dream and an idea into a "real" (*wirklich*) and "tangible" (*greifbar*) object.[50]

The leading metaphor used by the liberals to describe the nation after 1871 was *das große Ganze*, which has no direct counterpart in English and may be translated as the "big whole."[51] As *das große Ganze*, Germany represented a compact entity, turning the characteristics of pre-1871 inside out. The word *einheitlich* in its various meanings indicated the changes. The German state had now "standardized" regulations of trade and transportation, "uniform" monetary, measuring, and weight systems, a "central" diplomatic representation, and a "homogeneous" jurisdiction.[52] Germans themselves changed, and their new collective character represented "an indivisible consciousness, an indivisible feeling, an indivisible will, and an indivisible power."[53] The year 1871 signaled, therefore, the end of particularism and the beginning of a uniform national order.

As told by the liberals, the story of the birth of *das große Ganze* in 1871 had the makings of a fairy tale: in those days the German people changed all of a sudden, put past fragmentation behind, and a new nation was born. The year 1871 was Germany's baptism by fire, a rite of passage into national respectability. The war united Germans across religious, class, and regional divisions: "At that time religious confession did not matter. Shoulder to shoulder stood the factory owner and the worker, and the enemy's grenades hit the aristocrat as well as the peasant."[54] This experience molded provincials into Germans, as "the Prussian saw with joyful amazement how bravely his South German brother fought, and the Württemberger was astonished at what a loyal heart shone from the blue eyes of the Pomeranian: we became acquainted with one another and we learned to respect and love each other."[55] Indeed, "The soldiers did not wish henceforth to be Prussians and Bavarians, Saxons and Württembergers, but only German soldiers."[56]

The key word to describe the essence of the new Germany was the adjective "one" (*ein*) before nouns denoting the characteristics of the new nation. Usually, "one" appeared capitalized, to become "One" (*Ein*), deviating from grammatical regulations, and stressing the quality of *das große Ganze* as homogeneous. Thus in 1871 the nation was "forged into being One thing,"[57] as Germany was finally "One people, One army, One Reichstag, One German polity."[58]

According to the liberals, the experience of 1871 was the axis around which German history evolved. The rhetorical formulation of the event did not describe merely change but metamorphosis. The unification of 1871 was Germany's conversion and rebirth that cut German history in two, a *Stunde null*, zero hour, where German history stopped and began anew. The liberals appreciated the past in the national narrative neither for its own sake nor because it had led to the present, but because it served as an admonition against particularism and the absence of political unity. Their national narrative was not based so much on a quest for origins, as on emphasizing the present, *das große*

Ganze. It was not a history as genealogy, did not blur historical time, and consequently did not create a mythical German past.

The references in the national narrative to the German remote past, the period before the Thirty Years' War, were rare. This past was appreciated because of its ancientness, but was not perceived as a primordial one. The Middle Ages were evoked at times to enhance the present, thus confirming the fascination with this period during the Second Empire. Emperor Frederick Barbarossa and Emperor William Barbablanca were historical reference points as the reign of the new emperor fulfilled the legend of the medieval sleeping emperor who one day would save the German people.[59] Karl the Great (Charlemagne) was mentioned once in connection with the coronation of Emperor William I in Paris to show a return of a German emperor to the city.[60] On the whole, however, the references to the German remote past did not repeat often enough and with enough coherence to play a decisive role in the national narrative. The remote past was mentioned to remind the listeners of the long and important history of the German people, but it had the flavor of antiquity.

FEELING SWABIAN OR FEELING GERMAN?

What was the place of Württemberg in *das große Ganze*? Liberals faced the problem of integrating Württemberg history within a German narrative that praised national cohesion and uniformity. Oskar Fraas, the head of the Anthropological Association of Württemberg, formulated a response to this quandary that demonstrated a sense of uneasiness: "I want to lead you from the wide horizons of the German fatherland back to the narrow boundaries of the Swabian Heimat. Swabia is *after all* our old and beloved Heimat and we are *equally legitimized* to feel ourselves Germans, no less than Swabians, and Swabians no less than Germans!"[61] Reminding the celebrants that Swabia was "after all" their beloved Heimat, Fraas apologetically acknowledged the priority given to Germany over Württemberg in the national narrative. It was essential to stress their equal legitimacy precisely because the narrative failed to reconcile local and national pasts.

It is not that Württemberg was totally ignored. The speaker who followed Fraas, a gymnasium principal by the name of Jäger who was born in Württemberg but had already lived for many years in Cologne, toasted the "Swabian Heimat." He put the relations between any region and the nation poetically: "The day we celebrate today gave to each one of us again his narrow Heimat [*engere Heimat*]. Wherever a German man now celebrates Sedan Day, he can do it feeling that he is everywhere at home."[62] Jäger himself symbolized the Swabian who could feel at home after the unification even in Prussia. This reconciliatory way of putting the relations between Württemberg and Germany reminds us of the holiday's festival, which represented the nation within a local setting, but it was rather incongruent with the general idea of the national narrative where such references were too infrequent to create a modus vivendi between feeling Württemberg and feeling German.

The narrative of Württemberg history was based on truth, as well as invention and obliteration. Topics and periods that represented German unity and grandeur were preferred to those that represented disharmony. The Middle Ages, which was ignored as a source for constructing national origins, lent itself to connecting the history of Württemberg and Germany. Württemberg's support of Prussia in 1870–71 was viewed as a continuation of Swabia's loyalty to the Holy Roman Empire during the Middle Ages.[63] The Swabian origins of the Houses of Hohenzollern and Hohenstaufen were remembered in order to represent 1871 and the rule of the Hohenzollern over Württemberg as the return of a familiar past, not a victory of Prussia over Württemberg.[64]

The history of Württemberg between the Late Middle Ages and the modern era was hardly mentioned, perhaps because it was a fundamental stage in the formation of the Württemberg state. The significance of this period for German history, according to the narrative, was not the particular story of every state (Prussia being an obvious exception), but the nation's disunity. Thus the past of Württemberg in this period was mentioned only sporadically as part of the miserable national past of all Germans.

Modern Württemberg and German history presented more immediate, emotional, and controversial historical events that were difficult to integrate into a coherent story because during the nineteenth century the dominant attitudes in Württemberg about the German Question were very different from the solution of 1871. The Wars of Liberation of 1813–15 was remembered as an example of national rebirth, as Father Jahn, the founder of the gymnastic movement, and the poet Moritz Arndt provided an unforgettable lesson of patriotism. The unpleasant fact that Württemberg fought on the side of Napoleon against the Belle Alliance and Prussia in the Battle of Nations in 1813 was left unmentioned—a case of repressed historical memory that was better left in silence.

Above all, the German civil war of 1866 between Austria and the small German states including Württemberg, on the one side, and Prussia, on the other, was a nonevent. It was mentioned only rarely, in brief and superficial ways (for example, as the last act of disunity before the unification).[65] The origins and consequences of the war, and the mood of Württembergers before and after the defeat, were never discussed. The event was deformed to such a degree that celebrants planned how to transmit to the young generation the glorious memory of the wars of 1866 and 1870–71.[66] This did not correspond to the shock experienced by most Württembergers and by the royal house after the 1866 defeat. On 1 January 1867 the democratic *Der Beobachter* expressed poignantly the atmosphere of that year: "The signature of 1866 is called König-grätz. This is murder. Attached to the name of this Bohemian village is the total misery that befell us: the civil war, the division of the fatherland, the end of liberty in the North, and the loss of security in the South."[67] The memory of the civil war, an event that determined the future of Württemberg no less than the war with France, was erased.

Using obliteration and embellishment, the celebrants also produced a new memory of the attitude of Württemberg's king and royal house toward the German unification. Totally forgotten was Württemberg's traditional political support of Austria against Prussia as well as the popularity in Württemberg of the Third Way to solve the German Question. The national narrative praised the king for his support of Prussia, although it was well known in Württemberg and Germany that he opposed Prussia's dominance. The king's sentiments were remembered as "patriotic," which was questionable.[68] He was also remembered as happily renouncing in 1871 full sovereignty over Württemberg and as offering William I the emperor's crown during the coronation—sheer invented historical memories.[69]

The liberals argued that Württemberg's identity even gained by adapting to the new situation: "The regions and their dynasties lose nothing in terms of power and splendor when they fit into the big whole [ins große Ganze]; on the contrary, our peculiar Württemberg character gains its full significance only in harmonious collaboration."[70] Not everyone in Württemberg shared the idea that the land and its royal family retained after 1871 the power and splendor they had when Württemberg was an independent state, but this position was reiterated time and again in the celebrations. There was a strong contradiction between propagating a relationship of subordination between the nation and Württemberg, on the one hand, and, on the other, declaring the benefits to Württemberg derived by such relations. Thus the principle contained in the national narrative was a reevaluation of the role of local identity in German history and an attempt to create a national memory by largely disregarding local memory.

German histories before 1871—the events of 1813, 1866—resembled a mine-field for the construction of a national memory. Many events threatened to explode in contradictory meanings, many memories needed to be canceled, and many to be modified. The denouement of German history, according to the national narrative, was that 1871 was not the outcome of the German past, but the story of how Germans triumphed over their own past. The German past was not a guide for the German present.

Why did the liberals emphasize in the national narrative the present over the past in the representation of national identity? While the national narrative no doubt exaggerated the break with the past, this break nevertheless served to portray the liberals as a sort of national avant-garde in the battle against "enemies of the empire." The liberals boasted of the achievements they helped bring to German society after 1871: "Without Sedan [read: the unification], could Germany have had . . . the Reichstag, could we have had the direct, general . . . elections and the freedom of the press and of association? Could we have had a unified currency and a unified system of weights and measures? A unified system of law, transportation, and trade?"[71] Stressing the present and underplaying the past reinforced the liberals' perception of themselves as bearers of innovation, progress, and modernity, while depicting the liberals' opponents as being stuck in the pre-1871 world.

If the liberals repudiated the past in the national narrative, this perception was not their only way of looking at history. Sedan Day is a case in point that people have more than one way to construct an image of the past, and that they construct more than one image of the same past. It is well documented that Germans in the Second Empire perceived the Middle Ages as a historical model and predecessor to their period, emperor, and empire.[72] Among the groups that cultivated this myth in the arts, history, and monuments was the liberal bourgeoisie, the same group that led the Sedan Day celebration. Did the liberals in Württemberg deviate from the national pattern? This was improbable. Think of the celebrations on the Hohenstaufen near Göppingen, the prime location in Württemberg, and one of the classic locations in Germany, to pay tribute to the German medieval past. The liberals' perception of the medieval past, and of the past in general, was not determined by a false dichotomy whereby they either totally rejected or accepted it. Their perception changed according to the different objectives they gave the representations of the nation in the festival and in the national narrative. The myth of the sleeping medieval emperor who would awaken one day to save Germany suited the Sedan Day festival whose aim it was to connect local past with national sentiments, the local history and geography of Göppingen and the nearby Hohenstaufen mountain were thus linked to the idea of German nationhood. But in the context of the national narrative the liberals attempted to appropriate the nation by breaking with the past and emphasizing the present.

If the festival of Sedan Day as described in the previous chapter was a way of thinking about the nation through traditional images—by placing, say, the 1870–71 war monument in a symbolic texture celebrated since 1813 then the national narrative, the most innovative symbol in the holiday, was a way of thinking that could have originated only after the political change of 1871. The national narrative drew its strength from and was an outcome of the specific post-1871 political conditions in Württemberg when the liberals, being the main supporters of the empire in a *Großdeutsch* society, attempted to cash in symbolically on their political position by making the identification with the present, with the empire, the main element of a new national identity. By stressing in the national narrative the present instead of looking back at the past with nostalgia, the liberals translated their political experience, that is, the transformation of the DP and of Germany after 1871, into a symbolic representation. They viewed the past as a site of political disunion and powerlessness for the DP in Württemberg and for the German nation in Europe, while the present in comparison meant Germany's power among the nations and the liberals' new influence in local politics. In short, the liberals' political experience inspired the symbolic representation that was the national narrative. And if in the national narrative the liberals lay claim to speak for the nation in the name of the present as the supporters of *das große Ganze* and the metamorphosis of 1871, then this had clear consequences for the political meaning of national identity in Sedan Day: when a speaker talked to a liberal audience about *das große Ganze*, we can safely assume how everybody in the room understood the term—a liberal *große Ganze*. In short, *das große Ganze* was, in the context of Sedan Day, a metaphor of both exclusion from and appropriation of the nation.

Equally important in informing the national narrative, and complementing the metaphor of exclusion, was a discourse of national unity. If *das große Ganze* had only been a metaphor of exclusion and appropriation, the liberals could have been exposed to the accusation of disguising narrow, partisan interests as a national, general cause. They balanced the practice of exclusion with the posture of national solidarity: *das große Ganze* was at one and the same time a metaphor of exclusion and of national unity. As a metaphor of unity, *das große Ganze* represented the new, postunification national community—"forged into One"—where differences of class, religion, and region should ideally disappear following the battlefield experience in 1870–71. The discourse of unity represented the holiday as an identity project of the nation as a whole. Yet by legitimizing Sedan Day's identity project and the liberals who created it, the discourse of unity simultaneously delegitimized the holiday's opponents. The metaphors of exclusion and uniformity were thus woven together in the discourse of national narrative. The image of a uniform nation meant in fact a nation of liberals; the wish expressed in the national narrative to build a uniform national society corresponded on the symbolic level to the actual exclusion from the holiday of the majority of Württemberg society.

In this respect, the national narrative contained a utopian vision, being an image of a never-never land of a uniform national society where this did not exist. The revised histories of Germany and Württemberg provided a new national look to a local reality of particularism that was in fact altogether different. The history that elevated Germany over Württemberg was in a sense an antidote to local particularism and to the general view of the liberals as "Prussian." I should emphasize that by arguing that the national narrative was a representation of a never-never land I do not mean to undermine the effectiveness of the holiday or the sincerity of the liberals. On the contrary. An identity, every identity, is more effective and symbolically richer when it represents an image that transcends reality, that connects the present with lost worlds of the past and coveted worlds of the future. We shall see later why the holiday's symbolism failed.

The national narrative represented the ambiguous commingling of *Kultur* and *Macht*, culture and power, in the liberals' perception of national identity. While the liberals felt entitled to speak for the nation because of their *Bildung*, the self-cultivation of the German spirit, they also viewed decisive political action as the necessary factor that changed German history and made national unification possible. They contrasted this political will with the inaction of "poets and philosophers," thus referring, without a sense of irony it seems, to the term contemporaries employed to describe most often none other than themselves, the educated, intellectual, and professional liberal bourgeoisie. The term meant either a flattering attribute of a group that contributed enormously to German and European culture, or a pejorative characterization of an unworldly and apolitical group of people. But for the liberals *Kultur* and *Macht* were not mutually exclusive; rather, the two images constituted a discourse of national uniqueness. German *Kultur* referred to *Innerlichkeit*, to the spiritual qualities of the German people, to essence and authenticity contra image and appearance. The German spirit, or *Geist,* was contrasted with Western and especially British commercialism and superficiality, with the profit-oriented but spiritually vacuous British *Krämer-Nation*, nation of shopkeepers. At the same time the liberals portrayed national identity in the colors of progress and modernity, and Germany as a nation of great military and industrial might. Young Werther was, to be sure, important for the German *Geist*, but Bismarck's political and military exploits were no less significant. The complementary yet explosively ambiguous commingling of *Kultur* and *Macht* was a feature of national identity throughout imperial Germany.[73]

Kultur and *Macht*, culture and politics: the liberals seemed to have mastered both. They did not correspond to the idea of the Germans as *Dichter und Denker* who were removed from everyday reality and lacked the political spirit and commitment to act in their own best interests. On the contrary, they consciously established the holiday as a political tool to exclude their ideological rivals, as a political means to take symbolic possession of the nation. Yet if the liberals consciously established the holiday as a political tool, this tool was not democratic and pluralist. As a metaphor combining discourses of exclusion and national uniformity, *das große Ganze* obliterated the social, political, and religious variousness of Württemberg society. It allowed for political action, not for the representation of differences.

The liberal bourgeoisie constructed in Sedan Day two forms of representation to imagine the nation: the festival, discussed in the previous chapter, based on the past and stressing the locality, and the national narrative based on the present and stressing the nation. Relying on tradition, the festival delivered the message of the new nation-state through an almost reflexive familiarity with a festive discourse. The national narrative, in contrast, was iconoclastically innovative, suggesting in effect that the past cannot be trusted. The image of Germany in the national narrative reflected more closely the political and ideological divisions in Württemberg society about the unification and the legitimacy of the empire. This image was a result of the liberals' confidence and their leading position in local society after 1871, a sort of counterreaction to the strong particularist sentiments in Württemberg; it emphasized the German present, the empire, and the political novelty in national life. The second image of Germany, that of the festival, depicted local life and its connection to national history and was a result of traditional modes of thinking about and celebrating German nationhood; it connected the traditions of the local community with the innovations of the national present. The question that emerges is therefore apparent: were these two forms of representation contradictory and did they not in fact reflect the liberals' incongruous perception of the nation?

On this question we do not have explicit evidence in the sources of Sedan Day. We can formulate, by way of speculation, several hypothesis. Let us begin by assuming that the festival and the national narrative were indeed contradictory aspects of the liberals' perception of nationhood and localness. The contradiction in the liberals' image of the nation and the locality could be illustrated by the symbolic map established by the celebrants of the spaces where the festival took place, in and out of town.[74] The festival marked out a few places that shaped its significance: the stations of the procession, the war memorial, a natural site out of town. Because the festival's symbolic map was identical to traditional German national celebrations, the itinerary of the celebration, which mapped out the memory of the nation Sedan Day wished to immortalize, was more local than national. As a result, liberals produced in the national narrative an iconoclastic reading of local and national history, but did not carve out a new space to display it. They failed to establish either a space without history and memory, like the open-air space of the French Revolution, or a space with memory that would nonetheless stress the novelty of the nation-state. Because liberals used the old space in the traditional manner, the festival was always an appendage to the space established in national holidays in the past. The traditional space of the festival thus contradicted the idea of the birth of the nation as a sudden metamorphosis and instead characterized the nation as a body formed in a continuous and organic way. It interwove ancient and traditional memories with new historical associations (the war of 1870–71, the emperor) and established therefore a continuity between Württemberg and the nation, and between the past and the present. Participants, crisscrossing among the stations, tangibly mapped out this continuity. By fixing the celebration to a prearranged historical setting, the liberals provided a message of national roots and historical genealogy which the national narrative discarded. In short, while the national narrative emphasized the newness of the nation-state, the space chosen to celebrate the nation was full of ancient traces and old emotions. Moreover, in contrast to the national narrative, the itinerary of the festival established a symbolic covenant between the old locality and the nation through the movement from historic and local stations, such as church or marketplace, to new and national ones, such as a war memorial or emperor's monument. The itinerary of the spatial arrangement thus caused the meaning of the national narrative to disintegrate.

This is an elegant explanation, too elegant perhaps. It is attractive because it provides a clear explanation of a complex holiday. But human affairs are often messy and mixed up. The biggest drawback of this explanation is that it views localness and nationhood as mutually exclusive, and therefore concludes that their coexistence must be a contradiction. It assumes a simple and uncomplicated relationship between past and present whereby the representation of one is a substitute for the other. It appears more fruitful to interpret the festival and the national narrative as being complementary aspects of the liberals' perception of localness and nationhood. The liberals attempted to navigate between two shores—one promised a sense of pride stemming from tradition, the other promised a sense of pride stemming from innovation; one put the locality at the center of the world, the other put the nation. The two forms of representation matched all too well the liberals' mindset after the unification as Württembergers and as Germans. The liberals used both forms of representation to appropriate the nation and both forms grew out of their experience before and after 1871. The festival discourse, which had been celebrated by liberals in national holidays before the unification, represented their attachment to the past and to the community. The national narrative was a way to take advantage of the new political opportunities opened by 1871 to lay claim to speak for the nation.

In itself, the combination of local heritage (the festival) and national innovation (the national narrative) could have succeeded in reconciling the region and the nation, as happened later in the Heimat idea. But we can appreciate the possibility of opening a symbolic dissonance between the festival and the national narrative, namely between perceptions of localness and nationhood, the past and the present. Such a possibility was real. Where the narrative stressed novelty, the festival legitimized tradition. Where the narrative emphasized a national metamorphosis, the festival underlined national organic growth. Where the narrative insisted on the sole validity of the nation, the festival confirmed the power of local existence. Where the narrative maintained that all had changed in Germany, the festival showed that much had remained the same. The liberals, therefore, had to juggle two complementary representations so that they would coexist in a state of tension, but without breaking. And powerful tensions did exist, of two kinds. There existed the tension between using tradition while at the same time representing the nation, according to the interpretation of some of the holiday's opponents, as a substitute for, and not a complement to, local identity. This prompted the democrats to say that "We have people in Württemberg who ceased to be Württembergers, but instead became totally Prussian. These people support wholeheartedly the Sedan Day celebrations."[75] And there existed the tension between claiming to speak for the nation while at the same time excluding the majority of Württemberg society. Without popular support the liberals were in danger of losing the legitimacy to speak for the nation and of becoming not a national avant-garde as they had wished but an isolated group out of step with local reality. It is to these tensions that we turn now.

CHAPTER FOUR

An Unfulfilled National Community

I t comes as no surprise that some Württembergers opposed Sedan Day. The celebrants of the holiday attempted to create a sacrosanct public space and time, the violation of which was tantamount to a taboo; for them the allure of the holiday never ceased to work. But for the opponents of the holiday the allure never existed, as they refused to accept the essential presuppositions of the celebration as the "correct" representation of the nation. Their aim was to express an opposition that would be equally powerful, emotional, and authoritative as the celebrations of Sedan Day. The theater of war was the public sphere where opponents attempted to keep community symbols out of the celebration to show that the holiday represented a limited, partisan group and not the community as a whole.

While liberals based the holiday, as we have seen, on the common German tradition of national celebrations as a way to own local symbols and national tradition, democrats and Catholics resisted the use of this tradition for partisan political purposes. They were aware of the importance of the local image to the practice of the holiday and resented the local "look" of Sedan Day in the Children's Festival. The democratic *Der Beobachter* ran a satire on how to score a success in the organization of the celebrations. the first item on the list was planning a Children's Festival because thereafter popularity and triumph were ensured.[1] The joining of the Children's Festival with Sedan Day, although very successful, alienated many in Württemberg who regarded it as a manipulation of an old local festival for partisan political purposes.[2] In Catholic Gmünd the city council decided to celebrate the Children's Festival three days after 2 September to avoid a connection with the celebration of local Protestants.[3] The democrats took pains to untie the relations between past (Children's Festival), present (Sedan Day) and future (the youth) by calling upon the communities to leave the innocent children out of this "party demonstration."[4]

Democrats and Catholics confronted the liberals' attempt to tie the holiday with the unveiling of the 1870–71 war monuments. Setting the unveiling ceremony on the controversial date of the national holiday was a way for liberals to appropriate the memory of the unification and to mark those who did not celebrate Sedan Day as disrespectful toward the fallen sons of the community and of the nation. Uniting Sedan Day and the unveiling ceremony had a strong symbolic meaning because it gave the holiday a sort of official, communitywide approval. While some communities did choose Sedan Day to unveil the monument, many did not. Local authorities were reluctant to give an official blessing to a controversial holiday. In Kirchheim in 1873 the city council decided not to celebrate Sedan Day officially and the unveiling of the war monument was set on 31 August, while the liberals celebrated Sedan Day two days later.[5]

Another strategy of protest was to challenge the participation in the holiday of voluntary associations that included supporters and opponents of the holiday. One such challenge from within led the Veterans Association in Catholic Gmünd to refuse to take part in the celebration.[6] In Ravensburg bad blood almost caused a split after some members of the Singing Society refused to sing in the celebration. The supporters of the holiday in the society tried to change the statute so that it would enforce participation in future celebrations of Sedan Day, but the idea failed. Finally, to the disgrace of the holiday's supporters, some members sang in the ceremony and some stayed home; this destroyed the pretension of national unity.[7]

Individuals, too, found ways to express their opposition in public. Gottlob Egelhaaf tells in his memoirs of an unpleasant ceremony on 2 September at the Heilbronn gymnasium where he taught. In 1875 the principal, Dr. Julius Rieckher, asked the senior teacher Planck to take an active part in the school celebration of Sedan Day. Planck, a staunch *Großdeutscher*, steadfastly declined to cooperate, while Rieckher, a supporter of the holiday, tried without success to talk his lifelong friend into changing his mind. The ceremony took place but old Planck stuck to his guns. He stood through the entire ceremony silent and unapproachable, without providing the slightest sign of accessibility or approval. Having been a leading figure in the school for decades, his comportment was conspicuously noted, and the ceremony dragged along in a tense atmosphere.[8]

By far the most effective means to undermine the holiday, and the least documented, was also the most silent one: absenteeism. People went their usual way, opened their stores, worked the fields, or stayed at home. In Biberach and Ravensburg, Catholics did not even hold church services.[9] The continuation of everyday life in the midst of a national commemoration served as a public display of a taboo; it destroyed the allure of the holiday.

The holiday in Württemberg provoked two counterarguments. Catholics viewed Sedan Day as a threat to the national legitimacy of their religion, and therefore countered the holiday with religious arguments that concerned Germany as a whole. Democrats, in contrast, viewed the holiday as a threat mainly to the local and traditional Württemberg way of life, and their arguments concerned more specifically the future of Württemberg in the new Germany.

The German and Württemberg Catholics were conspicuously absent during the campaign for the national holiday in 1871–72. Fearful of a Protestant *Kleindeutschland* while, particularly in South Germany, harboring *Großdeutsch* sentiments, Catholics were initially cautious toward the Second Empire. But for Catholics these feelings did not require abstention from Sedan Day; Catholics had fought patriotically in the war against France and many viewed the nationstate as a just and inevitable solution to the German Question. They might have needed an encouraging sign from the authorities or from the promoters of the holiday, such as an invitation to join the celebration, for example. Their subdued position during the national holiday campaign in 1871–72 seemed to result from their suspicion of the prominence of certain Protestant protagonists, in particular Bodelschwingh and the Provinzialausschuss whose ideas, influenced by Pietism, linked German nationalism to Protestant religious revival.[10] The suspicion was warranted. Bodelschwingh never seriously planned to include Catholics and Jews in the celebrations.

The liberals determined the meaning of the holiday for Catholics when in 1873 they transformed it to the front line of the *Kulturkampf*.[11] Liberals used Sedan Day, their instrument to codify "correct" national behavior, to expose Catholics as enemies of the empire and national unification. The Catholics responded promptly: on 19 August 1874 Bishop Ketteler of Mainz announced the Catholic policy on the holiday. Ketteler stated first that Catholics were willing to participate in a true Sedan Day national holiday that would commemorate the victory at Sedan and would thank God for his guidance. But, he continued, the present version of a national holiday was false: this holiday did not "originate with the entire German people, but principally from one party [the National Liberal Party]. The holiday, therefore, did not develop from the collective consciousness of the people, but is too often an artificial creation. . . . This party . . . is at present at the forefront of the battle against Christianity and the Catholic Church."[12] Ketteler prohibited the clergy of his diocese to participate in the holiday, which was tantamount to a nationwide prohibition to all Catholics. Instead of celebrating Sedan Day, Catholics celebrated 16 June, the anniversary of the election of Pope Pius IX.[13]

Catholics in Württemberg followed the national pattern and shunned the celebrations whenever and wherever they could. For them 2 September was a business-as-usual day. In Württemberg communities the local church usually held a service on Sedan Day to pray for the fallen soldiers and to thank God for the victory. This innocuous participation was an act of piety toward the families of the dead soldiers and was not regarded by either liberals or Catholics as an expression of support for the holiday. The church services, which attracted only a handful of participants, were the only holiday observances in which adult Catholics participated.[14]

The most interesting factor about Catholics and Sedan Day in Württemberg is that for liberals and Catholics alike the "Catholic Question" relative to the holiday was connected to the *Kulturkampf*, although Württemberg did not experience a *Kulturkampf*. Liberals and Catholics in Württemberg used the language of the *Kulturkampf* to communicate about Sedan Day and, by extension, about German national identity. Catholics undermined the legitimacy of the holiday using religious arguments. Thus in Gmünd, a community with a proud Catholic tradition, the town council decided in 1873 not to celebrate Sedan Day because of the holiday's "un-Christian ideas."[15]

By making the *Kulturkampf* an ideological founding stone of the holiday in a region that experienced no such anti-Catholic campaign, the liberals showed both willingness to stick to their beliefs and consistency with the policies of German liberalism, even when these beliefs and policies were irrelevant to local life. But there was a price to pay. The liberals, by importing the *Kulturkampf* into the relatively peaceful fabric of local Catholic-Protestant relations, demonstrated an indifference to local conditions. It is safe to assume that Catholics in Württemberg would not have supported Sedan Day under any circumstances given the prominent role of German liberals in the *Kulturkampf*. But by making the holiday a stage for the *Kulturkampf*—against sentiments of democrats, conservatives, Karl I, Mittnacht, himself a Catholic, and, of course, the Catholics—the liberals demonstrated disregard of public opinion and popular beliefs in Württemberg society. They thus opened the possibility of the holiday and its celebrants becoming isolated, turning Sedan Day into an aberrant festival in a local world that was in fact quite different.

There was another reason why the liberals' import of the *Kulturkampf* seemed ideologically courageous but out of touch. The basic political principle in Württemberg from 1871 until the upheaval in the 1895 Landtag elections had been that national and not religious convictions shaped the political alignment. Even the *Kulturkampf* in Germany did not change that. Sedan Day in Württemberg was opposed by Catholics and Protestant democrats. As a result, in local terms, the absence of the *Kulturkampf* in Württemberg made the controversy between Catholics and liberals relatively marginal to the meaning of the holiday as a measure of local and national identity. Democrats often complained of the artificial use of anti-Catholic propaganda in Sedan Day when no *Kulturkampf* existed. The origins, the progress, and the results of the *Kulturkampf* were non-Württemberg, external matters that depended on Bismarck, the pope, and Windhorst, the Center leader. Liberals and Catholics in

Württemberg ignored in the *Kulturkampf* controversy the fundamental issue of local identity and how to place it within the nation. Catholics justified their opposition to Sedan Day in religious terms and legitimized their positions by claiming the right of religious freedom. This was a noble cause that also won the support of democrats in Württemberg, but as a whole the cause was too partisan to answer the dilemmas of local identity.

The democrats in Württemberg raised a very different argument against the holiday that concerned the foreignness of the celebration to local tradition. The democrats enjoyed the legitimacy of being part of the historic and the traditional core of Württemberg. They were, for the most part, Protestant, and the origins of their movement were in the geographical heart of Württemberg. Throughout its long history, the democratic movement boasted leaders who symbolized the essence of Swabia and the Swabian character, like the poet and writer Ludwig Uhland, whose name became synonymous with the Swabian homeland. The humble social composition of the movement, whose members were mostly petit bourgeois, gave it the aura of being an authentic people's movement, and the party was called People's Party, Volkspartei.[16] In short, democrats were the salt of the Swabian earth; their arguments against Sedan Day could be countered, but not disparaged.

In Württemberg democrats were the most outspoken opponents of Sedan Day. For democrats and liberals Sedan Day marked a continuation of their pre-1871 disagreement about the proper way to solve the German Question. Before 1871, liberals believed in freedom through unification (*Freiheit durch Einheit*) and supported Prussia's hegemony in Germany. Democrats, in contrast, believed in unification through freedom (*Einheit durch Freiheit*), opposed Prussia's hegemony, and defended Württemberg's independence and particular traditions. The democrats' critique of Sedan Day reflected their preunification arguments as they maintained that the holiday disguised national unification as individual liberty and that, like the empire, the holiday was militaristic and authoritarian.[17]

The democrats posited a clear and a simple postulate that became a serious obstacle for the reception of Sedan Day in Württemberg: the national holiday was a Prussian creation designed to obliterate Württemberg's traditions; the ideas of the celebrations had nothing in common with Württemberg's way of life. Sedan Day was an "official [read: imposed from above and not a popular, authentic celebration arising from the people], particularistic, Hohenzollern-Prussian holiday" that honored Prussia's victory of 1866 and left South Germans to remember their humiliation.[18] It was established by Prussians deliberately to remind South Germans of their subordination to North Germans in the empire, and, like other Prussian innovations, did not display people's inner feelings, but was "ordered" from Berlin.[19] Worse than the Prussians who originated the holiday were the Württembergers who celebrated it. They denied their origins and traditions for a new identity that rejected their Württemberg roots.[20] The democrats judged the liberals without mercy: Sedan Day developed into a "ridiculous farce" of Württemberg "'Prussians' who wished to become more Prussian than the Prussians themselves."[21] The celebrants of Sedan Day were derided as "our Prussians at any price,"[22] as "those who beg to become Prussians" (*Bettelpreußen*),[23] and their political name was changed from National Liberals into "national servitors" (*Nationalservilen*: of Prussia, naturally).[24]

These evaluations were a strong condemnation in Württemberg society. The reactions of the democrats reflected common anxieties among noncelebrants of Sedan Day after 1871 regarding the place of Württemberg in the new empire, in general, and the danger of Prussianizing the land, in particular. In their criticism democrats expressed the dignity of Württemberg's identity in spite of the defeat in 1866 and of the loss of full sovereignty in 1871. They rejected the idea of a uniform nation and questioned its benefit to the future of Württemberg. Their rejection was expressed in the *Beobachter* five days before Sedan Day in 1874 in an 1858 poem by Carl Gutztow: "Unification is a fine sound; but will [unification] be realized at the expense of our best character? / Who wants to advocate its case at such a price! / The German people is only a spiritual people / Its force lies in the soil that it defends, in its customs, language, and traditions."[25]

The sentiments about the dignity of Württemberg's identity found a deep resonance in Württemberg society. *Großdeutsch* supporters and loyalists to the Württemberg royal house effectively opposed the holiday behind the scenes. People like Mittnacht dictated the nonintervention policy of the state in Württemberg on Sedan Day. Conservative groups were also active against the holiday. Otto Elben, a leader of the Deutsche Partei, the editor of the *Schwäbische Kronik*, and an ardent supporter of Sedan Day, complained bitterly in his memoirs about the staunch opposition of conservatives to the holiday and about their decision to countercelebrate with a holiday commemorating Duke Christoph, Württemberg's ruler between 1550 and 1568 and a founding father of the Württemberg state. Duke Christoph was not an important enough figure to prompt any further celebrations; but commemorating his legacy during the years of Sedan Day symbolized for Württemberg conservatives a reaffirmation of their history.[26] Democrats and conservatives attempted, in a sense, to undermine the liberals and their image of the nation by evoking local identity. In an argument similar to that of Karl I in 1872—that by abandoning their Heimat the liberals "can be of help neither to the empire nor to Prussia"— they maintained that one must first be a good Württemberger in order to speak for the nation.

In contrast to the energetic opposition by Catholics and democrats, the socialists played a negligible role in the holiday in Württemberg where workers were few and not yet organized. The socialists criticized Sedan Day as chauvinistic and militaristic, while the celebrants blamed the socialists for being antinational and revolutionary. This animosity, however, was especially vivid in North Germany. Only in Eßlingen, which together with Stuttgart constituted the industrial center in Württemberg, workers refused to participate in the holiday and instead organized a meeting.[27]

Without Catholics, democrats, conservatives, or socialists, and lacking the support of the royal house and the government, the liberal bourgeoisie that celebrated Sedan Day was clearly a minority in Württemberg. The liberals were confronted by serious opposition from democrats and Catholics who, while excluded, did not seem inclined to support the holiday in the first place. They failed to enlist the support of the state and the king and raised indignation among conservatives. In fact, in celebrating Sedan Day, the liberals seemed isolated and the policy of exclusion appeared to have been a result of two contradictory aspects. On one level, the policy gave a clear demonstration of the liberals' self-conscious attempt to take symbolic possession of national identity. Celebrating in splendid isolation underlined the liberals' self-assigned role in Württemberg society as the voice of the nation. On a second level, however, the policy of exclusion also showed the logic of their wish to speak for the nation, while lacking a broad base of consent or popular support. By excluding from the holiday most of Württemberg society, the liberals were left with a holiday but without a nation. The democrats expressed this sentiment clearly in 1876 and then again in 1887: "Instead of saying that Sedan Day has developed year after year into a more authentic national holiday, it would be far more correct to say: into a more authentic National Liberal holiday."[28]

The policy of exclusion exposed the contradictory position of the liberals in Württemberg society after 1871. Assisted by their social status and political influence, the liberals claimed to represent the nation because their national stance stood out in a particularistic Württemberg society. But because Württemberg society was largely *Großdeutsch*, their holiday lacked popular support and became synonymous with a partisan political demonstration, not a people's national holiday. The reason for the liberals' success produced also, in a dialectical relation, their failure.

In principle, exclusion of one group by another in a national holiday should not pose a problem, for national holidays are symbolic forms of political, social, and cultural struggle. The Nazis, to take one obvious example, excluded from the national community a large section of German society: socialists, Communists, Jews, and homosexuals, among others. But their claim to speak for the nation was sustained by enthusiastic mass popular support and, after January 1933, by a state apparatus that violently imposed a racial worldview. The liberals in Württemberg enjoyed neither the political power to impose their holiday nor, most important, mass popular support. As a result they created in the holiday a contradiction between an exclusivity that bordered on isolation and the claim to represent the nation.[29]

The liberals' raison d'être in the holiday was to represent the nation as a whole, not a sectarian, factional idea. The national narrative represented a myth of unity—"One people, One army, One Reichstag, One German polity"—forged by the unification war. In that discourse of national unity the nation stood above class, religious, and regional divisions in German society. The battle of Sedan was admired because on this day "the contrasts between the political parties were silenced."[30] The liberals justified (they used this word specifically: *Die Berechtigung*) Sedan Day by arguing that the holiday stood above the parties, as in the speech of Dr. Karl Elben in 1887: "This commemoration day is not a celebration of a party or of parties. Similar to the German army [in 1870–71]—in which no differences existed between rich and poor, between intellectuals and artisans, between industrialists and workers, and no discrimination existed because of political or religious convictions—thus the celebration of Sedan Day, too, is a holiday of all the Germans."[31] And he continued: "Those who see Sedan Day as a political demonstration and mock the holiday exclude themselves from the celebrations (applause)."

In practice, however, the liberals behaved very differently. They openly supported their partisan political causes, be it the *Kulturkampf*, the Anti-Socialist Law, or attacks against the democrats. The speeches at the evening banquets resembled political campaigns, rather than an attempt to unite the nation around a common celebration.[32] Special publications for the holiday by the Deutsche Partei, such as "On the Occasion of Sedan Day" (1891), communicated particular political messages.[33] The partisan political character of the celebrations was acknowledged by contemporaries. The democrats called the holiday "an idea of National-Liberalism."[34] The *Beobachter* did not report on the celebrations in Heilbronn in 1875 because, explained the newspaper caustically, identical speeches would be held in the meetings of the Deutsche Partei before the runoff Reichstag election called for in mid-September.[35] Nine years later in 1884 the paper reported that six weeks before the Reichstag election in Tübingen the " 'national holiday' of 2 September was used again for partisan party politics and election purposes. The main speaker, Dr. Ramsler, rector of the nonclassical secondary school, did that in an unveiled manner."[36] In Reutlingen in 1886, similar members composed the Holiday Committee and the Electoral Committee of the *Kartel* Parties (liberal and conservative parties, supporters of Bismarck), a situation that attracted attention and drew criticism.[37]

Far from maintaining their claim of unity about the holiday as being above the parties, the liberals saw Sedan Day as an extension of the political arena. The *Tübinger Chronik* expressed this idea when it said that Sedan Day was not only a celebration, but a political war between good and evil, that is, the national forces and the "enemies of the empire."[38] This was a step short of saying that the holiday and the political arena were interchangeable means of reshaping the German nation. The policy of exclusion practiced on Sedan Day was a continuation of the Reichstag election campaigns that were seen as a means to combat "enemies of the empire." The image used by liberals to describe this election war was none other than the battle of Sedan. They maintained that after the political unification in 1871 election campaigns were the battleground for the inner unification of German society. The difference being that in 1870–71 they fought the foreign enemy, while in elections they were fighting the inner enemies.[39] This attitude was especially evident in the Reichstag election campaigns of 1878 and 1887 that presented elements for a recreation of the atmosphere of the great days of 1870–71.[40] In 1878, a political crisis broke out after the attempt upon the emperor's life. Bismarck dissolved the Reichstag and an acrimonious electoral campaign followed that centered on the Anti-Socialist Law. In 1887, Bismarck again dissolved the Reichstag and called for the *Septennat* elections that centered on the Reichstag's control of the military budget. The government fabricated a military crisis with France and conducted a poisonous campaign against the opposition. Gustav Siegle, the Deutsche Partei's candidate in Stuttgart, declared during the campaign of 1887 that "the situation is such that one instinctively thinks back to 1870."[41] The legacy of the unification war was mobilized to delegitimize political opponents. Turning Karl von Clausewitz's famous adage on its head, politics, and Sedan Day, thus became the continuation of the unification war by other means.

The liberals, on the one hand, justified the holiday as being for all the Germans and, on the other hand, coalesced the message in the celebrations of Sedan Day and in their political campaign. They dissolved the boundaries between the national holiday and party politics. The political expressions of the holiday—support of the *Kulturkampf* and of the Anti-Socialist Law, and propaganda against enemies of the empire—were not simply an appendage to its "real" message; rather, they became the message. Even the slogan of Sedan Day, "For Emperor and Empire," was identical to the political battle cry of the Deutsche Partei in the Reichstag elections of the 1870s and 1880s. When the liberals saw no discrepancy between the identity they created in Sedan Day and their partisan positions adopted in political life, they in effect posited the creation of national identity through not only the national holiday but also through their party politics. In short, in their behavior the liberals sought national identity in party politics although it was in fact the most divisive sphere of society.

By attempting to construct a national identity through their partisan politics without having the popular support and political power to back this mode of operation, the liberals exposed the holiday to the accusation of being a *Parteifest*, a partisan political holiday. That was a strong accusation in Württemberg and German society where *Parteifest* was a code word for acting against the commonweal, be it the commonweal of the community, of Württemberg, or of the nation.[42] In Württemberg and Germany the idea of partisan politics was synonymous with factions and particular interests.[43] No one could claim to speak for the nation by evoking the authority of a partisan political voice, only by evoking the voice of the community as a whole. Behind the democrats' statement that "Sedan Day has developed . . . into an authentic National Liberal holiday" was the conviction and the accusation that the true motives of the liberals in Sedan Day were power, manipulation, and personal gain in the guise of a disinterested national cause. Moreover, in this and similar statements the democrats minimized and ultimately destroyed the legitimacy of the holiday by reversing the meaning given to it by the liberals: they portrayed the liberals not as an avant-garde laying claim to speak for the nation, but as a fringe group that bracketed itself out of the national community.

Throughout the lifetime of Sedan Day the accusation of being a *Parteifest* accompanied it in Württemberg as it did in Germany. In his letter about Sedan Day in 1874 Bishop Ketteler denounced the holiday as having originated principally in the National Liberal Party.[44] The Social Democrats echoed the same theme in 1895 after Emperor William II's Sedan Day speech, in which he identified the socialists as "a gang, which is not worth bearing the name 'German.' "[45] In Württemberg opponents argued that the holiday was directed "more against the inner enemy than against the traditional enemy [France]."[46] As a partisan celebration, Sedan Day was excluded from the list of events that identified the community as a whole: in Catholic Ravensburg the town council decided unanimously against a celebration "because in light of recent experience the holiday appears to be a party demonstration against the majority of the inhabitants."[47]

For the "enemies of the empire" in Württemberg, the fusion of the holiday with partisan politics stigmatized Sedan Day and its national representation forever. The holiday did not have the legitimacy to represent the community and thus lost its legitimacy to represent the nation. In 1890 the *Beobachter* reviewed twenty years of celebrations in Württemberg and arrived at the following conclusion: "From year to year the meaning of this commemoration day has sunk lower. The reason is that from year to year the holiday has been constantly reduced to a purely private celebration of one or two parties that regarded themselves as the only patriots and as the specific German parties."[48] Even as opponents of the holiday came to terms with the Bismarckian empire, and the reality of the unification sank into people's minds, they refused to celebrate *this* holiday. The democrats expressed this sentiment as early as 1881: "The contention that Sedan Day is now harmoniously celebrated by all the parties is an insult that contradicts the evidence. To be sure, the empire and its constitution are generally recognized." Nonetheless, the democrats would always refuse to participate in this "one-sided partisan demonstration."[49]

The symbolic weakness of Sedan Day lay in the fact that it failed to create a sense of oneness among broad and diverse groups in German society. My argument is not that national identity must always be integrative; it is obviously a contested process, full of conflicts, reversals, and false starts. But a national identity is more durable and effective when it represents, for a broad section of the population, a common destiny that overcomes symbolically real social and political conflicts in order to give the illusion of a community to people who in fact have very different interests. It is significant that the holiday did not cut across even one of the fundamental division lines in German society, either religion, class, or politics. The only exception was the participation of petit bourgeois Protestants in small and medium-sized communities who joined as fellow travelers; but compared with the Protestant haute bourgeoisie who originated the holiday, this was a change in degree, not in kind. Instead of constructing a representation of the nation that would conceal through symbols real conflicts in German society, Sedan Day reproduced these conflicts. So, just as one did not expect a democrat to get up one morning and join the Deutsche Partei, one did not expect him to celebrate Sedan Day. It *was* a *Parteifest*.

The relations between politics and identity in the holiday illuminate the liberals' political culture. By dissolving the difference between party politics and national identity and by wishing to construct a national identity through party politics, the liberals, in effect, refused to sanction political divisions and refused to recognize what party politics really was—an arena that necessarily represented divisions, not national unity. While this argument may seem speculative, it should be remembered that the unwillingness on the part of the liberals to sanction political divisions was also displayed in the policy of exclusion and in *das große Ganze*, both of which represented an idea of a national community free of conflicts. By excluding their opponents, the liberals enjoyed in Sedan Day, for one day each year, the dream of a nation without divisions. But the consequence of refusing to sanction political divisions was to introduce conspicuous partisan politics into a field of national life that should in fact create, or appear to have created, consensus, namely a national holiday. For the liberals the boundaries of the political were not confined to its appropriate institutions and mechanisms such as parliament and elections, but were expanded to celebrations with the result that the holiday created a forceful political symbolism of power. But the liberals' political forms of thought and action in Sedan Day failed to create among Württembergers a *perception* of the German nation as a community that "regardless of the actual inequality and exploitation that may prevail in [it] . . . is always conceived as a deep, horizontal comradeship."[50] The logic of the liberals' claim to speak for the nation, while being unable to generate broad popular support, did produce the perception among the overwhelming majority of Württembergers that the holiday was a partisan political spectacle. The message of Sedan Day was inherently contradictory. The liberals claimed to be above the parties, but were in fact political. They claimed to originate a holiday for all the Germans, but were in fact exclusive. They claimed to speak for the nation, but were in fact partisan. They claimed to integrate, but spread in fact divisions. This message eroded and ultimately destroyed the legitimacy of the holiday.

THE 1890S AND THE END OF SEDAN DAY

Slowly by the end of the 1880s and more rapidly during the 1890s Sedan Day lost momentum. The holiday, which was celebrated with enthusiasm and stirred controversy in the 1870s and the 1880s, produced thereafter only boredom and apathy; former participants deserted the celebrations and former opponents stopped heeding the holiday. Few adults participated. In many localities the holiday was now centered only around school festivities, and when at the beginning of the 1890s the summer vacation was extended into the first week of September, the blow to the celebrations was fatal.[51] Manifesting the decline in the significance of the holiday, the towns of Geislingen and Ulm undertook in the mid-1880s to celebrate only every five years.[52] Although the holiday continued to be celebrated sporadically after the 1890s, it neither enjoyed popular support nor stimulated controversy.[53]

What was the place of Sedan Day and its originators, the liberal bourgeoisie, in the creation of national symbols in imperial Germany? An answer must begin with the recognition that, in spite of the strides cultural history has made in German historiography, studies of the symbolic and linguistic representations of power are very few. Compared with French historical studies, the leading historiography in this field, German history has nothing like the brilliantly illuminating studies of the symbolism of power by Mona Ozouf, Maurice Agulhon, Keith Baker, Lynn Hunt, and François Furet.[54] Very few studies of political festivals in Germany have employed the symbolic and linguistic approach to political representation that blends influences from cultural anthropology, poststructuralism, postmodernist literary criticism, and semiotics.[55] Still, an important interpretation has been formulated by Wolfgang Hardtwig, who has explored in numerous articles and books the symbolic representation of bourgeois political mentality in monuments and celebrations. Hardtwig has argued for the "considerable deficiency" of the bourgeoisie's political culture and national symbology in imperial Germany.[56] Caving in to the powerful state, the subservient German bourgeoisie represented in its "monuments and political celebrations Prussian—and monarchical—authoritarian motifs" that "shaped [its antidemocratic and militaristic] political mentality." This mentality was represented, for instance, in the Bismarck cult (often expressed in monuments) that "articulated the desire for a powerful and authoritative imperial chancellor."[57]

The danger in this approach is the implicit assumption that national symbols and political mentality were connected in a direct and unmediated way: that erecting a monument for Bismarck equaled sharing the statesman's political ideas. From this it becomes a short step to reading off a set of interconnected responses and attitudes: national symbols = William I, Bismarck, Sedan Day, Hohenzollern = militarism and authoritarianism. In essence, this interpretation assumes an uncomplicated relationship between form and consciousness. We cannot simply suppose that because people celebrated the *battle* of Sedan, Bismarck, and the emperor, the political meaning of their symbols was authoritarian.[58] This approach takes symbols literally and ignores the actual symbolic experience of the celebration; it overlooks the complex and often contradictory ways by which forms of symbolic representation are used to claim social, cultural, and political power.

Most unsettling of all, the evidence that emerges from the celebrations of Sedan Day does not support Hardtwig's interpretation. Whether the bourgeoisie's deficiency means that it lacked originality in creating national symbols or that it became the spineless tools of the authoritarian state, Sedan Day did not corroborate either of these arguments. The holiday, before it failed, showed the liberal bourgeoisie's initiative and imagination without a sign of symbolic or actual subservience to the Prussian state. The idea of the "considerable deficiency" of the bourgeoisie's national symbols implies that the bourgeoisie served the interests of the Prussian authoritarian state while neglecting its best interests. But the liberals originated Sedan Day in Württemberg to reinforce their identity as the symbolic possessor of the nation and not primarily to strengthen the authoritarian state. Moreover, their symbols in the festival and the national narrative did not appear as signs of deficient national symbolism; they were unsuccessful but not deficient. And it is worth mentioning that the liberals did not espouse in the holiday militaristic, *volkisch*, and nationalist ideology.[59] This interpretation is the wrong historical direction to follow when we attempt to understand the role of the liberal bourgeoisie in the production of national symbology in Germany and, more generally, the ways identities are made.

Identity, as I have attempted to show, is a relationship among symbolic representation, social practice, and political behavior. The postunification period provided a certain mode of relations between politics, culture, and society that characterized Sedan Day: the holiday reflected and shaped a specific liberal sociopolitical mode of action based on a position of political influence, ideological support for the 1871 solution for the German Question, and social distinction. In this period liberal notables attempted to redeem their cultural capital as supporters of pro-Prussian unification, and to redeem their political capital in a system of notable politics, into a leading role in shaping national identity. They succeeded, up to a point. They took control of the holiday in the 1870s and 1880s and claimed to have taken symbolic possession of the nation. But they created an innate mechanism of failure in the holiday, an unresolved tension between being exclusive to the point of being isolated and claiming to speak for the nation.

The innate mechanism of failure in Sedan Day was not accidental. It reflected the incapacity in the 1870s and 1880s to produce any meaningful discourse about localness and nationhood in Württemberg society. It is difficult to see how a national holiday of any kind could have succeeded in Württemberg after 1871. Particularism, anti-Prussian sentiments, Catholics' anxieties because of the *Kulturkampf*, the reservations of the king and the administration, and the time needed to digest the changes of 1866–71—all were formidable obstacles to finding a *via media* between the empire and Württemberg, between the nation and Catholics, democrats, and *Großdeutsche*. During the 1870s and 1880s, although Württemberg was part of Germany, the two were not integrated into a united whole, just as the local past and the national present faced one another in the holiday's national narrative as two distant and suspicious relatives.

Sedan Day failed, but its symbols are meaningful to our understanding of imperial Germany's political culture and national symbolism. When we concentrate on the images of Bismarck and the emperor in the festival and interpret them as a display of militaristic political mentality and attachment to the Hohenzollern, then the result is at worst a partial truth and at best predictable. But when we look at the symbolic experience of the celebrants and at the form of national representation they created—by taking cognizance of the ways they symbolically ordered space and time—then we find that the festival of Sedan Day was primarily a way to render the nation familiar, to internalize new national images, such as Bismarck and the emperor, by placing them within tradition. Here we see a fundamental symbolic meaning of Sedan Day and, as we shall see in Part II, of German local-national memory: the attempt to imagine the nation through the locality.

Sedan Day in Württemberg shaped and was shaped by the liberals' political culture, by the beliefs and expectations that molded their idea of the political. The *Sonderweg* thesis has argued that the liberals were politically passive and immature, and surrendered their best interest to the authoritarian state. Hardtwig has offered a version of this interpretation by arguing that the bourgeoisie's national symbolism in the German Empire showed its "progressive tendency to escape from reality, to avoid the constitutional, social, and political conditions and possibilities of practical politics."[60]

But the idea that the liberal bourgeoisie was politically passive and immature is unfounded. When we take a narrow definition of the political—that is, participation in the political process (elections, party and parliamentary activity) in order to promote one's interests—then there is no reason to doubt the political savvy of the liberal bourgeoisie in Württemberg. This conclusion is in agreement with a growing and important body of literature in the past decade that "rehabilitated" the political practice of the liberal bourgeoisie and has restored its historical capacity to think politically and act according to its best interests (for example, by allying with Bismarck after 1871 and rejecting a full-fledged democracy because of understandable fear of the biggest and most organized European working-class movement). Studies have focused on subject matters such as relations among the German parties, voting patterns and election campaigns, and the interaction between local and national politics.[61]

A cultural definition of the political—that is, the political as exercise of power through forms of symbolic representation—has been less frequently employed to understand German political culture. The liberals, by means of the policy of exclusion, attempted to create a new form of national representation that gave them exclusive power over national identity. Political power cannot be measured only by the ballot box or the ability to hold the reins of government. Neither in Württemberg nor in Germany could the liberals exert political power that equaled the power of Mittnacht and Bismarck. But using their position as the main supporters of the empire in Württemberg, they celebrated Sedan Day in an attempt to exert exclusive political control over national identity. For one short score of years in Württemberg they largely succeeded. This cannot be described as escaping from reality.

It cannot be described as pluralistic either. The liberals did not accommodate varied political opinions, social groups, or religious beliefs in the holiday. So can we fault them for being undemocratic? As far as we wish to understand the liberals' political culture this is, I think, a superficial judgment. Struggles over national identity are not an inclusive picnic, and we should not expect the liberals to behave any differently. And yet we should ask whether there is not a point where ideological conviction without any consideration of the larger world around seems out of touch. The liberals, after all, by excluding the majority of Württemberg society from the celebration, steadily undermined the legitimacy of the holiday. The liberals' behavior no doubt indicated a detached style of notable political culture. They were elitist, and viewed the populace and the Catholics with undisguised condescension. Living in a world governed by the values of education and property (*Bildung und Besitz*), they lacked a certain touch for the ordinary, average person. Their holiday lacked popular consent, and they lacked the will and methods to generate it. This was demonstrated most clearly in the liberals' attempt to introduce the *Kulturkampf* to Württemberg, disregarding the local political culture, the tradition of religious tolerance, and the position of just about all nonliberals in the region, from the king down to the humblest Catholic, conservative, and democrat. At the same time, while this evaluation is true, we should not ignore the larger context of the liberals' behavior in Sedan Day. As a cultural-political artifact, the holiday was a result of the existing opportunities and limits for constructing national identity in Württemberg in the 1870s and 1880s. The limits, as we have seen, were formidable: it is difficult to see how any national holiday could have succeeded and under what conditions democrats, Catholics, conservatives, and the king would have joined any national celebration. Under these conditions the liberals seized the opportunity to appropriate the nation. While the exclusionary holiday proved counterproductive in the long run, this was not evident in the 1870s. And we cannot fault the liberals for not seeing in the 1870s the reality of the 1890s.

Ironically, the liberals failed in Sedan Day not because they escaped from reality but because their symbolic representation was too close to reality—it never possessed the mystique and allure that goes beyond the here and now. They reproduced in the holiday the political and social divisions of German society in a way that made the holiday seem to opponents merely an extension of Deutsche Partei politics. Sedan Day did not create a multifaceted image of the German past that was a guide to the German present, especially to ways of reconciling tradition and modernity. The holiday's image of the nation was too unambiguous, present-oriented, and connected with 1871 to correspond either to the changing reality of German society in the Second Empire, or to provide a framework to imagine the German nation. It treated the empire more than the nation, *Kleindeutschland* more than the eternal existence of Germany, the transitory more than the mythical. The holiday's representation of the nation lacked the profundity needed in order to become a national common denominator: it lacked the depth of intellect to bridge the past and the present; the depth of feeling to construct new identities from old emotions; and the depth of meaning to encompass the variegation of pasts and memories that were the German nation before and after 1871.

It would be a mistake, however, to interpret the liberals' failure only in terms of symbolism of power. The liberals celebrated Sedan Day as long as the sociopolitical mode of action that produced it remained intact. When by the 1890s, Württemberg politics and society dramatically changed, Sedan Day first declined and ultimately disappeared as a representation of the nation. The issue of *Kleindeutschland* versus *Großdeutschland*, first of all, lost its prominence to social and economic issues. Even though anti-Prussianism remained a feature in Württemberg culture and politics (as late as the 1895 Landtag elections, the Volkspartei campaigned on a strong anti-Prussian program),[62] the 1871 solution to the German Question lost its poignancy as a divisive issue. Particularism had begun to disappear as an independent, political, and divisive force in German society. From the beginning of the 1880s democrats acknowledged the legitimacy of the empire and of the constitution. As the *Kulturkampf* effectively ended at the end of the 1880s, Catholics ceased to appear as a mortal enemy of the empire, and the Anti-Socialist Law ended in 1890. Moreover, during the 1890s the face of Württemberg politics changed. Social and economic discontent among peasants and petite bourgeoisie and their consequent shift of political support to new interest groups undermined the politics of liberal notables as the ties of deference broke down. Some Protestant peasants began to lean toward the Peasants League (Bauernbund), founded in 1893 as the local branch of the North German Agrarian League (Bund der Landwirte). Catholics organized in the local Center Party, and the increasing industrialization of Württemberg strengthened the Social Democratic Party (SPD) among workers. A new demagogic style of political campaigning and rhetoric mobilized voters on the local level. The main loser from these developments were the liberal notables. In the Landtag election of 1895 the Volkspartei and the Center Party, in its debut in Württemberg politics, soundly defeated the Deutsche Partei, which lost its dominant position after twenty-five years of uninterrupted majority. The Deutsche Partei sank from 64 percent of the votes in 1889 to 24 percent in 1895, while the Center Party won 23 percent and the Volkspartei became the biggest party with 32 percent of the votes. The pariahs of the 1870s and 1880s became the establishment. In the same elections, the first representative of the SPD was elected. The liberals produced in Sedan Day a representation of the nation based on exclusion and symbolic appropriation of the nation, yet this representation ceased to be a sociopolitical mode of action by the 1890s.

The 1895 political earthquake was part of a larger transformation in Württemberg society whereby the liberal notable bourgeoisie gradually lost its control of public life and its exclusive claim to speak for the nation. The real political integration of Württemberg and Germany took place, in a sense, not in 1871 but in 1895 when the local party structure finally corresponded to the national one. The nationalization of local politics meant the introduction of mass politics, the proliferation of associations organized from below, the enlargement of the public sphere, and consequently the end of notables' control on local public life. The nation itself was now appropriated successfully by rivals of the liberals, something that did not happen in the 1870s. This was displayed symbolically in the 1896 celebrations of the twenty-fifth anniversary of the foundation of the empire. As the two biggest parties in the Landtag, the Center Party and the Volkspartei had an important role in the celebrations. The democrat Friedrich Payer, after 1895 speaker of the Landtag, was assigned the keynote speech for the evening banquet in Stuttgart. Due to illness, he was replaced by Konrad Haußmann, another democratic leader, who delivered a sweeping patriotic speech.[63] The speech eloquently reflected the generational change toward national identity in Württemberg: it was Haußmann senior who composed the antiunification poem—"In spirit we are one / In the empire, though / When it will crumble / Home happily we'll go"—in 1874. The idea of the German nation as legitimately represented by the empire and *Kleindeutschland*, which was successfully appropriated by Sedan Day's liberals, became a common perception in the 1890s. The monopoly of national qualifications, which identified the liberals and Sedan Day, was obsolete in the 1890s because the society that produced Sedan Day—a society of profound localism, of notable politics, of reservations about the unification—ceased to exist. The memoirs of two political activists, one a member of the Deutsche Partei, the other of the SPD, illustrate the social and political transformations. The notable Otto Elben compared the 1870s with the 1890s with an evident sense of loss: "A feeling of security animated us then [after 1871]; who would have imagined where we would arrive twenty years later."[64] In contrast, artisan Gustav Kittler, an activist of the SPD in Heilbronn, described in a poem the period after the abolition of the Anti-Socialist Law: "The past is going down / The times are changing, and new life flourishes from the ruins."[65]

How representative was Sedan Day of general trends in German society in the 1870s and 1890s? The yardstick to evaluate this question should not be failure or success but the production and reception of the holiday's representation of the nation. When we look at the main celebration period, the 1870s and 1880s, the most striking phenomenon is the failure of the liberals to create in Sedan Day a sense of oneness. But if the liberals failed to produce a sense of oneness among diverse groups in Württemberg society, it was because such a sense did not exist in Germany during the 1870s and 1880s given the *Kulturkampf*, the Anti-Socialist Law, and, in Württemberg and other regions such as Bavaria, the misgivings of particularists. The Württemberg liberals' policy of exclusion followed the general trend in German society of orchestrated campaigns to discriminate against "enemies of the empire." The holiday thus fit well within a political culture that excluded from the national community entire groups and it is precisely this inability to find a symbolic common denominator that made the holiday representative of the 1870s and 1880s. After all, the holiday was not a production of a fringe group in Württemberg and German society but, quite the contrary, of a most distinguished social group and political party. The liberals' inability to create a holiday that would aggregate diverse groups only reflected the real ideological differences in German society about national identity.

Sedan Day in Württemberg enriches our historical view of the obstacles to national integration in the 1870s and 1880s. Historians have been aware of the challenge to reconcile local and national identity in this period, but have tended to emphasize the Catholic and the Socialist Questions as the most significant political problems on the way to national integration after the unification. Sedan Day in Württemberg demonstrated that the issue of local identity had been as political and as divisive as the "big" questions of the *Kulturkampf* and the Anti-Socialist Law. The difficulty of cultivating a successful discourse of localness and nationhood was part of the difficulty of cultivating any successful discourse of national integration in the 1870s and 1880s. Indeed, the rewriting of local history in the national narrative, while paying no attention to religious or class history, showed that the liberals regarded the issue of local identity and its integration to the national whole as particularly important.

Also the end of Sedan Day in Württemberg followed a well-charted national pattern. Concurrently with the decline of the holiday as a symbolic practice of exclusion was the termination on the national level of the *Kulturkampf* and the Anti-Socialist Law. Moreover, the dramatic political changes in 1895 in Württemberg were in fact, as we shall see in some detail in the next chapter, part of a general transformation of German society whereby the domination of notables on the political and public spheres was challenged by petite bourgeoisie, peasants, women, and other groups who had hitherto been largely politically passive. In this respect, the end of the sociopolitical mode of action that characterized Sedan Day was a national phenomenon.[66]

It is obviously important to highlight the representativeness of Sedan Day for general trends in imperial Germany, but we should not lose sight of the fact that Württemberg was not identical to Germany, and that we should not expect it to be. There were differences that made the story of Sedan Day a particular Württemberg tale. Two were especially important. Although the Deutsche Partei in Württemberg enjoyed local political successes through four Landtag election campaigns until 1895, the National Liberal Party lost its dominating position in German politics in 1878 when Bismarck switched alliances to the conservatives. The party remained a central player in national politics, but not as central as the Deutsche Partei in Württemberg. The second difference is closely connected. Divided into three parties, the Deutsche Partei, the Landespartei, and the Volkspartei, the Württemberg political universe emphasized the national stance of the Deutsche Partei and united all nationalists around it. The national political scene, in contrast, was a great deal more complex including conservative parties, the Social Democratic Party, and the Center Party. Under these conditions the National Liberal Party had to contend with a restricted pool of voters and, moreover, could not don alone the mantle of patriotism.

I would like, by way of conclusion, to place my interpretation of the construction of national symbolism in Sedan Day in relation to the interpretation that has emerged in French historical studies of the representation of political power. According to this interpretation, which has centered on the French Revolution, the meaning of the revolution lay in symbolic forms of political representation and discourse.[67] Shifting the meaning of the revolution from Marx to Tocqueville and from social structures to political culture, this approach has challenged (and ultimately demolished) the distinguished though increasingly rigid social interpretation of the French Revolution that understood the revolution in terms of preexisting social conditions and social processes, and that assumed that politics and culture were derivable from the more basic social phenomena. The new approach has opened new avenues for exploring the revolution as a popular political act and cultural creation—as the making of a revolutionary experiential political symbolism—that was not determined by the imperative of social conditions. What was revolutionary in the French Revolution was the creation of new symbolic forms of political representation. The influence of this illuminating approach is now widely recognized and my reading of Sedan Day owes much to it.

Yet it cannot be accepted uncritically. This approach, as Keith Baker argued and François Furet would doubtless agree, is based on the assumption that "political authority is . . . essentially a matter of linguistic authority" and that, moreover, "to the extent that social and political arrangements are linguistically constituted in any society, efforts to change them (or to preserve them) can never occur outside of language. . . . social and political changes are themselves linguistic."[68] The problem here lies not in what is being said but in what is being excluded. This interpretation is right that we cannot explain everything by the social structure. But that does not mean that one can explain everything by symbolic representations and linguistic structure.[69] Just like any other historical interpretation that is based on a single explanatory device (however complex it may be: think of the interpretative approach based on class and social structure), the symbolic-linguistic interpretation is destined to fail in capturing the complexity of people's lives in the past. If symbolic representations are constitutive elements of the social and the political, it is equally true that social and political forms of thought and action shape symbolic representations.[70]

Ultimately, the consequence of understanding historical events as well as "social and political arrangements . . . and changes" as having no meaning outside the symbolic representation is that we in effect postulate that such representations are self-referential and self-enclosed systems of meanings. It becomes impossible to explain why one system of representation replaces another without considering factors that are exterior to the representation—namely, social and political conflicts: it becomes impossible to explain change.[71] Moreover, by focusing on internal development of symbolic representation and linguistic structures, we run the risk of favoring textual analysis at the expense of illuminating political behavior and social practice;[72] we can thus easily lose sight of the experience of people in the past.[73]

If we apply the symbolic-linguistic approach to Sedan Day, we must conclude that the holiday failed because of internal contradictions in its representation of the nation. This is true, but it is only a partial truth. Sedan Day no doubt failed because of contradictions within the holiday's symbolic representations: there were the contradictions between the discourse of unity and the policy of exclusion, and there was the tension (and perhaps even contradiction, as we have argued) between the representation of national identity and local identity (the national narrative and the festival). These symbolic contradictions were essential to the failure of the holiday in Württemberg. But they are insufficient to explain the opposing meanings embodied in Sedan Day as a result of conflicts exterior to the representation. The symbolic representation of Sedan Day shaped the identity of Württembergers who engaged in producing, receiving, and rejecting it, but it was simultaneously shaped by the concerns of Württembergers over social, political, and cultural conflicts (the *Kulturkampf*, to give one notable example). These conflicts gave the symbolic representation opposing, unexpected, and at times contradictory meanings. A striking example was the democrats' opposition to the festival of Sedan Day that displayed the nation in local terms, a representation that, on the face of it, should have been agreeable to the democrats who championed local identity. They boycotted the festival not because they opposed giving the nation a local image but because they opposed the political use of this representation by the liberals. Moreover, the symbolic-linguistic approach is even less successful in accounting for the failure of the holiday in the 1890s and not before. Why did Sedan Day end in the 1890s when the contradictions in its symbolic representation were in place right from the beginning? It is difficult to see how the symbolic-linguistic approach can answer this query satisfactorily without considering factors outside the symbolic representation. As I have argued, the symbolic representation of the holiday fit social and political relations that governed Württemberg in the 1870s and 1880s and that rewarded the liberals. When these conditions changed in the 1890s, so did the destiny of Sedan Day. The new period produced a new perception of the locality, the region, and the nation—the Heimat idea.

PART TWO

Germany and Württemberg:
A Nation of Heimats

CHAPTER FIVE

A System of Knowledge and Sensibilities

Germans like to think of the Heimat idea as unfathomable, mysterious, and, above all, peculiarly German. In fact, the Heimat idea was not an inherent attribute of the German nation, but came to appear as such after the 1880s, representing the permanent identity of the local and the national communities, the immutable in the ups and downs of German history, the core of existence in every German. Heimat became immemorial because memory is short: an alleged timeless national memory, invented at the second half of the nineteenth century, for an alleged timeless nation, unified in 1871.

The Heimat idea has been usually interpreted either as a mythic German concept or as a human state-of-mind that longs for stability and human relations.[1] Celia Applegate has written an excellent study on the role of the Heimat idea in modern German society and culture.[2] Tracing the idea in the Palatinate (Pfalz) from the 1850s to the 1950s, Applegate sheds new light on its cultural invention and social origins and on the reformulations of the concept that placed the Palatinate and its inhabitants within the context of the nation for more than a century of political upheavals. Viewing the Heimat idea as a mediating concept between the immediate local life and the abstract nation, Applegate successfully shows the different ways in which Pfälzers used it "to rest finally on what both region and nation have in common."[3] What is striking in this study is its tone. Historians writing on German identity have often either bemoaned its missed opportunities or condemned its inevitable course. Writing with neither condescension nor condemnation, Applegate sets out to understand how "her" Pfälzers developed a sense of localness and nationhood and what kind of historical options and opportunities opened and closed before them at every historical juncture.

Building on the cases of the Palatinate and Württemberg and adding new

97

sources and evidence from across Germany, I would like to shift our attention to the status of the Heimat idea in the nation as a whole, to the relations between the various local and regional Heimat ideas. The Heimat idea did function as a mediator between the local place and the nation. But the existence of Heimat ideas throughout Germany, in every locality and region, calls for further investigation: what was the meaning of the local Heimat ideas considered collectively? My argument is that in imperial Germany the idea itself transformed also into an actual representation of the nation. The local peculiarities expressed in, for instance, Heimat museums and images made up through a process of stereotypization a representation of the German nation as a whole. The national Heimat idea possessed a national narrative and a national image and by representing interchangeably the locality, the region, and the nation, created in the mind of Germans an "imagined community."

The birth of Heimat as an idea that represented the locality and the nation was a result of a conjuncture of German and international conditions in the last decades of the nineteenth century. Germans manufactured Heimat as a set of shared ideas about the immemorial heritage of the German people in local and national history, nature, and folklore as, first of all, part of a European and North American response to modernity. To make sense of the transformation of landscape, the acceleration of social change, and the perceived growing separation from the past caused by progress and technology, Europeans and North Americans conserved the past, protected nature, and embraced often invented traditions to reaffirm the roots of the nation. Victorians yearned for the past so passionately that John Stuart Mill thought his fellow countrymen all "carry their eyes in the back of their heads."[4] This was not only a British characteristic, but one of the period as a whole.[5] As one of Germany's responses to modernity, the Heimat idea was a memory invented just when German society was rapidly changing, as a bridge between a past and a present that looked uniquely dissimilar. Heimat looked to the past for reassurances of uniqueness on the local and the national level in times of political, economic, and cultural homogenization: it emphasized the uniqueness of a locality with respect to national standardization, and the uniqueness of Germany with respect to European and North American standardization.

The national context of the production of the Heimat idea was nation building in times of great transformations in Wilhelmine Germany. What were the changes in Germany and Württemberg between the period of Sedan Day, the 1870s and 1880s, and the period of the Heimat idea that enabled the creation of Heimat as a new conception of localness and nationhood? To begin with, social and economic progress drew the local place and the nation together. The developments in education, transportation, and communications and the common experience in the market economy, military service, and national elections brought together the immediate local world and the imper-

sonal national one. While in the 1850s and 1860s important cities were connected to the railway network, in the 1880s and 1890s the local countryside and
small towns were connected to the nation.[6] The expansion of the press followed this pattern.[7]

Moreover, the last decade of the nineteenth century gave rise in imperial
Germany to a new public sphere and political culture. This transformation has
been in recent years the topic of a growing body of work.[8] The most striking
manifestation of the changing political perceptions was the increase in political involvement as shown by the increasing turnout at Reichstag elections,
which rose from 50–60 percent in the elections between 1871 and 1884, to 70–
80 percent in the following elections, reaching 85 percent in the last election
before the war in 1912.[9] The immediate visible result of the political participation was the expansion of the Social Democratic Party (SPD) after the end of
the Anti-Socialist Law in 1890. Furthermore, the transformation of political
culture was due to new political organizations among groups that had been
traditionally represented by notables and had therefore been inactive in national politics. In the 1890s the peasantry organized political pressure groups,
such as the Bavarian Peasant League, the Central German peasant movement
of Otto Böckel, and the Agrarian League, to represent their interests in the
parties, Reichstag, and government.[10] A host of other organizations also became active, as craftsmen, shopkeepers, petty entrepreneurs, and white-collar
workers were eager to defend their particular interests or the general cause of
the middle classes, the *Mittelstand*.[11] The *Mittelstand* and the rural protest
movements nourished the anti-Semitic parties that originated for the first time
during this period.[12] Furthermore, pressure from below for a more energetic
colonial and nationalist policy was exerted by newly founded radical nationalist organizations such as the Pan-German League (1891), the Society for the
Eastern Marches (1894), and the Navy League (1898), whose members had a
less eminent status than that of the notables.[13] And new civil associations,
which included the Evangelical League, the People's Association of German
Catholics, the German Peace Movement, and the German feminist movement,
changed the map of the German public sphere.[14]

The result of this hectic activity was pressure from below to make German
politics and culture more inclusive than before. The ferment in German politics among proletarians, peasants, and the middle classes and the changing
patterns of political campaigning and voting signaled the erosion of the politics of deference that had dominated since the 1860s and, consequently, of
notables' control of the political system. Similarly, the emergence of numerous
leagues and associations brought about the enlargement of the public realm
and the consequent end of the notables' domination of it. The changes during
the 1890s in the political system in Württemberg should be seen, therefore, as
part of this larger social and political transformation in Germany.

Knowledge and Sensibilities

The Heimat idea was a result as well as an answer to these significant changes in German society. The issues that dominated Sedan Day, such as *Kleindeutschland* and the legitimacy of the empire, became anachronistic around 1890, and *Großdeutsch* ideas became irrelevant. Imagining the nation in preunification political terms became obsolete. Instead, a new local-national memory was introduced by the German bourgeoisie that represented the nation as an interconnected network of local identities. It reflected two social-cultural trends. On the one hand, petite and provincial bourgeoisie, who became increasingly active in the growing public sphere, expressed in the Heimat idea their demand to become acknowledged members of the nation. The Heimat representation of the nation, postulated on the importance of every local identity, however small and unimportant it might have been, gave voice to the social and geographical periphery of the German bourgeoisie. On the other hand, the Heimat idea functioned for the German bourgeoisie as a whole as a unifying national memory, a never-never land that was impervious to the political and social conflicts that characterized Wilhelmine Germany.

I use the terms Heimat memory and Heimat idea interchangeably, to describe the symbolic Heimat representation of the past embedded in the context of social action. The notions indicate a process by which Germans "Heimatized" the nation, making it an everyday mental property and creating a visual image of it in their minds.

What are the sources used in this study to establish how the Heimat memory was created and received? I attempted to overcome the problem of evidence in the study of collective memory by using a wide array of sources. Too often the conclusions drawn about collective memory from an analysis of a single artifact that represents the past, say, a historical museum, are incongruent with the limited evidence the source actually provides about social practice and cultural perceptions. I explore the Heimat idea through documents and printed material of local, regional, and national Heimat associations, notably historical, as well as nature and folklore associations. Also consulted were dictionaries of the German language and of regional dialects from the first half of the nineteenth century to the twentieth century, *Heimatbücher*, or Heimat books, that described the history, nature, and ways of life of the community, along with school textbooks. The importance of literature in the construction of memory is expressed by the analysis of popular poems written during World War I that were a source to the collective perception of the nation. In addition, I use stories and poems about the Heimat by known writers such as Hermann Hesse. The development of Heimat into a national idiom is also explored on the basis of a questionnaire I sent in 1990 to local Heimat museums, from which I received more than 100 responses. Finally, a corpus of 300 Heimat images in postcards, posters, Heimat journals, local newspapers, and other sources underlines the significance of iconographic production to understand the mentality of people in the past. By comparing different sources, we can verify our findings drawn from one source with evidence drawn from another. The variety of sources makes it possible to explore the Heimat memory as a comprehensive cultural, social, and political phenomenon, treating it as a unit of complementary parts, such as images, museums, books, and the like, that contributed to a single effect, a simultaneous representation of the locality, the region, and the nation.

HEIMAT HISTORY:
"VIVID, CONCEIVABLE, POPULAR"

At the turn of the century local communities in Germany and Württemberg began to publish a new kind of book about their identities and traditions, *Heimatbuch*. The Heimat book was written by the local priest or schoolteacher, the authoritative transmitter of history in the community, and, unlike some scholarly books, was a clearly written and well-illustrated publication destined for the family and the school. The books described the locality and the area according to three fields of knowledge: the history from the times of the Germanic tribes to the present; the nature, geography, fauna, and flora; and the ways of life and thought of the inhabitants, their character, and traditional customs. Heimat books appeared everywhere in Württemberg, from the metropolis Stuttgart to provincial Giengen an der Brenz, where there were 3,459 inhabitants in 1914, when a Heimat book was published. The Heimat book became one of the principal vehicles of the new Heimat idea, a symbol of local identity, prompting many communities to publish one as a sign of self-respect.

Yet the Heimat books were not really that novel since they employed the methods and subject matters of the traditional *Ortsgeschichte*, or local history, also written by the local priest or teacher and known at least from as early as 1819.[15] At this period, in addition, the history-nature-folklore formula to describe local identity was used by government agencies whose task was to collect data in order to increase the state's control over the economy, the society, and the population. Such a new institute was founded in Württemberg in 1820, the Department for Statistics and Topography (Statistisch-Topographisches Bureau) that began in 1824 to publish a series of statistical, ethnographic, and historical descriptions of regional districts, entitled *Beschreibungen* (Descriptions).[16] The Association for Studies of the Fatherland, Verein für Vaterlandskunde, founded in 1822, (fatherland meant here Württemberg, not Germany), whose aim was to study Württemberg's "history, statistics, and topography," also generated local studies based on this formula.[17] The popularizers of the Heimat idea, therefore, employed methods and subject matters that had been established in Württemberg for decades.

The Heimat books, however, were not identical to old topographical descriptions of a local community or a region. Heimatlers took traditional ways of thinking about and modes of representation of the local and regional community and gave them a whole new meaning by connecting them to the nation in ways that were unpredictable before 1871. Local historical studies and historical associations existed in Württemberg long before the 1880s, but only thereafter could the Heimat movement proudly proclaim, as did Ellwangen's Historical and Archaeological Association in 1910, that "The old times have awoken again. . . . The call for Heimat research and Heimat protection has become the motto on the gates of the new century."[18] Wilhelm Seytter, an author of a Heimat book about Stuttgart, explained the kind of history cultivated by Heimatlers:[19]

> As a Heimat study, this book imparts not only bare historical knowledge, but aims at animating the Heimat by enlivening its history. . . . By looking at Heimat's simple and daily life [Kleinleben], Heimat history is being stripped of learned academic scholarship, and becomes vivid, conceivable, and therefore popular. Heimat studies should, indeed must, encompass the whole of life, for description in miniature [Kleinmalerei] is its essence. While history rushes to generalize from concrete facts, and surveys mountains and valleys at a glance only to get a general impression of the landscape, Heimat studies enter affectionately into people's simple and daily life, down from the ivory tower of scholarship into the valleys and meadows of civil, family, and even personal life. . . . Heimat is not a prosaic system of concepts, and Heimat studies are not a logical theory. Heimat has been given to us by the disposition of our ancestors. . . . [It resembles] a damask of decorated fantasy.

For Seytter, obviously, Heimat history was different from professional history, which he viewed, according to the common nineteenth-century approach, as a scientific system of concepts and methods. Heimat history, in contrast, was a system of sentiments that combined knowledge and sensibilities.

The cultivation of Heimat history did not depend on theoretical rigor but on stirring up empathy and loyalty with the locality and the nation. Emotional awakening was the aim no less than in-depth understanding. The detachment demanded from historians for an impartial evaluation was the antithesis to Heimat history, which was personal and direct.[20] That is why the Heimat was often addressed in the second person singular: "O you [Du] my Heimat, you my native land / How my heart has turned to you full of love!"[21] Anthropomorphizing Heimat was seen as neither ridiculous nor preposterous, but elicited instead an intimate relationship with it. Thus a reader of a Heimat book was not an outside observer to an unfolding of facts, but always an integral part of the narrative, the landscape, and the history. "It is a bright May morn-'ing," opens a Heimat book for Kirchheim unter Teck, "I would like to take you by the hand, dear reader, and to lead you into the quiet splendor of the valley's spring."[22]

Like every history, Heimat history appreciated the past for what it bestowed on the present; after the 1880s Heimat provided roots in an ever changing world. As Seytter wrote, Heimat was "given to us by the disposition of our ancestors." Ellwangen's Historical Association expressed the idea of Heimat as the embodiment of stability: "[In the past people said] that it is better to draw a line over the past. . . . [But] the nerve-racking bustle of world transportation has begotten again the yearning for the old Heimat."[23] Heimat history, with its mixture of facts and literary narrative, reaffirmed the value of the past, while progress threatened to obliterate it.

Although Heimat history looked back at the past, it did not express a reactionary idea of returning to it, but a bridge between the past and the present. Professor Karl Johannes Fuchs of Tübingen University, the chairman of the Bund für Heimatschutz in Württemberg und Hohenzollern (The League for Heimat Protection in Württemberg and Hohenzollern) and a national leader of the Heimat movement, defined Heimat in the foundation ceremony of the Bund in 1909 as a mode of communication between the past and the present: "The main tasks of Heimat protection have originated from the daily industrial development of Württemberg. Heimat protection means to work so that industrial capitalism will cease to destroy the old, on the one hand, and, on the other hand, that a new artistic culture, equal to the old, will be created. Using local architecture, factories can fit into the landscape just as well as train stations."[24] Fuchs did not wish to substitute the present with an idyllic past, but to construct a modus vivendi between the progress of the present and the traditions of the past.

In particular, Heimat history looked in the past for reassurances of local uniqueness in a period of national homogenization. The program of the Regional Committee for Nature Conservation and Heimat Protection (Landesausschuß für Natur- und Heimatschutz), founded also in 1909, declared that its tasks were "to emphasize and to stress the peculiarities of local character in the different areas of Württemberg."[25] Armed with hometown patriotism, localities probed their history and propagated their uniqueness. "Should we consider a university town like Tübingen less suitable than Rottenburg to have a historical association," asked the *Tübinger Chronik* rhetorically, when Tübingers debated whether to establish a historical association. "Who will write the history of Tübingen, the Rottenburgers? . . . [No!] Only Tübingers can feel bound to dedicate their time and money to study Tübingen's history."[26] Thus every locality wrote its own Heimat history, emphasizing its own historical importance and inheritance: the people of the small town of Tuttlingen took care of the ruins of Honburg castle, destroyed in 1642, and those of Kirchheim remodeled the Reußenstein ruins.

Building on local history, Heimat historians connected local peculiarities to German national identity. This was expressed at the fiftieth anniversary of the Archaeological Association of Württemberg that was celebrated in 1893 in Stuttgart in conjunction with the annual convention of the Archaeological Association of Germany (Deutscher Altertumsverein) to honor Württemberg: "We must set up a very wide concept of archaeology [*Altertum*]. It should include not only megalithic graves, castles, and Middle Age findings, but also the most recent periods . . . and even the future. The common ground for all these endeavors is the love of the Heimat and the fatherland. Also here in Maulbronn [Württemberg] we stand on historical ground. The recollections go back to the most beautiful times of the Swabian emperor, the Hohenstaufen. Another family of rulers that originated in Swabia, the Hohenzollern, now rules over Germany."[27] Heimat history wove the past, present, even the future, of Swabia and Germany into a coherent history, which highlighted both the distinctiveness of the part (that is, Swabia) and the oneness of the whole (Germany). Heimatlers' aim was not to show Württemberg's glory, but Württemberg's peculiarity in an age of national standardization and the place of this peculiarity within the homeland. Herwarth von Bittenfeld, a mercenary from a distinguished Swabian family, joined the Prussian army of Frederick the Great after serving in Sicily and Hungary, thus symbolizing Swabian courage, good judgment, love for the fatherland, and the converging histories of North and South Germany. Eduard Mörike, a poet and writer, represented Swabian intelligence, sensitivity, and love for nature, also characteristics of Germans.

As a whole, the cultivation of Heimat history from the 1880s constituted a change in the traditional pursuit of local history in Württemberg. The foundation of the first historical associations in Württemberg—in Rottweil (1831), Ulm (1841), Rottenburg (1852), Schwäbisch Hall (1847), and the Württembergischer Altertumsverein, or Archaeological Association of Württemberg (1843)—was influenced by the brothers Grimm, as well as romantic ideas about German history, and Freiherr von Stein, the founder of the Society for Ancient German History (Gesellschaft für ältere deutsche Geschichtskunde).[28] The associations were small, closed clubs of academically educated notables, that is, Catholic and Protestant civil servants, ministers, doctors, teachers, lawyers, and army officers, who saw themselves as keepers of local history. They were usually dilettante historians who devoted their free time to history, and thought of their task as "salvaging" and "collecting" archaeological findings.[29] Their main activities were to excavate archaeological sites and to study the ancient past of Roman and German settlements in their areas. Indicative of their historical scope was, in many cases, the word "archaeology" as understood in *Altertum* instead of "history," that is, *Geschichte*, in their title.[30]

The Heimat movement, in contrast, was a wide civic movement of socially and professionally varied groups. While members of the old associations continued to be active, Heimat history was cultivated after the 1880s by a growing number of bourgeois professionals who occupied the emerging public sphere. Among the members of the Bund für Heimatschutz in Württemberg, for instance, were architects, landscape architects, sculptors, gallery directors, booksellers, and painters.[31] Lawyers, ministers, and doctors worked with an increasing number of newspaper and journal editors, museum professionals, librarians, and archivists.[32] Educators, who were highly representative in the movement, exemplified the variegated bourgeois social character of the Heimat movement: the Heimat idea was a common denominator between the distinguished Professor Fuchs from Tübingen, and G. Eppinger, a teacher in small Fellbach (population 5,561) who wrote a Heimat book.[33] In the Hall district, a group of four teachers of diverse status, wealth, and professional authority cooperated in writing a Heimat book; the group consisted of the district's school inspector, a teacher in the town's girls school, and two village headmasters from Rieden (population 757) and Vellberg (population 1,141).[34] Also religiously the Heimat movement was varied. Bourgeois Catholics and Protestants were active in historical and Heimat associations, such as the Bund für Heimatschutz.[35] Children of both faiths learned from school textbooks about the Heimat ideas.[36] And Heimat books were published for Catholic, Protestant, and mixed communities.[37]

Moreover, contrary to the old historical appreciation of the past in Württemberg, the Heimat movement changed the social destination of local history from scholars and the elite to the public at large.[38] The immediate indication of this change was the geographical expansion of the institutional cultivation of local pasts. In comparison to the old historical associations that were founded in several towns of relative importance, after the 1880s new historical associations were founded in, for example, Backnang (1884), Cannstatt (1896), Ludwigsburg (1897), Heidenheim (1901), Ellwangen (1904), and Neu-Ulm (1908).[39] The Bund für Heimatschutz had in 1911 members from 74 communities, though the number varied from 1 member in Herrenalb to 458 in Stuttgart.[40] More important, historical perceptions changed. Heimatlers widened the range of their historical interests beyond archaeology, excavations, and ancient history to encompass recent history and every aspect of local *Geschichtskunde*, or local Heimat studies, exploring, in Seytter's words, "daily life" in "vivid, conceivable, and popular" ways. That Heimat historians adopted a new, more self-conscious attitude to history was also indicated when new associations were named historical association (*Geschichtsverein*) instead of archaeological association (*Altertumsverein*), and old associations added the word "historical" to their name, like the Archaeology Association in Rottweil that was renamed in 1912 Historical and Archaeological Association of Rottweil.[41]

The significance of Heimat history was considerably larger than this, however. The Heimat movement changed the civic purpose of local history by popularizing it through museums, lectures, newspaper inserts, popular publications, school activities, and an increasing number of associations such as beautification societies (*Verschönerungsvereine*), associations for the promotion of tourism (*Fremdenverkehrsvereine*), and the regional Bund für Heimatschutz and Committee for Nature Conservation and Heimat Protection. The popular Heimat books, written to publicize to natives and foreigners the locality's singularity in German and Württemberg history, were designed for use in schools and especially in the family circle. In schools the *Heimatkunde* (Heimat studies) entered the curriculum in the 1890s exposing Württemberg children to local history in a new key. And between 1871 and 1918 nineteen Heimat museums that displayed local history to local inhabitants and tourists, often free of admission charge, were founded in Württemberg. Predictably, a museum was founded in the capital Stuttgart, but perhaps more significant for the popularization of Heimat history was the museum founded in Bad Waldsee in 1915, where there were only 3,200 inhabitants. As a whole, Heimat historians developed new modes of communication and display of local history, which was public, visible, and accessible, and constituted a change from the traditional pursuit of local history in Württemberg.

An indication of the widening of historical interests and the opening up of a public sphere of historical activities was the active role of the state. An important task of Heimat history was the preservation and protection of historical sites within the framework of the ongoing industrial and urban development. The state-financed Committee for Nature Conservation and Heimat Protection coordinated these efforts among state ministries, local authorities, and civic associations. In addition, the Ministry of Education and Religious Affairs, and state agencies connected to Heimat preservation, took it upon themselves to instruct schoolchildren and the public about their Heimat activities.[42]

Before the 1880s, public interpretation of the past was determined by an exclusive group of notables, either professional or dilettante historians, organized in a handful of historical associations. It was the Heimat movement, however, that diversified the geography, social origins, and public pursuit of historical activities, opening a new public sphere for the transmission and display of local history. History, once a territory reserved for the local and scholarly elite, was now popularized, simplified, and packaged for mass consumption. The new Heimat historical knowledge reflected a reconstitution of the public realm in Württemberg and, by extension, the notables' progressive loss of their dominant place as public interpreters of local history.

The diversity of the Heimat movement resulted in the Heimat idea having different meanings for different people. For Seytter, Heimat history was a popular endeavor, not devoid of antielitism, expressed in the idea that "Heimat history is stripped of learned academic scholarship." Professor Fuchs, in contrast, a founder of the learned, haut bourgeois Bund für Heimatschutz, applied to Heimat history and Heimat conservation the methods and knowledge of professional scholarly disciplines. His plan of "Using local architecture [so that] factories can fit into the landscape just as well as train stations" called for the cooperation of professional architects, urban planners, historians, and city and state authorities. Nevertheless, Heimatlers shared the belief in the singularity of local identity and in the capacity of the Heimat idea to represent this singularity and to reconcile it with a notion of Germanness.

The history sections of school textbooks exemplified the shared belief of the Heimat idea as a representation of local and national belonging. School textbooks were an important vehicle to transmit the Heimat idea and, as a medium of inculcation, reflected general trends in society.[43] Written for children, the textbooks presented material in an uncomplicated way and, therefore, provided a notion of the Heimat idea reduced to its most essential elements. The textbooks are thus an excellent source to explore the production and meaning of the Heimat idea in Württemberg between 1871 and 1914.

The Heimat idea was not mentioned in school textbooks until 1895. Given that it took about a decade until new concepts found their way into school curriculum, this date corresponded with the beginning of the production of the Heimat idea in the 1880s. From the 1860s to the 1890s, in fact, it seemed that history passed unnoticed in Catholic and Protestant textbooks in Württemberg; they remained unchanged, apart from an additional section about the war of 1870–71. Textbooks did not distinguish among world, European, German, and Württemberg history and presented them in one long chapter. Thus, the chapter "From History and Human Life" (*Aus Geschichte und Menschenleben*) in an 1874 Protestant textbook discussed diverse topics such as ancient Egypt, Socrates, the destruction of the Jewish temple, Jesus Christ, Mohammed, Frederick Barbarossa, old Swabia, Columbus, Luther, Frederick the Great, the French Revolution, Napoleon, and the unification of 1870–71.[44]

History sections changed in 1895 when the concept of Heimat was used for the first time to describe Württemberg. A 1895 Catholic textbook, for example, discussed the history of Württemberg, in a chapter entitled "The Universe," separately from the history of Germany, Europe, and the world. Among the poems and stories, the opening item was a story "The Heimat."[45] The 1910 edition of this textbook tied the Heimat idea and Württemberg regional identity even more explicitly.[46] The elusive title "The Universe" disappeared and instead Heimat appeared in a chapter entitled "From Geography and the Life of the Peoples of the Earth" (*Aus der Länder- und Völkerkunde*).[47] The first section, "From the Heimat," combined Württemberg history, folklore, and nature, the classic Heimat topics. Significantly, educators did not deem it necessary to teach about regional Heimat identity when Württemberg was an independent state and its distinctiveness from other German regions was evident. But twenty-four years after the unification, at a period when national uniformity threatened to render all Germans equal, regardless of their different pasts and traditions, Württembergers did find it necessary to teach their children the attributes of regional belonging. The change in the representation of Württemberg history in school textbooks in 1895 reflected a turning point in the shaping of Württemberg regional identity.

The Heimat idea received additional meaning in textbooks issued in 1909–10 when it was attached to the nation as a whole. The same 1910 Catholic textbook presented German history, for the first time, in a separate chapter entitled "From the Past of the German People."[48] The section included three items with "Heimat" in their titles including a poem by Prince Emil von Schönaich-Carolath, "At Home" (*Daheim*), about feeling at home in the German homeland. A similar theme appeared also in the 1909 Protestant textbook. The chapter "From Our Heimat Land Württemberg" (*Aus unserem Heimatland Württemberg*) was followed by "From the German Fatherland" (*Aus dem deutschen Vaterland*), which commenced with a poem that identified Germany as Heimat: "Ah, this beautiful land, it is my Heimat / it is my beloved German fatherland!"[49]

HEIMAT NATURE:
POETICALNESS AND PRACTICALITY

Württembergers looked not only backward, to their past, but also around, and what they saw there was the beautiful Swabian landscape, a landscape so rich and varied to affect natives and travelers alike: a mixture of a range of mountains, small and round hills, ravines, and valleys. Heading northbound from the snowy Swabian Jura and Lake Constance, one crosses the second highest plateau in Europe, 600 meters high (second only to the 800-meter Castilian plateau in Spain), replete with brooks, woods, and green meadows. Just as Württembergers set out to make the past a hospitable country in an age of constant change, so they set out to make nature such a country in an age of unprecedented environmental transformation. They treated nature with an ambiguous combination of poeticalness and practicality: they cherished nature for its ageless qualities, its beauty, the passion and the awe it inspired, and they appreciated nature for its new role in a mass society; it was a potential gold mine, an attraction for tourists, a source for local profits.

New appreciation of nature was carried by the *Verschönerungsvereine*, the beautification societies.[50] The first society in Württemberg was founded as

A NATION OF HEIMATS

early as 1838, in Drackenstein, followed by one in Tübingen (1842), in Heidenheim (1843), and several others. They were still few and far between, part of a
growing awareness of nature and its place in modern life. In Württemberg and
in Germany beautification societies were a nationwide phenomenon. By 1870
twenty-two societies were founded, although not all had maintained constant
activity. Thereafter they proliferated rapidly: another fourteen societies in the
1870s, seventeen in the 1880s, nine in the 1890s, and eleven between 1900 and
1914. On the eve of World War I, beautification societies in Württemberg were
active in about seventy localities, from the capital Stuttgart, with 286,218 inhabitants in 1910, to small Tettnang, which had 2,675 inhabitants in 1905 when
a society was founded.[51] The societies' aim was to "beautify the town and its
surroundings."[52] They attempted to draw a locality and its environment together, whereas under "environment" they included both nature and historical
sites. In towns they established parklands, planted trees, set up benches, and
erected monuments and fountains; in nature they renovated historical ruins,
maintained castles, and set up paths for hikers.

The new appreciation of nature, similar to trends in the cultivation of
Heimat history, was a bourgeois civic movement. Among the 1,475 members of
the Beautification Society in Stuttgart in 1885, for example, 30.3 percent came
from the commerce and manufacturing sector, including bankers, industrialists, innkeepers, restaurateurs, as well as merchants, shopkeepers who sold
wood, wine, fish, furniture, and others.[53] An additional 23.6 percent of the
members came from the civil service and military, while 12.2 percent were
rentiers, 5.4 percent educators and clergymen, and 12 percent (category III)
came from various middle-class professions. These categories, which together
comprised 82.7 percent of the membership, indicate that the society drew its
support overwhelmingly from the economic and intellectual bourgeoisie. Petit
bourgeois artisans made up only 6.7 percent of the members, workers did
not participate, and the agricultural sector was represented by 8 winegrow-
ers. Women were underrepresented in the society; there were altogether 112
women members, or 7.5 percent, 103 of whom were classified as widows. It is
safe to assume that widows joined the society as an extension of the social
milieu of their late husbands.

The Stuttgart society shows, in a pattern similar to historical associations,
the professional diversity of the Heimat movement. The social profile of the
society in Stuttgart, the capital and the seat of the royal family, was predictably
high, including some of the most powerful and prestigious people in Württemberg: members of the royal court and royal theater, and the distinguished
Otto Elben, Julius Hölder, and Stuttgart's mayor, who served on the society's
standing committee. Located in a socially differentiated urban center, the society became the place to be for local haute bourgeoisie at the expense of the
participation of the lower segments of society. In this respect, the social reality

in Stuttgart was exceptional among hometown Württemberg communities. When we look at the membership of beautification societies in smaller and more representative communities it becomes evident that the Heimat movement comprised more varied middle-class groups.

Take Schramberg, for instance, where 93 members founded the Beautification Society in 1881.[54] Being a typical Württemberg hometown with 4,571 inhabitants, Schramberg shows particularly well the diverse middle-class origins of the societies in the region. Among the 93 members, 29 percent came from the commercial and manufacturing sectors, 5.3 percent were civil servants, 7.5 percent were educators and clergymen, and an additional 7.5 percent comprised a group of middle-class professions including a physician, a newspaper editor, a photographer, an architect, a surveyor, and two painters. These categories together comprise 50.4 percent of the total membership, which means that, similar to Stuttgart, the members of the Schramberg society came predominately from the economic and intellectual bourgeoisie and that the Schramberg society also included the local bourgeois notables such as the mayor, the curate, two local priests, four teachers, and leading entrepreneurs. One social difference between the societies of Stuttgart and Schramberg can be easily explained. The society in Stuttgart had a larger number of civil servants and military personnel, the latter not represented in Schramberg at all, because Stuttgart was the seat of local government.

The most significant social factor, however, was this: compared with the composition of the society in Stuttgart the percentage of petit bourgeois artisans in Schramberg, including, for instance, a cooper, a tailor, a blacksmith, a saddler, a cutler, two cabinetmakers, and seven bakers, was notably higher, 23.6 percent in Schramberg compared with only 6.7 percent in Stuttgart. The inclusiveness of Schramberg's society was also reflected in the membership dues, 20 pfennigs a month, or 2.20 marks a year, an affordable amount to middle-class citizens, compared with a payment of at least 4 marks a year in Stuttgart.[55] Together, the mixed bourgeois groups of Schramberg's society and the haute bourgeoisie of Stuttgart's society made up the social origins of the Heimat movement in Württemberg, a movement that extended from the petite bourgeoisie, to educated professionals, entrepreneurs, up to the higher echelons of local officeholders.[56]

Overall, the social profile and prestige of beautification societies were slightly lower than that of historical associations. Participation in historical associations depended on education and was thus reserved mainly for university-educated bourgeoisie, the *Bildungsbürgertum*, whereas participation in a beautification society required, regardless of education, mainly a lively interest in the well-being of the town. Furthermore, the mixed social origins of beautification societies were also an outcome of the growing commercialization of nature that drew to the societies innkeepers and restaurateurs, shopkeepers and artisans, merchants and entrepreneurs, all of whom sought to cash in on the new appreciation of nature.

Most beautification societies in Württemberg resembled the society of Schramberg, not Stuttgart.[57] In this sense, the geographical diffusion of Württemberg societies in Stuttgart, in medium-sized towns, and in small hometowns reflected the mixed bourgeois social origins of the Heimat appreciation of nature and, more generally, of the Heimat idea. But what were the power relationships between the center and the periphery? Was there a hierarchical pattern according to which the Stuttgart haute bourgeoisie originated the Heimat idea and later diffused it to petite and provincial bourgeoisie in small and medium-sized communities? The geographical pattern of foundation of beautification societies in Württemberg does not support this hypothesis. Württemberg had one big city, Stuttgart, and a number of big towns or regional centers, such as Heilbronn, Ulm, Eßlingen, and Gmünd. Also important were Tübingen, thanks to its university, and Ravensburg, the Catholic center. Between 1842, the foundation of a society in Tübingen, with 9,016 inhabitants, and 1861, the foundation in Stuttgart with 75,260 inhabitants, associations were founded also in small Heidenheim, a town of 4,726 inhabitants in 1843 when a society was established, in Blaubeuren, where there were 2,068 inhabitants in 1858, and in Winnenden, with 3,037 inhabitants in 1860. The same pattern continued in the 1860s: societies were founded in towns such as Heilbronn and Ulm, both in 1863, and Eßlingen in 1867, and in peripheral localities such as Saulgau in 1862, which had 2,775 inhabitants. Indeed, preceding these towns were the small localities of Kirchheim (1864, 5,548 inhabitants), Leonberg (1867, 2,136 inhabitants), Schorndorf (1869, 3,515 inhabitants), Mergentheim (1869, 2,999 inhabitants), Rottweil (1869, 5,447 inhabitants), and Ehingen (1870, 3,547 inhabitants). This pattern persisted in the following decades. In the 1880s Waldsee with 2,812 inhabitants and Mengen with 2,441 inhabitants preceded Ravensburg and Gmünd, which were immediately followed by Münsingen, which had 1,699 inhabitants in 1890 when a society was founded. The Heimat idea originated in both central and peripheral localities, by members of the royal court and by a saddler from a small community.[58]

In the 1880s the attitudes of societies and of Württembergers toward nature changed from a focus on beautification into active reclamation. Societies began to act regionally as well as locally, and planned common activities.[59] In one such meeting in Eßlingen in 1888 beautification societies from seven towns founded the Swabian Jura Association (Schwäbischer Albverein), which propelled the message of Heimat nature to the four corners of Württemberg and attracted 30,000 members before World War I.[60] The Black Forest Association of Württemberg (Württembergischer Schwarzwaldverein), founded several years before in 1884, had similar influence. The associations cooperated in organizing outdoor activities and in diffusing through newspapers and journals the Heimat's treatment of nature. A network of paths covering all Württemberg was established and the associations organized periodic excursions and hikes that took town dwellers into the countryside. This was the norm even in associations that had no connection to nature; the Schiller Gymnastic Association, for instance, comprising six districts in the Marbach-Ludwigsburg area, organized regular *Wandertage*, or hiking days, to cultivate the idea of the Swabian Heimat.[61] In addition, in 1887 an elementary teacher from Stuttgart, Karl Gottlob Lutz, founded the Teachers Association for Natural Science in Württemberg (Lehrerverein für Naturkunde in Württemberg), whose interests outstripped narrow scientific topics and promoted the uniqueness of Swabian and German nature. In a convention of German teachers in Stuttgart in 1894, Lutz gave a lecture entitled "Forest as a Community of Life" and the association organized an exhibition called "The German Forest." Appropriately, the organ of the association was called "From the Heimat."[62] Beautification societies also participated in the publication of Heimat books.[63] As the notion of Swabian nature changed and became identified with Heimat, outdoor activities and a fascination with nature became a staple of Württembergers' life.

It would be a mistake to view this attraction to nature as simply antimodern, as a romantic attachment to bygone times, for this interpretation fails to recognize the multiple meanings of the Heimat idea that, as a perception of nature, attempted to reconcile tenderness with worldliness, looking backward to the past with looking forward to an age of progress. To begin with, the Heimat idea of nature was an idea formulated by city and town dwellers, people who observed, studied, and vacationed in natural settings but did not draw their living from them. Even in small communities, where boundaries between nature and town were blurred, the daily life of people was not determined by nature but increasingly regulated by the pace and rhythms of agents of modernity such as the railway and the nearby factory. The origins of Heimat in urban and modern habitat was most evident in the modern concept of time that governed Württembergers' treatment of nature: outdoor activities were determined by the modern organization of work and its accompanying realm of leisure time. Württembergers left town and city to enjoy nature only when work restrictions and public and civic duties allowed, mostly on weekends or on holidays. The Heimat treatment of nature was based, therefore, on the modern possibility to choose one's attitude and behavior toward nature: whether you take a hike or prefer to stay home, hiking is entertainment, not a momentous decision. Such privilege was diametrically opposed to the essence of nature and of its accompanying human activity, agriculture, which is determined by climatic and biological laws, rhythms, and conditions.[64]

Heimat's modern notion of time—and the ideas of conservation of nature, improvement of its look, and the need to *return* to it—derived from the fundamental conditions in which Heimat was originated, namely the state of being extraneous to nature. Heimat looked at nature from outside, wishing to take some part in it, but not being determined by it. When beautification societies declared they want to "beautify the town *and* its surroundings," they in fact underscored the difference between the two. Württembergers who lived in towns and cities praised nature, but had no intention of moving. Just as Heimat history did not endorse a return to bygone times, so Heimat nature did not recommend abandoning the towns and cities for life in the countryside. In fact, instead of immersing themselves in nature, Württembergers did their best to control it by cleaning, marking, mapping, improving, and propagating it. Under their hand nature became a planned, functional site in modern society for outdoor activities, relaxation, and vacation. A symbol of their command was the lookout tower, which was erected by virtually every self-respecting beautification society that wished to attract tourists. The high tower dominated the surrounding landscape and emphasized the betterment, and consequently control, of nature by the nearby town's inhabitants.

The case of the lookout tower in Kirchheim unter Teck exemplified Heimatlers' perceptions of nature. Heimatlers were sincerely committed to the conservation of nature and of nature's authenticity and they were as sincerely committed to improve nature's look according to contemporary perceptions of beauty and attractiveness. This characterized the attitude of beautification societies toward castles and ruins, which were often regarded more as lucrative sites than as historical objects. The lookout tower in Kirchheim presented a familiar Heimat mix of ancient ruins, a commercial spirit, and an artistic touch to improve nature's look. After its foundation in 1864, Kirchheim's Beautification Society maintained the local ruins whose tower was a source of local pride; the ruins were open to the public after the construction of a protective roof and the renovation of the cellars. By the 1880s, the growing number of visitors suggested the economic potential of the ruins, and led the society to enhance their appeal. Improvements of the ruins' surroundings were followed by a plan to build a new medieval-style tower on the remains of the old one; the designers were concerned with an accurate historical rebuilding of the tower, but also with the appearance of authenticity in the eyes of contemporaries. The impressive new tower, which was 30 meters high and 4.80 meters in diameter, was unveiled in 1889 in a big local and regional celebration attended by 3,000 participants. The king sent a telegram. In 1890 Kirchheim had 7,391 inhabitants. The lookout tower lived up to the rosiest expectations and became a tourist attraction in Württemberg.[65]

What was most evident in the modern appreciation of nature was the relentless commercialization of it. The opening sentence of the 1884 statute of the Württembergischer Schwarzwaldverein declared that "the aim of the association is to enhance tourism."[66] Beautification societies were founded with the explicit intention to mobilize nature to the city's prosperity; the society of

Eningen, a town of 3,470 inhabitants, was founded in 1885 in order "to attract tourists, especially in the summer period, and, if possible, to establish Eningen as a climatic health resort."[67] After the turn of the century it was common for beautification societies to merge with associations for the promotion of tourism. Nature provided towns and cities the opportunity to cash in on the increasing interest in traveling that began to be broadly diffused at the turn of the century.

Another development attested to Heimat's appreciation of nature. The naturalization of Heimat quickly found its way into Heimat books and, of course, school textbooks, those sensitive barometers of Heimat consciousness. In the books, Heimat nature was a mixture of geology, climate, flora and fauna, and geography. It was presented in a matter-of-fact, scientific language, which left little place for romantic imagination.[68] The story of geological strata or of the region's animals in the past and present was not the object of romantic effusions.

And yet, just as Heimat history was more than history, so Heimat nature was more than simply geology and economic profit. To describe Heimatlers as technocrats of nature is as unjust as describing Heimatlers as antimodern. For all its commercialization and regulation, local and national nature remained for Heimatlers a territory replete with beauty and memories, distinguished from nature in other parts of the world: this was their nature, their habitat, as locals, Württembergers, and Germans. Through poems, stories, travels, and conservation, Heimatlers cherished and cultivated a poetic side of nature, which was fundamental to Heimat sensibilities. For Heimatlers nature embedded the "peculiarity" [Eigenart] and the "remarkableness" [Merkwürdigkeit] of the German local and national Heimats.[69] The bond between German territory and history provided for Heimatlers the historical-ideological justification, in contrast to the environmental justification, for nature conservation and Heimat protection. Thus the Bund für Heimatschutz in Württemberg vowed to "protect the *natural and historical* peculiarity of the German Heimat."[70]

The poetics of nature connected the local community with the national community, and endowed the national community with a sense of homeyness that became the hallmark of the Heimat idea.[71] Tangible, visible, and therefore easier to identify with than history, Heimat nature aroused immediate sentiments of local and national belonging, attaching coziness to the local and national territory through descriptions of mountains, valleys, and rivers. The language of poetic nature lent itself easily to sentimental and gushy descriptions—"O you, my Heimat, valleys and hills / In my soul you will always be."[72] Used in local and national contexts, Heimat nature underscored the affinity between man, nature, roots, region, and homeland.

As a yearning for nature that originated from the comfortable dwellings of modernity, Heimat's treatment of nature combined sentimentality and modern pragmatism. For Heimatlers, nature was simultaneously poetic and scientific, just as history was simultaneously literary and scholarly. This mixture between a "system of sensibilities" and a "system of knowledge" was the reason for Heimat's appeal and claim for authenticity.

HEIMAT ETHNOGRAPHY:
COMMEMORATING THE GOOD OLD DAYS

Having embraced local history and nature, Württembergers set out to infuse Heimat with life, and particularly with the Württemberg way of life. They cultivated a Württemberg ethnographic consciousness, Heimat folklore, that encompassed every aspect of traditional manners, customs, and life-style. Heimat folklore added to Heimat history and nature an important human factor by concentrating on the ways in which people in Württemberg lived and thought. Simultaneously, looking back to traditions helped define the origins of Württemberg society, a topic that became ever more urgent as German society rapidly changed. While Heimatlers adopted a most European and German solution to the search for origins by looking for the essence of Württemberg's identity mainly in rural folk life, it is significant that they found it also in burgher folk life in German hometowns. Württembergers established an ethnographic knowledge through a systematic effort, emanating from academic and nonacademic circles, including historical associations, Heimat writers, and Heimat museum activists, to collect, catalog, study, display, promote, and invent folk traditions. These studies in Württemberg followed the pattern set by Heimat history, whereby amateurs as well as scholars, middle classes as well as notables, cultivated Heimat folklore. At the turn of the century a host of associations contributed to folklore studies, such as the Württemberg Folklore Association (Württemberg Vereinigung für Volkskunde), the Association for the Preservation of Popular Folk Costume (Verein zur Erhaltung der Volkstrachten), and the Bund für Heimatschutz.

How vast the interests of Heimat ethnographers were can be gauged from a study organized in 1899 by the state's Royal Statistical Office (Königliches Statistisches Landesamt), the Württemberg Folklore Association, and a group of professors and ministers, headed by Professor Karl Bohnenberger of Tübingen University. Their project was to collect all the popular traditions in Württemberg in the past and the present. For that purpose they distributed to ministers and teachers across the country a detailed questionnaire. The whole of life was included: nourishment, clothing, habitation, law and administration, rituals, festivities, songs, legends, dialects, beliefs and superstitions, manners at home and work, and many others; it was a genuine field questionnaire of anthropologists. The response was enthusiastic, and more than 600 questionnaires were sent back from as many localities. The Württemberg Folklore Association processed the data, and the first findings were published soon afterward in the *Württembergische Jahrbücher für Statistik und Landeskunde.*[73]

Folklore was used and understood in various ways. Some ethnographic studies followed well-known and established academic methods; for academics like Bohnenberger, work was conducted under the principle of *wie es eigentlich gewesen ist.* But invention was integral in the cultivation of ethnographic consciousness. For Heimat as a "system of sentiments," Truth was never a goal. Traditions could be invented, providing they conformed to contemporary notions of ancientness, peasant and burgher culture, and Swabianness. One of the most successful and durable inventions was the Swabian *Tracht,* or folk costume.[74] Traditional society in Württemberg before the second half of the nineteenth century maintained strict and elaborate dress regulations in the village community. Apparel represented accurately one's social status, occupation, and wealth. One could tell a minister in Württemberg from a peasant not only by the functionality of the person's clothing, but also by specific articles of clothing: for instance, a minister never wore leather trousers or a red peasant vest. Regulations also existed within a social group: rich peasants who owned cattle wore a silver miniature cow attached to a silver chain on their leather trousers. The color, shape, and material of apparel visually classified social hierarchies. This had changed with the transformation of the society of estates into a society of classes. Traditional ways of dressing disappeared as city and country moved closer, peasants turned into workers, and urban fashion became a status symbol. Technological innovations in the processing of textiles resulted in mass production of cheap cotton clothes that were more comfortable to wear than linen. The studies on Württemberg's districts (*Beschreibungen*), published by the Department for Statistics and Topography, reported as early as the 1830s on the decline of traditional costumes. After midcentury most traditional clothes disappeared into cupboards and chests of drawers.[75]

But not for long. In their search for identity and origins, Württemberg's Heimatlers counterresponded to monotonous modern apparel by dusting off the traditional colorful peasant dresses. They called the traditional costume *Tracht,* a word originated among the urban bourgeoisie that no peasant could understand.[76] The most famous *Tracht* invented in Württemberg was of the village Betzingen.[77] The painter Robert Heck discovered the village and its *Tracht* in the 1850s. But Betzingen's *Tracht* moved to the local and national center stage only after 1861. That year the village, having the good fortune of being located between two important local towns, Reutlingen and Tübingen, was connected to the railway system. As a result, city dwellers, in search of peasant authenticity, soon discovered Betzingen, and a group of artists, called the Betzinger School, painted numerous pictures of Betzingen's colorful *Tracht.*

Technological innovations helped popularize the *Tracht*, when at the end of the century photographers, such as Paul Sinner from Tübingen, replaced painters.

The growing production of paintings and photographs of Betzingen's *Tracht* is interesting because in the second half of the nineteenth century almost no one there wore traditional costumes. The village minister reported in 1865 that traditional peasant costumes were rarely seen.[78] In fact, many Betzingers were workers, and labored at the local factory or in Reutlingen. But Heimatlers were not distracted by such considerations. Betzingers who posed wearing traditional *Tracht* were dressed up especially for the occasion and some of them were workers.

If few wore *Tracht* in Betzingen, how then did Heimatlers reconstruct it? Before they disappeared, traditional costumes in Betzingen were very elaborate. Villagers had special articles of clothing designed specifically for weekdays, for social purposes or celebrations, and the like. To complicate things further, social groups wore different costumes on similar occasions. The Heimatlers simplified this myriad of costumes by constructing a few prototypes, and packaging them for mass consumption: what was important were the colors of the costume, not its historical accuracy. The invented tradition of *Tracht* was very popular: the sections on local *Tracht* became a staple of Heimat books;[79] the Association for the Preservation of Folk Costume was founded;[80] and postcards and Heimat museums displayed the *Tracht*. Soon, the commercialization of *Tracht*, that is of tradition, was in full swing. Villagers understood that by selling at town markets in traditional dress they associated freshness and health with their products.[81] Others sold the old costumes from grandmother's closet for high prices.[82] And photographers sold pictures, taken only weeks before, of "authentic" *Tracht* from the good old days.

Heimat folklore integrated many single local traditions into a whole, Württemberg ethnography, that was more than the sum of its parts; local *Tracht* thus gave rise to *schwäbische Tracht*, pure historical invention.[83] Ethnography was a means of exploring the Württemberg collective identity. Bohnenberger, the head of the project to collect Württemberg's traditions, explained that "What we strive after [in this project] concerns the entire land," because Württemberg's traditions were a popular patrimony that connected generations of Swabians and epitomized their "collective character" (*Volkscharacter*).[84] This belief in a common patrimony and character was the reason that Heimatlers in Württemberg engaged in folklore studies, and that Heimat books included chapters about traditional "collective character and ways of life" (*Volkscharacter und Volksleben*), delineating particular dialects, dresses, dances, foods, costumes, and manners.[85]

The purpose of Heimat folklore, similar to that of Heimat history and nature, was to reconcile Württemberg and German identities. A classic case was the study of Swabian dialect, *Mundart*. Language embodied Swabian distinctiveness: "The language of our people offers one of the most important means to know its peculiarity. . . . [Our language] still streams in the localities of our Heimat with its blend of power, originality, nativeness, and simplicity."[86] The Swabian dictionary published in 1904 symbolized this uniqueness. At the same time, language embodied Germanness. The editor of the dictionary, Hermann Fischer, declared in the introduction that the history of Swabian dialect was part of the history of German philology.[87] Folklore provided, for laypersons and scholars, a concept to understand the German way of life as comprising regional ways of life. Like Heimat history and Heimat nature, folklore was a representation of Germany based on the metaphor of whole and parts: areas in Württemberg had different dialects; together they formed the Swabian dialect; and all the regional dialects constituted the German language.

Heimatlers used folklore studies to find a common denominator between the young and old generations that, in the changing modern world, often seemed to draw apart. A 1913 Heimat book for Reutlingen explained: "This book is intended to be a companion to the family circle, where one gathers around the companionable fire, where small hands lay on grandmother and grandfather's laps begging for a story, where on Sunday afternoon father wanders with the children in field and forest. The stories in this book bind us with past generations, with their anxieties and creations, thoughts and sentiments. The stories also greet the present generation that is now away from the Heimat [meaning, perhaps, workers who migrated to cities]."[88] Heimat folklore served as a link between generations by emphasizing the longevity of traditions, real or invented, thus connecting the past and the present.

Heimat folklore reconstructed Württemberg and German identities by looking backward to the past, but this reconstruction was not synonymous with being backward-looking and antimodern. In search of identity, people often look back to the past as a source of validation; the question is, How is the past used within an eclectic reconstruction? Heimat folklore never embraced the past completely. Some traditions were not good for anything, as a Heimat book for Heidenheim declared in 1914: "We need not shed tears about the disappearance of quite a lot of the old customs and manners of our ancestors. For often they were surrounded with hideous superstitions and were rather immoral and abusive. One hopes that with the course of time they will be buried once and for all."[89] Heimat folklore thus appreciated the progressive results of modernity.

Furthermore, in addition to peasant traditions, Heimat folklore also cultivated the traditions of hometown burghers. If the Heimat idea preferred a rural society as the locus of national origins it is also because German society before the second half of the nineteenth century was an agrarian society. Nevertheless, Heimat folklore, as a set of social and cultural attributes, was also employed to study urban communities. Wilhelm Seytter, who defined Heimat as a "system of sentiments," also defined his book about Stuttgart as a "Heimat study."[90] It includes stories and legends about the city, such as Stuttgart's *Tracht* in the past, or children in the Middle Ages, and was, in fact, a Heimat folklore of Stuttgart's burghers, destined for a bourgeois readership in Stuttgart at the turn of the century.[91]

Heimatlers thus never simply adored the past; for them the past was both venerated and passé. Through Heimat ethnology, similar to Heimat history and nature, they appreciated the past for the origins it bestowed upon the present and for its modern application, namely profit. Nowhere was this combination better displayed in German society than in tourism, which was a representation of a locality, a region, or the nation that mixed, for the enhancement of the traveler's pleasure, illusion and reality, historical facts and historical inventions. After the turn of the century, tourism became a major vehicle to diffuse the Heimat idea. The International Travel and Tourism Exhibition was opened in Berlin in the Zoologischer Garten on 1 April 1911 with the participation of Württemberg. At the entrance to Württemberg's pavilion stood a red-cheeked, life-size woman doll dressed in a Black Forest *Tracht*. Small neat windows, adorned with flowers on the sills, imparted a traditional and intimate look. Two big wooden doors led to a Black Forest coffee room and a wine cabinet from Eßlingen. There, visitors seated at peasant wooden tables were served coffee and hot chocolate by *Tracht*-dressed blond Swabian women. At one corner stood a big stove, a wooden frame where dishes dried, and a long and winding wooden bench. On the wall behind hung tiles of "primitive" peasant art and colorful peasant pottery. German peasants could have learned a great deal from this representation, not about the peasant way of life, but about urban and modern ideas of what the peasant way of life had been. This hodgepodge of objects was meant to appeal to an urban public who viewed folklore with the same fascination it viewed foreign countries. The reports emphasized how enchanted Berliners were to see the *Tracht*—they carefully inspected the pointed caps, silk aprons, colorful breast cloths, and the taffeta bows on the women's hair—which, after all, were about as common in the metropolis's streets as a traditional dress of an African tribe.[92]

Tourism was an especially suitable field to construct an imaginary representation of folk life because the main purpose of tourist representations was to convey not historical accuracy but a world that was different from everyday life. The necessity of attracting consumers and making money obliged tourism to appeal to common perceptions. The new Heimat folklore after the 1890s fit the need of consumer society to produce images of the past, tradition, and society that would be marketable, appealing, and easy to grasp. Heimat folklore, and in a sense the idea of Heimat in general, was an illusion about the

past, just as tourism was a short illusion of freedom, adventure, and enchant-
ment in a life that was usually less heroic. In the words of the *Schwäbischer
Merkur*: "It was a fortunate idea to build the Heimat café because it arouses
such lovely travel illusions."[93] The success of the Berlin exhibition led travel
associations and state agencies in Württemberg to organize a similar exhibition in Stuttgart a year later, dedicated exclusively to Württemberg. Featuring
similar folklore themes as in Berlin, the Swabian Exhibition for Travel and
Tourism was visited by 70,000 people and was a resounding success. The
exhibition's catalog opened with a poem by Ludwig Finckh—"To Heimat."[94]

When we think about the meaning of Heimat folklore, it is worthwhile
bearing in mind that while Heimatlers collected traditions, they did not plan
to imitate them or to use them as a blueprint for a new organization of society.
Some traditions, like the *Tracht*, ended up in Heimat museums with a caption
for ignorant visitors. Others became topics for scholarly books or found their
way into popular Heimat books. The display of these traditions was not intended as users' manuals but as an evocation of a disappearing world. Heimat
folklore—the collection, invention, and display of traditions—was in a sense
also a way to commemorate, and to come to terms with, past ways of life and
thought in Württemberg. And like every commemoration, it included an element of mourning and loss.

HEIMAT AND MODERNITY: PROGRESS AND LOSS

The times had been changing, declared a Fellbach Heimat book in 1908 looking back at the past half century of industrial development, and the Heimat
idea was a German response to explain this change.[95] How did Heimatlers
appreciate the transformation of German society from an agrarian into an
industrial society? Did Heimat sentiments foster fundamentally anti-industrial
and antitechnological ideas about a return to a primeval and pure state of
society? One answer can be found in a 1914 Heimat book of Heidenheim
district, *Our Heimat in the Past and the Present*, which described small Giengen
an der Brenz (population 3,459):[96]

> Similar to the cities, we find also in rural communities a welcome increase
> in prosperity . . . everywhere and in almost every field of life we feel a
> sound progress. . . . Communication has increased in the entire district
> very rapidly, and the transportation of people and goods has developed to
> a degree that was unthinkable a few decades ago. . . . One writes and
> speaks over great distances in a flash. Even in the smallest locality there is
> a public call-office. Motorists and bicycle riders rush with alarming speed
> raising dust between valleys and hills. In fact, soon Heidenheim will have

an airship hangar and aviation center. A special picture of our valley will be offered to the coming generations when the canal connecting the Neckar and the Danube will cross it. Then the localities on the Brenz, provided with locks, cranes, and disembarkation areas, will draw the heavy cargo steamers. New jobs will be created, new factories will be established. Some old things will disappear and new life will flourish out of the ruins. Our times, to be sure, never halt [*Nie ermüdend steht ja unsre Zeit stille*].

Passages such as this have been ignored by scholars who until recently have interpreted the Heimat idea as wholly antimodern, as a conservative idea that idealized the rural past and ignored modern reality.[97] A first step to reverse this view has been the perceptive analysis of Applegate about the incompatibility between the Heimat movement in the Palatinate and antimodern tendencies in German society.[98] The perceived contradiction between the Heimat idea and modernity is a result of the putative dichotomy between modern and anti-modern. But this dichotomy fails to take into account the ambiguity of modernity and of Heimatlers who simultaneously mourned the past while applauding the material progress and cultural opportunities promised by modernity.

Instead of viewing modernity and the Heimat idea as oppositional, Heimat lers commonly attempted to strike a modus vivendi between the preservation of national roots and the continuation of modernity and the prosperity it promised. The working program of the Regional Committee for Nature Conservation and Heimat Protection thus declared:[99]

> Heimat protection and nature conservation does not mean to restore and maintain retrogressively, artificially, and under every circumstance the old at the expense of the new. It does not mean to impede the progress and achievements of the new age in agriculture, architecture, transportation, industry, commerce, technology, and the like. Instead, Heimat protection and nature conservation want to prevent, with a spirit of moderation, harmful side-effects of a rapid economic development. . . . Heimat protection and nature conservation mean to harmonize the challenges of progress and the preservation of Heimat's individuality, beauty, remarkableness, and venerableness.

Heimat thus both glorified the past and celebrated modernity.

The Heimat idea also reflected the sense of loss felt by Germans as a result of modernity that produced the feeling and the condition of being mentally and physically extraneous to the "old Heimat." The Heimat idea was a German form of mourning the past, the disappearing "good old" ways of life. In an essay about his native hometown, *Heimat. Calw*, Hermann Hesse painfully and perceptively recognized that "I would not have had to write about Calw, had I stayed in this beautiful town. But to stay was not my destiny."[100] Leaving one's old town behind, either physically or by fashioning a modern way of life, created the Heimat longing for the world of yesterday.

The Heimat idea had also outright antimodern meaning, though it was rather insignificant to the larger meaning of the movement in Württemberg and Germany. The mixture of land, nation, origins, and uniqueness lent itself to appropriation by reactionaries in every European national movement. In Germany the *Heimatkunst* (Heimat art) movement of Adolf Bartels and Heinrich Sohnrey's German Association for Agrarian Welfare and Heimat Care (Deutscher Verein für ländliche Wohlfahrts- und Heimatpflege) saw the Heimat idea as the epitome of rural society and as an antithesis to modern, industrial society. Bartels and Sohnrey were never interested in the regional characteristics of the Heimat idea. Their notion of Heimat had negligible influence in Württemberg and Germany, where the Heimat movement emphasized the coexistence of local and national identities and the reciprocity between tradition and modernity.

The Heimat idea was modern because the hallmark of modernity has never been this inexorable, onward-moving progress toward technological proficiency and political freedom that has been obsessively demanded from Heimatlers and Germans. Rather, modern concerns, as Marshall Berman described, "are moved at once by a will to change . . . and by a terror of disorientation and disintegration, of life falling apart." To be modern is to be "both revolutionary and conservative. . . . We might even say that to be fully modern is to be anti modern . . . it has been impossible to grasp and embrace the modern world's potentialities without loathing and fighting against some of its most palpable realities."[101] In this light, the Heimat idea—combining an attraction to and celebration of progress with an anxiety over technological change, and a yearning for a past of putative wholeness and authenticity—seems at the center of Germany's experience of modernity.[102] Heimatlers were not antiquated traditionalists but knowledgeable observers of and participants in Germany's modernity project. The Heimat idea was a representation of the social world that embraced and fretted about modernity. When we acknowledge that representations of the social world are components of social reality, then we can see that Heimat was not a dream about a return to a bucolic world, but an ambiguous perception of modernity, ambiguous like modernity itself.

Nevertheless, if historians have paid too much attention to the myth of *Blut und Boden* (blood and soil) at the expense of the experience of modernity in German society, an opposite approach, that is, ignoring the yearning for the past, is not helpful either.[103] The modernity of the Heimat idea is so interesting, so modern one might say, because Heimatlers fascinatingly commingled progress with tradition, the airship hangar with *Tracht* folklore, the fear of losing one's identity and the promise of progress. Heimatlers were people who could remember what was it like to live in a world before the forces of technology and capitalism transformed it. They fondly carried the image of this world in the back of the mind as an antithesis to the contradicting and confusing industrial society, but they also enthusiastically embraced the modern life.

Furthermore, the Heimat idea was an idea of modernity that never lost sight of human beings, either of their ways of life and thought in the past or of their capacity to influence and change modern society in the present. In spite of the impersonalism of modern society, and perhaps because of it, Heimatlers sought to reclaim the individual and believed that through education, instruction, and civic activity one could ameliorate modern society. This, I believe, is a significant factor in understanding not only the meaning of the Heimat idea and German modernism in the past but also of the experience of modernity in the present. Berman discusses two types of conception of modernity. On the whole, thinkers in the nineteenth century embraced modernity enthusiastically while grappling with its contradictions, ambiguities, and disorientation. It was a perceptive, self-conscious, and creative reception, of which the Heimat idea is but one demonstration. In contrast, twentieth-century thinkers tended toward "rigid polarities and flat totalization."[104] Modernity is either saluted or else cursed. It is either hailed by the Italian futurists as the inevitable change that is "hacking an abyss between those docile slaves of tradition and us free moderns" or else somberly viewed by Max Weber as an "iron cage." Michel Foucault, who contributed perhaps more than any other thinker in the past decades to our thinking about modernity, has of course seen modernity as a sort of prison where it is impossible for mankind to be free. In *Discipline and Punish* the prison becomes a metaphor for modern society, which is a "carceral network" where there is no escaping outside and no freedom inside: "The carceral network does not cast the unassimilable into a confused hell; there is no outside. It takes back with one hand what it seems to exclude with the other." Man in modern society is entrapped in the carceral network (which always remains impersonal in Foucault's writings), which has a way of making its power seem natural and legitimate: the prison is "linked to a whole series of 'carceral' mechanisms which seem distinct enough—since they are intended to alleviate pain, to cure, to comfort—but which all tend, like the prison, to exercise a power of normalization." In this society the idea of one's freedom of action is a fanciful illusion. The octopusian carceral network is everywhere, "in its compact or disseminated forms, with its systems of insertion, distribution, surveillance, observation." Foucault's rhetorical question is therefore to be expected: "Is it surprising that prisons resemble factories, schools, barracks, hospitals, which all resemble prisons?"[105] Foucault's bleak view of modern society is wrong not because it is so pessimistic, which is irrelevant, but because it obliterates any possible effect of human agency. His is a view of modern society that is hermetically sealed from changes, where people live in a sort of a sleeplike state, with neither control nor much understanding of the world around them. But like every interpretation of history that consigns human beings to the role of passive, manipulated spectators, this interpretation is bound to fail to embrace the richness of people's lives in the past, and the consequences of the vicissitudes and contradictions of human action. It is significant to note that in spite of their manifested disagreements, Foucault and the scholars who criticized Heimat for not being modern enough, in fact have much in common. They have viewed modern society as an unconditional totality, either progressive and onward-looking or depressing and oppressing. But it is worthwhile remembering that history is (also) what happens to people when scholars formulate another theory about the world. And history, even in modern society, is also made by the surprises and unintended consequences that human actions and beliefs produce. If there is something we can learn from Heimatlers, it is not some sort of a naive belief in progress but the idea that, in spite of the disorientation caused by modern society, meaningful life can be breathed into this society, if only one is willing to take the challenge.

A NATION OF HEIMATS

CHAPTER SIX

A National Lexicon

ONE, TWO, THREE . . .
A THOUSAND GERMAN HEIMATS

*T*he concept of Heimat in imperial Germany did not halt at the Swabian borders. At the root of the Heimat idea were developments that made Württemberg only one regional actor in a large national play about modernity and national integration. The Heimat idea transformed concepts of history, territoriality, and association. On the one hand, the German hometown changed because it could not live with the accelerated transformation of society, that is an integral part of the modern world.[1] Technology obliterated the awesome power of natural space, and from the train's window yesterday's horizons and yesterday's natural boundaries disappeared quickly.[2] The nation-state and the capitalist economy expanded both time and space, thus changing the traditional community, once closed within itself, and irreversibly connected it to the world.[3] On the other hand, the alteration of time and space did not simply obliterate the old community; it revived it as well. Overwhelmed by modernity, people looked back at the old local community, real or imagined, as a point of orientation. At the very moment Germans experienced the unlimited expansion of time and space, they invented the "old Heimat" as a secure and eternal site. While the historical accuracy of this "old Heimat" was, as we saw in the preceding chapter, a matter of degree and opinion, modernity did change the old community, in real life, only to reinstate it intact, and at times "improved," in the imagination.

In one respect the expansion of time and space was limited, however. Historians have usually viewed the unification in 1871 as a social and political turning point in German history. It is often forgotten that 1871 mapped the temporal and spatial dimensions of the German homeland. From an amorphous domain divided up into kingdoms, the nation turned into a territorially defined state. Time and space obviously transcended Germany's borders, but they had a particular symbolic meaning within the homeland because the territorial nation was inhabited by a population that believed it had shared a past, a future, and a unique character that no other national population had. The invention of the local and national Heimat ideas was a symbolic response to the post-1871 temporal and spatial demands of the homeland. The Heimat idea provided a symbolic national common denominator among different regions, their inhabitants and territories. And it provided the nation a link between past, present, and future in a period of rapid mutation, introducing coherence and causality to local and national histories. After 1871, at the historical meeting point between the requirements of national integration and the conditions of modernity, Heimat become a key concept in German culture and a central word in German discourse. The logic of Heimat was that it represented a community, real or imagined, tangible or symbolic, of people who shared a transcended common denominator. In imperial Germany the idea of a Heimat community extended from a small, tangible community of people with face-to-face social relations, to an imaginary national community that contained millions of people.[4] It embodied the intimacy of closed places and the abstraction of the homeland, integrating the space, time, and character of the old community with the abstract notion of region and nation.

After the 1880s new Heimats seemed to spring up daily in the German homeland. Heimat meant Germany, as in Deutscher Bund Heimatschutz. Heimat also meant region, as in Bund für Heimatschutz in Württemberg und Hohenzollern, Schlesischer Bund für Heimatschutz, and other organizations for almost every German province and region. Heimat meant district, as in the Heimat book *Heimatkunde für den Oberamtsbezirk Göppingen*.[5] Heimat meant city, as in Wilhelm Seytter's *Unser Stuttgart*. It meant town, as in *Reutlinger Heimatbuch*. And it meant small town, as in a Fellbach Heimat book.[6] Everywhere one looked in Germany, there lay a Heimat, which became the ultimate metaphor in German society for roots, for feeling at home wherever Heimat was—the homeland, the region, the hometown. Thus, one's Heimats were simultaneously, say, Reutlingen, Swabia, and Germany. How many Heimats were in the German Empire? One, two, three . . . a thousand?

THE WORD AND THE ORGANIZATION

We like to think of "Heimat" as a word denoting local territory that is immediate and tangible—a hometown, a village, or home itself.[7] Between the 1880s and the 1940s, however, Germans understood the word Heimat to mean both local and national territory invested with sentiments of familiarity, and felt at home at both the *weitere Heimat*, the large Heimat, and the *engere Heimat*, the

A NATION OF HEIMATS

narrow Heimat. *Die deutsche Heimat,* or the German Heimat, which sounds today awkward, anachronistic, or even incomprehensible, was a common and intelligible expression, the imagined national homeland.

Because Heimat has been associated with home and origins, it is tempting also to think of the word and its meaning as immutable. For Carl Jacob Burckhardt, Heimat, a unique creation of the German "spirit of the language" (*Sprachgeist*), aroused timeless and ahistorical feelings.[8] In the past two centuries, however, the meaning of the word Heimat changed with the vicissitudes of the German nation. Germans today understand Heimat as having a local meaning and have forgotten that fifty years ago Heimat meant something else; one hundred years ago Germans understood Heimat as having a national meaning and had forgotten that in the 1850s this meaning did not exist. The meaning of Heimat in the past two hundred years thus appears to have made full circle defining local territory in the first half of the nineteenth century when a German nation-state did not exist, local and national territory in the period of the nation-state, and local territory again after 1945 following the bankruptcy of German nationalism and the dismemberment of the nation-state.

Before the nineteenth century Heimat commonly meant the parental home or the farm property. *Ausland,* or foreign country, described the fields beyond the farm boundaries. The word *Heimweh,* or homesickness, became popular only after 1800. The dictionary of the brothers Grimm defined Heimat as (1) yard (*Hof*) and house, (2) land or region where one was born or is living, and (3) as having symbolic associations in expressions such as the Christians' heavenly kingdom or the animal kingdom.[9] According to the third definition, Heimat symbolized the place where one really belonged, though this place was either heaven (for man) or nature (for animals) but not the nation-state.[10] Generally, Heimat was used in the first half of the nineteenth century as a legal concept—*Heimatrecht,* or law of domicile;[11] the 1852 Brockhaus lexicon explained under "Heimat" the different laws of domicile in the German states, Austria, England, and France.[12] Heimat defined in these cases concrete spatial and temporal conditions, as well as precise legal and social relations.

The transformation of the word Heimat into a symbolic representation of the nation is documented in dictionaries. While most dictionaries fail to indicate why changes in the meaning of a word have occurred, they can be useful in documenting what have been the changes. If a dictionary is a good source to finding the meaning of a word in society, we must be aware that it may not record all the meanings of a given word. For example, the slang meaning of a word may not appear in certain dictionaries that are deemed "respectable." It is therefore important to examine dictionaries that represented different social discourses to find out the pattern in the meaning of a given word.

In 1939, a German dictionary, *Trübners Deutsches Wörterbuch,* was commissioned by the Study Group for German Word Research (Arbeitsgemeinschaft für deutsche Wortforschung) to replace the famous Grimm dictionary, deemed too scholarly and not popular enough, and to explore the linguistic and cultural meanings of words.[13] The page-length entry "Heimat" advanced one simple point: "Fatherland as the larger Heimat."[14] Compared with its meaning as house and yard, Heimat was enlarged to encompass the entire nation. Moreover, Heimat, both local and national, conveyed emotions that were absent a hundred years before: "Where no love exists to enduring Heimat, there is no love to fatherland either."[15] The transformation of Heimat from a concrete entity of house and yard into a symbolic representation of Germany, an abstract entity, meant the nation took symbolic possession of the concepts of space, time, and kin. The Heimat idea created real social relations and emotional bonds where these had not necessarily existed, among millions of Germans, and among a thousand Heimats.

This transformation of the meaning of Heimat was also demonstrated in regional dictionaries of dialect (*Mundart*), themselves products of the new Heimat consciousness. Dialects have been more resistant to change than the German language, and several German dialects have maintained to the present the original meaning of Heimat as house.[16] The discovery that some German dialects did express the new Heimat consciousness is, therefore, significant. The *Bayerisches Wörterbuch*, the *Wörterbuch der Elsässischen Mundarten*, and the *Wörterbuch der Ostfriesischen Sprache*, published between 1872 and 1899, defined Heimat as one's most immediate habitat—home and yard.[17] Some forty years later, the *Pfälzisches Wörterbuch*, whose main research was conducted between 1925 and the late 1930s, and the *Hochdeutsch-plattdeutsches Wörterbuch*, whose research was completed in 1938, added to the original meaning of house and yard the identification of Heimat with fatherland, and of *Heimatliebe* (love for one's Heimat) with *Vaterlandsliebe* (patriotism).[18]

The transformation of Heimat's meaning from a local into a national habitat was especially clear in Koolman's *Wörterbuch der Ostfriesischen Sprache* and Buurman's *Hochdeutsch-plattdeutsches Wörterbuch*. Buurman based his study on Koolman's etymological dictionary published in 1879. Fifty years of Heimat consciousness separated Koolman and Buurman, and it was evident. While Koolman defined Heimat as house and yard, Buurman provided the most articulate definition of Heimat's new meaning: "Fatherland—the bigger Heimat." Once house and yard, now the whole nation became one's habitat.

By comparing these dictionaries we can date the change in Heimat's meaning. A dictionary is ten to twenty years late in recording changes in language because it takes time until a new meaning of a word becomes common knowledge and finds its way into a dictionary, and it takes a few more years until a dictionary is published. The meaning of Heimat in dictionaries changed between the turn of the century to the 1920s. We may conclude, therefore, that the meaning of Heimat in German society changed in the last ten to fifteen years of the nineteenth century.

There is a great difficulty, however, in the way we have so far put the relation between the Heimat idea and its origination, for we have implicitly assumed that the Heimat idea was new because the word and notion were new. This way of reasoning derives from the conviction that things exist only once they can be articulated and have a name. Following this logic one might conclude that *Homo sapiens* did not exist before paleontologists discovered its skeleton. The novelty of the Heimat idea in German society needs to be demonstrated in more than words alone, in changes in social behavior and social organization. Did the change in the meaning of Heimat correspond to a particular social mode of action? Or did the word remain a dead letter? Jean-Paul Sartre wrote in *Les temps modernes* that "action and thought are inseparable from organization. People think as they are structured. They act as they are organized." What was, then, the organization of Heimat memory in German society?

Institutions gave Heimat memory a structure and an organization that was decisive for its reception. In the Heimat institutions, Germans carried, cultivated, and propagated the Heimat memory and their activity gave memory social continuity and regularity. Germans organized the Heimat idea in a network of associations. Local associations, such as beautification societies and historical, folklore, and nature associations, were organized in regional bodies: the Württembergischer Schwarzwaldverein or the Bund für Heimatschutz in Württemberg und Hohenzollern. These in turn were organized into national bodies, notably the Deutscher Bund Heimatschutz, or the German League of Heimat Protection, founded in 1904. This network corresponded to the constitutive metaphor of the Heimat idea—the metaphor of the whole and its parts—and was consciously perceived as such by Heimatlers. *Heimatschutz*, the periodical of the Deutscher Bund Heimatschutz, wrote in 1915: "Unity is the aim of the Deutscher Bund Heimatschutz. Its regional associations and chapters correspond to the federal states in the German Empire. The Bund should *integrate* their individual achievements, for this is the only way in which the Bund, like the empire of 1871, can fulfill its work."[19] The interlocking structure of national and regional associations, in which the national Deutscher Bund Heimatschutz comprised the independent local Heimat organizations, represented the relationship between the oneness of the German Heimat and the multitude of local Heimats. Confirming Sartre's observation, Heimatlers established Heimat organizations in a pattern that accorded with their image of the nation. For Heimat national memory, the organization was the message.

On the eve of World War I the geographical diffusion of the Heimat idea reached every corner of Germany. Regional Heimat organizations sprung up nationwide, and by 1915 all the important German regions prided themselves on having one. Most Prussian regions and provinces founded Heimat organizations between 1906 and 1910: Lower Saxony (1906), Mecklenburg (1906), Cologne and the Rhine (1906), Brandenburg (1907), Schleswig-Holstein (1908), Pomerania (1910), Silesia (1910), Hessen-Nassau, and Westphalia (1915). They joined Heimat organizations in Bavaria (1902), Lippe (1907), Saxony (1908), Württemberg and Hohenzollern (1909), Baden (1909), Hamburg (1910), and Eisenach (for Thuringia, 1911).[20]

The idea of making the nation one's symbolic habitat received an organizational affirmation with the creation of the Deutscher Bund Heimatschutz on 30 March 1904 that manifested the idea of the *Deutsche Heimat*, the national Heimat idea. The statute of the organization opened with a declaration that "the aim of the association is to protect the evolving natural and historical uniqueness of *the German Heimat* [*die deutsche Heimat*]."[21] Similarly, the founding members of the Bund pledged in "A Call for the Foundation of a Bund Heimatschutz" to protect "the Heimat itself, our *German* land, the fertile soil of our civilization." And they articulated their task in the following words: "We therefore create an association that covers all of Germany . . . in order to protect from further damage *the German Heimat*."[22]

The three-tiered organizational structure of the Heimat idea fit perfectly the symbolic representation of the nation as a composition of local, regional, and national Heimats. From the local to the regional to the national level, associations merged to form bigger organizations that informed new kinds of Heimats and brought together more Germans. It is a mistake, however, to view the three levels of local, regional, and national Heimat organizations as a reflection of a gradual process of Heimat invention from the local to the national level. Rather, a different Heimat scale emerges: the foundation in 1904 of the Deutscher Bund Heimatschutz slightly preceded the foundation of some local and of all but two of the regional Heimat associations (in Bavaria and Lower Saxony). The simultaneous foundation of the regional Heimat associations and the national Deutscher Bund Heimatschutz within a period of thirteen years (1902–15) reflected the *simultaneous* invention of the local and the national Heimats.

Similar to the word "Heimat," Heimat organizations point to the change in Heimat's meaning during Wilhelmine Germany. Particularly important for Heimat organizations were the years 1902–15. Local associations such as the beautification societies and the historical associations already existed during the first half of the nineteenth century. But, as we saw in the previous chapter, toward the end of the century their message changed, their number substantially grew, and eventually they became connected to new regional and national associations that were founded only after the turn of the century, explicitly named "Heimat" for the first time. The new organizations reflected the new appreciation in German society of Heimat as an image of the nation. But whose appreciation exactly? It is to the Germans who produced the Heimat memory that we have to turn now.

HEIMAT: THE BOURGEOIS HOMELAND

Who took part in Heimat organizations? Who produced the Heimat memory? While until recently the social composition of the Heimat movement in Germany has been a neglected topic, we now possess several studies that shed light on the subject. Emerging from these studies is the unmistakable conclusion, which corresponds to our discussion of Württemberg, of the bourgeois social origins of the Heimat idea. William Rollins's analysis of the membership of Heimatschutz organizations of several regions shows that two classic bourgeois groups were especially representative among Heimatlers.[23] The *Bildungsbürgertum*, the quintessential bourgeois group in German society,[24] made up 51.4 percent of the 9,051 Heimatlers.[25] They were academically educated civil servants, lawyers, doctors, educators, clergymen, and professionals, such as writers, newspaper editors, journalists, architects, and artists, who increasingly occupied the growing public sphere in German society. The *Wirtschaftsbürgertum*, the economic bourgeoisie of merchants, industrialists, entrepreneurs, and manufacturers, made up 27.2. percent. That Heimatschutz was predominantly a movement of the intellectual and economic bourgeoisie is further supported by the meager participation of other major social groups in German society—the working class, the nobility, artisans, and the agricultural sector.[26] Werner Hartung, who studied the Heimat movement in Lower Saxony between 1895 and 1919, reached very similar conclusions: "An analysis of the social structure of the Heimatbund Niedersachsen proves a downright preponderance, a sort of monopoly, of diverse bourgeois groups in the cities and countryside. While workers and artisans do not appear at all in membership lists, 'peasants' or 'farmers'" made up only 1.5 percent.[27]

The valuable contributions of Hartung and Rollins fail to embrace, however, the full measure of the Heimat idea's diffusion in German society because they neglect the production and reception of the idea in small communities in favor of focusing on Heimat organizations that represented big cities and entire regions. This appears a significant drawback because when we take into consideration local Heimat associations (such as beautification societies) we must conclude that, while the Heimat movement had "a decidedly middle-class profile," it cannot be described only as having "a tendency in the direction of high prestige."[28]

Hartung interpreted the Heimatschutz as an antidemocratic, antimodern, and conservative movement produced "from above" by "the German Empire's bourgeois intellectual and power elites" to maintain their control on society.[29] As a result of this interpretative point of departure, Hartung has mainly focused on Heimat activities of the Lower Saxon elites in the cities of Braunschweig, Bremen, and Hannover, which was the seat of the regional Heimatbund Niedersachsen, while ignoring the popular production, diffusion, and acceptance of the Heimat idea. This is unfortunate, for as a local study Hartung's book could have been particularly suitable to explore the making of the Heimat idea in medium-sized and small communities by bourgeois groups and professionals who did not belong to the empire's elites. There is a direct historiographic link between viewing the Heimat idea as a calculated reactionary political and ideological tool and placing the social origins of the idea among the elites.[30] Once we abandon this tendentious evaluation, we can appreciate the diverse bourgeois social origins of the Heimat idea.

As for Rollins, he explored the Heimatschutz movement through the words and actions of the people around the Bund Heimatschutz who normally came from cultural and urban centers. Among the nine Heimatschutz organizations whose social composition he analyzes, five were regional Heimat associations that habitually comprised Heimatlers with a tendency to high social prestige. Rollins's aim in his study is to explore the "Heimatschutz proper," that is, Heimat protection manifested in environmentalism and organized in the Deutscher Bund Heimatschutz. As such his findings are accurate as well as important to differentiate among various manifestations and meanings of the Heimat idea. But his argument in favor of separating the Heimatschutz from the general Heimat movement is artificial. It is impossible to understand Heimatschutz outside the larger context of the popular production, manifestations, and artifacts of the Heimat idea in Germany from the 1880s on. One result of Rollins's narrow focus is that his thoughtful discussion of environmentalism neglects the meaning of Heimat as local, regional, and national identity. In the end, that Heimatschutz and Heimat movement belonged essentially together is shown by Rollins's own definition of Heimatschutz, as "comprised of groups involved in serious efforts to maintain an area's unique natural or historical ambiance," a definition which fits perfectly local folklore, as well as historical, and beautification associations of the Heimat movement.[31]

The question as to who produced the Heimat memory must be answered therefore by looking at regional and national Heimat associations but also at associations at the local level. Only two local studies of the Heimat movement are available, both dealing with South Germany: Applegate's study of the Palatinate, and the findings presented in the previous chapter about Württemberg. Obviously, we need additional local studies in order to draw comprehensive conclusions about the social composition of the Heimat movement in Germany. Nevertheless, the information at hand clearly indicates a social pattern, namely that the Heimat movement comprised bourgeoisie of socially diverse groups. Historical associations in Württemberg tended to comprise the local educated bourgeoisie (*Bildungsbürgertum*), while beautification societies, which spread to small communities, included the petite bourgeoisie. In the Palatinate, the membership of the Pfälzerwald Verein (Palatinate Forest Association), the region's "Heimat association par excellence," drew especially from the petite bourgeoisie, the cities' new white-collar workers, while haut bourgeois notables continued to play a leading role in the association. The membership of beautification societies leaned toward a majority of lower middle-class artisans and professionals, who brought to the societies their wives and daughters. And whereas the Heimat historical museum in Speyer was an enterprise of the educated bourgeoisie, the local notables, the museum simultaneously "reflected a popular and inclusive conception of local culture that had much in common with the civic activism of the beautification societies and the Pfälzerwald Verein."[32]

Although the difference in wealth and social status between Heimatlers was enormous—between, say, a member of Stuttgart's royal theater and an artisan from Schamberg—together they produced the Heimat idea. The production and reception of the Heimat idea like that of the national idea itself, question the notion that cultural cleavages and cultural common denominators are necessarily organized according to social divisions constructed beforehand. The idea of Heimat defies an attempt to explain cultural originations in social structures. Instead, it was a popular representation of the nation, not in the sense that it was from below instead of from above, a dichotomy that should be avoided, but in the sense that it was produced, carried, and received by diverse bourgeois social groups, both from below and from above. Heimat stemmed from *l'Allemagne profonde*, from dozens of provincial localities and big cities that boasted a historical association or a Heimat museum.

The Heimat idea functioned as a common denominator among middle-class Germans in cities, towns, and hometowns, who, often being leaders of the community, stood at the crossroads of the great projects of German society after 1871: modernity and nation building. In Heimat memory they found a way to reconcile local with national identity, and local and national pasts with modernity. Whether through vocabulary changes or through Heimat organizations, Heimatlers attempted to transform the impersonal nation into something manageable, intimate, and "small." Their method was to transform the localness of history, nature, and folklore into a concept of nationhood. They had to perform one of the miracles of nationalism, namely to convert the peculiarity of the community into a single image of the nation. One way to perform this miracle was to found Heimat museums that, existing across Germany, represented the peculiar community, yet in their totality were a representation of the nation as a whole. What image of the nation did the peculiarity of local life reflect?

Between 1890 and 1918, 371 Heimat museums were founded in Germany.[33] This number of local historical museums is impressive even for a large and populated country like Germany. Definitive numbers for the pre-1890 period are unavailable, though partial evidence illustrates a clear pattern by which the post-1890 wave of Heimat museums constituted a quantitative as well as a qualitative change with respect to foundations of local historical museums in preceding decades.[34] In the regions that constituted West Germany, 14 local historical museums were founded before 1871, 15 between 1871 and 1880, and 31 between 1881 and 1890. Altogether, 46 new museums were founded between 1871 to 1890 compared with 371 between 1890 and 1918.

The pattern of foundation of Heimat museums reflected the production and reception of the Heimat idea in Germany. Compared with hundreds of local history museums founded during the German Empire (1871–1918), only a small number of such museums were founded before 1871. Until the 1870s, museums of local history were founded mostly in big or important centers of culture and politics and only rarely in provincial localities.[35] The systematic cultivation of local identity was thus closely connected to the national unification in 1871. Moreover, the determining years for Heimat museums corresponded to the formative period in the construction of the Heimat idea demonstrated by dictionaries, Heimat books, and associational behavior—1890 to 1918 in general and 1900 to 1914 in particular. Based on Haef's information, 15 Heimat museums were founded in the 1870s, and 31 in the 1880s. The increase compared with that in the pre-1871 period was too tenuous to be considered a national phenomenon. A qualitative leap forward occurred in the 1890s, when, based on Karasek's information, 76 new museums were founded, a pattern that continued in the 1900s with 178 additional museums. And in a growing crescendo, the immediate years before World War I, 1910 to 1914, saw the foundation of 103 museums. Only the war arrested this formidable proliferation. Between 1900 and 1914, therefore, 281 new museums were established, 75.7 percent of the total of new museums between 1890 and 1914.[36] Heimat museums were founded in all regions by both Catholics and Protestants.[37]

More than a trend, the 371 new Heimat museums constituted a mania. Germans knew how to self-ridicule their obsession. Reporting on a foundation of a Heimat museum, the celebrants of carnival in Göppingen presented a "German Catalog for the Collection of Rare and Ancient Fooleries" (*Selten- und Alterdummheiten*, a word play on *Selten- und Altertumheiten*, rare and ancient objects), including Eve's apple and the last tear of Lot's wife.[38] That Heimat museums became a target of satire in Wilhelmine Germany is a measure of the extent to which they turned into familiar artifacts of the national culture.

How are we to interpret this museum mania?[39] Heimat museums reflected the diffusion of the Heimat idea in German society. It is not surprising, therefore, that until recently the dominant interpretation of the Heimat museums phenomenon emerged from the understanding of the Heimat idea itself as reactionary and antimodern. A good example is Martin Roth's important study of Heimat museums in the Weimar Republic and the Third Reich.[40] Roth, who has viewed the republic's Heimat museums as a "connecting link" between the "nationalistic museum politics of Wilhelmine Germany" and "*Volkstum* ideology of National Socialism," has argued that Heimat museums in imperial Germany were "a self-representation of a national-chauvinistic bourgeois culture."[41] Founded by the bourgeoisie, Heimat museums constituted "a flight from social reality into irrationalism" by displaying the romantic ideal of an agrarian national community and cultivating the values of antimodernism, that is, hatred of big cities and opposition to the labor movement.[42] It is interesting to note how close is this argument to Karasek's Marxist-Leninist interpretation of Heimat museums as "an instrument of the ruling classes" created "to diffuse nationalistic and chauvinistic ideas in the interests of the bourgeoisie." Also Karasek criticizes the representation in Heimat museums for "completely ignoring historical reality," as the museums represented "a romantic transfigured image of German rural life, which never existed."[43]

The premise of this approach is questionable. Roth and Karasek assume that Heimat museums had an obligation to represent the existing "social reality." By social reality they presumably meant the social and political conflicts in imperial Germany, the effects of industrialization, and working-class culture. Karasek viewed the absence of such representation as manipulation; according to Roth, it was the failure to cope with reality; both considered it antimodern. But it should be asked whether a representation of the present, that is, of industrialization and its effects, is the most important thing in a historical museum and whether it is the most revealing factor about the meaning of the museum. The expectation that a Heimat museum, a site of identity that represented the local past, would reflect reality is misplaced. Identities are meaningful not because they provide an accurate representation of reality, but often precisely because they distort it. The result of comparing the representation of Heimat museums to "reality" and finding it wanting is that the subjective meaning of the exhibit, the curator's intentions, and the visitors' experience is largely lost, while concepts like subterfuge, irrationalism, and manipulation take center stage as explanatory devices.

The point here is not to deny the existence of reactionary ideas among theoreticians and founders of Heimat museums. Heinrich Sohnrey actively supported the creation of Heimat museums.[44] Rather, the point is that Sohnrey and others like him were in fact marginal in the Heimat movement, whether we look at the national organization Deutscher Bund Heimatschutz, or at

Württemberg and the Palatinate. Sohnrey cannot stand for the entire Heimat movement or the Heimat idea. Moreover, even if we accept for the sake of the argument the fact that Heimat museums indeed represented a romantic rural past and reflected a chauvinistic bourgeois mindset, these characteristics are not sufficient to identify the bourgeoisie as turning away from social reality into irrationalism. In order to prove *this* one must show that the bourgeoisie cut off social ties, ceased to behave according to the prevalent social norms, and descended into a behavior that was counterproductive to its best interest. But instead it can be argued that the bourgeoisie, by silencing in the museum the identity of the working class, behaved rationally given its struggle with the labor movement: it appropriated the local and national pasts and claimed symbolic ownership of national identity. The bourgeoisie may have been reactionary, a point that will be determined in the following pages, but its political, social, and cultural behavior in Heimat museums cannot be seen as out of step with reality.

Another major problem with this approach is the silence concerning the relations between the single museum and the meaning of Heimat museums viewed collectively. Roth and Karasek assume correctly that behind the separate establishments of museums in hundreds of communities lie common purpose and common meaning. Bourgeois Germans set up in Heimat museums a set of images and ideas with which to understand the German past and present. But Roth and Karasek ignore the methodological problem as well as the interpretative potential of the relationship among the hundreds of single histories which made up a single national history. They assume that the representation in the single museum was, in the mind of Heimatlers, the nation writ large without discussing the fundamental aspect of the Heimat museum phenomenon, namely that it articulated, based on the metaphor of whole and parts, the relationship between the locality and the nation, between hundreds of divergent local histories and one single national history. They do not show how the single museums actually created a national meaning and how Heimatlers related in practice and theory the local and the national. As a result, what is mostly missing in those studies is a serious discussion of local identity, which seems to be taken for granted and to be perceived as less revealing than the "hard facts" of the professed reactionary social and political functions of the museum.[45] This is a critical omission because the Heimat museums phenomenon, 371 local history museums founded in the era of deeply felt nationalism, is a classic case of how Germans constructed perceptions of localness and nationhood.

Heimat museums should be interpreted as part of the larger development of the Heimat idea in imperial Germany, as a mode of communication to reconcile localness and nationhood, the past and the present, tradition and modernity. As a national phenomenon, Heimat museums constructed a particular local Heimat identity that could be placed within the national Heimat. The fundamental factor of Heimat museums was that although they represented hundreds of different local pasts, their representation shared basic common denominators in terms of objects displayed, content, and meaning. Heimatlers, by displaying everyday life instead of big historical events, ordinary people instead of the elites, and the historical origins of the community, constructed a pattern to understand national history, a national narrative. By reclaiming the local pasts, they in essence represented the locality as the location of the origins of the nation.[46]

The proliferation of Heimat museums in Wilhelmine Germany was directly influenced by the rise of *Volkskunde* as an academic discipline and museum practice. *Volkskunde*, or folklore, a term first used by the English William John Thoms in 1846, was an anthropological and ethnologic representation of the cultural identity of a community. The popularity of *Volkskunde* is intimately associated with Rudolf Virchow, who led the 1889 foundation in Berlin of the Museum of German Popular Dresses and Everyday Life House Products (Museum für deutsche Volkstrachten und Erzeugnisse des Hausgewerbes), which was essential to the development of Heimat museums just as the 1852 foundation of the German National Museum (Germanisches Nationalmuseum) in Nuremberg was essential to historical associations and museums.[47] The museum, according to a statement by the founding committee headed by Virchow, was to shed light on the material culture of the German people: "how it made and built its houses, how it designed its farms and villages, yards and fields, how it kept the rooms, kitchen, and cellar, and how the household was managed."[48] Transcending the celebrated museum tradition that displayed high art produced by the perceived culture-carrying groups in society, the museum aimed at combining the spheres of art and of work. Virchow wrote that "there is no distinction between history of culture and history of labor, for no one can say where art begins and the work of everyday life ends."[49] The collection of the Berlin museum included sections on dwelling, household, dress, nutrition, art and trade, commerce and transportation, and objects of popular beliefs and traditions. The museum, which was joined by an association of Volkskunde and a scientific journal, mixed a number of intellectual and political influences. The European colonial expansion, and the consequent meeting with exotic and "primitive" peoples, led to the development and refinement of anthropology and ethnology, which were in turn used to study one's own people.[50] In terms of more specific German influences, *Volkskunde* owed an intellectual debt to the Herderian idea of a national community sharing a common culture and traditions, and to a whole century of folklore research from the brothers Grimm to the invention of the Betzinger folk dress.

Applying the basic principles of the folklore museum, Heimatlers founded Heimat museums as, first of all, sites of local identity to reclaim the local past.

The demand for local museums came both from national leaders of the Heimat movement and from local Heimat activists in the communities. Robert Mielke, an important figure in the Deutscher Bund Heimatschutz, demanded a Heimat museum in every German village "in order to increase the love for Heimat and to arouse the sense of the cultural development of the narrow Heimat in large sections of the population."[51] Most often the initiative to set up a museum came from the local bourgeois Heimat association, be it the historical association or beautification society. In the town of Weinheim (population 12,500), the museum committee decided to found "a Heimat history collection" to display "the culture and history of our beautiful Heimat."[52] The common pattern was that an association initiated the establishment of a museum, which was shortly thereafter supported, or at times taken over, by the local authorities.[53]

The social origins of Heimat museums provide further support to the argument presented already about the production of the Heimat idea by diverse bourgeois groups. Museum activists were always social and cultural leaders in the community—teachers, civil servants, merchants, and liberal professionals—but while they belonged to the intellectual and economic bourgeoisie in big cities and towns, they tended to come also from the petite bourgeoisie in small and medium-sized communities. In these communities, such as Weinheim, artisans can also be found among the activists.[54] The very diffusion of Heimat museums into small communities underlines the diverse bourgeois character of the phenomenon. Heimat museums in cultural and political centers such as Stuttgart, Hamburg, and Berlin, where museums could rely on lavish support by the local patricians and municipality, were the exception among the hundreds of museums. The overwhelming majority of Heimat museums were founded in small and medium-sized communities that had to cope with "provincial" challenges.

The first such challenge facing museum activists in these communities was to find items to exhibit in the museum. Since they rarely commanded the financial resources to buy exhibits, museum activists invented less expensive ways: the great majority of exhibits were donated by distinguished local citizens who possessed archaeological collections or by others who happened to have an object of historical value. Activists mobilized the entire community, as in Prien am Chiemsee and Schwandorf, both in Bavaria, by going from house to house in town and countryside and asking for contributions.[55] The results of these extemporized procedures to found a Heimat museum were twofold: the inventory of exhibits was determined by coincidence, rather than by a systematic historical approach, and it was possible to establish a Heimat museum, even in a small community, in a very short time.[56] All that was needed was a popular determination to conserve the past; this was aplenty in the German Empire and so were the number of Heimat museums.

While Heimat museums were founded with a mix of enthusiastic improvisation, that attitude also dominated the perennial problem of their location. Localities, particularly small ones, were not equipped to offer exhibition space for a museum that often was founded instantaneously. Local authorities helped by making available one or two rooms in the town hall or the school, but often Heimat museums were located in such uncommon places for a historical museum as hospitals, inns, restaurants, and, in one case, an old wool warehouse.[57] Frequently, after a few years of activity, museums had to be moved because of lack of exhibition space, and the move provided an opportunity to improve the location. Activists sought to locate museums in buildings with historical significance in order to stress, if ever there was a need, the symbolic connection between their museum and the locality's identity.[58]

While the humble location of Heimat museums indicates the determination of activists to exhibit the past at all costs, even under unfavorable conditions, it primarily underscores their belief in the importance of the museum to all members of the community. In contrast to the old national historical museums in big cities, such as the German National Museum in Nuremberg, which were directed by members of the upper classes and imposed scholarship and elitism, a local Heimat museum communicated a public and broad idea of culture.[59] This was expressed in the mode of exhibition, a humble space crammed with exhibits, that was informal, unpretentious, and did not impose strict social manners and etiquette. To encourage popular participation museum activists often set open hours on Sundays, which permitted working people to visit the museum on the day of repose, and entrance was free or fees were minimal (20 pfennigs, for example).[60] Heimat museums quickly gained popularity and respect among inhabitants of a locality and its environs as a symbol of the community. Five hundred people visited the Heimat museum in Weinheim on its opening day in 1906, while in a small village near Reutlingen the highest honor the teacher awarded first-rate pupils was a visit to the town's Heimat museum.[61] Among the attractions of the 650th anniversary celebration of Herborn in 1901 was the Heimat museum special exhibition that was open for five weeks and attracted 6,000 people.[62] Historical associations and archaeological associations in small communities dedicated most of their time and activities to the museum because other professional activity was limited. Typically, in Ramsdorf, a ritualistic visit to the Heimat museum preceded every meeting of the Archaeological Association.[63] Museums often became centers of historical information and communication, apart from the exhibition itself. Thus, in Leer, in Friesland, a library and an archive were founded adjacent to the museum where historical lectures were regularly held.[64]

Heimat museums embodied, first of all, the locality. In Oettingen the museum exhibited "how the Ries and its inhabitants have lived in the past and how they live in the present."[65] The past history of even the smallest community was worthy of collection and exhibition, as Oettingen's museum activists explained: "Although some may think that in the Ries there are no historical objects to collect, we are nonetheless convinced that even here there are plenty of interesting historical objects to find and to preserve."[66] Every locality in Germany deserved a museum, as Th. Bruß, one of the founders of Reinfeld's (Holstein) Heimat museum convincingly explained in 1913: "The foundation of a Heimat museum in Reinfeld cannot be objected because Reinfeld belongs to the category of localities that has had, as everybody knows, a long history."[67] Every community in Germany had, as everybody knew, a long history and Heimat museums therefore proliferated rapidly, legitimizing local history and identity. Activists often argued that since other localities had already established museums, theirs should follow suit.[68] The very existence of a local Heimat museum symbolized the worthiness of one's local past and, conversely, to be a locality with no Heimat museum was perceived almost like admitting to having no significant history. Once a Heimat museum became a symbol of local identity, why should a community live without one?

The significance of Heimat museums, then, was as sites of identity where Heimatlers represented the past. How they conceived the past of the community lay in great measure in the criteria according to which they collected objects of the past and later displayed them. The museum activists in Oettingen, who believed that even their small locality possessed "plenty of historical objects," were true to their words and collected the following items: coats of arms and heraldic figures; documents, deeds, and indentures; drawings, engravings, and oil paintings; objects of guilds; all kinds of arms; stoves, tiles, pottery, and kitchenware; plaques, photographs, old games, local maps; folk dresses and pictures of them; all kinds of furniture; ornaments; genealogical albums, epitaphs, and pictures of ancestors; prehistoric and archaeological findings; coins, medals, seals, and stamps; "miscellaneous" such as locks, shoe buckles, spoons, knives, rings, boxes, and natural science materials.[69] These objects, representative of Heimat museums across Germany, emanated from people's lives in the community—the private and the public spheres, the home, the work, and the family.[70] Behind this museum conception of displaying simple and seemingly unimportant objects lay a self-conscious intention to represent the past, and the community, as an everyday life experience.[71] *Museumskunde*, the leading German journal of museology, commented on the museum in Celle, considered a model of the genre since its foundation in 1907: it symbolized " 'courage for simplicity and everyday life' applied to one's own Heimat and people. . . . The huge number of often entirely artless and in themselves uninteresting utensils and tools are linked through a shared, purposeful idea. . . . [T]he museum exercises an extraordinary strong, uniform, and unified impression. The astounded visitor asks himself how was it possible that the German museum world could carelessly ignore for so long these simple facts and foundations of our existence."[72] Heimat history, whether practiced in the museum or in historical associations, articulated what Wilhelm Seytter defined, as we have seen in the previous chapter, the "simple and daily life . . . the whole of life . . . the description in miniature."

Together with the principle of everyday life, Heimatlers sought to represent in the museums the origins of the community.[73] "The aim of the museum [in Kaufbeuren] is to provide the people of the Algäu a picture of their ancestors' life and culture."[74] For Wilhelm Bomann, the founder of the Celle museum, the representation of the life and work of the locality's ancestors provided "a source of true moral education."[75] The quest for origins as "a source of moral education" was a direct result of modernity that changed the physical environment and opened a growing cleavage between the present and past. Thus the foundation of the Heimat museum in Föhr, founded in 1908 on a North Friesland island, "was a cultural necessity to save that which is still savable from the material and spiritual historical property of the island. The purpose of the museum is to preserve the memory that has been irretrievably lost."[76] By "origins" and "past" Heimatlers meant the entire past, from prehistory to the most recent past. Heimat museums were not limited to one period, and entertained a variety of origins, for, as historical-anthropological sites of identity, they displayed history particular to the community. Thus in Lübeck, the Protestant port city of Buddenbrooks merchants, the museum represented church and bourgeois art and culture from the Middle Ages to about 1860. In Oberammergau in Bavaria, the emphasis was on local Catholic church history and the traditional art of wood carving.[77]

The representation of origins came in two basic modes. The first was common in many communities that established a museum during the Heimat museum mania. The image of the Heimat museums at Weinheim (fig. 1) is an excellent source that reveals the meaning of the exhibition of the past. The *Weinheimer Anzeiger* explained that the town "sets up a Heimat history collection, a cultural-historical place that displays the life of old Weinheim. This is not an easy task, however, for much has been neglected. Many valuable objects of the culture and history of our beautiful Heimat were sold to foreign people. . . . In spite of this, there is a warehouse here, some old closets and chests there, with old objects from the ancestors' period. They can be collected and appropriately organized to fulfill the ideal task of having our grandchildren go back to the time" of the ancestors.[78] The image from the Weinheim museum shows that exhibits were accumulated one near the other, on the floor and on the walls, in exemplary order, but that the exhibitions as a whole were not organized according to historical yardsticks, namely classified according to periods and themes, appreciating the uniqueness of each period. Heimat museums like the one in Weinheim displayed a collection of undifferentiated objects from the past, lacking selective categories. Collecting the past tout

Figure 1. The Heimat museum in Weinheim, 1909. The objective of the exhibition was to enable the youth to experience the time of their ancestors. Heimat museums represented the nation's origins by displaying a collection of undifferentiated objects from the past. (Courtesy of the Museum der Stadt Weinheim)

court, museum activists displayed it as a vast country with no frontiers, where one could move freely back and forth as one wished; the past became a continuous, indistinctive entity. This representation of the past was essentially ahistorical, for history appreciates the people and events of the past for their uniqueness; it values chronology and the intrinsic differences between periods, and is like the river in Heraclitus's adage, "You cannot step twice into the same river." Leveling the differences between the past and present, Heimatlers constructed in the museums a narrative of origins, which is always an ahistorical narrative.[79]

The second mode of representation of origins was based on reconstruction of previous modes of life, of the material and spiritual ambience of peoples in the past. Common scenes from the life and times of the community included a peasants' room (*Bauernstube*) displaying, among others, a stove, furniture, and folk dress; a burgher study (*Bürgerstube*) displaying a desk, an inkstand, books, and a cabinet; and a guild's room (*Zunftstube*) with documents, emblems, flags, and working tools.[80] Unlike the leveling of past and present evident in Weinheim, the historic-ambience rooms represented history in a linear and forward-moving direction, thus creating a local narrative of history. The

A NATION OF HEIMATS

Figure 2. The Heimat museum in Weinheim, ca. 1910. One mode of representation of origins was based on reconstruction of the material and spiritual ambiance of Germans in the past. The historic ambiance rooms represented history in a linear and forward-moving direction, thus creating a local narrative of history that linked Germans in the Second Empire with their past. (Courtesy of the Museum der Stadt Weinheim)

local narrative was reinforced as most communities displayed in Heimat museums the continuity of their history since the ancient period. Local history began with the Germanic tribes, such as the Franks and the Alemanni, represented in archaeological exhibits, advancing to the Middle Ages, with displays of weapons, coats of arms, and heraldic figures, progressing to the life of hometown inhabitants in the early modern period, and finally to the recent past.

The two modes of representation of origins often coexisted in one museum. The museum in Weinheim displayed in one section the past as a country with no frontiers, while in another a rather linear narrative of archaeological findings: the Lorcher Codex of 775, which contains the earliest mentioning of Weinheim; documents from the Middle Ages, the oldest from 1356; a guild's room and a peasants' room (fig. 2).[81] These two conceptions were not contradictory but complementary, as each cultivated in its own way a sense of the past as a narrative of origins, a narrative whose aim was to link the Germans in the Second Empire with their past.

The aim of Heimatlers was to overcome the inherent strangeness between the past and present and to connect the visitor intimately with the past. A Heimat museum was a sort of a time machine that transported the visitor into the mood and frame of mind of his or her ancestors. That is why Heimatlers described the representation of the past in the museum as "theatrical," aimed at "bringing closer the spirit of the past in an emotional way."[82] The museum in Lübeck was considered successful because it let the visitor "experience the state of mind of old times."[83] Of course, one could not experience the past or ignore the difference between past and present. Connecting the German present with the German past called on the visitors to use their imagination as travelers to the past. This must have been the meaning of the description of the peasants' room in Weinheim as a "fantasy *Stube*."[84] Given this approach to the past, Heimatlers often interpreted quite generously the task of displaying history in the museum. The museum activists in Föhr, whose museum was considered to be a representative of "the principle of a Heimat museum in all its purity and rigorousness," had the museum built as a characteristic North Friesland peasant house. "An accurate copy of a peasant house was not recommended, however, since such a house was hardly suitable for exhibition purposes."[85] The peasant house was thus remodeled to fit modern standards of exhibition. Also the display rooms of peasants, guilds, and burgher life, which provided a general image, an impression, of traditional ways of life, at times comprised objects from various centuries, paying little attention to their historical connection. This anachronism and the exhibition of undifferentiated objects diluted the notion of time in the past and connected Germans in the Second Empire with their ancestors.

What was the meaning of Heimat museums viewed collectively? Using diverse sources, listening to declared motivations, and interpreting the meanings of Heimat symbolic representations, we can provide a convincing answer. It would be inconceivable to think that in imperial Germany, in an era that saw national identity as a centerpiece of one's existence, Heimat museums produced hundreds of disparate and unconnected local histories. Heimat museums were part of the Heimat idea that emphasized local uniqueness only to reinstate this uniqueness into a larger national whole. They shared two important factors: they displayed everyday life objects and they told the story of local origins. Heimatlers created in the museums a visual lexicon of local past, common denominators with which to understand every local history. Significantly, Heimatlers' discourse of local individuality never materialized into a really unique mode of representation. Heimatlers often justified setting up a museum with the argument that, since other localities already had a museum, their own also deserved to display the past. Underlying this argument was the idea of the worthiness and uniqueness of local past. And yet, with all the talk of uniqueness, Heimat museums represented identity through a shared pattern of objects and narrative. Local individuality was articulated in a museum language of similitudes. Some activists were quite explicit about using a familiar pattern of exhibition. In Krumbach (Bavaria), at a meeting about Heimat preservation attended by 600 inhabitants, district official Ernst Riedl sought to establish a Heimat museum of the Krumbach district "based on the model of other districts."[86]

German tourism involving the Heimat museums reflected the creation of a shared and commonly understood lexicon of local representation. The Heimat movement encouraged Germans to travel in their Heimat and to Heimats across the nation. Traveling was seen as a "very serious cultural task," whereby one enriched his or her horizons by learning and experiencing the local culture, history, and nature.[87] Communities often listed among the reasons for the creation of a Heimat museum the economic benefits of attracting tourists. The Sylter Association in the North Sea island of Sylt founded a museum in 1903 "in order to preserve the past from disappearing and to offer an attraction for the increasing flow of tourists."[88] In Miesbach the potential success of a Heimat museum among tourists became a factor in deciding whether to establish a local museum or not. The founding committee decided to "try out an exhibition," preferably in the tourist season, to see how popular the museum would be.[89] And tourists did visit Heimat museums, so much so that in Bad Tölz (Bavaria) tourists visiting the local museum outnumbered the local inhabitants.[90] Behind the attempts to attract tourists to museums and behind the tourists' visit was the assumption that tourists know how to "read" the particular history of a given community and to relate this history to their own experience. The museum represented a history that was familiar in a general sense, as well as unknown. The visitors knew something about the history of Bavaria, but most likely they knew very little, if at all, about Bad Tölz's history. Whether in Bad Tölz or in Sylt, German tourists interpreted local histories according to a representational lexicon familiar from their Heimat museum back home. In a Heimat museum not their own, German tourists saw a variant of their history, an everyday life history of origins only with the different local peculiarities thrown in.

There was a third significant factor shared by all Heimat museums: they represented the identity of a community of people who shared a past and a present. The community in question was not only the local community, but also an intangible community that extended to larger territories and inclusive identities. Heimatlers talked about "Heimat museums in the narrow sense," which meant a museum of the locality proper, and Heimat museums of larger territories.[91] While they set up local Heimat museums, they also set up district Heimat museums, such as the district museum in Hadersleben, and Heimat museums representing an entire province, such as the museum in Bautzen, Saxony, representing the area of Oberlausitz.[92] The concept of Heimat museum as a representation of identity was expandable, and enabled Heimatlers to place the local past within regional and national history. The museum in Rheydt, founded in 1906 in Westphalia, was a good example for Heimatlers' museum practice that connected the local past to larger historical identities. The museum represented three Heimat identities by including three collections: the "larger collection area" of the Rhineland and Westphalia regions, the "restricted collection area" of the nearby cities of Düsseldorf, Aachen, and Cologne, and the "narrow collection area" of the town of Rheydt itself.[93] The concept of a Heimat museum connected the locality to the district, to the region, right up to the nation. Kurt Freyer, the author of the *Museumskunde* article on the district Heimat museum in Hadersleben, articulated the relationship among the local, district, regional, and the so-called central museums (Zentralmuseum). The latter were museums located in big centers of politics and culture that often display national history, such as the German National Museum in Nuremberg and the Roman German Central Museum (Römischgermanisches Zentralmuseum) founded in Mainz in 1852. The central museums obviously possessed special importance. They enjoyed national stature and rich collections and were the first historical museums in Germany. Connected to these museums, and functioning as "complementary" to them, was the "extended net of small and very small museums, the local and district museums and the museums of the provinces."[94] Local Heimat museums were viewed as telling a history that, while representing local particularity, was not isolated from the larger national history, but a constitutive element of it.

The precise role of the different territorial Heimat museums was a subject of debate among museum professionals in Wilhelmine Germany. Gustav Brandt, an important museum expert and frequent contributor to *Museumskunde*, argued somewhat rigidly that a Heimat museum should be restricted to display only the history of its precise territory. Otherwise, for instance, a local museum might end up displaying objects that properly belonged in a regional museum. "Where the activity of the regional museum ends begins the task of the district museum and [where its task ends begins the one of] the local museum."[95] The intricacy of the debate, which was academic and was taken by professionals who attempted to classify (to box is a better term) Heimat museums according to perceived scientific categories in order to achieve uniformity, is of no immediate relevancy to the argument made here. Local activists, in any case, usually followed their own rather haphazard methods. What is important to note is that the theoreticians of Heimat museums, while engaging in a debate of what to exhibit where, assumed a priori the existence of a meaningful connection between local museums and a national past. This was never debated. Thus Brandt constructed in his articles a theoretical edifice of local, district, regional, and central museums, each with different exhibitory tasks, but all connected in a common scope—to present German history and preserve the past. If Heimat theoreticians attempted to decide what was appropriate to display in local museums, they never doubted that the museum's local representation was important to sustain the edifice of national history.

Museum activists saw the local museum, and local history, as transcending the limited spatial and temporal borders of the single community. In a symbolism that is reminiscent of the foundation of local, regional, and national Heimat associations, local Heimat museums were followed by district, regional, and central museums. The local museum represented something more than the local history actually displayed there. It became a sort of foundation for the history of larger entities. An article in *Museumskunde* on the Celle museum argued that modern developments in transportation and communication "squander quickly the local customs and traditions that characterized the multiform German people. . . . That is why the significance of Heimat museums for the history of our [German] people will grow in the course of time."[96] Heimat museums, according to the author Bernard Müller, were important to understanding the history of the nation. Moreover, in his essay Müller implicitly argued that the sum of local Heimat museums made up the national history of Germany. As such, local museums came to represent a historical narrative that stood for the nation as a whole, offering a key to understand German history as a story of everyday life history of origins.[97]

In Heimat museums the nation was never far from the Heimatlers' thought and concerns. Embarking on setting up a museum, the Schwabmünchen Historical Association defined its task as a "patriotic undertaking."[98] In Heidelberg, the museum was viewed as "a factor in the cultural life of the nation and locality."[99] More specifically, Heimatlers articulated the idea that through Heimat museums the nation can be loved and its history understood. The Heimat museum in Jever was established in order to "advance the local archaeology and—through this activity—the love for Heimat and for the German fatherland."[100] Even more telling is the sentiment expressed in 1917 by the director of Emmerich's Heimat museum, Ferdinand Goebel: "The German people possess a high degree of historical sensibility [*Sinn*]. Let us take care that this sensibility takes root also through our Heimat museums for the well-being of our fatherland." In other words, the local Heimat museum ought to have represented the historical meaning of the German people and not exclusively and simply of the people of Emmerich. A principal of a local education institute, Goebel was not a museum professional like the rest of the contributors to *Museumskunde*. Indeed, the editor of the journal saw fit to add a concluding remark that "The style of this article diverges from the usual [scientific] tone of this journal. I decided not to efface the personal, colorful tone of the article because it gives a lively idea of the way many of our Heimat museums came into being."[101] Goebel, a passionate man, expressed from his heart an idea that museum professionals thought to be too "soft" to be presented in a learned journal, but with which, as the editor made clear, they agreed. Gustav Brandt's intellectual edifice of classified local, district, regional, and central museums meant as much, but he did not bring himself to say as much explicitly. To return to the question that opened this discussion, What was the meaning of Heimat museums viewed collectively? Local Heimat museums represented local history and also the nation as a whole, constructing a narrative of everyday life of origins with which to imagine the nation.

Answering the questions, Who are we and where did we come from?, bourgeois Heimatlers defined in Heimat museums an idea of the nation, its origins, and its members. Whether Germans were represented as the descendants of the ancient Germanic tribes or of townsmen from the Middle Ages, Heimat museums endowed the new nation-state with the mark of time immemorial. They supplemented the myth of origins told by other Heimat artifacts. A Catholic school textbook in Württemberg described Hermann the Cheruskian, who led the Germanic tribes to victory in the year A.D. 9 in a decisive battle over the legions of the Roman general Varus in the forests near present-day Hannover, as determined "to free his subjugated fatherland from the Romans. . . . Without Hermann's courage and devotion Germany would have had foreign language, customs, and laws, would have become a Roman province, and would have ceased to be among the independent European countries."[102] A Fellbach Heimat book provided a straightforward historical periodization: "After the expulsion of the Romans, *the Germans* moved into their places of residence."[103] A classic myth of origins, the Heimat idea explained the present by looking back to the most distant past; Germany's independence in 1871 was thus a result of a battle that took place 1,862 years before.

German national origins had, of course, specific human and geographical coordinates. Origins lay in provincial places and in their local histories, a notion that made the Heimat idea an anticentralist representation of the nation; this German past, which comprised the multitude of local histories, emphasized the diversity of the nation, and was a pluralist conception of history. Moreover, Heimatlers advanced an innovative approach to represent the Germans who inhabited this local-national history: the everyday life of the common people.[104] Heimat activists not only exhibited objects of everyday life, from a spoon to a dress, but also set out to record popular historical memories. In Vilsbiburg the museum committee collected people's memories of "interesting, historical, or local events, for example, from the Napoleonic Wars," a project we now call oral history.[105] The habitat of common people was reconstructed, as in the Heimat museum of Scheeßel, founded in 1913 in Lower Saxony, which had a fully equipped peasants' house of 1830.[106] And also the *Stube* displayed everyday life. This comprehensive approach to everyday life included peasants, burghers, and members of the guilds, the majority of small-town inhabitants before industrialization.

Neither the search for national origins nor the idea that they existed among the common folk were peculiar to Germany in nineteenth-century Europe. What is interesting in the Heimat idea is the way in which the Germans imagined the nation as an elaborate combination of national origins with local and everyday life history. This provincial image of the nation enlarged local existence to its ultimate imaginary boundaries by transforming local history into national history. Heimat thus connected the abstract nation with the personal local existence by making national history as tangible as local history; Heimat nationalized local history by, in fact, localizing national history.[107]

At this point we should consider the two major arguments raised in the historical literature against Heimat museums: that they did not represent social reality, and that they did represent, by ignoring working-class culture and displaying a rural never-never land, a reactionary identity. First, social reality. It appears clear that to look for historical reality in a Heimat museum is like looking for an accurate rendition of the past in a historical film. Both represent a basic historical storyline determined by artistic license to change some facts and obliterate others in order to create a distinct understanding of the past. A Heimat museum was essentially an artistic representation of the past and not a representation based on the practice of historicism and positivism. Truth was never an issue in Heimat museums. Heimatlers did not intend to provide a comprehensive and accurate representation of social reality, whether in the remote past or in imperial Germany. The past was a malleable material to construct identities, where imagination molded historical accuracy. As such, Heimatlers represented the past in the museums in a way that corresponded to the practice of Heimat associations. Behind the Föhr museum, which invented a traditional peasant house to satisfy modern standards of exhibition, lay the principle that led to the invention of the Betzinger *Tracht* and to the renovation of the lookout tower in Kirchheim unter Teck.

Was this necessarily reactionary? Heimat museums were faulted for not representing working-class culture, but when we consider that the museums were dedicated to the display of origins this argument is put in another light. In itself the representation of origins was not inherently antimodern and certainly did not include only peasant life. Communities with a distinguished town culture represented it splendidly. Heidelberg proudly and consciously housed the museum in an eighteenth century burgher house. The museum in the Baltic Sea merchant town of Lübeck told the story of a thriving burgher culture, art, and maritime achievements.[108] Most museums, in fact, displayed a mix of rural and town culture, of peasants' and burghers' ways of life. The question is why should we expect to find working-class culture in a Heimat museum in the first place? No doubt, some Heimat museums included a representation of the recent past. For example, the exhibition in Lübeck ended at the threshold of the present, in 1860, and the peasants' house in Scheeßel was from the 1830s. In theory, therefore, Heimat museums could exhibit the process and human consequences of industrialization. But the essence of Heimat museum was as a *Volkskunde*, historical museum, as a representation of the past not the present. Heimatlers intended to record in the museums the community's ways of life that had been disappearing during the transformation into modernity; within this framework there was little place for industrialization and the working class. Heimatlers could not construct a myth of national origins based on the machine and the factory, the constitutive elements of modernity. They needed to make use of the elements provided by the past: peasants, burghers, Germanic tribes. Invention also had its limits, for one could not place the working class in medieval Germany. But, and this was the main point, they could have used the symbols of modernity to construct an additional, complementary identity to the myth of origins. This was not incongruent with Heimatlers' perception and embracing of modernity, as we have seen in the previous chapter. It would have meant, however, a dramatic political and cultural reconciliation with the working-class movement, and the de facto recognition of the legitimacy of the Social Democratic Party to take equal share in the governing of Germany. This would have meant a significant break with bourgeois sentiments before 1914. The German bourgeoisie's refusal to set up in imperial Germany *Volkskunde* museums to represent working-class culture and ways of life was not so much connected to antimodernism as to deep-seated antisocialism.

Heimat museums were, of course, sites of control, social, political, and cultural. To understand the trends evident in the Heimat museum phenomenon, both within the bourgeoisie and between the bourgeoisie and other social groups, we must place the image of the nation represented in Heimat museums within the tradition of historical museums in Germany. The first historical museums in Germany were founded under the dual influences of romanticism and nationalism, when history became a national, in contrast to provincial, endeavor, as well as a vehicle to affirm national roots and uniqueness. This change in national consciousness was expressed by the brothers Grimm, as well as by the foundation by Freiherr von Stein in 1815 of the Society for Ancient German History, and by the establishment of numerous historical associations in Germany, of which there were twenty-four by 1832 and sixty by 1846. It was also expressed by a new concept of historical collections. Before the nineteenth century, collections stood for the rulers not for the community, and belonged in their private *Kunstkammer*. The new historical museum stood for the awakening German nation and its renewed connection with the past: it was a public space, established in a central location in big cities, a means to cultivate national history. Prussian Chancellor von Hardenberg initiated the foundation in Bonn in 1829 of the Rhine-Westphalia Archaeological Museum (Museum rheinisch-westfälischer Altertümer) "in order to cultivate and support the significance of the fatherland's soil," and Hans von und zu Aufsess, under the aegis of King Ludwig I of Bavaria, established in 1852 the German National Museum in Nuremberg, both museums concentrating on German culture of the Middle Ages.[109] In this same year the Roman German Central Museum was founded in Mainz, exhibiting Germany's prehistory and ancient history. Many German states followed suit, and in Württemberg the Royal Archaeological Collection (Königliche Altertümersammlung) was founded in 1862 with similar national ideas.[110] Founded before the unification of 1871, and opposing a reality of a divided Germany, these museums represented a growing national sentiment. They personified the change in German national consciousness, from the French Revolution to 1871, from a nation of German states into a national community and an organic whole.

The 371 Heimat museums founded between 1890 and 1918 were, in the words of Kurt Freyer who conceptualized the relations between local, district, regional, and central museums as an "extended net," "counterbalance and complementary" to the big museums.[111] The national museums were established by the upper classes, the haute bourgeoisie and the aristocracy, for the educated public, providing public spaces dominated by strict, elitist, and often snobbish social manners. Local Heimat museums, in contrast, were established for the general public, as shown in their humble locations, simple exhibitions, and nonscholarly representations of the past. While national museums were located in cities that were cultural and political centers, Heimat museums were located in large and small localities, often on the periphery. National museums pertained to urban Germany, Heimat museums dominated the cultural landscape of German hometowns. What distinguished the phenomenon of Heimat museums was their foundation in dozens of small, peripheral, and "unimportant" localities. Schwabmünchen was no Berlin, Bad Tölz was no Nuremberg. Yet each town also deserved a museum. Heimat museums reflected the perception that the authenticity of local identity depended on it being displayed in the locality, however marginal the locality might be. Outsiders, whether scholars, upper classes, or big museums, could not represent authentically the essence of this past, as Th. Bruß from Reinfeld explained: "Valuable documents and historical objects of our locality, dispersed in provincial and regional museums, lose their meaning in big collections."[112] The nation was in the details, in the province.

Two "counterbalancing and complementary" social trends are evident in the transformation of the image of the nation. On the one hand, a Heimat museum gave a voice to bourgeoisie and petite bourgeoisie on the margins of the nation and reflected their pressure from below to become legitimate and dignified members of it. Heimat museums were produced in a period of change in German society that saw the enlargement of the public realm and the progressive loss of domination of the notables over provincial life and, by extension, over the public interpretation of the local and the national pasts. The meaning of a Heimat museum was clear to the people of Rain: "A reason to establish a Heimat museum is obvious to the 'small people' [*dem einfachen Mann*]: who is interested in, for example, the portraits of old Rain families? In the Heimat museum we should assemble in exhaustive manner, if possible, what reminds us of the ways of life of our ancestors."[113] The historical significance of the Heimat museum phenomenon was the enlargement of the social and the geographical narratives of German history by adding to the history of great men, events, and political centers the experience of the "small people" who lived in the provinces and had nothing "historical" to report.

A Heimat museum presented, like the Heimat idea, an alternative to an elitist, educated, and centralist image of the nation that excluded the geographical and the social periphery of the German bourgeoisie. The best illustration of the popular identity represented in Heimat museums was the unscientific and often chaotic way of collecting and displaying objects. The unprofessional premises and conditions of Heimat museums created for Rain's ordinary citizens a friendly social and cultural space, while, at the same time, outraged some well-educated museum experts in Wilhelmine Germany. Gustav Brandt was one of the most prolific museum professionals before World War I to make the case against improvised Heimat museums: "While we can trust that the big museums of our province, led by experts, are run in a professional way, we cannot express a similar confidence about the increased number of district and local museums. The foundation and direction of these museums, which have recently spread on the earth of our Heimat like mushrooms, often lack entirely insight and responsibility. One cannot avoid the impression that the museum is an amateurish play by little-occupied men and not an undertaking that involves a serious aim and endeavor in the public interest. The results lie in front of everyone's eyes: meaningless and useless unpleasant lumber-rooms where valuable objects are not preserved but perish."[114] Heimat museums were, of course, meaningful, but their meaning did not correspond to Brandt's high museum standards. For other Heimatlers, all museums, from the most chaotic to the model of the genre in Celle, were sites of identity whose task was to provide an image of the past, not a factual account of it. Heimatlers in small localities wanted to set up a location, any location, to admire the local past without setting standards they could not possibly have met. Theirs was not a scientific enterprise that followed the rules and confirmed the reputation of the nineteenth-century belief in the truthfulness of science to represent the world. And that is why, perhaps, Heimat museums became a widespread and popular site of identity across provincial Germany.

On the other hand, the Heimat museum phenomenon represented an integrative social force within the German bourgeoisie. It would be an exaggeration to present the pressure from below of bourgeoisie and petite bourgeoisie in peripheral locations as a sort of a class war against haute bourgeoisie in central cities. It is important to remember that by producing the Heimat idea Heimatlers in small and provincial localities wished to expand the idea of the nation to its provincials, but did not propose a blueprint for social revolution against the upper classes and big cities. Heimat museums proliferated after 1890 because Heimatlers, whether bourgeois and petit bourgeois in provincial localities or haut bourgeois of the Deutscher Bund Heimatschutz, manufactured a new reading of German history as a network of interconnected local identities. For every Brandt who felt his professional credentials and expertise threatened by the amateurs who "lacked insight and responsibility," there was a Robert Mielke, a leader of the Deutscher Bund Heimatschutz who supported a Heimat museum in every German village. In his articles Brandt in fact conceded the broad support the Deutscher Bund Heimatschutz gave the Heimat museum phenomenon.

Haut bourgeois and petit bourgeois Heimatlers strongly perceived their role in society as the keepers of the German past. In Heimat museums, where they defined the nation's origins, they attempted to appropriate the nation's past. As such, the museum provided an integrative function within the bourgeoisie by differentiating it from other groups and underlining its uniqueness in society.[115] Bourgeois activists enjoyed the status of organizers and initiators of Heimat museums, which reinforced their local authority as leaders and educators of the community.[116] They claimed the right to hand down its history and traditions to the youth, who took an active part in museum activities thanks to teachers who were often museum activists, and also to inner-migrants who settled in the locality.[117]

HISTORY AND MEMORY

Heimat museums displayed the national past as a past that was eclectic, not comprehensive; popular, not elitist; local, not centralist; a simple past, easy to grasp, whether one was a historian or not. It is fruitful to take this image of the past as a point of departure to explore the relations between collective memory and history. Like every collective memory, the Heimat idea was ahistorical: it collapsed the differences between past and present by linking the ancient Germanic tribes with the people of the Second Empire; it was anachronistic by viewing the origins of German nationalism among the ancient Germans; it was topocentric by concentrating on a few episodes and ignoring concepts of continuity and change; and it stemmed entirely from the obsessions of the present. It may be argued, therefore, that the Heimat idea proved the intrinsic contradiction between history and collective memory so forcefully argued by Maurice Halbwachs.[118]

Yet the Heimat idea shows precisely the opposite, namely the bond between history and memory. Preoccupation with national origins was a venerable topic in the nineteenth century among professional historians. In Germany an\ entire school set out to rewrite history in a national, Prussian, and immemorial key. Heinrich von Treitschke's *Das deutsche Ordensland Preußen* (appropriately translated into English as the *Origins of Prussianism*) was explicitly written in 1862 to forge a common German past where this did not exist: "There is hardly even an outline sketch to convey to the mind of a South German boy an intimation of the most stupendous and fruitful occurrence of the later Middle Ages—the northward and eastward rush of the German spirit and the formidable activities of our people as conqueror, teacher, discipliner of its neighbors."[119] For Treitschke, "the German spirit" (read: the Prussian spirit) was an unbroken chain that linked the civilizing mission of medieval Prussians in Eastern Europe to a South German boy in 1862. His quest for origins is reminiscent of the Heimat idea's national narrative, although the Heimat idea emphasized different kinds of origins, of course. Treitschke went on to find the roots of modern Germany in the Middle Ages: "[T]he Germans are so much at one with their history, as to be simultaneously very old and very young, with the result that our early days, our days of long, long ago, are not a burden on our shoulders. . . . modern Germany as a great power is firmly established upon the very soil on which was erstwhile upbuilded what was a New Germany to our forefathers, the Baltic great power of the Middle Ages. Who can understand the innermost nature of the Prussian people and the Prussian State unless he has familiarized his mind with those pitiless racial conflicts whose vestiges, be we aware of them or not, live on mysteriously in the habits of our people."[120] Treitschke explained the history of Germany with a notion that was basic to the Heimat memory as well—the persistence of the mysterious innermost German nature. The ways of German national memory and national history converged rather than separated. History, in contrast to memory, requires that we respect chronology and avoid anachronisms, that we take no notice of the present, however difficult it is, and avoid imposing our values on the past. But Treitschke's history, like the Heimat memory, was not without these attributes.

The fusion between history and memory in the nineteenth century was not at all surprising. The nation-state set up a new historical memory, through commemorations, monuments, and the like, wherein the national historian "enjoyed a status of a priest of culture . . . [who] made the symbols concrete."[121] Thus the notion of national origins amateurishly displayed in Heimat museums and books received its professional investiture by historians who shaped national memory by creating such legends as Hermann the Cheruskian and the alleged timeless German character that "live[s] on mysteriously in the habits of our people." Searching for a national identity sanctioned by the authority of the past, historians, like Heimatlers, attempted to obscure the chasm between the past and the German Empire. Treitschke's history and the Heimat idea were thus two complementary interpretations of the search for national origins and a common past. History and memory were different images of the past in German society that at times converged and in other times separated, but always influenced each other. The fundamental lesson we can draw from the discussion of history and memory is that history is a developed and organized form of collective memory, not its contradiction.[122]

Nevertheless, history and memory were not identical images of the past. There were also interesting differences between them in imperial Germany. The most obvious one is that while Treitschke viewed Germany as a bigger Prussia, the meaning of the Heimat idea was based on a pluralist image of the nation that reinforced regional diversity. Stuttgart was not Berlin, Württemberg was not Prussia—and both were proud of it. Heimat provided an image of the nation as an integrative idea of local and regional cultures. Other differences follow logically from the Heimat idea's emphasis on pluralism and diversity. Heimat history and museums were an approach to everyday life of ordinary people, thus becoming a popular representation of the national past that contradicted the official and professional concept of history, which saw its meaning in great men, kings, battles, and diplomatic events. Although *Volkskundler* embraced the history of the common burgher, this view of history remained marginal among professional historians. Heimat historians provided, in a sense, a rudimentary version of *Alltagsgeschichte*, history of everyday life, and of oral history, thus forming an impressive idea of history from below when it was not a current method among professional historians.[123] Moreover, showing innovation and imagination, Heimat historians sought to understand the past by using everything Germans produced including seemingly trivial objects such as a chair and a spoon, thus going beyond historians' reliance on official documents. In that respect the evaluation of the Heimatler Seytter—that "Heimat studies enter affectionately into people's simple and daily life, down from the ivory tower of scholarship"—rings true. It is understandable why for him the history produced by the likes of Treitschke "rushes to generalize from concrete facts, and surveys mountains and valleys at a glance only to get a general impression of the landscape." The Heimat idea, in contrast, was an image of history with a human dimension. And because the everyday is human, the national history of everyday life bequeathed an idea of Germany that was tangible and familiar.

To introduce a more speculative tone to our discussion, the Heimat museum phenomenon leads us to reflect on the different ways the past is important in modern society. The urge to represent the past, demonstrated by Heimatlers in the foundations of hundreds of local museums, has been a most common activity in modern society.[124] Heimatlers' search for origins reflected the growing gap between the past and the present, characterized by the unprecedented "acceleration of history."[125] The Heimat museum was their invention to mediate between the past and the present, to bridge the gap between yesterday and today, by displaying that which, according to Weinheim's museum activists, "today disappeared completely from our memory."[126] Heimatlers undoubtedly felt strongly about the importance of the past in the making of their identity. But it would be a mistake to interpret the urge to represent the past as meaning only an outright affirmation of the importance of the past in modern society, for this argument assumes in an uncomplicated way that people have only one idea of the past. In the drive to establish Heimat museums we can see the dual perception about the past that emerges in modern society as a result of the acceleration of history. On the one hand, Germans remembered and celebrated the past in Heimat museums as an ideal of roots and stability in a period of rapid and unpredictable changes; the past was important because it was different from the present. On the other hand, the past was *so* different from the present that it became incongruent with its anxieties and desires, a sort of exotic Other. The frenetic conservation and exhibition of the past before it would forever disappear meant that a way of life ceased to be a social reality and became, instead, a museum display. Only by displaying the past could people still remember it. This may explain why Heimatlers often represented in the museums whatever happened in the past of the community, and not simply what was important in that past. The main criterion to exhibit an object was its pastness, it being a wondrous object from a "foreign country." Thus, we may see in Heimat museums the *simultaneous* praise of the past as being crucial to one's identity and wonder of the past's exotic otherness. I don't think that these two perceptions are mutually exclusive; they seem more like the constituents of modern perception of the past, as people commingle two lines of thought: they speak and think about the world in metaphors of innovation, change, and reinvention, and they also obsessively look back at the past to evaluate that which has been lost. The two perceptions—praise of the past and wonder of its otherness—display the dialectical relations between past and present, between roots and modernity, that characterized the Heimat idea. The Heimat idea yearned for the past not because it was antimodern but because it originated from modernity.

The modern "acceleration of history" lengthened the past and shortened the present, for even the past of twenty or thirty years ago seemed different and worthy of conservation. That is the reason why museum activists collected photographs, which, in Oettingen in 1906, could at best record past life of a few decades. Heimatlers exhibited in the museums ways of life that disappeared, whether two centuries or two decades ago. Thus Schwabmünchen, a century-old center of a textile cottage industry that disappeared in the second half of the nineteenth century because of technological innovations and change of market routes, dedicated most of its Heimat museum, founded in 1913, to the life and work of weavers. Although many inhabitants still remembered this period, it became part of the past because it ceased to be an integral part of the community's way of life.[127]

Pierre Nora correctly observed that memory develops when a social practice diminishes and disappears, for we need to remember that which is no longer alive. Nora also argued that history and memory were united before the development of scientific history in the nineteenth century and have been split since, and he distinguished between a premodern memory as a social practice, a milieu of memory, and a modern memory as voluntary and deliberate.[128] This distinction, however, seems artificial as it posits, in a quite nostalgic way, an alleged authentic and organic premodern memory and an alleged premeditated modern memory that has been cut off from social practice. It implicitly assumes that memory in the premodern era never represented disappearing social practices, although Europeans in early modern Europe represented the ancient Greeks and Romans. It implies, perhaps unintentionally, that modern memory is consciously designed, while the premodern one evolved organically and is therefore more authentic. Perhaps more important, we should not forget that the representation of a past, say, in a museum becomes a social mode of action even when the represented past is of a social practice that disappeared. The effectiveness of memory in the life of a social group is measured in terms of it becoming a representation that drives people to social action—to found a museum, to set up an association, to write a book, to celebrate a holiday. In other words, the representation of a social practice that disappeared is in itself a social practice. By making the Heimat memory into a social mode of action through books, museums, organizations, and associations, and, not least, through changing the meaning of the word Heimat, Heimatlers formed a bourgeois social milieu of memory.

CHAPTER SEVEN

The Nation in the Mind

*A*thousand Heimats dotted Germany, each claiming uniqueness and individuality. Calw's history was not like Stuttgart's, Reutlingen's nature was different from Bonn's, and the Swabian Heimat was unlike any other. Germany became a nation of Heimats: Reutlingen was a Heimat with regard to other German cities, Swabia with regard to other German regions, Germany with regard to other nations. By using the metaphor of the whole and its parts, the idea of Heimat harmonized the heritage of local identities and the single national identity. Wilhelm Seytter understood the Heimat idea as a Matryoshka doll of small and big Heimats: "The origins of patriotism are in large part founded in the smaller Heimat, in the surroundings of the Heimat locality. The small Heimat embodies for the child the whole fatherland. . . . Later he will learn what connects the Heimat district with the [national] whole."[1] This was a diametrically opposed metaphor of whole and parts to Sedan Day's *das große Ganze*, which emphasized the univocal identity of the nation. The inherent meaning of the Heimat metaphor emphasized plurality, as every Heimat was a site of different memories and dreams.

And yet together the Heimats informed the ideal of one, unique nationality. The metaphor of whole and parts also implied a hierarchy of Heimats since the German Heimat comprised all other Heimats. There were, in fact, three groups of Heimats, local Heimats, regional Heimats, and the German Heimat, and this hierarchy meant a plurality with strings attached. Each level had to accommodate the integrative requirements of the next. So, for example, Württemberg's history obliterated the memory of the 1813 and 1866 wars. Each level of Heimats represented a larger and more diverse aggregation of Germans, and was therefore more abstract and symbolic, less specific and tangible, in order to maintain as wide a common denominator as possible. Nowhere was this more evident than in the iconographic image of the nation in Germans' minds. Bourgeois Germans defined in Heimat museums, books, and associational activity the spatial and temporal, and the natural and geographical, attributes of the homeland. It follows logically that the homeland had a distinctive "look" in their minds, and it is precisely this look that is the topic of this chapter. If the effect of the Heimat idea in German society was its ability to function as a national stage for local diversity, how did a thousand Heimats make up *one image* of the nation?

In the symbols and repositories of memory such as museums, monuments, and school textbooks, the iconographic representation of national territory faces peculiar problems. One can see how a historical event is being obliterated from school textbooks, and thus from a national memory, but can one possibly obliterate a landscape, a tangible territory whose existence can be verified at any moment? A representation of national territory is, in a sense, similar to the *Annales* conception of history. While the image of the third level of *histoire événmentielle*, of wars, kings, and political events, can be easily manipulated, it is more difficult to manipulate the image of the first level of geography and topography, history's *longue durée* that molds people's identity. The landscape of the Swabian Heimat would never resemble, after all, the flatlands of Eastern Prussia. What was the process, then, by which a single iconography came to represent the multitude of landscapes that existed in the German homeland? What kind of scenery did the Germans have in mind when they thought and talked about the homeland?

The sources reveal immediately that images were an integral part of the Heimatlers' conception of the Heimat idea. Was it not more persuasive and exciting to show an image of nature, for example, in order to explain the importance of its protection instead of describing it in words? The Heimat idea virtually called for visual representation to transmit the notions of nature, landscape, territoriality, and folklore. Heimat images were diffused across the length and breadth of Germany through postcards, newspapers, journals, publications of Heimat associations, school textbooks, Heimat books, Heimat museums, and the like. The diffusion of Heimat images reached its peak when associations for the promotion of tourism adopted and propagated the Heimat idea as an image of the nation: Heimat images became a necessary part of local, regional, and national travel guides, and posters of Heimat were placed in all German train stations and public places.

Images corresponded to a common metaphor used by Heimatlers to describe their work: "The main activities of the new Bund [für Heimatschutz in Württemberg und Hohenzollern] were, first of all, to instruct. . . . It meant, above all, *to open the eyes* of wide sections of the population . . . through various lectures and *exhibitions*. . . . At that time [before 1914] one had first *to learn to see* again [what Heimat sensibilities meant], for the correct look is not obvious. How easily one can 'over'look, even things that were already perceived. . . . In short, it deals with images."[2]

The Bund für Heimatschutz regularly held lantern lectures and after 1913 its secretary, Professor E. Lörcher from the School of Architecture, established the Swabian Photograph, a special library collection of Heimat photographs about such topics as landscape, history, and architecture, which was borrowed by schools, communities, and associations. Typically, the Bund's publications *Mitteilungsblätter* and the journal *Schwäbisches Heimatbuch* were published in quarto pages to fit the size of pictures;[3] the handsome volume in big format, *Volkstümliche Kunst aus Schwaben*, edited by a leading Heimatler, the *Landeskonservator* (head of the state's preservation activities) Dr. Eugen Gradmann, had 500 images in 106 pages; and the Heimat publication *Augen auf* (Eyes opened) was eulogized for its instructive name.[4]

The sources of the Heimat idea virtually force the historian to explore the Heimat iconography. The Heimat image was not the only iconographic representation of the nation in Germany before and during World War I. It was an allegory that symbolized the local and the national worlds and that integrated through iconographic stereotypization of Germans and Germany. There were obviously other allegories of the nation with different meanings; this field of research is still underexplored and we need more studies to elucidate the various imageries of the nation and the relations between them. The following chapter is based on close to 300 Heimat images produced mostly between 1880 and 1918. The majority of this corpus consists of images of local Heimats in Württemberg, while a substantial minority depicts the national Heimat, mostly images from World War I, and a third group represents the regional Heimat. I compared the local and regional Heimat images produced in Württemberg with the national Heimat images produced in Germany in order to find the pattern of Heimat iconography. Württemberg was used, therefore, as a test case for local and regional Heimat images across Germany. It is safe to assume that there existed variations in local and regional Heimat images, based on different traditions and landscapes, but the unequivocal iconographic connection between local and regional Heimat images produced in Württemberg, and national Heimat images produced in Germany, leaves no doubt about the essential paradigm of the Heimat image.

We should consider the status of the various Heimat images as a documentary source. I regard the collection of Heimat images as a serial document, namely a document that consists of several parts which make up a coherent whole. The serial document is chronologically organized and submitted to analysis through selected, controllable indicators. The foundation of this mode of proceeding is the homogeneous, comparable, and repetitive quality of the images. The collection is built on the basis of research of two bodies of sources: those directly connected to the Heimat idea as found in Heimat journals, books, associations, and history books, and the general pictorial production in Germany in that period found in posters, postcards, paintings, drawings, and images from tourist guides. We thus overcome the danger of explaining the Heimat iconography tautologically by using only material from within the production of the Heimat idea, and are able to connect Heimat and its iconography to larger social processes and cultural traditions in Germany.

Although images provide new and different insights to the field of historical research compared with traditional sources, historians still tend to base their studies almost entirely on written sources. The exceptions only prove the rule.[5] But the use of iconographic evidence by historians is also fraught with dangers. When historians use a written text they know that the meaning of it can be inferred only through intermediaries, through selected indicators that make it possible to control the evidence and formulate an interpretation. In short, the text cannot speak for itself. This fundamental principle is not always applied to iconographic sources, where images are believed to give direct information, without intermediaries, about modes of life and thought of people in the past. The result is, as Carlo Ginzburg observed, that the historian thus reads into the images "*what he has already learned* by other means, or what he believes he knows, and wants to 'demonstrate.' "[6] For historians the means of interpreting images has often been through the title, description, or commentary appended to them, while it should be the works of art themselves. Furthermore, when we attempt to understand the social and political meanings of the Heimat images we face a great problem of interpretation because artistic style can never be a reliable guide to social and political developments, to values and beliefs. Thus Heimat images of the nation did not represent workers and have therefore been interpreted as reactionary. By the same logic, however, we can conclude that Nazi and fascist images, which did represent workers, conveyed progressive ideas. Both conclusions are based on a simplistic explanation of political values in symbolic style.

I attempt to overcome these obstacles by subjecting the Heimat images to iconographic analysis, the method of art history originated by Aby Warburg and developed by his student, Erwin Panofsky.[7] This method sets out to overcome the limits of the formalistic tradition in art history that understood works of art merely in terms of style (colors, lines, and the like) and that viewed the main analytical task of art historians as that of establishing the relations between works of art. The iconographic method, in contrast, seeks to reconstruct the relations between a work of art and the social experience and collective mentality of a given society. It explores the meaning of an artistic representation by placing it within a historical context, by analyzing the ideas and values embedded in and symbolized by its imagery. For Panofsky, a society produces two sets of iconographic symbols: the limited one classifies the consciously produced symbols, such as the eagle in German art signifying the empire and its power; the deeper one explores "those underlying principles which reveal the basic attitude of a nation, a period, a class, a religious or philosophical persuasion."[8] Panofsky never established a methodical approach to explore these "underlying principles," but suggested that they be controlled on the basis of "documents bearing witness to the political, poetical, religious, philosophical and social tendencies of the personality, period, or country under investigation."[9] Because the Heimat image was not a cultural artifact *an sich*, but part of the Heimat system of values in German society, the meaning of Heimat images can be controlled on the basis of the findings in noniconographic Heimat artifacts, such as Heimat museums, books, journals, and the like. We avoid the risk of circular argumentation that stems from using only documents related to the Heimat image by also considering general German pictorial production, which provides a controllable intermediary between German society and the Heimat image. In other words, our sources provide an intermediary between the historical conditions and the artistic representation.

CITYSCAPE, REGIONSCAPE, NATIONSCAPE

The Heimat iconography was based on the cityscape, an overall depiction of a human settlement and its landscape, usually of a hometown, and less frequently of a village. The Verein für ländliche Wohlfahrtspflege in Württemberg und Hohenzollern (The Association for Agrarian Welfare in Württemberg and Hohenzollern) identified specific iconographic features as belonging to a Heimat image in a comment on the picture *Tübingen* (fig. 3) by Walter Strich-Chapell, a painter of refined landscape in the style known as lyric impressionism, who became a leading artist of Württemberg landscapes and Heimat images before World War I, and who in 1909 made the symbol for the Bund für Heimatschutz: "The beloved old Swabian Muse town lies before us as *a type of Swabian Heimat*. This image of the town forcefully combines into a peaceful view! The old castle, golden by the warm evening sunshine, mirrors in the Neckar river. . . . the town and its surrounding silently integrate into the atmosphere. . . . A school can hardly choose a better image to show the children *a typical image of a Swabian town*."[10]

The case of the Verein, the local branch of the antimodern and antiurban Deutscher Verein für ländliche Wohlfahrts- und Heimatpflege that was originated in North Germany and headed by Heinrich Sohnrey, illustrates the diffusion of Heimat images among bourgeoisie of different political persuasions and social status. The Verein was a typical patronizing bourgeois association that acted among peasants. Its members, upper-class people in the cities and petite bourgeoisie in the villages, saw their mission in educating the presumed naive peasant, unaware of the national traditions he possessed, in order to halt the migration from the countryside to the cities. They appreciated the importance of pictures as a means of education, and often used lanterns in *Heimatabende*, evenings of lecture, discussion, and other activities organized for the peasants. The Verein purposefully chose certain pictures over others, and lengthy articles appeared in the *Schwäbische Heimat* about the "correct" pictures for peasants. The availability of the images was controlled by organizing special exhibitions that alternated from village to village, where pictures in various sizes were sold in reasonable prices.[11] In spite of the antimodern Heimat message of the Verein, it diffused in Württemberg the Heimat images produced by the Bund für Heimatschutz that never shared its ideas.

While *Tübingen* depicted a specific community, the effectiveness of Heimat iconography depended on forming a typology of every German community. The founder of the Deutscher Bund Heimatschutz, Professor Paul Schultze-Naumburg, wrote a book at the beginning of the century, *Die Entstellung unseres Landes* (The disfigurement of our country), that quickly became a best seller (third edition in 1909 totaling 50,000 copies), a seminal text of Heimat ideas in Germany, synthesizing popular feelings about the preservation and protection of the national heritage in landscape and architecture. Schultze-Naumburg himself was an architect whose style combined "traditional accents in a downright fundamental modern building."[12] He was among the founders in 1907 of the *Deutscher Werkbund*, where artists, architects, writers, industrialists, and politicians, among them Friedrich Naumann and Theodor Heuss, aimed to bring together art with technology and industry. Schultze-Naumburg occupied the nationalist position in this group, emphasizing the neoclassic architecture of the new modernity; his was an attempt, albeit a conservative one, to combine tradition and modernity.[13]

Out of 78 pages the book included 75 pictures, in accord with Schultze-Naumburg's philosophy about Heimat images: "Only few people direct their eyes to distinguish sharply between good and bad in our present existence. I would like, therefore, to show a series of pictures of, on the one hand, the country we inherited and, on the other hand, the country we have been making of it. Side by side, the pictures should show this [development] graphically."[14] Appropriately, the first picture in the book represented the essence of a German Heimat (fig. 4): "We all know exactly what one understands under the word *heimatlich*. When we look at any village or small town, towns that have existed and still exist in Germany by the thousands, our heart fills with pleasant emotions before the magic of this *heimatlich* German impression."[15] The Heimat image of Schultze-Naumburg was a town with no name, a location with no geographical, political, or territorial attributes. The anonymity of the town made the image an iconographic pattern of all German Heimats.

Especially interesting in this respect is the monthly series *Heimatgruß* that was published in Württemberg from 1905 by the Protestant Society in Stuttgart as a local edition of the Evangelisches Gemeindeblatt für Württemberg. The text of the four-page newspaper, which was immediately diffused in ninety towns and villages, was identical in all localities and so was the name of the newspaper *Heimatgruß*, but from the name of the locality: *Heimatgruß von Heerberg, Heimatgruß aus Bubenorbis-Neunkirchen*, and the like. The logo of every newspaper included the name and an image that represented the community (figs. 5–6). Significantly, although the images intended to show the uniqueness of every Heimat, they looked remarkably similar. We can, for example, imagine Steinheim (fig. 5) represented by the image of Ötlingen-Lindorf (fig. 6). It is also worth noting that figure 5 represents three localities, whose appearance in reality was, of course, not identical. Lacking the distinct silhouette of the individual community's townscape, these images became interchangeable. Many newspapers displayed the Heimat image only as a local house, a church tower, or landscape and some houses. As a whole, the images depicted the iconographic inventory of a Heimat: local houses, church tower, cityscape, and the surrounding nature and landscape. Similar features, in various forms, colors, style, light, and perspective, appeared in all Heimat images.[16]

An image from 1913 published in a local newspaper in Württemberg represented the Heimat idea in its purest form, a stereotype of all German communities. Figure 7, consisting of a silhouette cityscape of a small community with a church tower surrounded by nature, was entitled *A Heimat Image*—note the unspecified "a," which meant an image of a generic German Heimat that could fit anywhere in the homeland.

The importance of the Heimat iconography, however, was its capacity to represent what was otherwise unrepresentable, namely the regional and national territories. One of the founding acts of the Bund für Heimatschutz in Württemberg und Hohenzollern in 1909 was to ask Strich-Chapell to paint its symbol and by extension the image of the Württemberg Heimat (fig. 8). Dominating the foreground was a handsome half-timbered house (*Fachwerk Haus*), while the locality's houses and church tower were visible behind, directing the viewer's eyes to the landscape that stretched along a brook, into the horizon. That image was the official symbol of the Bund für Heimatschutz and was tremendously successful in Württemberg; the poster was hung in all train stations, offices, big hotels, and restaurants. What is interesting in this Heimat image is that while it conformed to the real landscape of Württemberg (you simply could not paint the Baltic Sea as Swabian Heimat), the composition was totally invented: the house, the locality, and the landscape did not exist in reality because Strich-Chapell combined elements from two different places in Württemberg, the Höfingen castle near Leonberg and the area of Sersheim, where he lived.[17] Significantly, the Bund had to disappoint many Swabians who wished to visit the location depicted in the image; although the Heimat image was totally manufactured, it nevertheless successfully evoked authentic Heimat sentiments.[18] Indeed, by being unidentified with a specific locality and landscape, the Heimat image worked even better, for it thus symbolized all the localities in Württemberg. A comparison with Schultze-Naumburg's image is revealing. Only the title of the territory distinguished between the regional and the local Heimat images: the form and iconography were similar.

During World War I there was an intense effort to continue the "Heimatization" of Germany, with the aim of constructing a collective image of the homeland. This period proves especially fruitful for exploring the national Heimat iconography. In the crucible of war, Germans embraced the symbols, values, and ideals that, in their view, most clearly united them. If Heimat had become part of the Germans' collective memory before 1914, then, logically, they would employ it during the war. A means of fostering solidarity presented itself in the campaigns for war loans (*Kriegsanleihe*), which obviously appealed to the most common, familiar, and uniting national symbols. For the Germans on the home front, subscribing to the war loans simulated participation in the real war: "We donate to the army all the means that are necessary to defend the holy German soil."[19] A pamphlet for the Sixth War Loan portrayed dramatically the feelings of angst and hope the war elicited, and which the war loan iconography had captured: "The decision in this war is getting closer, the well-being of your [*Deiner*] Heimat, your relatives, and your own fate depends on the result of this war loan."[20] The poster in figure 10, entitled "Protect Your Heimat," presents a Germany of small hometowns, and two factories, in harmonious relationship with nature, an image of a tranquil and local national existence. Similar motives appear in other posters: "Loan Your Money for the Protection and Defense of the Heimat!" (fig. 9) and "War Loans: Defying the Enemy, Protecting the Heimat" (fig. 11). The poster in figure 12 features in addition an inferior poem: "Unweakened weapons / Richest harvest wreath / Create in the Heimat / Brightness in all eyes."

Heimat iconography in the war also appeared in images that did not bear the title "Heimat," but that represented Germanness, the essence for which one fought. A poster of the Ninth War Loan (fig. 13), "It Concerns Everything We Love," showed a soldier guarding Germany represented by hometown houses, church towers, and a mother with a child. In 1915 Fritz Boehle painted a poster (fig. 14) that was strongly influenced by Dürer's engraving "St. Michael" (1508). Below the horse's belly we see the German homeland that the German knight defends, a familiar Heimat image.

These posters appeared across Germany and were published in newspapers and on postcards that popularized Heimat images of the nation, some as

Feldpostkarte to communicate between the front and the rear, others as greeting cards for Christmas and the New Year.[21] The bond between the Heimat idea and the poster as a vehicle of memory appeared to be foreordained. Originated in France, in the 1890s the artistic poster spread around the world.[22] The first real poster in Germany appeared in 1896 for a Saxon exposition of arts and crafts in Dresden, *Die alte Stadt* by Otto Fischer. The new awareness of the social, cultural, and economic potential of the artistic poster was linked to the rapid development of commerce and marketing; gradually, artists painted posters, and poster illustrators were recognized as artists. Combining aesthetic and advertising values, the poster popularized ideas and commodities through colors, graphics, and texts, fostering an identification with a commodity, be it a cigarette or an automobile; it thus possessed an intrinsic value as a means of disseminating ideas and stimulating emotions. Could Heimat sensibilities also be produced on posters as any other commodity intended for public display and containing a message that was aimed to move the viewer? The Great War, which demanded unparalleled devotion for the nation, accelerated the transformation of the Heimat image into a commodity and the poster into a producer and disseminator of Heimat belonging.

Before 1914, the European states did not deem the illustrated poster an important propaganda tool; posters were used to announce government orders, and the lifeless black and white words only underscored the visual contrast with commercial posters. This changed rapidly during the first months of the war, as the belligerent states began to use the illustrated poster to recruit soldiers, lift morale, and encourage the population to lend money to the nation.[23] The best poster artists were now recruited to draw the war-illustrated posters. The case of Lucian Bernhard exemplified the bond between the Heimat idea, the poster, and the commercialization of national feelings. Bernhard (1883–1972), who studied at the Munich academy, was introduced to the art of the poster in Berlin and became, together with Ludwig Hohlwein, the most important poster artist in Germany. Before World War I he opened new paths for the advertising poster, the *Sach Plakat* (object poster), displaying a simple image of the commodity with a text, also simplified into a clear and short slogan. During the war Bernhard made many designs for the war loan campaigns, such as figure 13, applying the *Sach Plakat* system to advance the Heimat idea: the combined image of the mother, the child, and the hometown generated strong emotions, the text was reduced to its clearest expression, "It Concerns Everything We Love," and the people, one hoped, would buy the war bonds.[24]

Let us examine another privileged source of the history of mentality: literary sources, poems to be exact, provide a way to understand the meaning, reception, and power of this collective image of the nation in German society. Literary sources have been regarded by scholars as fundamental representations and vehicles of collective memory. A model of the genre is Paul Fussell's *The Great War and Modern Memory*, which is based solely on British literary sources. Typically, the war gave rise to a flood of literary works by people from all walks of life, soldiers at the front and civilians at the rear. The most popular literary genre, by far, entailed poems published for mass consumption, in small, cheap booklets made of cheap paper. Their diffusion was widespread, and booklets by the tens of thousands were printed and sold in Germany and at the front. The booklets themselves proclaimed the popular origins of the poems. One dust jacket, for example, announced that the poems therein were collected from newspapers around the country and selected according to the degree to which they expressed the sentiments in Germany and at the front.[25] Responding to the serious situation of Germany, the poets rhymed patriotic poems, swearing to defend the fatherland. The booklets were intended to lift morale both at the front and at home, and they were embedded with *Vaterlandsliebe*. Even the names of the booklets indicated the status of the Heimat idea in the public mind. One series of nine volumes dealing with different topics was entitled *Around the Heimat. Pictures from the World War*. Another booklet was named simply *The Heimat: New War Poems*.[26] Obviously, in these booklets Heimat meant Germany.

The Heimat poems can be considered a kind of a written comment on the Heimat images. "A kind of"—for Heimat images were most probably not in front of the eyes of the soldiers and citizens who wrote the poems. Precisely this, however, makes the poems such a revealing indication of the reception of Heimat images in German society because the descriptions in the poems were remarkably similar to the images of the national Heimat.

In the patriotic, military, and unstable environment of the war the idea of Heimat represented in war poems the eternal German community, an ideal, small community that embodied intimacy. A poem entitled "Heimat" described the idea:[27]

. . . Is this not the Heimat?— September's meadows.
Over there, clear golden rays pierce the air.
Mowed fields. The strong scent of the harvest.
And a chain of hills, like bowed giants,
On the horizon. With round, red knob
Rises dignified the Heimat's church tower.
The trees hang satiated and loaded with fruits.
The peasants' wheat accumulates in golden swaths.
This is the Heimat!

We don't know whether Julius Berstl, the poet, indeed lived in a village, or whether the village's church tower had a round, red knob, but this is of course irrelevant. What is important is the description of warmth and familiarity, a description that arouses immediate recognition. Does not this poem sound like the description of figure 11?

The leading symbol of the Heimat community, local, regional, and national, was the church tower, the symbol of the spiritual and intimate community. In Heimat poems and images the church tower was usually not described in detail, so as not to resemble a specific one.[28] Every German could easily think of his or her locality's church tower, for every German locality had one. Before high buildings dotted the urban landscape, church towers were the highest, most visible and dominant architectural feature in the German skyline. Returning to the locality, one saw the church tower from afar and sighed with happiness; leaving it, one looked back to see the tower and cherish the memories. The church tower evoked the sound of bells, a traditional symbol of a community. Bells rang to summon the community, on Sundays and holidays, and to announce important news; theirs was a sound of human activity and human society. The church tower was a center of communal life, a pivotal location for one's relations to man and God. Although it was a dominant feature, the church tower was never too imposing; it was noticeable enough to emphasize human community, and yet modest enough to express the harmonious relations between nature and man. The church tower, moreover, historically old, represented history itself, the roots of the community.

In World War I Heimat iconography became such a collective notion in German society that minimal features sufficed to convey its message. In the poster competition in Stuttgart for the Seventh War Loan, a poster of Karl Sigrist, "To Be Strong in the Heimat," was selected among 193 works (fig. 15). An article in *Das Plakat* explained its meaning: "A correct assessment of the population's mood, which today can be mobilized to subscribe to war loans above all because of the hope for a quick peace, led most of the artists to avoid warlike iconographic elements, depicting instead the coming peace or the secured peacefulness of the Heimat, protected by the army." Sigrist's poster reduced Heimat iconography to its most essential elements, "understandable to everyone": an oak tree, a symbol of roots and security, robustly planted on the ground.[29] Another poster of Sigrist, which won the second place in the Eighth War Loan competition organized in 1918 by the Verein der Plakatfreunde, took the Heimatization of Germany even further. His poster showed an eagle and a dove flying above Germany, represented as landscape only; this was the German Heimat which needed no further comment (fig. 16). The art of Sigrist, a Swabian born in Stuttgart in 1885, also showed the meaningful link between the local and regional Heimat images produced in Württemberg and the national images produced in Germany. Although participation in Stuttgart's Seventh War Loan competition was restricted to Swabians, Sigrist's poster "To Be Strong in the Heimat" shows that the artist's Swabian identity did not stand in the way of his German identity. Instead, one identity enhanced the other.[30]

Because the Heimat iconography was in itself common and simple, not every cityscape image aroused Heimat sentiments. The context—Heimat publications, explicit captions, or the artist, such as Strich-Chapell, who was known as a Heimat painter—determined the values attached to the image. The Heimat image was mostly produced by artists and members of the regional and national Heimat organizations, giving it a bourgeois upper-class profile. But it was also diffused by organizations that included petite bourgeoisie, such as the Verein für ländliche Wohlfahrtspflege and the Protestant Society in Stuttgart. And it became familiar through Heimat literature such as the *Heimatschutz* and *Schwäbisches Heimatbuch* (the journals of the national and Württemberg Heimat associations) that was directed to upper-class readership; local newspapers such as *Heimatgruß* that were directed to inhabitants of villages and small and medium-sized towns; and posters and postcards, a cheap, popular, and effective means of diffusion, that were directed to all.

HOMO GERMANICUS

What kind of Germans inhabited the Heimat image? Originated by the bourgeoisie, it may be tempting to interpret the Heimat image as a national symbol of class domination. It appears, however, that what needs to be explained in Heimat images is not bourgeois symbols of superiority, but the absence of pretense and pretentiousness, and the simplicity of form and style which evoked authenticity. Bourgeois Heimatlers avoided in the Heimat image class elitism and class snobbery: they did not aestheticize the peasantry, the working class, poverty, or bygone times, nor did they depict the upper classes as the backbone of the nation.

Indeed, produced by bourgeois Germans, the Heimat images did not depict them or almost any other Germans, thus implicitly rejecting an appropriation by a specific social, political, religious, or regional group. Typically, the images were devoid of religious superiority, as the dominant church tower designated neither a Catholic nor a Protestant church. In this respect, the Heimat image was democratic and equal, not in the sense of legal and political rights, but because it was an image of Germany that excluded no one, and, in theory at least, included all. Indeed, Heimat became a popular image of the nation in German society precisely because its missing element was society itself. It represented no social relations, no social context, and no social scenes in the workplace or the town; and where no social context exists, social conflict disappears. Heimatlers did not portray workers or bourgeois because in Germany this would unavoidably suggest a solution, and thus would politicize the

Heimat image. Because the Heimat image did not represent a social context, it also avoided social accusation (against workers, for example). The integrative function of the Heimat idea is evident here.

Moreover, the banal artistic style of Heimat images was itself a statement against class snobbery. Figures 4–6, but also 9–11, were distinguished by the simplicity of form, structure, perspective, and composition. Some Heimat images seem to have been purposefully drawn to look like a work of laypersons, not artists, such as A Heimat Image (fig. 7). In artistic terms the Heimat image was poor and unsophisticated, but this only enhanced its effect as an integrative vehicle in German society, for it was an image understood by all, educated and Philistines, intellectuals and provincials, petit bourgeois prone to trendiness, as well as sophisticated artists such as Strich-Chapell. The importance of the Heimat image lay in neither aesthetic nor artistic values, but in providing a graphic image of the nation in Germans' minds.

While Heimat images described an indeterminate German person, they pursued symbols of unity and coziness, which were easily applicable to every Heimat. The Heimat idea informed a structure of sentiments and images with which people could grasp the idea of a nation, and therefore, in order to be effective, this structure had to include personal and recognizable experiences which were immediately familiar and capable of being projected onto bigger entities. The community was the core symbol; it led to the related symbols of home and family, both evoking togetherness. There were good reasons why the home became a leading metaphor for the nation because the origins of the ideas of home and Heimat had much in common. Similar to the invention of Heimat, the invention of the home in the nineteenth century as an intimate point of orientation was a response to the expansion of space, the acceleration of time, and the growing individual mobility.[31] Home, as the community of family, and Heimat, as the national community, were sites of unity, of shared past and future, and of a collective memory, which were distinguished from all other homes and nations. And for bourgeois Germans in the Second Empire, the values of home and family and the sentiments they aroused were associated with women.

The connection between home and Heimat transformed women, always accompanied by children, into the human protagonists of the Heimat. "[The soldiers] thought of Heimat, wife [Weib], and home," was a common description of Heimat in poems, as was the combination "Heimat, wife, and child."[32] Typically, figure 13 shows a mother and her child as symbols of the Heimat. The connection went beyond the specific conditions of the war, when men were at the front and women at home. Sentiments of harmony were best expressed in the private spheres of home and family, assigned to and dominated by women and associated with commonly perceived feminine sensibilities.

The connection Heimat-home-coziness-woman was, therefore, a logical one. The metaphor of home was constructed through the description of women as wives and mothers and through the evocation of special moments that symbolized harmony in the life of a family. Sunday and Christmas were the most popular. For one soldier on the western front, home was embedded in the following memories:[33]

Sunny Sunday!
When the bells ring at home,
When chorals sing to heaven,
When mother's intense prayers
beg to God for us out there
  Holy Sunday!

. . . . . .

Don't you hear the Heimat's bells
Blissfully transcending the horrible present?
Yes, today is Sunday!

This poem also demonstrates the predominance in the Heimat idea of female metaphors, which transfigured and appropriated male metaphors. In German society Sunday's activities were usually male metaphors because on this day the father, free from work, could spend time with his children. We saw an example of this in chapter 5, when a Reutlingen Heimat book urged the teaching of Heimat values "on Sunday afternoon [when] father wanders with the children in field and forest." But Sunday activities also became female metaphors, like the praying mother in the preceding poem. The logic of Heimat sensibilities led it to be associated with what contemporaries believed to be female sensibilities. Just as the home and the family were women's domain, so was Heimat. At home women represented a point of orientation for all the members of the family. While men worked during the day and were absent from home, women stayed home to care for the family nest. While men were on the move, women were fixed to one place. In a changing world, home-family-woman were symbols of stability. The Heimat idea used these symbols in the same way and projected their meaning onto the nation as a whole. The image of the family-home-Heimat was powerful because it was uneventful: an image of the simple things one took for granted, of kinship, commitment, and continuity.

People in the Heimat poems were anonymous, and had roles of mother, father, wife, and child, but no name, address, or face. Men usually appeared when needed to complete the nuclear family, but not as a key symbol. Even when an extended family was evoked as a metaphor for the nation, men served only as supporting actors, as in the following case of the author's father:[34]

I am thinking of you, silently on guard,
My distant Heimat valley,
Of father and of mother
Ever so many times

' All the little birds are sleeping

. . . .

Now sleep you too, my lovely child—
Tomorrow,
Yes, tomorrow is the battle!
I am thinking of you, faithfully on guard,
My silent and beautiful maiden.

To be sure, there were Heimat poems and stories that identified their heroes. But the effectiveness of the Heimat idea increased when it remained undefined in as many areas as possible. The important message in Heimat images and poems was not what kind of Germans inhabited the Heimat, but that they were Germans; whether they were Swabian or Saxons, workers or bourgeois, Catholic or Protestant was irrelevant. That is why there were almost no real people in the Heimat images; the knights in figures 10 and 14 were, of course, not contemporaries.

The common denominator among the occasional persons who did appear in Heimat images was the personification of timelessness. The iconography did not include workers or bourgeois, who were associated with modernity, but instead showed peasants and mothers, working at humble domestic chores (figs. 11 and 13). Since nothing ever happened in the images of the national Heimat and no specific German occupied the images, they became a stage in which every German could direct the action in his or her mind. The images were powerful because they were, in a sense, empty. Paradoxically, therefore, the image that was the epitome of German local-national memory was the most abstract of all, elevating national forgetfulness to its highest level. Imprinting the idea of Heimat in their minds, bourgeois Germans ceased to associate the nation with real social and political processes, and viewed it as immemorial. It is to the concept of time in Heimat images, therefore, that we have to turn now.

THE GERMAN HEIMAT: ILLO TEMPORA

In the Heimat idea bourgeois Germans strove to make sense of German history; the Heimat image, similar to Heimat museums and books, told the story of national origins. With no specific locality and inhabitants, with no social context, Heimat images represented the national community as an eternal community, beyond time, thus creating a chain between the German past, present, and future. The Heimat image displayed no historical rules, no historical evolution, and no intention to foretell history; it arrested the flow of history, thus enlarging it to encompass German history from time immemorial. Heimat poetry followed this pattern. The ellipsis opening Julius Berstl's poem "Heimat"—". . . Is this not the Heimat? September's meadows"—suggests that Heimat had a long history before he or the reader encountered it. Heimat conveyed the feeling of having always been there. Some images were general enough to fit the present and the past (figs. 3–9, 12, 15–16). Perhaps the best example is figure 10, where two factories point to the modern era, while at the same time the armored person protecting Germany was certainly not a contemporary. The image, therefore, leveled past and present, obscuring the chasm between them. The same is true for figure 14.

The interpretation of the Heimat image as a representation of Germany that leveled past and present agrees with previous findings from sources like Heimat museums and books. In imperial Germany, a period of historical self-consciousness that attached great meaning to images of the nation, the Heimat image without history and social relations was bound to demand explanation. Heimat iconography was an allegory that represented feelings of national belonging more effectively than it displayed social conditions, and provided a common denominator that social and political life denied Germans. The meaning of the Heimat image comes into sharp focus when we consider that the social and political purpose of the image was connected, in some ways at least, to the knowledge and information it conveyed—and the Heimat image conveyed remarkably little information about imperial Germany's economy, politics, culture, and people. Why was the Heimat image so empty, if not in order to reconcile the unreconcilable, to build a common denominator among Germany's diverse and opposing social, political, and religious groups? The image did convey that this territory was the land of the Germans, thus transforming, like every national idea, banality into metaphysics.

But even this allegory about the collectiveness of national belonging communicated a certitude about Germany's historical future and therefore presented one way of organizing German society as the only legitimate one. Produced by the bourgeoisie, the Heimat image conformed to some of their social and political ideas. Although in certain respects the Heimat image was democratic, popular, and open for various interpretations, it also represented an immobile nation, and therefore implicitly reinforced the existing order in German society. The Heimat image projected a conflict-free German society that symbolically represented the bourgeoisie's refusal to resolve the problems of equality and democracy in German society by sanctioning their political differences with the working-class movement.

Few words in the German language arouse such profound sentiments of time-lessness as "Heimat." But ideas become immemorial because memory is short. Precisely how short was the Germans' memory in the case of the Heimat idea? Stripped of the Heimat sensibilities associated with it, the local Heimat image was in fact a cityscape, a *veduta*, an old and venerable style in European painting that went back, as a genre, to the Renaissance and which had flourished in Württemberg around 1800. The *veduta* is an overall depiction of a human settlement, a village, a town, or a city, and its landscape that aims at topographic accuracy without loosing the artistic touch. Fashionable among wide circles of the bourgeoisie, the *veduta* in South Germany at the nineteenth century had a fixed formula, whether describing Swabia, Bavaria, or the Rhine. A clean, precise, and reliable picture aiming to capture one's habitat in a natural and geographic area, the *veduta* showed in the foreground fields, roads leading to the locality, and people at various activities, at the center the locality, with a background of landscape and bright sky.

Although the Stuttgart academics and the official art establishment in Württemberg rejected the *veduta* images after 1800 in favor of the ideal, classic, and historic landscape painting, the public enthusiastically embraced these images.[35] The Georg Ebner publishing house in Stuttgart played an important role in the reproduction of *veduta* pictures and published between 1816 and 1825 in big format the *Views of Württemberg* (Ansichten aus Württemberg) and later small engravings in numerous copies under the title *Recollections or Interesting Views of Württemberg*. By the 1830s *veduta* images enjoyed widespread diffusion thanks to lithography that replaced etching and engraving; the Royal Lithographic Institution was founded in Stuttgart and similar institutions, large and small, were common in localities all over Württemberg. The works of Eberhard Emminger (1808–85), the prominent painter of Württemberg's *veduta* images in the nineteenth century, exemplified the artistic style of the *veduta* and allow us to understand the affinities and the differences between the *veduta* and the Heimat images (fig. 17).

As if to correspond to the *bürgerlich* character of the Biedermeier period (1815–48), the *veduta* of this period, showing attention for details and devotion to accuracy, described the world of ordinary people, an immediate and personal world, devoid of heroes and pathos; realism and veracity characterized these images, not affectation and foppishness. The secondary particulars at the front of the picture, an essential feature in the *veduta* images of this period, helped communicate these values by describing local people, usually accompanied by animals, at work or at leisure: one woman is by the fountain near the crucifix and another, carrying a basket on her head, walks with a child (fig. 17); others walk their dog on a hill overlooking the lively street scene in the town below.[36] Other features characterized the *veduta* images. Neither the artist nor the viewer was part of the painting, but were outside observers, looking over the town from an imaginary hill outside it. The sky often covered one-third to one-half of the image, and the perspective of the sky above and the fields, people, and roads leading to the town below led the viewer's attention to the center of the picture, where the town's houses, churches, and walls were visible. Finally, the weather in the *veduta* images was always warm and desirable; storms, rain, and snow were not represented.

At that period the cityscape image was already attached to the *Beschreibungen*, the books that sketched the state of economy, history, architecture, urban development, and natural surroundings in Württemberg's localities and districts, and which anticipated the *Heimatbücher* that appeared later in the century. The frontispiece of the *Beschreibungen* showed a cityscape image of the district's capital. The images of Ehingen in the *Beschreibung des Oberamts Ehingen* (fig. 18), published in 1826, and in *Das Königreich Württemberg. Beschreibung nach Kreisen, Oberämter, und Gemeinden* (fig. 19), from 1907, show the extent to which Heimat images owe a debt to old cityscape iconography. Only the drawing style and the three factory chimneys distinguished the image of Ehingen in 1907 from Ehingen in 1826; the town's fundamental social and economic transformation during these eighty-one years was not expressed. The iconographic pattern of the *Beschreibungen*'s images from the 1820s to World War I obscured the distinction between the past and the present. Moreover, the link between the community description in the *Beschreibungen* and the cityscape image means that this image associated history and identity of a community before the full-blown development of the Heimat idea in imperial Germany.

After the 1850s the style and the production of cityscape images underwent a change that eventually connected it to Heimat images. New technologies influenced the future of the cityscape images in contradictory ways. The lithographic process made the images literally household items, and also small hometowns had a proper lithographer who produced local cityscapes in his workshop. Concurrently, the invention of photography rendered the topographic cityscape image obsolete, for whatever the image depicted, the photograph captured better. Cityscape images, therefore, began to appear less detailed and more metaphoric: people and animals disappeared, only the main outline of the community's silhouette was depicted, and general landscape motives were preferred over precise designs. The Heimat image took over this metaphoric image of the locality and many of its iconographic and formal features, such as the perspective, the point of view of the artist and the viewer, and even the pleasant weather, a prosaic but not irrelevant point. Underlining the continuity between it and traditional German painting, the Heimat image even persisted in depicting the community from the traditional point of view of the artist: the two images of Ehingen were drawn from the exact same position, while in Tübingen the castle had regularly dominated cityscape images (fig. 3). Most of these artistic points of view of cityscape images went back to the German cityscape painting tradition of the sixteenth century,[37] and because neither the style nor the image of the *veduta* was innovative, each associated history and tradition in imperial Germany.[38]

Heimatlers, however, also altered the traditional cityscape image in order to suit it to the conditions of the modern nation-state; thus people were usually removed from the Heimat image because they identified it in terms of time, class, religion, and the like. The Heimat idea, therefore, was neither a clear-cut German tradition nor a clear-cut invented tradition, but rather both, a reinterpretation of an existing tradition that included a fabrication. Heimatlers invented the very idea of the longevity of the Heimat idea, but did not invent the Heimat iconography. Instead, they chose the venerable tradition in German art of cityscape and landscape iconography because it represented a German community and, being connected to topographical descriptions, had been already associated with its history, nature, and customs. Yet after 1871 they gave this tradition a whole new meaning—the image of the nation as a local metaphor. Heimatlers thus took old notions unconnected to the nation and endowed them with new significance that gave the nation the appearance of ancientness.

While the connection between the local Heimat image and the German cityscape tradition appears evident, did the cityscape image ever represent a large and impersonal territory before the Heimat idea? Did cityscape images in Württemberg compose, in one image, a regionscape, being thus a forerunner of the regional and national Heimat image? A travel guide for Württemberg, written by Dr. Julius Bernhard and published in 1864, entitled *Historical, Picturesque, Statistical, Topographical, and Economic Guide Book for Württemberg*, was a true precursor of the Heimat books. Bernhard's travel guide, small in size but including more than 400 pages of detailed descriptions, set out to capture Württemberg's uniqueness: "Swabia has always belonged to the countries that enjoyed the reputation of being great marvels of nature; indeed, in the Middle Ages one did not hesitate to call Württemberg the paradise of Germany. . . . In terms of domestic institutions and state structures Württemberg is second to no country in the world, and in terms of natural beauty, archaeology, architecture, art, industry, and the like it contains as many remarkable objects as any other country."[39] The gem of the travel guide was a nearly one-meter folding map of Württemberg, the size of a page, an intersection of the region depicting its landscape, localities, and people (figs. 20–21). While the text of the travel guide described Württemberg accurately, the image was obviously a symbolic representation; Stuttgart, for instance, is depicted as a locality of several houses and a church tower. The localities were similar, even identical, in form and style, and only the names at the bottom of the image differentiated between them. All the communities were depicted as small hometowns, surrounded by landscape, and this human and manageable dimension projected mutatis mutandis to Württemberg as a whole.

This image of Württemberg was published in 1864, before Königgrätz and Sedan. Cityscape and landscape iconography in German society and culture, therefore, symbolized emotional links and impersonal territories before the foundation of the nation-state. Heimatlers took this kind of image after 1871 and applied its symbolic heritage to the local and regional Heimat ideas as well as to Germany as a whole. How similar are the localities in Bernhard's travel guide with *A Heimat Image*, the *Heimatgruss* images, and, as we shall see, the *Gruss aus* postcards (figs. 5–7 and 22–24)!

SPACE I: NATURE AND LANDSCAPE

The combination between cityscape and landscape was the essential feature of Heimat iconography. In German historical literature it has been common to regard the German attraction to nature as a cultural heritage of German romanticism, as proof of Germans' attraction to myth and to the irrational. According to this view, the use of landscape and nature as a representation of the German nation reflected antimodern values because it excluded a representation of urban and industrial society. Produced by the Junker landed aristocracy and its bourgeois allies, according to one scholar, the political purpose of this representation was to control and manipulate the lower classes.[40] This approach to the relations of nation and landscape has been based, however, on an uncomplicated attempt to explain artistic style in social structure.[41]

It appears tempting to understand the Heimat iconography of landscape along the lines of a recent interpretation of the English picturesque painting. This artistic style was widespread between 1740 and 1860, when the agrarian and industrial revolutions radically transformed the landscape of the British isle. The landscape depicted by the picturesque painting was the opposite of the one produced by these revolutions. Through a depiction of rustic landscape and the aestheticization of poverty and rural life, the picturesque painting reflected, it has been argued, an attempt to escape from the harsh reality of the industrial revolution.[42] Was the meaning of the German Heimat landscape similar to that of the English picturesque painting? What kind of nature did the bourgeoisie represent in the Heimat image?

Let us answer this question by looking at the kinds of landscape Heimat image did *not* represent. A fundamental development in landscape painting took place in the seventeenth century under the French painters Nicolas Poussin (1593/4–1665) and Claude Lorraine (1600–1682), who painted ideal and heroic landscapes—large-scale biblical or mythological scenes. Heimat land-scape, in contrast, was neither heroic nor idealistic: it did not depict a pasto-ral paradise and ancient historical scenes, or, for that matter, any historical themes; it did not enhance nature aesthetically and morally, or use literary references to the classical Gods and heroes to transform reality into myth. In contrast to heroic and idealistic landscape, Heimat images avoided sentimen-tality. Heimat landscape was also not an Arcadian landscape for it was not a representation of rustic and pastoral life, and it lacked the myth and unreality often displayed by music and poetry that are fundamental to an Arcadian landscape.

Above all, Heimat landscape was not romantic. Although romanticism in-cluded several iconographic elements that were close to the Heimat image, and which the Heimat iconography later used, it was different from it. Caspar David Friedrich and Phillip Otto Runge, the great romantic painters, empha-sized the landscape itself, a tree, a rock, or a mountain, not the relations between humankind and landscape that in Heimat images represented interest in all people, humble and otherwise. They depicted a sublime idea of land-scape, representing God's eternal being in contrast to man's transient exis-tence; in romantic paintings the protagonist experiences rapturous emotions in a journey that leads far and away from our mundane world. These values had nothing in common with Heimat's simplicity and down-to-earth values of the common man; romanticism showed how nature overwhelmed man, Hei-mat showed how man and nature complemented each other. The difference between romanticism and the Heimat image was demonstrated in romantic cityscape images. Friedrich's *veduta* of his hometown *Wiesen by Greifswald* (the 1820s) exemplified this.[43] Drawn in the familiar artistic tradition of the cityscape, it showed Wiesen and its surrounding landscape. Yet Friedrich's cityscape aroused feelings unknown to a Heimat image. It showed the city at dawn, in contrast to the blue sky and good weather of Heimat images, and it conveyed an eerie atmosphere of expectation and dream, which was alien to Heimat images, enhanced by the mist and the fog that blurred the city's sil-houette.[44] Romanticism based the essence of art on the idea of the artist-genius, of creativity that was unique, whereas the Heimat image elevated ba-nality to a state of art. While Heimat images also conveyed a touch of nostalgia, it was a candid and human nostalgia that every person could identify with. Heimat images took the sublime out of landscape, representing the locality, the region, and the nation as a friendly and intimate environment, and above all as territories fit not for heroes, but for every German.

Heimat poems offered a similar picture. They depicted the nation as a community within nature, and in harmony with nature. Trees, fruits, gardens, brooks, hills, and the earth were made part of the representation of the na-tion.[45] This landscape had human dimensions, and its elements inspired companionship between man and nature. Nature that inspired awe, such as big mountains and rivers, that challenged—or seemed to defy—men and women was left out. Nature in the Heimat idea was, to use a current expression, user-friendly. Heimat cultivated a poetic view of nature that connected the local community with the national community, and endowed the national community with a sense of homeyness.

SPACE II: THE HEIMAT HOMETOWN

When Julius Berstl wrote ". . . Is this not the Heimat?—September's meadows" the ellipsis that opened his poem indicated that he thought certain things about the Heimat may never be known. Being indeterminate and eternal, the Heimat was perforce mysterious; but never too mysterious to be misunderstood as a symbol of Germany and Germans. To be effective Heimat needed to maintain a fine balance between being somewhat chimerical, on the one hand, and comprehensible, on the other. As in the poem "From the Mist, Shining, Rise, the Heimat":[46]

First it was only the golden knob on the tower.
Then appeared bright houses through the swaths,
Blossoming gardens, trees, loaded with fruits:
From the mist, shining, rises the Heimat.

Even in the midst of mist, Heimat needed to convey the image of a community where Germans lived. Although Germans have liked to think of Heimat as full of mystery, it in fact possessed just the right amount of mysteriousness to become both enchanting and utterly mundane.

This was exemplified by the choice of the hometown as the human settlement to represent the German Heimat, epitomized in the *Gruss aus* postcard series that began to appear in the 1880s. Through the postcards the bourgeoisie linked two of their originations: modern mass tourism and Heimat national memory. The postcard is one of the things in life one takes for granted; but, in fact, the invention of the postcard reflected a distinctly modern form of communication. The first postcard was issued on 1 October 1869 by the Austrian Post Office. Germany followed suit on 1 October 1870 and 45,000 postcards were sold on the first day. During the 1870s most of the European and North American countries joined Austria and Germany.[47] In a world moving increasingly faster, the form of a letter became inappropriate to communicate short messages because of the elaborate etiquette connected with it, while the postcard called for short, informal, and direct messages. By eliminating the envelope, the postcard also eliminated the veil of secrecy, privacy, and personal property associated with letters. It is not surprising, then, that some members of the upper classes saw the postcard as degrading because it was a popular and democratic mode of communication.[48] The image on the postcard popularized whatever it depicted. Cheap, small, and produced for mass consumption, the postcard contradicted snobbishness and elitism; the iconography of the postcard broke with high artistic culture by displaying uncomplicated graphics, marvelous colors, and everyday subjects by artists who until then were slighted by the official art world. The democratic social function of the postcard was not, of course, equivalent to liberal and humanist world views, but rather to a form of communication independent from the domain of the privileged, accessible to all. The ideas which the images diffused represented society's rich mosaic of beliefs, values, and identities: Jewish and Christian holidays, socialist and nationalist ideas, frivolous topics such as the circus and critical topics such as World War I. As a form of social communication, the postcard vulgarized and divulged ideas through images.

The invention of the postcard was linked to the change in European travel habits. Mark Twain, an avid traveler who visited imperial Germany, wittingly observed that "Seventy or eighty years ago Napoleon was the only man in Europe who could really be called a traveler . . . but now everybody goes everywhere."[49] People went places and sent postcards. The *Daily Mail* ironically commented about the impact of picture postcards on Germans when on holiday: "The picture postcard is one of the vital elements in German life. . . . the object of the German's travels is not so much enjoying himself in a place as enjoying saying he has been there—adding it to his repertory. . . . Highland or low, the whole nation plays with the picture postcard as one German. It is the exact summery of the German holiday."[50] This behavior, one must add, was not peculiarly German. It seems that little has changed since the turn of the century: the traveler's maxim remains, I sent a postcard, therefore I traveled. And in a slightly different rendition, If it is Tuesday, it must be Munich.

The postcard made distant places seem closer by putting the world at everybody's fingertips. The invention of the postcard made possible the expansion of knowledge of close and faraway lands. By receiving picture postcards, one was familiarized with places one had never visited. The postcard and the development of European travel at the turn of the century made it possible to feel at home in heretofore unknown territories. Was this not also the function and mode of operation of the Heimat idea that made Württembergers feel at home everywhere in Germany? The social functions of the postcard—communication, popularization, democratization—agreed with those of the Heimat idea.[51] Heimatlers mobilized the postcard in the services of the Heimat idea— both artifacts originating, developing, and reaching their peak between the 1880s and 1918—by displaying Heimat themes such as *Tracht* and Heimat museums,[52] and above all typical Heimat images. The postcards thus put the national Heimat, nay a thousand German Heimats, at Germans' fingertips.

Before 1914, the bond between tourism and postcards produced one of the most successful picture postcard series, the "*Gruss aus* . . ." (Greetings from . . .) series.[53] The *Gruss aus* displayed places and cities. (Sometimes it displayed a variety of events and entertainment as, for example, Greetings from the Circus.) Around 1900 the *Gruss aus* postcards were available as tourist attractions around the world. In Germany, the period between the mid-1880s and mid-1890s saw the transformation of the single-color postcard into cards in splendid colors produced by chromolithography. These cards showed, most often, a general view of the locality, and often included several distinguishing elements of the place such as the *Tracht*, the church, and the main street.[54]

The *Gruss aus* postcards were published in German localities as self-promoting images that represented the community, often initiated by publishing houses, tourist associations, or the local authorities for purposes of profit and to promote tourism. The bourgeoisie gave its locality in the *Gruss aus* postcards the classic Heimat image, the cityscape. The Heimat image of Steinheim from the *Heimatgruss* newspapers (fig. 5) is remarkably similar to the *Gruss aus* postcards from Altheim (fig. 22; in this case the image looks indeed identical) and Nagold (fig. 24); the form and iconography of *A Heimat Image* (fig. 7) are familiar from *Gruss aus Herrenberg* (fig. 23). The *Gruss aus* postcards represented images of localities of different size, climate, landscape, architecture, and urban topography. But what makes these images so interesting is the preservation of the Heimat form and iconography. Figures 22–28 show typical postcards from the turn of the century of seven localities in Württemberg, ordered according to their size. In examining this *Gruss aus* picture postcard series, from small Altheim to the capital Stuttgart, we observe how the clean cityscape image dissolved the differences among the localities. Can one tell Stuttgart, 253,100 inhabitants in 1905 (fig. 28), from Waiblingen, which had only 5,997 inhabitants (fig. 25)? The pictures of the small communities, such as Altheim and Nagold, accorded more or less with reality and reflected their size and number of inhabitants. But the discrepancy between the image and the reality grew in proportion to the size of the locality. Heilbronn was depicted in figure 27 as a peaceful and small community, almost bringing to mind a medieval town. To enhance the Heimat effect a second image was added to the postcard, an oak tree symbolizing origins, and within its roots a Heimat landscape. At the turn of the century, however, Heilbronn was far from being *this* kind of a community, but was instead a developing town with 40,000 inhabitants, factories, and social conflicts emanating from rapid industrialization. These relations between iconography and reality were true for all the *Gruss aus* images of localities larger than a small town (Göppingen and Stuttgart, for example, in figs. 26 and 28).

In fact, the *Gruss aus* Heimat image represented an idealized community regardless of the real size of the locality because it avoided displaying the social consequences of modernity in imperial Germany. Local Heimat images froze time by avoiding the description of the inhabitants and of social action, thus enabling every (at least bourgeois) citizen of Heilbronn to identify with its image. But national integration alone did not determine the *Gruss aus* image. The idealized image was also an intrinsic part of the development of tourism and the commercialization of memory. The *Gruss aus* series never showed the poverty-stricken working-class neighborhoods that sprung up around the cities and the inhuman conditions in the workplace. But this was, after all, expected: was not one of the principles of tourism to sell a world of marvels? Bourgeois tourists preferred visiting Heilbronn's Historical Museum in the old slaughterhouse, instead of the poor working-class neighborhoods at the city's outskirts.[55] A tacit agreement enveloped bourgeois producers and consumers of the local Heimat images: the former wished to represent the locality as a never-never land in order to attract tourists, enliven the economy, and develop the town; the tourists wished to avoid seeing the social consequences of capitalism and to remember instead the achievements of bourgeois culture: museums, recreation, and the like. Since the postcard was "the exact summary of the German holiday," could it represent something other than a beautiful picture with which to remember it? The bourgeoisie thus perpetuated the diffusion of Heimat images by producing *Gruss aus* images in its own locality and consuming as tourists the *Gruss aus* images of others.

The local Heimat image was an idealized community, yet it was neither a reactionary image nor was it completely devoid of the notion of historical time. The choice of the hometown as the human settlement to represent the German Heimat deserves an explanation. While it seemed reasonable that the hectic and bustling city could not symbolize a Heimat, it was significant that the village never dominated Heimat images either. Typically, although Schultze-Naumburg mentioned the village as "*heimatlich*," he showed a Heimat image of a hometown. If the Heimat image really wished to project a rural atmosphere it had to represent that which distinguished rural life from city life, namely agricultural activities and the cycle of the natural world such as the changing of seasons and climatic conditions. These elements, however, rarely appeared in Heimat images, and when they did (fig. 11), they never formulated an iconographic pattern. One reason was that the village did not encompass the complexity of modern life like the town because it did not associate the progress *and* the dislocation embedded in modernity. Had the Heimat idea been an outright concept of antimodernism, the iconography of the village could have been felicitous. The image of the town, however, was more appropriate to embrace the hope and the fear of modernity, standing midway between the village and the city, the past and the future.[56]

A cultural artifact of modernity, the Heimat image, while being abstract enough to allow every German to find his or her local Heimat and memories, was also a believable picture of Germany, as the depiction of landscape and industry showed. Bourgeois Heimatlers represented in Heimat images a landscape as an urban experience, attempting to merge nature and urban life, which increasingly separated in the nineteenth century, into one universe. What is remarkable in many Heimat images was the rejection of deindustrializing Germany. The symbols of modernity were frequently included in local Heimat images: big bridges in Heilbronn;[57] factory chimneys in local and national Heimat images (figs. 10, 19, 25, 26, 28);[58] and the train, usually a toylike display of the locomotive, wagons, and smoke (fig. 23). There was no direct opposition between the reality of the industrial nation and the image of it, but the Heimat image did embellish the nation by representing the vehicles of progress, such as a bridge, a train, and factories, while avoiding the negative consequences of modernity. The Heimat image thus displayed the nation as an idealized community, though within certain limits of reality and progress. It oversimplifies to think that Heimatlers were antimodern because they did not represent in Heimat images the appalling conditions of the lower classes, while ignoring the significant fact that Heimatlers did represent Germany as a rural *and* industrial community. Heimatlers were ambiguous about modernity; they embraced it, but with some reservations. This position, as I have argued, cannot be interpreted as antimodern. It is rather the hallmark of modernity.

We have previously seen that most of the associations and artists who produced the Heimat images were active and lived in cultural and political centers and had an upper-class bourgeois profile. The postcards changed this by enlarging the social production and diffusion of the Heimat image. While the Verein für ländliche Wohlfahrtspflege in Württemberg und Hohenzollern diffused Heimat images in small communities, these images were not an origination of the communities themselves. The postcard, on the other hand, like the Heimat museum, popularized the Heimat idea in small and peripheral localities, and was a representation of the small community and the nation produced by small-town bourgeoisie. The spread of the Heimat iconography accorded with other Heimat artifacts, such as books, museums, and associations, as a social mode of action of the German bourgeoisie.

Heimat images appeared in German society on posters and postcards in war and peace, cheap local newspapers, refined pictures, popular Heimat books, and other means; they were displayed in public spaces like streets, train stations, restaurants, and classrooms and privately at home when one received a postcard or read a newspaper. Unlike representations of the nation such as a national holiday, like Sedan Day, the Heimat idea did not need a special time, space, or event to be called to mind; one could simply send a postcard. The humble sources of Heimat iconography and the pedestrian occasions in which it appeared exemplified that the Heimat image brought the nation to mind anytime and anywhere.

German society before and during World War I was not, of course, a small community at peace with nature and itself, but a burgeoning industrial state rife with social and political tensions. In the historical literature, the hometown and the intimate qualities of the Heimat idea have been viewed as a flight from modern reality. What kind of a symbolic representation of the nation was it, it has often been asked, when no similarity existed between the signified and the signifier? But this position seems to misunderstand the role of the Heimat idea in German society. It is important to keep in mind the motivations of bourgeois Heimatlers behind the construction of the Heimat idea. The Heimat image did not represent the offensive characteristics of modernity. But why should it, actually? Heimatlers did not set out to write a report on the social conditions of the German lower classes in the wake of industrialization but to construct a national identity, a symbolic common denominator. They never intended the Heimat idea to reflect reality precisely or to provide a completely accurate portrait of German society. Identities are not suppose to do this. The Heimat idea functioned successfully as an integrative symbol because it was an ideal that kept reality at a safe distance, giving a respite from everyday social and political conflicts. If nations were made aware of their inner conflicts and differences all day long, they would never hold together. The Heimat idea provided a never-never land, where bourgeois Germans found a second Germany, impervious to social and political conflicts, one of harmonious relationships, to compensate for the deficiencies of the first, and real, Germany.

The emphasis on indeterminate nature, people, and locality in the poems and images led to the representation of the nation as a generic Heimat, which was crucial to the reception of Heimat in German society as an imagined national community that embraced the individual Heimats. To fit every Heimat in Germany, the German Heimat had to fit no specific one. To enable every German to imagine his or her own individual Heimat, the German Heimat had to fit any place and no place. A clearly defined national Heimat would have been unable to convey the meaning of unity *and* diversity, to harmonize the single nation with the multitude of local and regional identities. Heimat iconography dissolved the local, regional, and national spaces and became an interchangeable representation of these communities. Through it Germans concretized the impersonal regional and national territories represented as local communities; the image thus transformed localness into a concept of nationhood.

The attributes of the national Heimat raise the question, Was there a difference between Heimat, on the one hand, and *Vaterland* and *Nation*, on the other? A comprehensive analysis cannot be offered here, but some reflections, by way of informed hypothesis, may be illuminating. These three words described the German people and the territory of Germany, but their meanings were not identical. While fatherland and nation represented Germany as the one and only, Heimat represented Germany as the one and the many. Heimat's meaning was interchangeable between local, regional, and national levels. Fatherland and nation, although ambiguous as well, did not seem to have shared Heimat's depth of meaning. They did not seem to have matched the rich imagery of the Heimat idea. Fatherland and nation, which brought to mind Germany's borders, territorial integrity, and political or military system, represented Germany as something fixed. Heimat, which brought to mind history, traditions, and landscapes, was, in contrast, infinitely adaptable. Arguably, Heimat was easier to understand and to identify with than fatherland and nation. As Ernst Jünger wrote in "The Battle as Inner Experience," an essay about his participation in World War I, "State and nation are unclear concepts, but what Heimat means, this you know. Heimat, it is a feeling."[59]

The areas where Heimat, on the one hand, and fatherland and nation, on the other, played out their differences most clearly were war and gender. Heimat was a representation of the nation informed by what contemporaries regarded as feminine sensibilities. Fatherland and nation, in contrast, conveyed masculine qualities, such as courage, combativeness, and competitiveness. Fatherland and nation, therefore, could go to war, while Heimat could never do that. One could say "the fatherland (or the nation) declared war on France," but to say "the Heimat declared war on France" made no sense. Similar to values like family and community, Heimat was something one fought for, never something that participated in battle.[60] The images demonstrated this clearly by placing war outside the Heimat; the sword (figs. 9 and 12) and the person (fig. 10) protect the Heimat, but they are not part of it. Heimat was the antithesis of war and to all that war represents: havoc, suffering, disorientation. At the same time, war underlined the identity between Heimat and women: both stayed away from battle, in the rear—subjects of dreams and fantasies, personifying the home to which men yearned to return and the just cause for which men fought. Heimat and fatherland were as incongruous as Heimat and war, like women and war.

These contradictory representations of the nation were nevertheless complementary. Nations, like people, have more than one face. Heimat and fatherland described Germany at different conditions and situations. Fatherland presented it at war, as an empire, as an energetic and expanding society, whereas Heimat presented it as a peaceful community.[61]

THE NATION AS A MENTAL PROPERTY

"Is it possible that all these people know, with perfect accuracy, a past that never existed?" asks Rainer Maria Rilke's hero, Malte Laurids Brigge.[62] Every nation, and Germany between 1871 and 1918 was no exception, sets up imaginary pasts. Societies invent pasts continuously, which brings us back to the questions posed at the outset of this book: Why is it that some pasts triumph while others fail? Why do people prefer one invented past over another?

One factor in the success of the Heimat idea and the failure of Sedan Day concerns the profundity of representation. Sedan Day was too close to the present and was dependent on temporary and fleeting political events and states of mind. The Heimat idea, in contrast, extricated the German Empire from the here and now and projected it into the immemorial past. Such an idea of Germanness was applicable, in theory, at least, to all Germans at all times. It emphasized eternal themes with which to understand national history, namely local and everyday life. And it was not so much about specific events, as about the immutable in the fluctuations of German history. Sedan Day associated the unification in 1871, a specific temporal and spatial event; Heimat, on the other hand, associated roots and traditions.

Moreover, a local-national memory was more effective when it appeared beyond social and political conflicts. While every collective memory is political, the appearance of being above ordinary and daily conflicts renders it authentic, perhaps even mystical. The holiday and the Heimat idea were both vehicles used by the bourgeoisie to appropriate the nation. But Sedan Day failed because it was too closely and explicitly identified with a specific political worldview, with transitory political conflicts and alliances, with soon-to-be-forgotten political issues. The political image of Sedan Day divided the Germans within the nation into the liberals opposite the Catholics, democrats, socialists, and royal particularists, while the image of the Heimat idea set the Germans apart from other nations. It represented, as we have said, a conflict-free, never-never land.

Sedan Day, as the creation of the liberal notables, was also identified with snobbery and elitism. The notables never intended to obtain popular support for the holiday, which remained socially isolated. The Heimat idea, in contrast, not only associated German roots in the imagination, but actually stemmed from *l'Allemagne profonde*, from hundreds of provincial localities where Heimatlers founded a museum, set up an association, and wrote a Heimat book. Any successful national identity in the modern era not only must be received by the populace, but also must be perceived as emanating from and representing the populace.

The different fate of the Heimat idea and Sedan Day is particularly interesting because both had been originated and carried by the German bourgeoisie. Although we cannot assume a straightforward agreement between a social class (bourgeoisie) and a political idea (liberalism), this global view of the local-national memory shaping is based on the bond in German society between liberal worldview and bourgeois life-styles.[63] When we look at the period of imperial Germany as a whole, the presence of the bourgeoisie in the field of local-national memory shaping is palpable. It appeared inventive and resourceful, even in Sedan Day when it failed. This picture does not support the until recently common view in German historiography of the bourgeoisie as out of touch with reality and duped by the authoritarian state. But it is significant to emphasize the inverted relationships between bourgeois political visibility and symbolic success. In Württemberg until 1895 the liberals enjoyed political victories. The holiday reflected a liberal sociopolitical mode of action based on a position of social distinction, political influence, and ideological support for the 1871 solution for the German Question. But the liberals' political success and ideological advantage as champions of the unification was the seed of their failure, for what undid Sedan Day was the partisan political use of the holiday and the policy of exclusion. In contrast, in the volatile and unstable political universe of Wilhelmine Germany, the bourgeoisie did not enjoy political influence and unity in the same way the liberals did with the Deutsche Partei in Württemberg until 1895. As a result, the bourgeoisie's use of the Heimat idea as a symbolic representation of power to appropriate the nation was less evident. Through the Heimat idea it claimed hegemony in German society in ways that, compared to Sedan Day, were more subtle and indirect. The Heimat idea was not connected to one political party in the same way Sedan Day was; it was open to appropriations by various political movements. Its political message was implicit and ambiguous. Thus, the attempt of the bourgeoisie to lay claim to speak for the nation was more successful because its partisan political interests were less evident. Some years ago David Blackbourn argued in a seminal essay about the role of the bourgeoisie in imperial Germany that the bourgeoisie supplanted weakness in the political field by exerting its "discreet charm" in civil society and culture as the most effective way to claim hegemony.[64] The findings of this study support Blackbourn's argument from a perspective he did not discuss: the symbolism of power and the construction of a local-national representation.

Still, there was one important symbolic common ground between the representations of the nation in Sedan Day and the Heimat idea, namely the importance of the local community. The celebrants of Sedan Day's festival based the collective image of the nation on the local community, although the specific conditions in Württemberg after 1871 made this symbol ineffective. The idea of the local community as the cradle of the nation was not invented in the Heimat idea, but was, from 1871, a core metaphor with which Germans imagined the nation.

Yet it was the Heimat idea that brought this imagination to fruition. Two images from World War I epitomized the representation of the nation as a Heimat. One image perfectly displays the constituents of the Heimat iconography, the second its ultimate abstractness. Figure 30, entitled "Do You Want This? Defend Your Land," is a poster featuring the hometown, the church tower, the train, the factory chimneys, and the merge of landscape and industry. In short, the Heimat local image of Germany. Figure 29, *"Barbarenland"* (Barbarians' country), with double quotation marks denoting irony and pain, was an iconographic answer to the Allies' propaganda describing the Germans as the modern Huns. The picture appeared in the journal of the Deutscher Bund Heimatschutz in the campaign to support German prisoners of war: "Send . . . [our prisoners] *characteristic images of our Heimat.*"[65] The development of the Heimat iconography between 1871 and 1918 reflected the capacity of Germans to think the nation, to grasp its abstract image. Is this not an answer to the question posed at the outset of this study: what was the image with which Germans imagined the nation?

Heimat iconography takes us beyond the banal reiteration of the by-now classic definition of the nation as an imagined community by telling us what was the image of people's imagination of the nation. Benedict Anderson has observed that national communities should be distinguished "by the style in which they are imagined," but he has not identified these styles.[66] Heimat was one such important style, showing Germans' imagination of the nation as a local metaphor.

My main argument has been that Germans imagined nationhood as a form of localness. The Heimat idea was not simply an aggregation of discrete Heimats, but became a representation of the nation itself. This argument differs from Celia Applegate's view of the function of the Heimat idea in German society as a mediator between local and national identity. Applegate has argued that the Heimat "movement was not a national phenomenon at all, but a regional, even a local one."[67] But in the historical and national self-conscious era of the German Empire there was another context to Heimat activities, namely the nationwide symbolic construction of the Heimat idea as a representation of the nation. Through a process of stereotyping German regions and the Germans themselves, the Heimat idea became synonymous with the German nation. This process, I believe, gave the Heimat idea its main historical meaning in this period.

Originating from modernity, the Heimat idea changed concepts of space, time, and kin, which brings us back to the question posed at the outset of this study: how did Germans internalize the nation? Applegate has argued that "The evolution of Heimat as a concept followed the shifting hierarchies of belonging, from hometown to territorial state to nation."[68] The process of internalizing the nation was, as I have attempted to show, more spasmodic and unmethodical than the linear progression, from the small to the big, from the locality to the nation, from the tangible to the abstract, that is implicit in Applegate's argument. In these pages we have seen the construction in a few years of a new idea of Germanness that has been generally regarded as originating at a far earlier date. We have seen the one score years before the Great

War as determinant in the formation of German local-national memory. And we have seen that the articulation of the nation in images, organizations, and the topics of history, nature, and folklore emerged through a *reciprocal* and *simultaneous* changing of perceptions about abstract national life and an immediate local one, as Heimat became a symbolic depiction of the locality, the territorial state, and the nation at one and the same time.

Popular wisdom has perceived Heimat as an idea representing a fixed place, one place, connected to a limited social and territorial space. Heimat represented also this, but its significance between 1871 and 1918 depended on being anything but fixed: it was a flexible and ambiguous concept that depicted different places at the same time. The potency of Heimat as a national symbol lay in its capacity to depict different levels of one's existence, thus allowing the placement of the individual and locality within the context of greater communities, larger territories, and bigger developments—within the context, in other words, of the projects of nationhood and modernity. Ironically, if Heimat succeeded in symbolizing an intimate and closely knit community, it was only because it represented at the same time large territories and impersonal social relations. Had Heimat symbolized only the local place, it would have disconnected the locality from the larger processes around it. Heimat gave meaning to local places not because it represented them, but because it represented them *as part* of the world around—of the nation, of modernity—and this was possible only by constructing an interchangeable image of local and national German communities.

Figure 3. Walter Strich-Chapell, *Tübingen*, 1903, chromolithography. This view of Tübingen depicting local houses, church tower, cityscape, and the surrounding landscape was hailed as a typical image of any Swabian town.

Figure 4. The first illustration in Paul Schultze-Naumburg, *Die Entstellung unseres Landes*, 2d ed. (Munich, 1907), 8, photograph. This townscape had neither a name nor political or geographical attributes. It became a stereotypical Heimat representation of any German community.

Figure 5. Townscape in *Heimatgruss von Steinheim a.A., Sontheim im St. Küpfendorf, Gnannenweiler u. Neuselhalden*, 1909. (Courtesy of the Württembergische Landesbibliothek Stuttgart)

Figure 6. View of Ötlingen-Lindorf, *Heimatgrüsse aus Ötlingen-Lindorf*, 1910. These townscapes represented the individual community by using the Heimat iconographic inventory: local houses, church tower, cityscape, and the surrounding landscape. The stereotypical Heimat representation replaced the distinctive silhouette of each community. (Courtesy of the Württembergische Landesbibliothek Stuttgart)

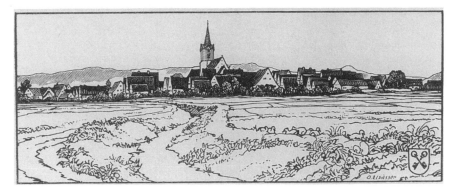

Figure 7. O. Elsässer, *Ein Heimatbild* (A Heimat image),
in *Heimatklänge aus der Gemeinde Bempflingen und Kleinbettlingen*
(March 1913): 3. A representation of the generic local German Heimat.

Figure 8. Walter Strich-Chapell, *Württembergischer Bund für Heimatschutz*, 1909, poster. A generic view visualizes here the imagined regionscape of Württemberg. (Courtesy of the Graphische Sammlung der Staatsgalerie Stuttgart)

The Nation in the Mind   193

Figure 9. Hugo Frank, *Leiht euer Geld für der Heimat Schutz und Wehr!*
(Loan your money for the protection and defense of the Heimat!), 1914–18,
poster. *Das Plakat* 9 (September–November 1918): 248. The Heimatization of
Germany: the German Heimat as an ensemble of small hometowns in
harmonious relationship with nature. The national Heimat became a rallying
collective image to mobilize the financial and emotional resources of Germans
in World War I. (Courtesy of the Staatliche Museen zu Berlin,
Preußischer Kulturbesitz Kunstbibliothek)

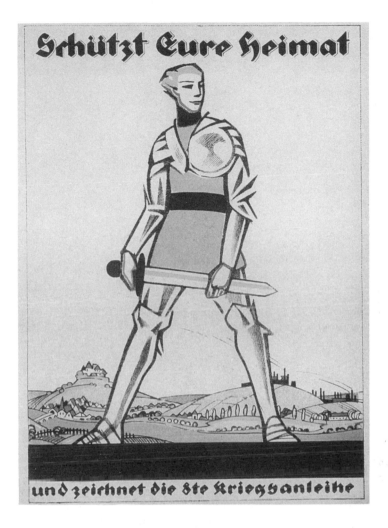

Figure 10. Elisabeth von Sydow, *Schützt eure Heimat* (Protect your Heimat),
1914–18, poster. *Das Plakat* 10 (March 1919): table 29. The Heimatization of
Germany: the Heimat image commingled features of modernity, such as the
factories on the right, and of the German past, such as the knight defending the
Heimat. Some Germans may have associated the knight with the adolescent
Siegfried of Wagner's opera. By dissolving the distinction between past and
present, the Heimat image represented the nation as immemorial. (Courtesy of
the Staatliche Museen zu Berlin, Preußischer Kulturbesitz Kunstbibliothek)

The Nation in the Mind

Figure 11. Wilhelm Schulz, *Den Feinden zum Trutz/der Heimat zum Schutz*
(Defying the enemy, protecting the Heimat), 1914–18, poster. *Das Plakat* 10
(January 1919): table 23. The Heimatization of Germany: the nation imagined as
a local, village community. The rustic symbols that are so prominent here were,
however, rarely used in Heimat iconography to represent the nation.

Figure 12. Euringer, *Kriegsanleihe* (War loan), 1914–18, poster. *Das Plakat* 9
(January 1918): table 27. The Heimatization of Germany: the Heimat image
represented interchangeably the local, regional, and national territory. (Courtesy
of the Staatliche Museen zu Berlin, Preußischer Kulturbesitz Kunstbibliothek)

The Nation in the Mind   197

Figure 13. Lucian Bernhard, *Zeichnet die Neunte! Es geht um Alles was wir lieben*
(Subscribe to the ninth! It concerns everything we love), 1914–18, poster. *Das
Plakat* 10 (January 1919): table 17. The representation of Germany as mother and
child was often associated with Heimat iconography. (Courtesy of the Staatliche
Museen zu Berlin, Preußischer Kulturbesitz Kunstbibliothek)

Figure 14. Fritz Boehle, *In Deo Gratia* (Thanks be to God), 1915, poster.
By World War I the representation of the nation as Heimat was common
in German society. Heimat iconography appeared in images that did not
bear the title "Heimat," but that represented Germanness. Here the knight
defends Germany, represented as a Heimat under the horse's belly.
(Courtesy of the Trustees of the Imperial War Museum, London)

Figure 15. Karl Sigrist, *In der Heimat stark sein* (To be strong in the Heimat), 1917, poster. *Das Plakat* 9 (January 1918): table 29. As Heimat iconography became a collective notion in German society, minimal features sufficed to arouse the emotions and identification associated with the Heimat idea. Sigrist reduced Heimat iconography to its essential elements: an oak tree, a symbol of roots and stability, robustly planted on the ground. (Courtesy of the Graphische Sammlung der Staatsgalerie Stuttgart)

Figure 16. Karl Sigrist, *Zeichnet Kriegsanleihe* (Subscribe to the war loans),
1918, poster. This poster took the Heimatization of Germany even further:
an eagle and a dove flying above Germany represented as landscape only.
(Courtesy of the Staatliche Museen zu Berlin,
Preußischer Kulturbesitz Kunstbibliothek)

Figure 17. Eberhard Emminger, *Ansicht von Gmünd aus Nordosten*
(View of Gmünd from the northeast), ca. 1850, engraving. The cityscape image,
veduta, was an iconographic precursor of the Heimat image.
(Courtesy of the Museum für Natur und Stadtkultur, Schwäbisch Gmünd)

Facing page: These two images show the extent to which Heimat images in
imperial Germany owed a debt to old cityscape iconography. Only the drawing
style and the three factory chimneys distinguished the two images; the town's
fundamental social and economic transformation during the eighty-one years
was not expressed. Used by Heimatlers, the cityscape iconography tended to
obscure the distinction between past and present. (Courtesy of the
Württembergische Landesbibliothek Stuttgart)

A NATION OF HEIMATS

Figure 18. The frontispiece of *Beschreibung des Oberamtes Ehingen*
(Stuttgart, 1826), engraving.

Figure 19. *Ehingen* in *Das Königreich Württemberg. Eine Beschreibung nach
Kreisen, Oberämter und Gemeinden*, ed. Königlisches Statistisches Landesamt,
vol. 4 (Stuttgart, 1907), 102.

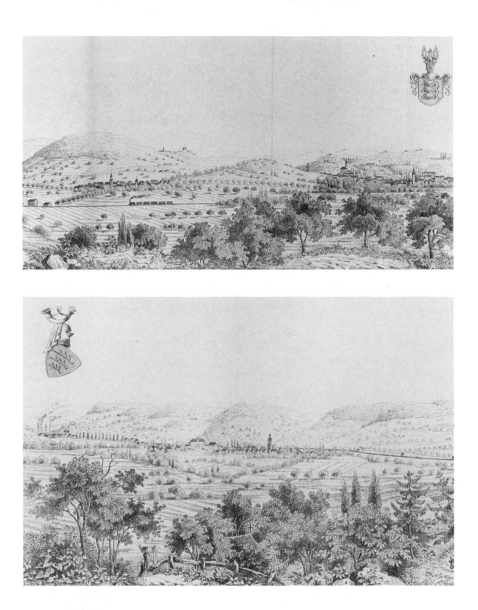

Figures 20–21. Map of Württemberg, details, in Julius Bernhard,
*Reisehandbuch durch Württemberg und die angrenzenden Länderstriche der
Nachbarstaaten. Historisch, pittoresk, statistisch-topographisch und industriell*,
2d ed. (Stuttgart, 1864). Cityscape and landscape iconography in Germany
symbolized emotional links and impersonal territories before 1871. The images
here represented Württemberg as a regionscape of small hometowns surrounded
by landscape. Heimatlers took this kind of image after 1871 and applied its
symbolic heritage to the nation as a whole. (Courtesy of the
Württembergische Landesbibliothek Stuttgart)

Figure 22. *Gruss aus Altheim* (Greetings from Altheim), postcard, 1906. The *Gruss aus* tourist postcards, which were extremely popular in Germany around 1900, used the classic Heimat image, the cityscape. Its effect was to dissolve the differences among the localities. It created an idealized German community, though often within the limits of reality: witness the factory chimneys. (Courtesy of the Geiger Verlag, Horb a.N.)

Figure 23. *Herrenberg*, after 1899, postcard. (Courtesy of the Haus der Geschichte Baden-Württemberg, Sammlung Metz)

The Nation in the Mind

Figure 24. *Gruss vom Nagold. Gauturnfest und Fahnenweihe* (Greetings from Nagold. District Gymnastic Celebration and Inauguration of the Flag), 1905, postcard. (Courtesy of the Geiger Verlag, Horb a.N.)

Figure 25. *Gruss aus Waiblingen* (Greetings from Waiblingen), 1906, postcard.

Figure 26. *Gruss aus Göppingen* (Greetings from Göppingen), turn of the century, postcard. Göppingen as the commingling of landscape and industry.

Figure 27. Karl Schilling, *Gruss vom 29ten Allgem. Liederfest des Schwäb. Sängerbundes, Heilbronn 1910* (Greetings from the 29th General Choral Festival of the Swabian League for Singers, Heilbronn 1910), postcard. Heilbronn as a peaceful community, bringing to mind a medieval town.

The Nation in the Mind 207

Ansichtskarten mit goldgeprägtem Sonnenauf- oder -untergang waren um die Jahrhundertwende außerordentlich beliebt, sie sind heute ausgesprochene Raritäten. Verhältnismäßig kleine Auflagen bedingen die Seltenheit dieser Panoramakarte mit einer Zeichnung Stuttgarts von Südost.

Figure 28. *Gruss aus Stuttgart* (Greetings from Stuttgart), turn of the century, postcard. Although Stuttgart had 253,100 inhabitants at the beginning of the 1900s, the city's representation here is not different from that of Waiblingen (fig. 25), which had only 5,997 inhabitants.

Figure 29. *"Barbarenland"* (Barbarians' country), 1914–15, engraving. *Heimatschutz*, ed. Deutscher Bund Heimatschutz, 10, no. 1 (1915): 18. The image was an iconographic answer to the Allies propaganda in World War I describing the Germans as the modern Huns. The abstractness of this Heimat image reflected the capacity of Germans to conceive of the nation. (Courtesy of the Württembergische Landesbibliothek Stuttgart)

A NATION OF HEIMATS

Figure 30. *Wollt ihr dieses? . . . Schützt Euer Land* (Do you want this? . . . Defend your land), 1914–18, poster. This image beautifully displays the constituents of the Heimat iconography: the hometown, the church tower, the train, the factory chimneys, and the merge of landscape and industry.

Heimat, Germany, and Europe

e end, then, where we began: with nationhood as a concept that transforms people's notions of kin, history, and space. Was the Heimat idea between 1871 and 1918 sui generis in Europe, thus supporting the argument about Germany's special historical path (*Sonderweg*)? I would like to reflect, by way of conclusion, about the possible implications of the Heimat idea to this perennial question of German historiography. It appears that while the constituents of the Heimat idea, such as the quest for origins and the sensitivity to the environment, were common in Europe their combination was specifically German.

Recent research on the construction of national identities shows that the concerns, the issues, and the symbolic depictions of Heimat were familiar phenomena throughout Europe in the age of "mass-producing traditions."[1] National individuality was articulated in a European symbolic language of similitudes. Among these similitudes were the mixture of pride stemming from tradition and from innovation in the representation of the nation, the mixed reactions to modernity as agent of progress and producer of anxiety and nostalgia, and the emphasis of national uniqueness. Heimat looked back at the past as a source of authority to define the identities of Württemberg and Germany. In Europe, this was the sign of the times: the French saw themselves as direct descendants of the Gauls, Italians of the ancient Romans. As for England: "What is clear is that during 1880–1920 the conviction that English culture was to be found in the past was stabilized."[2] The construction of an imagined national community by searching for national origins was not peculiar to Germany.

The related representation of women and nationhood was a familiar constituent of national identity, too. The association of women with coziness and home was prevalent at that period in Europe and North America.[3] Similar to the Heimat idea in Germany, also in England nation, home, and woman were related metaphors.[4] And by linking Heimat and women and by opposing them to war, the Heimat idea voiced a common perception among men, women, and feminists in Germany and Europe, namely that women were inherently inclined to peaceful behavior and were intrinsically against war.[5]

The Heimat movement's treatment of nature, which has often been interpreted as a proof of Germans' attachment to romanticism and antimodernism, should in fact be viewed within the context of modern European attitudes toward the environment. In 1912 Stuttgart hosted the Second International Congress for Nature Conservation (Zweiter Internationaler Kongress für Heimatschutz) after the first congress was held in Paris in 1909 and called Premier Congrès International pour la Protection des Paysages.[6]

In Germany, the congress was organized by the Deutscher Bund Heimatschutz, in France by the Société pour la protection des paysages de France. In its 1904 manifesto, in fact, the Deutscher Bund Heimatschutz justified its foundation by pointing to the creation a few years before of similar associations in England and France.[7] Different words—"Heimatschutz" and "protection des paysages"—conveyed closely related meanings: nature conservation. Awareness of the devastation of nature resulting from new technologies was widespread in Europe. Not beyond every Heimatschutzer lurked the specter of an antimodern and romantic German, although beyond modern technology lurked the danger of the destruction of nature. The Heimat idea was part of a European response to the environmental challenge posed by modernity.

Moreover, Heimat iconography and its vehicles, the postcard and the poster, appeared so European as to undermine the German artistic contributions. The *Gruss aus* postcards were a worldwide phenomenon, and similar Heimat images appeared as representations of cities and towns in many countries. The cityscape was a common European style and the drawing technique of Heimat images was used all over the continent.[8] Furthermore, during World War I, patriotic posters in several belligerent countries presented the nation as a combination of landscape and human settlement. An unknown British artist painted a poster entitled "Your Country's Call. Isn't This Worth Fighting For? Enlist Now," which displays a Scottish soldier pointing to an appealing rural scene: thatched cottages, colorful gardens, and hedgerows, the homeland threatened by the enemy.[9]

And yet the Heimat idea was also unlike other national representations of the period. While the constituents of the Heimat idea were common in European culture, their combination made Heimat special. The Heimat idea was more than the sum of its parts: its singularity in European culture was the merging of local, regional, and national identities in one representation of the nation. While the connection between localness and nationhood has been common in national symbolism, Germans appeared to set themselves apart by finding in these relations an essence of German national identity. The Heimat iconography representing the nation as a local metaphor was not emulated by other Europeans. Sporadically, British, French, and Italian posters represented the nation during World War I as a Heimat image, but they were few and far between, never making an iconographic pattern. The British poster just mentioned, "Your Country's Call. Isn't This Worth Fighting For? Enlist Now," was an exception that proved the rule.[10] The nation was evoked by all in World War I, often symbolized as a lion in Britain and a women in France. Only in Germany, it appears, an iconography of landscape and cityscape as a representation of the nation became a common symbolic capital.[11]

As a symbolic representation of the nation, the Heimat idea reformulated the meaning of its European constitutive elements. Take, for example, the interplay between "paysage" and "Heimat": while demonstrating a common denominator between Heimatlers and Europeans, it also emphasized differences. "Paysage" in German is translated as "Landschaft," not as "Heimat"; the use of the word "Heimat" in this case shows that the preservation of nature was only one element of the Heimat agenda, and in fact the significance of the Deutscher Bund Heimatschutz for German identity went beyond nature conservation. Moreover, the Heimat idea gave significant symbolic meaning to its constituent parts, which independently were often less important. The *Gruss aus* postcards, for instance, received a special meaning in Germany because of their association with the Heimat idea, symbolizing not simply a locality, as in other countries, but a locality as part of the nation.

The Heimat idea was unique, in the same way that every historical event, process, or production is, but within the ordinary European development of constructing national identities between 1871 and 1918. Nothing in its development before 1918 predetermined the course of German history after 1933. The question to ask about German history as a *Sonderweg* has never been whether a certain political, social, or cultural phenomenon was peculiar, for every country has peculiarities, but whether the development of German history as a whole was inherently different from that of other European histories. The development of Germany during the Second Empire corresponded to European development in areas that historians have been quick to interpret as German peculiarities—attitudes toward nature, modernity, and nationhood. The Heimat idea as a German local-national memory is an important indication that German history of this period corresponded to the general European political, social, and cultural development.

The debate on the peculiarities of German history continues, as does the belief of nations in the peculiarity of each nation's character. In that respect, the Heimat idea and the *Sonderweg* approach have something in common, namely the idea of German peculiarity. Heimat was invented between 1871 and 1918 as the essence of German authentic national character; the *Sonderweg* thesis has been, in a sense, a historiographical manifestation of the same idea.

I have attempted in this study to explore nationhood's depth of meaning without preconceived reproach. Some readers, I am certain, would object to this approach on the grounds that men and women have in the past two hundred years perpetrated unspeakable acts of terror in the name of nationalism. I can understand this view, though I do not share it; this evaluation of nationalism is true, but it is only a partial truth. At the beginning of this study I observed that we should think of nationalism as a mode of religion, not as a political ideology such as fascism and liberalism. Let me use again the analogy between religion and nationalism. Throughout history people used religion to justify the worst kind of policies. Are we, then, to conclude that because of the Saint Bartholomew's Day Massacre, the Thirty Years' War, anti-Semitism, and other forms of bigotry religious beliefs are always superficial and perhaps even murderous? Obviously, this view is unsuitable to capture the complex and profound role religion plays in human society. And it is worthwhile reflecting that, as our century comes to a close, nationalism and religion are the two worldviews capable of mobilizing people worldwide, not communism, liberalism, or fascism. One of the most remarkable phenomena in the study of nationalism is the discrepancy between most people's heartfelt belief in their homeland and the belittlement of nationalism's depth of meaning by some scholars and laypersons. Even scholars who have taken nationalism seriously have too often explained it by concentrating on one variable such as ethnicity or economic progress. For most if not all people, however, nationhood includes the whole of life, and what makes the Heimat idea so interesting is that it reveals the profundity of the national idea.

Of course, speaking of German nationhood in terms like "depth of meaning" immediately recalls another period, raising perturbed thoughts; and it should. Some readers would also object, I am even more certain, to the portrayal in this book of German nationhood without a trace of the Nazis, racism, and the *Volk* ideology. I can understand the political, cultural, and especially moral grounds for this view, but as a historian I cannot accept the underlying assumptions behind it. We should not comprehend the nationhood of imperial Germany as an antechamber to the one of 1933. German nationhood before 1933 had various political, cultural, and ideological applications, representations, and meanings. It was relevant for Germans in more than one way. Marc Bloch, who discussed in his book *The Historian's Craft* "The Idol of Origins," conveys my view faithfully: "In any study, seeking the origins of a human activity, there lurks the same danger of confusing ancestry with explanation."[12]

Thinking about the depth of meaning of nationhood brings to my mind two different opinions about the sense of national belonging. Arthur Schopenhauer condemned nations sarcastically and without a bit of fondness when he said: "Each nation makes fun of the others, and all of them are right."[13] Johan Huizinga, in contrast, had a more profound view than Schopenhauer. He took cognizance of the conflict between nations but at the same time appreciated what the national idea represents for most people:[14] "Our awareness of our own country flourishes in the sphere of recollections of childhood and nostalgia for the past. It arouses the scent of pine trees and plowed fields and sandy beaches. . . . Every cultured and right-minded person has a particular affection for a few other nations alongside his own. . . . Summon up an image of such a nation, and enjoy it. . . . You perceive the beauty of its art . . . you experience the perturbation of its history, you see the enchanting panoramas of its landscape . . . you smell the scent of its wines . . . you feel all that together, stamped with the ineradicable mark of that one specific nationality that is not yours. All of this is alien to you—and tremendously precious as a wealth and luxury in your life. Then why controversy, why envy?"

In spite of the seeming difference between Schopenhauer's condemnation of nationalism and Huizinga's affection for it, nationalism should be seen as a combination of both attitudes. One should remember that every nationalism, one's own included, is historical, and as such ephemeral, here today, gone tomorrow (though tomorrow may be in two hundred years); it is not eternal, superior, and unique in ways that legitimize terrorizing other peoples. A nation is right to make fun of others' authenticity, but it has to know how to make fun of itself, too; it is the seriousness with which nationalists take themselves that is so perilous. And yet, as Huizinga described so well, our nations are also locations for such fond memories, with unmistakably unique smells, sights, lights, and tastes, a place we call home. It seems a daunting task to bring these tendencies to coexist in peace. And in the end it is everybody's responsibility to make it happen.

Notes

Beob.   *Der Beobachter*
HStA   Hauptstaatsarchiv Stuttgart
Sch.Kr.   *Schwäbische Kronik*
Tu.Ch.   *Tübinger Chronik*
WDS   Württembergische Drucksachen. The number refers to a box.

CHAPTER ONE

1. The two most influential studies have been Anderson, *Imagined Communities,* and Gellner, *Nations and Nationalism.*

2. Deutsch, *Nationalism and Social Communication.*

3. Smith, *Ethnic Origins of Nations;* Hobsbawm, "Introduction: Inventing Traditions" and "Mass-Producing Traditions."

4. Weber, *Peasants into Frenchmen.*

5. Hobsbawm, *The Age of Empire,* 148.

6. Anderson, *Imagined Communities,* 5. Ernst Kantorovitz argued as much in 1951 in a brilliant, though forgotten, article, "*Pro Patria Mori* in Medieval Political Thought."

7. An illustration of this problematic state of the research was the excellent study by Anderson, who treated the nation "in an anthropological spirit, as kinship or religion," but failed to discuss the relations between the imagined national community and other imagined communities that exist in the nation such as regional and religious.

8. See Berdahl, "New Thoughts on German Nationalism." See also the review essays by Eley, "Nationalism and Social History," and by Mommsen about the study of nationalism in German social history, "Nation und Nationalismus."

9. See, for example, Böhme, *Deutschlands Weg.* For the study of nationalism as the history of an idea, see Kohn, *The Idea of Nationalism.*

10. Two of the founding texts of the *Sonderweg* view are Wehler, *The German Empire,* and Dahrendorf, *Society and Democracy.*

11. In the *Sonderweg* historiography the manipulation of national feelings is termed "social imperialism." For a critique of this view see Eley, "Defining Social Imperialism."

12. The seminal text is Blackbourn and Eley, *The Peculiarities of German History.* See also

Nipperdey, "Wehlers 'Kaiserreich.'" On the *Sonderweg* debate see Retallack, "Social History with a Vengeance?"; Fletcher, "Recent Developments in West German Historiography"; Moeller, "The Kaiserreich Recast?"; and Evans, "The Myth of Germany's Missing Revolution."

13. Some representative studies are Evans and Lee, *The German Family*; Moeller, *Peasants and Lords in Modern Germany*; and Evans and Lee, *The German Peasantry*. The literature on women has expanded in recent years faster than on any other topic. See the English-language bibliography in Fout, *German Women in the Nineteenth Century*, 385–95, and *Journal of Women's History* (Spring 1991): 167–72.

14. For the contributions and problematics of *Alltagsgeschichte*, see Eley, "Labor History, Social History, *Alltagsgeschichte*," and Lüdtke, *History of Everyday Life*.

15. For an overview on the state of the concept and the research, see Wachtel, "Memory and History"; Joutard, "Mémoire collective"; Nora, "Mémoire collective" and "Entre mémoire et histoire" (English translation "Between Memory and History"); Lowenthal, *The Past Is a Foreign Country*, 185–259; Gillis, "Memory and Identity"; Hutton, *History as an Art of Memory*, chap. 1, "Placing Memory in Contemporary Historiography."

16. Bergson, *Matter and Memory*; Proust, *Remembrance of Things Past*; Goody, *The Domestication of the Savage Mind* and "Mémoire et apprentissage dans les sociétés avec et sans écriture"; Bastide, "Mémoire collective et sociologie du bricolage."

17. Halbwachs, *Les cadres sociaux*, *La topographie légendaire*, and *La mémoire collective*. In English see Halbwachs, *The Collective Memory*, and the recent translation *On Collective Memory* by Lewis Coser. On Halbwachs's formulation and use of collective memory, see Hutton, *History as an Art of Memory*, chap. 4.

18. Several discussions with the late Amos Funkenstein helped to refine my argument. See his illuminating article "Collective Memory and Historical Consciousness."

19. Extremely influential has been the magisterial work edited by Nora, *Les lieux de mémoire*, vol. 1: *La République*; vols. 2–4: *La nation*; vols. 5–7: *Les Frances*. For a critique of Nora's approach, see Englund, "The Ghost of Nation Past." Traditional Jewish and novel Israeli memories have been the topic of some important studies by Yerushalmi, *Zakhor*; Zerubavel, *Recovered Roots*; Sivan, *The 1948 Generation*. For an English essay on Sivan's concept and application of collective memory, see "To Remember Is to Forget." The unfading interest in World War I has produced some noteworthy studies: Fussell, *The Great War and Modern Memory*; Mosse, *Fallen Soldiers*; Gregory, *The Silence of Memory*; Winter, *Sites of Memory*.

20. I use "local-national memory" to denote the memory Germans constructed to reconcile localness and nationhood. It should be differentiated from other memories in German society such as class and religious memories.

21. Collective memory is, by definition, simultaneously a structuring of historical forgetfulness. Silence, obliteration, and lies are part of the production of memory. As Ernest Renan observed in a seminal essay: "Forgetting, I would even go so far as to say historical error, is a crucial factor in the creation of a nation." Renan, "What Is a Nation?," 11. For a good discussion of national forgetfulness, see Valensi, "Silence, dénégation, affabulation." See also Yerushalmi, Loraux, et al., *Usages de l'oubli*; "Politiques de l'oubli," a special number of *Le genre humain*; Anderson, *Imagined Communities*, chap. 11; Burke, "History as Social Memory," 108–10.

22. Peter Burke poses this question in his discussion of social amnesia. See Burke, "History as Social Memory," 108.

23. The ability to penetrate the everyday level of collective memory depends, obviously, on the use of appropriate sources. In her study of Zionist invented tradition, Yael Zerubavel

used, among others, jokes, popular songs, public school textbooks, plays, poems, children's stories, and the experience of trips to Masada and Tel Hai.

24. I am interested in the image of the nation in the mind of Germans during the relatively ordinary and calm period of 1871 to 1914, no less than in the tumultuous and violent period of war and revolution. This stands, in a way, in contrast to the view of Émile Durkheim, whose views on social solidarity were never far from my mind when I thought of nationhood, who saw the creation of sacred rituals as taking place especially during periods of historical "effervescence" such as the French Revolution. In *The Elementary Forms of the Religious Life* Durkheim explored what was considered the most primitive religious group of his time, the Australian aboriginals, in an attempt to understand the inherent and immutable traits of human society. His conception of religion assigned a fundamental role to the notion of the sacred, epitomized by rituals whose purpose was to "awaken certain ideas and sentiments, to attach the present to the past or the individual to the group" (423). According to Durkheim, society makes objects sacred especially during periods and historical events of "effervescence," of renewal and creation, when "under the influence of some great collective shock, social interactions have become much more frequent and active. Men look for each other and assemble together more than ever. That general effervescence results which is characteristic of revolutionary or creative epochs." (Cited in Hunt, "The Sacred and the French Revolution," 27.) The problem I see with this approach is that it neglects the evolution of national sacredness, of national imagination, in period of calm when routine behavior is the order of the day.

25. Halbwachs, *La topographie légendaire*. The recent translation *On Collective Memory* includes the "Conclusions" of this book.

26. A recent exception is Schama, *Landscape and Memory*.

27. Le Goff, *La naissance du purgatoire*; McDannell and Land, *Heaven: A History*; Vovelle, *Immagini e immaginario nella storia*.

28. Anderson, *Imagined Communities*, 15.

29. One problem with the rigorous definition of collective memory as recollections of the past is that collective memories which do not evoke a specific historical event or period, such as a collective image of a nation, have often been left unexplored. It is in this spirit that I suggest broadening the notion of collective memory and combining it with the notion of imagined community.

30. Kammen, *Mystic Chords of Memory*, 10.

31. The literature on Holocaust memories is enormous, and continues to grow. On the memory of Holocaust survivors see, for example, Langer, *Holocaust Testimonies*. For an overview of the Historians' Dispute, see Maier, *The Unmasterable Past*. On the representation of the Holocaust in monuments, see Young, *The Texture of Memory*. On the creation and transmission of the image of the Holocaust in West German cinema, see Kaes, *From "Hitler" to "Heimat"* and "History and Film"; Santner, *Stranded Objects*. See also Hartman, *Holocaust Remembrance*.

Saul Friedlander has been a dominating presence in the study of Holocaust memory. He has worked through his personal memories in an acclaimed autobiography and has contributed in a series of influential books and articles to shaping the field of Holocaust memories. See *When Memory Comes; Memory, History, and the Extermination of the Jews*; and "Die Shoah als Element in der Konstruktion israelischer Erinnerung."

32. Refining our understanding of collective memory, Allan Megill has distinguished three ways in which memory has been used by scholars: to recover personal, experiential recollections (such as of Holocaust testimonies); to denote tradition, or cultural knowledge (in this respect we should distinguish between participation in a cultural practice that

symbolizes an alleged historical past, such as the Seder, and memory of the historical past); and to denote commemoration, where most of the recent studies of celebrations, museums, and national symbols fall. In reality, of course, a clear cut distinction is often impossible. The celebrants of Sedan Day commemorated the unification of Germany as an event they personally experienced and they also attempted to invent a national tradition, namely to create and transmit a new form of cultural knowledge about the local and national pasts. I am indebted to Allan Megill for sharing with me his text "Memory," in *Encyclopedia of Historians and Historical Writing* (1997, forthcoming).

33. Nora, "Entre mémoire et histoire," xvii.

34. Halbwachs, *The Collective Memory*, 78–87, 105–7. On Halbwachs's conceptions of history and memory, see Hutton, "Collective Memory and Collective Mentalities."

35. Nora, "Entre mémoire et histoire," xvii, xx–xxx.

36. In addition to the literature mentioned in note 31, it should be emphasized that German historians of *Alltagsgeschichte*, a rendition of history of everyday life, used collective memory in their oral history studies. Important in this regard is the work of Lutz Niethammer on the experience of Nazism and of the aftermath of World War II in popular memory. Niethammer, *Lebenserfahrung und kollektives Gedächtnis*; *"Die Jahre weiß man nicht, wo man die heute hinsetzen soll"*; *"Hinterher merkt man, daß es richtig war, daß es schief gegangen ist"*; and *"'Normalisierung' im Westen."* Also important is the work of Detlev Peukert. See "Ruhr Miners under Nazi Repression."

37. In other fields of German historiography the study of memory is still in its inception. For political symbolism in the German Empire, see Hardtwig, "Erinnerung, Wissenschaft, Mythos." For a nineteenth-century connection between memory and museums see Crane, "(Not) Writing History: Rethinking the Intersections of Personal History and Collective Memory."

38. It is Eric Hobsbawm's merit to have suggested the importance of invented traditions to understanding modern European history. See Hobsbawm, "Introduction: Inventing Traditions" and "Mass-Producing Traditions."

39. Elias, *The Germans*, 2. Elias understood "national character," which he enclosed within quotation marks, as evolving through time: "a people's national habitus is not biologically fixed once and for all time: rather, it is very closely connected with the particular process of state-formation they have undergone. Just like tribes and states, a national habitus develops and changes in the course of time." Ibid.

40. Sheehan, *German History*, 1.

41. With historical hindsight we know that the memory of the nation-state shaped in 1871 has remained to this day the principal way for Germans to imagine the nation. There were two important attempts to redesign German nationhood in the twentieth century: the *Anschluß* in 1938 and the annexation of territories to the Third Reich between 1939 and 1945, and the existence of two Germanies between 1949 and 1990. The unification of 1990 demonstrated that, in spite of these attempts, Germans' idea of the nation-state has remained connected to the boundaries of 1871.

42. Evans, *Death in Hamburg*, 1–2.

43. Mommsen, "History and National Identity," 575.

44. "Peculiarity"—but similar to the peculiarities of other nations. In my view neither this nor other peculiarities that existed between 1871 and 1914 predetermined 1933.

45. See Robbins, *Nineteenth-Century Britain*.

46. The regional variegation of the German Empire was also a reflection of power relationships between Bismarck, William I, and the Prussian army, on the one hand, and the German states, on the other, relationships that in themselves were influenced by particular-

ist identities. Significantly, in 1871 Bismarck did not attempt to incorporate the German states into Prussia—that is, to depose the German princes as he did in Hannover and Hessen-Nassau, which were annexed to Prussia in 1866—because he recognized that such an attempt would lead to armed resistance and popular revolt based on sentiments of local identity and anti-Prussianism. For Bismarck's annexationist policy in 1866, see Schmitt, "From Sovereign States to Prussian Provinces."

The regional diversity of the European nation-states has been for too long passed over by historians who saw themselves as delegates of the indivisible nation. British historiography has been for a long time dominated by the conception that English history was British history, thus ignoring Scotland and Wales. Contra this assumption, Linda Colley argued in *Britons* that "Great Britain was invented only in 1707" with the Act of Union that united Scotland with England and Wales, and that the new national identity did not replace old loyalties as "Britishness was superimposed over an array of internal differences," but without obliterating the distinct Welsh, Scottish, and English identities. See Colley, *Britons*, 6, 373. See also Kearney, *The British Isles*. In German historiography the idea of the centralized nation was expressed in the notion that the German Empire was Prussia and Prussia the German Empire. James Sheehan has observed of the historiographical tendency, now in decline, to treat the German Empire as a centralized state that "It is remarkable that France, Europe's most centralized nation, has been dissolved by its historians into regions, while Germany, Europe's most fragmented polity, is treated as if it were a cohesive entity." In "What Is German History?," 21.

47. This sentence has usually been attributed to Massimo d'Azeglio, prime minister of the Kingdom of Sardinia before Cavour, who allegedly said it after the Italian unification. A new study on Italian nationalism, however, has recently revealed that the famous sentence was uttered by Martini. See Soldoni and Turi, *Fare gli Italiani*, 1:17.

48. On Württemberg before the French Revolution, see Vann, *The Making of a State*, and Wilson, *War, State, and Society in Württemberg*.

49. Sauer, *Napoleons Adler über Württemberg*, 78–125, 273–80, and *Der schwäbische Zar*, 238–381.

50. Not all the Swabians resided in Württemberg; some lived in Bavaria. Not all the Württembergers were Swabians; a minority of Franconians lived on the border with Bavaria. This study focuses on the Swabians (Protestants and Catholics) in Württemberg and how they refashioned their regional identity after 1871. This was obviously the major regional-identity problem in Württemberg. Therefore, the term "Württembergers" in this study does not include the Franconians in Württemberg and the term "Swabians" does not include the Swabians in Bavaria.

51. See Wehling, "Barock—bäuerliches Oberschwaben," 131–32.

52. See *Beob.*, 6.10.1875.

53. Schmahl and Spemann, *Geschichte des 2. Württembergischen Feldartillerie-Regiment*, 110.

54. Dieter Langewiesche has written a fine study of the democrats and liberals in Württemberg, and the possibilities of Germany's historical development between 1848 and 1871. See *Liberalismus und Demokratie*.

55. Cited in Langewiesche, *Liberalismus und Demokratie*, 18.

56. Henning, "Liberalismus und Demokratie im Königreich Württemberg," 66.

57. Bosl, "Die Verhandlungen über den Eintritt der süddeutschen Staaten in den Norddeutschen Bund," 148–63.

58. The existence of separate regional armies within the German army was significant, and the army's role as a means of national integration of soldiers from different regions

deserves to be further studied. On the army in Württemberg see von Gleich, *Die alte Armee*; Von Graevenitz, *Die Entwicklung des württembergischen Heerwesens*; Forstmeier and Meier-Welcker, *Handbuch zur deutschen Militärgeschichte*, 4, pt. 1: 205–11; 4, pt. 2: 283–89; Craig, *The Politics of the Prussian Army*, 219; Sauer, *Das württembergische Heer*.

59. Elben, *Lebenserinnerungen*, 159–60.

60. On Mittnacht see Kleine, *Der württembergische Minister-Präsident*; on Württemberg's policy, Binder, *Reich und Einzelstaaten*.

61. Bachem, *Geschichte und Politik*, 347.

62. Elben, *Lebenserinnerungen*, 163–64.

CHAPTER TWO

1. *Sch.Kr.*, 6.9.1873.

2. *Sch.Kr.*, 3.9.1884. A similar theme in *Sch.Kr.*, 4.9.1880.

3. On Arndt's song see Rohlfes, "Geschichte im Gedicht," 766–67.

4. *Sch.Kr.*, 4.9.1897.

5. *Beob.*, 2.9.1873.

6. The study of political festivity in Germany is still in its inception. The pioneering study is Mosse's *The Nationalization of the Masses*. For other studies on national celebrations, see Düding, Friedemann, and Münch, *Öffentliche Festkultur*; Lehnert and Megerle, *Politische Identität und nationale Gedenktage*; Hettling and Nolte, *Bürgerliche Feste*; Schellack, *Nationalfeiertage in Deutschland*; and Sperber, "Festivals of National Unity." See also the general overview of Grimm and Hermand, *Deutsche Feiern*.

7. *Kindheit und Jugend*, 2:8.

8. Schieder, *Das deutsche Kaiserreich*, 76–77, 125–53, first drew attention to the holiday in the context of nation building in Germany. In the 1960s two articles appeared on the motivations of Pastor Bodelschwingh in originating the holiday by Georg Müller, "Friedrich von Bodelschwingh und das Sedanfest," and Lehmann, "Friedrich von Bodelschwingh." A short discussion followed of the working-class movement and the holiday by Conze and Groh, *Die Arbeiterbewegung in der nationalen Bewegung*, 110–13, and H. Müller, "Die Deutsche Arbeiterklasse und die Sedanfeiern." Mosse, analyzing the holiday as a political ritual, set the tone since 1976 in the Sedan Day historiography (*The Nationalization of the Masses*, 90–93, 95–96, 124, 142, 170). His ideas on the holiday have influenced Baeumer, "Imperial Germany as Reflected in Its Mass Festivals," and Schellack, *Nationalfeiertage in Deutschland*. For a summary of Schellack's argument, see "Sedan- und Kaisergeburtstagsfeste."

9. Mosse, *The Nationalization of the Masses*, 91.

10. Baeumer, "Imperial Germany as Reflected in Its Mass Festivals," 66. See also Mosse, *The Nationalization of the Masses*, 89.

11. Mosse, *The Nationalization of the Masses*, 91; Baeumer, "Imperial Germany as Reflected in Its Mass Festivals," 66; Eley, "Army, State and Civil Society," 103; Schönhagen, "Ich wüßte keinen besseren Wegweiser," 28.

12. Baeumer, "Imperial Germany as Reflected in Its Mass Festivals," 66. Schieder was more cautious in his observations by acknowledging the popularity of the holiday and its importance as a nonofficial celebration; but he, too, stressed its military character, "especially in Berlin" (Schieder, *Das deutsche Kaiserreich*, 77).

13. Baeumer, "Imperial Germany as Reflected in Its Mass Festivals," 65–66; Schellack, "Sedan- und Kaisergeburtstagsfeste," 284–85.

14. Bauemer, "Imperial Germany as Reflected in Its Mass Festivals," 65; Mosse, *The Nationalization of the Masses*, 96.

15. On the emperor's birthday celebration, see Schellack, "Sedan- und Kaisergeburtstagsfeste," 286–92, and especially Wienfort, "Kaisergeburtstagsfeiern."

16. Adresse an S. M. den Deutschen Kaiser und König von Preußen, in Schieder, *Das deutsche Kaiserreich*, 132. Other participants came from Breslau, Weimar, Altenburg, Gotha, Wiesbaden, Königsberg, Leipzig, Bremen, Hannover, Stettin, Hamburg, and Rostock, underlining the role of Prussia and North Germany in the initiation of the holiday. Schieder included in his book a valuable collection of documents pertinent to the holiday.

17. Ibid., 133.

18. Lehmann, "Friedrich von Bodelschwingh," 546. Both newspapers emphasized the need for a German national holiday to celebrate the unity of the post-1871 nation in contrast to previous disunity. The *Kirchliche Gemeindeblatt* stated that "We don't want the national holiday to be celebrated on a separate day in every state and province in Germany as happened in the past. We want all Germany [to celebrate] on the same day." See Lehmann, "Friedrich von Bodelschwingh," 546.

19. James, *A German Identity*, 88–89

20. On the Reichstag see Haltern, "Architektur und Politik."

21. Tittel, "Monumentaldenkmäler von 1871 bis 1918," 235–36.

22. Hardtwig, "Geschichtsinteresse, Geschichtsbilder, und politische Symbole," 62

23. Letter of Grand Duke Frederick to his cabinet, 17.8.1872, in Schieder, *Das deutsche Kaiserreich*, 146.

24. Ibid.

25. Bericht des badischen Gesandten Frh. von Türkheim an den badischen Staatsminister Dr. Julius Jolly, 23.1.1873, in Schieder, *Das deutsche Kaiserreich*, 151.

26. Lehmann, "Friedrich von Bodelschwingh," 546.

27. Letter of the king to the Ministry of the Interior, 28.8.1872, in HStA, E 151a, no. 2932.

28. Ministry of the Interior, 28.8.1874, in HStA, E 151a, no. 2932.

29. Letter of the king to the Ministry of the Interior, 2.9.1874, in HStA, E 151a, no. 2932.

30. Minutes of Stuttgart City Council, 22.8.1872, in HStA, E 151a, no. 2932. See also *Sch.Kr.*, 24.8.1872.

31. Elben, *Lebenserinnerungen*, 206. Some communities in Württemberg—Nürtingen, Tübingen, and Biberach, among others—celebrated Sedan Day in 1872 (*Beob.*, 7.9.1872; *Tü.Ch.*, 4.9.1872; *Sch.Kr.*, 5.9.1872). But the general experience was appropriately described by the *Schwäbische Kronik*, the most important newspaper in Württemberg and ardent promoter of the holiday: "The plan to transform Sedan Day into a national holiday failed this year" (*Sch.Kr.*, 6.9.1872).

32. *Beob.*, 7.9.1872.

33. Cited in Langewiesche, *Liberalismus in Deutschland*, 128. This feeling was joined by a sense of emptiness after the great events of the unification, expressed by von Sybel in the same letter: "How will we live hereafter? . . . Where from should a person of my age find a new meaning to life?" Langewiesche's book is an excellent guide to the history of German liberalism. See also the good collection edited by Jarausch and Jones, *In Search of a Liberal Germany*.

34. Blackbourn, "Progress and Piety," 145–51. For the liberals' condescending attitude toward Catholics during a case of the Blessed Virgin apparition in the 1870s, see Blackbourn, *Marpingen*, 250–67. On the *Kulturkampf* and German national identity, see Smith, *German Nationalism and Religious Conflict*, 17–49.

35. *Sch.Kr.*, 29.8.1876.

36. *Beob.*, 18.8.1874.

37. Nürtingen, *Beob.*, 7.9.1872; Giengen an der Brenz, *Beob.*, 12.9.1872; Kirchheim unter Teck, *Sch.Kr.*, 2.9.1873.

38. *Beob.*, 1.9.1874. In Tübingen common folk went their ordinary way when the town's rich and famous engaged in festivities (*Beob.*, 9.9.1875); see also Schönhagen, "Ich wüßte keinen besseren Wegweiser," 29. A similar report about Heilbronn can be found in *Beob.*, 31.8.1876.

39. *Beob.*, 27.8.1873, 6.9.1873, 11.9.1872.

40. In Schorndorf the highest officials of the district showed up at the celebration (*Beob.*, 8.9.1876); in Oehringen the main operator was the *Stadtvorstand*, a high state official responsible for the locality and its environs (*Beob.*, 1.9.1874); in Tübingen the *Stadtvorstand* announced the celebration and invited the citizens to participate (*Sch.Kr.*, 2.9.1873).

41. It is worthwhile remembering just how provincial Württemberg and Germany were well into the empire. In spite of the accelerated urbanization in the last third of the nineteenth century, the overwhelming majority of Württembergers still lived in small towns and villages, as the data in Table 1 attest. Even toward the end of the century, in 1890, most of the holiday celebrations took place in small and medium-sized communities. The second biggest city in Württemberg after Stuttgart with 139,817 inhabitants in 1890 was Ulm, which lagged significantly behind with 36,191 inhabitants. Apart from Stuttgart, therefore, Sedan Day was celebrated in communities of between 2,000 and 36,000 inhabitants. Only four towns (excluding Stuttgart) exceeded 20,000 inhabitants; seven had between 10,000 and 20,000 inhabitants; sixteen had between 5,000 and 10,000 inhabitants; and numerous others had less than 5,000 inhabitants. (As everywhere in Germany, the Württemberg authorities provided remarkably detailed statistics about a large number of social developments. Statistics of the patterns of population growth in communities with over 2,000 inhabitants between 1871 and 1890 appeared in the *Statistisches Jahrbuch des Königreiches Württemberg*, 1893, 4.) The situation in Germany after 1871 (see Table 2) was basically similar to that in Württemberg, with the exception that there was a gradually widening gap in the level of urbanization.

42. Bausinger, "Volkskundliche Anmerkungen zum Thema 'Bildungsbürger,' " 211.

43. See Egelhaaf's autobiography, *Lebens-Erinnerungen*.

44. This brings to mind the conditions of the Russian nobility. Only 1 percent of noble families in Russia lived in the opulent Tolstoyan world of *War and Peace*; many of the noblemen and noblewomen did not resemble Natasha and Pierre but their peasants.

45. Associations had a similar role in national celebrations before 1871. See Düding, "Nationale Oppositionsfeste," and Mosse, *The Nationalization of the Masses*, 127–54.

46. Nipperdey, "Verein als soziale Struktur"; Blackbourn, "The Discreet Charm of the Bourgeoisie," 195–98.

47. For example, in Ravensburg and Tübingen (*Beob.*, 9.9.1875 and 13.11.1875).

48. Blackbourn, "The Discreet Charm of the Bourgeoisie," 225.

49. I use the term "liberal-bourgeois notables" to denote the liberal notables as a whole, the haute bourgeoisie and the petite bourgeoisie.

50. *Beob.*, 18.1.1872.

51. *Beob.*, 12.6.1872.

52. *Beob.*, 14.1.1871.

53. See the "Introduction" by Langewiesche, 34, and the diary entry from 2.3.1879 in Langewiesche, *Das Tagebuch Julius Hölders*.

Table 1. Size of Württemberg Communities, 1871–1910

| | Percent of Population | | |
Number of Inhabitants	1871	1890	1910
Fewer than 2,000	69.3	61.2	50.0
2,001–5,000	14.2	15.4	14.4
5,001–20,000	10.0	11.2	14.6
20,000 or more	6.5	12.2	21.1
100,000 or more	—	6.9	11.7

Source: Hohorst, Kocka, and Ritter, *Sozialgeschichtliches Arbeitsbuch*, 43.

Table 2. Size of German Communities, 1871–1910

| | Percent of Population | | |
Number of Inhabitants	1871	1890	1910
Fewer than 2,000	63.9	53.0	40.0
2,001–5,000	12.4	12.0	11.2
5,001–20,000	11.2	13.1	14.1
20,000 or more	12.5	21.9	34.7
100,000 or more	4.8	12.1	21.3

Source: Hohorst, Kocka, and Ritter, *Sozialgeschichtliches Arbeitsbuch*, 43.

54. I am thinking here of course of the title of Maurice Agulhon's study *The Republic in the Village: The People of the Var from the French Revolution to the Second Republic.*

55. *Kindheit und Jugend*, 1:25.

56. Ibid., 2:8–9.

57. *Sch.Kr.*, 5.9.1875, 5.9.1877, 6.9.1881. *Beob.*, 26.8.1875. Processions took place across Protestant Württemberg, with variations according to local preferences. As a whole, a picture emerges of zest and dynamism as celebrants marched in towns up and down, back and forth, morning, afternoon, and evening. See reports about processions in towns: *Sch.Kr.*, 5.9.1875, 6.9.1876, 4.9.1895. *Beob.*, 11.9.1872, 6.9.1873, 27.8.1874, 9.9.1875, 8.9.1876.

58. *Sch.Kr.*, 4.9.1885.

59. Düding, "Das deutsche Nationalfest von 1814," 85.

60. See Mosse, *The Nationalization of the Masses*, 77, 83–90, 131; Brandt, "Das studentische Wartburgfest"; Foerster, "Das Hambacher Fest 1832"; and Noltenius, "Schiller als Führer und Heiland: Das Schillerfest 1859." Sperber discusses the shared tradition of national celebrations in the case of the festivals of the 1848–49 German Revolution in "Festivals of National Unity," 135–37.

61. Sperber, "Festivals of National Unity," 135.

62. Ibid., 137.

63. For the role of associations in national celebrations before and after 1871, see Mosse, *The Nationalization of the Masses*, chap. 6.

64. The rhetoric of the festival is the topic of the next chapter.

65. In the years immediately following the war of 1870–71, many localities in Württemberg had a monument built to commemorate the soldiers who died in the war, either its

own sons or German soldiers from other regions who died in the community's hospital. Monuments varied according to a town's size, prosperity, and importance. Small towns planted a linden tree, put a plaque in the church, or used a natural object, like a rock, as a war memorial. The most common symbolic form of monuments was an obelisk in the cemetery. Many places had combinations of several commemorative monuments. On war memorials in Württemberg for the wars of 1866 and 1870–71, see Rieth, *Denkmal ohne Pathos*, 12–13; Weißer, *Denkmale der Filder*, 104–5; Gradmann, "Kriegerdenkmäler," 19, 24–25, 33. For the general problematics of war memorials, see Koselleck, "Kriegerdenkmale als Identitätsstiftungen."

66. For Marbach and Isny: *Sch.Kr.*, 5.9.1875; Riedlingen: *Sch.Kr.*, 5.9.1875; *Beob.*, 27.8.1875. The same happened in Dizingen, *Sch.Kr.*, 5.9.1874.

67. For the unveiling ceremony, see *Sch.Kr.*, 4.9.1872.

68. Appropriation of the memory and legacy of the fallen soldiers proved a powerful weapon not only in the unveiling ceremonies, but also in subsequent years, when the monuments continued to play an important role in the celebrations. In Stuttgart the opening act of Sedan Day was a ceremony on the evening of 1 September at the foot of the war memorial in Fangelsbach cemetery, an imposing Germania, standing on a sarcophagus, unveiled in 1874. The participants' list read like the city's who's who: the war minister, the highest officers of the police and the XIII Württemberg Army Division, the mayor, members of the city assembly and city council, representatives of the Landtag and the Reichstag, the highest clerical authorities, the city troopers, and numerous associations. The crowd assembled at the cemetery gates and at six o'clock, as bells in and around the city rang heralding the beginning of the holiday, the procession moved slowly toward the monument. A black ribbon was attached to the numerous flags and ensigns, wreaths lay beside the monument, and a baldachin in black-white-red colors awaited the speaker. See *Sch.Kr.*, 3.9.1873, 3.9.1875, 3.9.1881, 3.9.1887, 2.9.1890. The monument was later destroyed in World War II. For its image and description, see *Stuttgart. Führer durch die Stadt*, 43–44.

Stuttgart was the only place in Württemberg where the war monument's iconographic representation was a figure (in this, as in other cases, the capital represented the exception rather than the rule in Württemberg). The story of Tübingen's monument was common in many communities. The local medical association, in cooperation with citizens and clergymen, decided during the war to erect a monument commemorating the soldiers who died in the town's hospital. Every aspect of the structure, form, and decoration of the monument was minutely discussed. The monument was an obelisk, the old Egyptian symbol of eternity and glory that was the customary tomb monument of the period and typified the majority of war memorials of 1866 and 1870–71. The inscription on the obelisk expressed national ideas and sentiments for the first time on a tomb monument in Tübingen. The unveiling ceremony occurred on 6 August 1872, the second anniversary of the Württemberg army's victory in the battle of Wörth, and a month before the first celebration of Sedan Day. In the following years, a 2 September evening ceremony at the foot of the monument was the holiday's major outdoor act. On the form of war monuments, see Fontana, *Der deutsche Krieg von 1866*. On the making of the monument in Tübingen, see Schönhagen, "Ich wüßte keinen besseren Wegweiser," 26–28, 45–49. On Tübingen's monument celebrations in the holiday see *Tü.Ch.*, 4.9.1875, 5.9.1876, 4.9.1878, 4.9.1880, and 4.9.1890. The war memorial played a central role in every Württemberg town. See, for example, Hall and Reutlingen, *Sch.Kr.*, 5.9.1875; and Heilbronn, *Sch.Kr.*, 6.9.1876.

69. One among many examples, *Sch.Kr.*, 7.9.1887. On the importance of the war veterans'

bequeathing the war memory, see Schönhagen, "Ich wüßte keinen besseren Wegweiser," 28; Düding, "Die Kriegervereine im wilhelminischen Reich"; and Blessing, "The Cult of the Monarchy," 362.

70. *Sch.Kr.*, 7.9.1873.

71. Nipperdey, "Nationalidee und Nationaldenkmal"; Hardtwig, "Soziale Räume und politische Herrschaft." For a similar development in France, see Agulhon, "La 'statuomanie' et l'histoire" and "Imagerie civique et decor urbain."

72. *Sch.Kr.*, 4.9.1893; *Beob.*, 6.9.1893; *Fest-Ordnung für die Feierliche Enthüllung des Kaiser Wilhelm-Denkmals*, WDS: 71; Jacobi, *Heilbronn*, 41.

73. *Sch.Kr.*, 8.9.1890. Isny's 1875 war memorial, a simple stone in the cemetery, and the 1890 memorial, an imposing eagle symbolizing the German Empire's might situated in a public place, demonstrate the change in the public concept and use of war monuments. The 1870s war memorials were erected in cemeteries or in natural sites, whereas in the 1890s, as a result of the transformation of civic society and the enlargement of the public sphere, local notables placed war monuments in public places.

In general, war monuments were immediately incorporated into the procession's route. In Reutlingen, in the years following the erection of the emperor's monument, the procession marched through the city to the monument's square where a ceremony was held (laying of a wreath, speeches, singing), only to continue to the marketplace, where the "traditional" ceremony took place. See *Sch.Kr.*, 3.9.1895.

74. *Sch.Kr.*, 2.12.1884, 12.1.1886, 16.2.1886, 22.7.1886, 27.7.1887, 16.6.1892, 21.6.1892.

75. *Sch.Kr.*, 3.7.1887.

76. *Beob.*, 22.6.1892.

77. *Sch.Kr.*, 22.7.1886. And see *Beob.*, 22.6.1892, and *Sch.Kr.*, 3.7.1887.

78. The statue adorns Tuttlingen no more. It was donated in 1916 for the war effort and was melted to produce guns. For a description and an image of the statue, see *Kleiner Führer durch Tuttlingen und Umgebung*, 10, 12.

79. *Sch.Kr.*, 3.9.1895.

80. On the symbolic significance of fire in German celebrations, see Mosse, *The Nationalization of the Masses*, 40–41.

81. In Heilbronn the Veterans Association held a torchlight procession which culminated in singing by the Choir Society, surrounded by a romantic scenery of fire and shadows (*Sch.Kr.*, 6.9.1876). Members of the Gymnastic Association in Reutlingen organized a torchlight procession accompanied by music. Marching through the city's main streets, they arrived at the marketplace where a torch play was staged whose main protagonist was Emperor William II. Again in Reutlingen, modernity was mobilized to propagate the holiday: the Cyclist Association rode in and around the city with colorful lampions on their bicycles (*Sch.Kr.*, 4.9.1890 and 5.9.1892). And in Eßlingen, upon returning at evening from the traditional holiday's excursion, celebrants marched through the streets singing the "Watch on the Rhine" (*Sch.Kr.*, 6.9.1876). See also the torchlight processions in Weinsberg (*Sch.Kr.*, 5.9.1874).

82. *Sch.Kr.*, 7.9.1887.

83. *Sch.Kr.*, 4.9.1874. The editor of the *Schwäbische Kronik* conveyed similar ideas in his memoirs (Elben, *Lebenserinnerungen*, 207).

84. For the importance of the school festivities in the celebrations, see Schellack, "Sedan- und Kaisergeburtstagsfeste," 279, and Schieder, *Das deutsche Kaiserreich*, 76–77.

85. *Sch.Kr.*, 4.9.1880, 6.9.1881, 3.9.1884, 4.9.1884, 3.9.1886, 3.9.1887.

86. The Mozer and Krockenberg kindergarten in Stuttgart, *Sch.Kr.*, 4.9.1880.

87. *Sch.Kr.*, 4.9.1881, 3.9.1884, 2.9.1890.

88. A typical incident happened in Aalen. The supervisor of the Catholic schools prohibited the pupils to participate in the celebrations, and ordered instead a class in Catholic catechism (*Sch.Kr.*, 4.9.1887).

89. *Sch.Kr.*, 4.9.1881, 3.9.1886, 4.9.1888.

90. *Sch.Kr.*, 3.9.1884. See also *Sch.Kr.*, 3.9.1887.

91. *Sch.Kr.*, 3.9.1885. And *Sch.Kr.*, 4.9.1885.

92. *Sch.Kr.*, 2.9.1883. Same motive: *Sch.Kr.*, 2.9.1892.

93. *Sch.Kr.*, 6.9.1881.

94. *Sch.Kr.*, 3.9.1882, 4.9.1880, 4.9.1884.

95. *Sch.Kr.*, 4.9.1885, 4.9.1888.

96. *Sch.Kr.*, 4.9.1881.

97. *Sch.Kr.*, 4.9.1887.

98. *Sch.Kr.*, 3.9.1882. The play was also staged in Eßlingen, *Sch.Kr.*, 6.9.1881. Other plays staged in the holiday were Christian Dietrich Grabbe's *Kaiser Friedrich Barbarossa*, Goethe's *Hermann und Dorothea*, and Kleist's *Hermannsschlacht* (*Sch.Kr.*, 5.9.1876, 4.9.1880, 4.9.1887). Similarly, adults staged tableaux vivants at evening banquets. See *Brackenheim. Heimatbuch*, 165.

99. Chapter 5 discusses how and why the history of Württemberg and Germany in school textbooks changed in the 1890s.

100. See Kennedy, "Regionalism and Nationalism," 13–17.

101. For the history of the Children's Festival in Württemberg see the chapter "Kinderfest in Blaubeuren" in Imhof, *Blaubeurer Heimatbuch*; in general, Petzoldt, *Volkstümliche Feste*, 146–85. May (Maien) Day does not point to a celebration in the fifth month of the year, but designates greens, birch foliage, and spruce branches that people used for decoration, regardless of the time of year (Petzoldt, *Volkstümliche Feste*, 148).

102. Petzoldt, *Volkstümliche Feste*, 146.

103. Some of the many communities that celebrated Sedan Day in conjunction with the Children's Festival were: Calw, *Beob.*, 22.8.1873; Weinsberg, *Sch.Kr.*, 5.9.1874; Schwaigern, Ettenhausen-Bartenstein, Weikersheim, Urach, Nagold, *Sch.Kr.*, 5.9.1875; Biberach, *Sch.Kr.*, 10.7.1875; Schorndorf, *Beob.*, 8.9.1876; Langenburg, *Sch.Kr.*, 3.9.1880; Bietigheim an der Enz, Hermann, *Geschichte der Stadt Bietigheim*, 221; and Heidenheim, *Beob.*, 2.9.1874, whose tradition of the festival is described by Schweier, "Die Geschichte des Heidenheimer Kinderfests," 232–38. In Riedlingen, 2 September 1877, united three celebrations: Sedan Day, the Children's Festival, and an unveiling of a war memorial (*Sch.Kr.*, 5.9.1875). In 1877 the town council officially decided on a permanent joint celebration of Sedan Day with the Children's Festival (*Sch.Kr.*, 1.9.1876, 5.9.1877).

104. *Sch.Kr.*, 6.9.1876.

105. *Sch.Kr.*, 6.9.1876 and 6.9.1877.

106. *Sch.Kr.*, 4.9.1880.

107. *Sch.Kr.*, 3.9.1887. For other outings, see ibid., 4.9.1887.

108. *Sch.Kr.*, 3.9.1875.

109. Bartenstein, *Sch.Kr.*, 5.9.1874; Göppingen, *Sch.Kr.*, 7.9.1875; Hoheneck, *Sch.Kr.*, 6.9.1876; Tuttlingen, *Sch.Kr.*, 9.9.1876. Like other popular festivals, Sedan Day gave free reign to actions that were normally not sanctioned by society. Shootings and fireworks were common during the celebration and citizens complained that youths took advantage of the day to misbehave. See *Beob.*, 6.9.1873, 3.9.1875, 8.9.1876.

110. Hobsbawm, "Mass-Producing Tradition," 274. For a similar argument about the

prime importance of Wilhelmine Germany over the Bismarckian period in producing national symbols, see also Blessing, "The Cult of the Monarchy," 362, about Bavaria.

111. Hardtwig, "Bürgertum, Staatssymbolik, und Staatsbewußtsein," 272.

CHAPTER THREE

1. *Sch.Kr.*, 26.3.1871.

2. As supporters of Bismarck's German policy before 1871 and as Bismarck's main political allies in the 1870s, the liberals reaped political benefits from the *Kleindeutsch* unification also on the national level. The introduction of a national political system in 1871 propelled the National Liberal Party to a series of victories that made it in the 1870s the leading political party in the empire. In the first Reichstag elections in 1871 the party won 125 seats out of 382, and in 1874, 155 seats out of 397 (39 percent of the votes). See Eley, "Politica dei notabili," 468.

3. For results of Landtag and Reichstag elections in Württemberg, see Große and Raith, *Beiträge zur Geschichte und Statistik*, 27, 44.

4. Kleine, *Der württembergische Minister-Präsident*, 32.

5. On the national level the party did not fare as well. In the Reichstag elections in 1877 and 1878 the National Liberals suffered from Bismarck's shift of policy toward protectionism and an alliance with the conservatives; consequently, the Reichstag representation of the party declined to 128 (1877) and 99 (1878). In spite of this political retrogression, the party maintained its central role in German politics. During Bismarck's chancellorship, only the 1884 election was unsuccessful—a meager 51 seats. This result was reversed in the 1887 elections, when the party gained 99 seats and 22 percent of the votes. These changes affected the Württemberg liberals, as optimism in the 1870s changed to a more sober, shall we say realistic, mood in the 1880s.

6. Kleine, *Der württembergische Minister-Präsident*, 44.

7. On the social and political composition of the Landtag and on Mittnacht's policies, see Kleine, *Der württembergische Minister-Präsident*, 56–58; Simon, *Die württembergischen Demokraten*, 47–49; and Nipperdey, *Deutsche Geschichte, 1866–1918*, 2:614–15.

8. Henning, "Liberalismus und Demokratie im Königreich Württemberg," 69.

9. Ibid., 73.

10. Sheehan, *German Liberalism*, 165.

11. Kleine, *Der württembergische Minister-Präsident*, 57; Simon, *Die württembergischen Demokraten*, 51.

12. In general, the leaders of both parties were bourgeois notables, while rank and file included diverse middle-class groups. But the social composition of the VP centered on the petite bourgeoisie, while the DP organized mainly the economic and intellectual bourgeoisie, although it also found strong support among the petite bourgeoisie. This evaluation is confirmed by Friedrich Payer, the lifelong leader of the Württemberg and the German Volkspartei: the social composition of the democratic movement was "small merchants and peasants, also salaried employees. As a rule, civil servants and the so-called notables stayed away from the party. The industrial workers played at the time [1871] still a relatively minor role in South Germany. . . . In general, the party was first and foremost a representation of the petite bourgeoisie." Cited in Simon, *Die württembergischen Demokraten*, 25. On the social composition of the liberal and democratic movements in Württemberg, see also Langewiesche, *Liberalismus und Demokratie*, 370–77.

13. Kleine, *Der württembergische Minister-Präsident*, 56.

14. On these divisions in Württemberg society, see Sheehan, *German Liberalism*, 127, 225. The national division went back to the 1860s when the future of Germany dominated the political scene.

15. On the emergence of the Center Party in Württemberg, see Blackbourn, *Class, Religion, and Local Politics*, chap. 2.

16. On the working-class movement in Württemberg until 1878, see Schmierer, *Von der Arbeiterbildung zur Arbeiterpolitik*. On the SPD during the Anti-Socialist Law, see Rieber, *Das Sozialistengesetz und die Sozialdemokratie in Württemberg*.

17. "Im Geist sind wir bei Euch / Doch leider auch im Reich. / Geht dieses aus dem Leim, / Kehrt jeder fröhlich heim." Simon, *Die württembergischen Demokraten*, 13.

18. Kleine, *Der württembergische Minister-Präsident*, 30–31.

19. Ibid., 17. On the king's attitude to Prussia and the unification, see ibid., 12–18.

20. Elben, *Lebenserinnerungen*, 169.

21. *Sch.Kr.*, 4.9.1878.

22. *Beob.*, 31.8.1872.

23. *Sch.Kr.*, 4.9.1880.

24. For example, *Sch.Kr.*, 7.9.1875 and 2.9.1890.

25. *Sch.Kr.*, 5.9.1876. See also *Beob.*, 7.9.1880.

26. *Beob.*, 10.9.1875 and 5.9.1876.

27. *Sch.Kr.*, 4.9.1875. See also *Sch.Kr.*, 4.9.1879.

28. See *Tü.Ch.*, 5.9.1874, 6.9.1874, and *Beob.*, 25.12.1874. The story did not finish there. Haller, who felt his reputation tarnished, published his version of the events, taking a half page in the local *Tübinger Chronik*, and pressed charges against Walcker for defamation. Three months later the court ruled Walcker guilty and obliged him to pay 20 thaler to Haller as well as the expenses of the trial.

29. The Deutsche Partei organized the celebrations every year in, for example, Heidenheim (*Sch.Kr.*, 5.9.1883), Heilbronn (*Sch.Kr.*, 5.9.1882), Reutlingen (*Sch.Kr.*, 5.9.1884), Göppingen (*Sch.Kr.*, 5.9.1884), Gmünd (*Sch.Kr.*, 2.9.1891), Stuttgart (*Sch.Kr.*, 3.9.1897), Cannstatt (*Sch.Kr.*, 3.9.1900), and Tübingen (*Tü.Ch.*, 4.9.1898, and Schönhagen, "Ich wüßte keinen besseren Wegweiser," 29). The Fortschrittspartei organized the celebrations in Eßlingen (*Beob.*, 3.9.1875) and the Deutsche Partei in Singen (*Beob.*, 5.9.1876) and Ulm (*Beob.*, 2.9.1873).

30. In Heilbronn (*Beob.*, 31.8.1876) and Reutlingen (*Beob.*, 1.9.1874), for example.

31. *Beob.*, 9.9.1884.

32. *Tü.Ch.*, 2.9.1885.

33. *Beob.*, 5.9.1880. See also Schönhagen, "Ich wüßte keinen besseren Wegweiser," 26–29.

34. The amount had to be at least 12 kreuzer. See *Sch.Kr.*, 1.9.1874. The unification of the currency became law in 1873 and, after a transition period, was made obligatory on 1 July 1875. Before the unification of the currency 1 gulden was worth 60 kreuzer. Jaeger, *Die deutschen Reichsmünzen*, 7, 76–78.

35. *Tü.Ch.*, 30.8.1893.

36. On the celebrations of Sedan Day and bourgeois respectability, see Hull, "The Bourgeoisie and Its Discontent," 252–53.

37. The words used to describe the period were "humiliation" (*Schmach*), "contempt" (*Verachtung*), and "humbleness" (*Niedrigkeit*). See *Sch.Kr.*, 4.9.1880, 3.9.1892, 3.9.1894, 3.9.1895, 20.1.1896, and *Tü.Ch.*, 4.9.1884.

38. *Sch.Kr.*, 5.9.1876, 4.9.1877, and *Tü.Ch.*, 6.9.1881.

39. *Tü.Ch.*, 8.9.1876, 4.9.1879, 3.9.1880, 4.9.1884, 4.9.1886, and *Sch.Kr.*, 3.9.1873, 4.9.1877, 4.9.1880, 4.9.1885, 4.9.1887, 3.9.1892, 3.9.1894, 3.9.1895, 3.9.1897. Most of the words begin with the prefix *zer* that means "going asunder" or "apart."

40. *Tü.Ch.*, 4.9.1885. See also *Tü.Ch.*, 8.9.1876, 4.9.1886, 5.9.1988, and *Sch.Kr.*, 3.9.1894.

41. *Tü.Ch.*, 4.9.1884. See also *Tü.Ch.*, 5.9.1888.

42. *Sch.Kr.*, 4.9.1877.

43. *Sch.Kr.*, 3.9.1894.

44. *Sch.Kr.*, 3.9.1895.

45. *Sch.Kr.*, 3.9.1894.

46. *Sch.Kr.*, 3.9.1894. On the place of poets and philosophers in German history, see also *Sch.Kr.*, 4.9.1885.

47. *Sch.Kr.*, 20.1.1896.

48. *Tü.Ch.*, 2.9.1885, and *Sch.Kr.*, 4.9.1880. See also *Sch.Kr.*, 4.9.1877, 4.9.1878, and *Tü.Ch.*, 4.9.1879.

49. For example, *Sch.Kr.*, 4.9.1875, 4.9.1877, 4.9.1880, 3.9.1892, and *Tü.Ch.*, 5.9.1888.

50. *Sch.Kr.*, 3.9.1892.

51. Because the "big whole" sounds odd in English, I prefer to use the German *das große Ganze*.

52. *Tü.Ch.*, 4.9.1884, 5.9.1888, and *Sch.Kr.*, 3.9.1892.

53. *Sch.Kr.*, 4.9.1885.

54. *Sch.Kr.*, 4.9.1885. Similar descriptions appeared also in *Sch.Kr.*, 4.9.1878, 2.9.1890, 3.9.1892, 3.9.1895, and *Tü.Ch.*, 3.9.1880.

55. *Sch.Kr.*, 3.9.1895.

56. *Sch.Kr.*, 4.9.1885.

57. *In Eins geschmiedet*, *Sch.Kr.*, 4.9.1880.

58. *Sch.Kr.*, 4.9.1875. See also *Tü.Ch.*, 3.9.1880, 5.9.1888, and *Sch.Kr.*, 3.9.1875, 3.9.1876, 4.9.1877, 4.9.1879, 2.9.1890, 3.9.1892, 3.9.1894.

59. See, for example, *Sch.Kr.*, 4.9.1879, 4.9.1880, 3.9.1892.

60. *Sch.Kr.*, 3.9.1894.

61. *Sch.Kr.*, 4.9.1877. Emphasis added.

62. *Sch.Kr.*, 4.9.1877.

63. *Sch.Kr.*, 4.9.1879.

64. *Sch.Kr.*, 4.9.1879, and *Tü.Ch.*, 4.9.1886.

65. *Sch.Kr.*, 4.9.1876, 4.9.1877, 3.9.1892.

66. *Sch.Kr.*, 4.9.1880.

67. *Beob.*, 1.1.1867.

68. *Sch.Kr.*, 4.9.1875.

69. *Sch.Kr.*, 4.9.1878.

70. *Sch.Kr.*, 4.9.1887.

71. *Tü.Ch.*, 6.9.1881.

72. Borst, "Barbarossa Erwachen."

73. See Eksteins, *Rites of Spring*, 64–89.

74. Mona Ozouf discusses insightfully the notion of a symbolic map in *Festivals and the French Revolution*, 126–36.

75. *Beob.*, 2.9.1873.

CHAPTER FOUR

1. *Beob.*, 12.9.1875.

2. *Beob.*, 26.8.1873, 27.8.1873, 14.8.1874.

3. *Sch.Kr.*, 1.9.1875, 4.9.1875, 5.9.1875, 8.9.1875.

4. *Beob.*, 22.8.1873, 21.8.1874. The democrats tried to counter the conspicuous importance of the youth in the festival by arguing that only children participated in the holiday.

5. *Sch.Kr.*, 2.9.1873.

6. *Sch.Kr.*, 1.9.1874.

7. *Beob.*, 13.11.1875. In Tübingen a similar split took place in the Gymnastic Association (*Beob.*, 9.9.1875).

8. Egelhaaf, *Lebens-Erinnerungen*, 35–36.

9. *Sch.Kr.*, 5.9.1877.

10. Lehmann, "Friedrich von Bodelschwingh," 557–66.

11. On Catholics and Sedan Day, see Sperber, *Popular Catholicism*, 225–27; Blackbourn, "Progress and Piety," 153, and "Catholics and Politics in Imperial Germany," 207. On German nation building and Protestant-Catholic conflicts, see Smith, *German Nationalism and Religious Conflict*.

12. Ausschreiben des Bischofs von Mainz, die Sedanfeier betreffend, 19.8.1874, in Schieder, *Das deutsche Kaiserreich*, 152.

13. Sperber, *Popular Catholicism*, 226; Schieder, *Das deutsche Kaiserreich*, 129–30.

14. Pupils had more opportunities to participate, as we have seen. A word about Catholic services on Sedan Day and Ketteler's prohibition to participate is in order. As long as further research on Sedan Day in other parts of Germany is not available, it is difficult to ascertain whether Catholic services on 2 September were peculiar to Württemberg, perhaps a result of the absence of the *Kulturkampf*, or a common Catholic behavior throughout Germany to honor the fallen soldiers and their families. The second hypothesis seems more plausible.

15. *Beob.*, 3.9.1873.

16. Democrats sarcastically called the Deutsche Partei "Party of the Masters" [*Herren-Partei*] (*Beob.*, 26.10.1884).

17. *Beob.*, 3.9.1873, 6.9.1873, 27.8.1874, 8.9.1875, 9.9.1875. There was also an international level to the arguments against the holiday, namely that the choice of the battle of Sedan as a national holiday was an affront to the French people that would hinder the possibility of reconciliation between Germany and France (*Beob.*, 27.8.1874).

18. *Beob.*, 4.9.1873.

19. *Beob.*, 4.9.1873 and 14.8.1874.

20. *Beob.*, 4.9.1873.

21. *Beob.*, 31.10.1875. See also *Beob.*, 1.9.1874.

22. *Beob.*, 18.8.74 and also 3.9.1873, 6.9.1873, 9.9.1875.

23. *Beob.*, 3.9.1873.

24. *Beob.*, 2.9.1873. In addition, their newspapers were called "reptile press" (*Beob.*, 14.8.1874).

25. *Beob.*, 27.8.1874.

26. Elben, *Lebenserinnerungen*, 208–9.

27. *Beob.*, 6.9.1874.

28. The phrase appeared in *Beob.*, 9.9.1876, and again with identical words on 30.8.1887.

29. That liberals were unable to impose the holiday is an advantage for the historian who seeks to interpret the motivations of the Sedan Day celebrants. Because the liberals did not possess the means to coerce people into participating, unlike for example Communist regimes on 1 May, those who celebrated the holiday were motivated by inner convictions (though of varied kinds, of course). In contrast, it is more difficult to gauge the real sentiments of East Germans who were bussed to the 1 May celebrations and were ordered to be happy in the name of the socialist revolution.

30. *Tü.Ch.*, 2.9.1886.

31. *Sch.Kr.*, 4.9.1887. For the idea of the holiday above the parties, see also *Tü.Ch.*, 8.9.1876, 3.9.1880; *Sch.Kr.*, 4.9.1878, 4.9.1880, 4.9.1887; and *Beob.*, 4.9.1878.

32. For example, *Sch.Kr.*, 5.9.1876, 4.9.1878, 4.9.1879, 3.9.1881, and *Tü.Ch.*, 2.8.1885.

33. *Beob.*, 8.9.1891.

34. *Beob.*, 3.9.1873.

35. *Beob.*, 12.9.1875.

36. *Beob.*, 12.9.1884.

37. *Beob.*, 9.9.1886

38. *Tü.Ch.*, 2.9.1885.

39. Schönhagen, "Ich wüßte keinen besseren Wegweiser," 28–29.

40. On the similarity between the war of 1870–71 and the election campaigns, see, for 1878, *Sch.Kr.*, 6.6.1878, 2.7.1878, and *Beob.*, 9.6.1878, and for 1887, *Sch.Kr.*, 23.2.1887, 26.2.1887, and *Beob.*, 4.2.1887, 16.2.1887, 12.3.1887.

41. *Sch.Kr.*, 1.2.1887. The atmosphere at the victory banquet for Siegle was likened to the burst of emotions that followed the victory in the battle of Sedan (*Sch.Kr.*, 23.2.1887).

42. A *Parteifest* may have no negative implication when it means a celebration of a specific party when the party does not claim to speak for others.

43. Not only in Wurttemberg, of course. This was, for example, the perception of politics in France during the revolution. See Hunt, *Politics, Culture, and Class in the French Revolution*, 44.

44. Ausschreiben des Bischofs von Mainz, die Sedanfeier betreffend, 19.8.1874, in Schieder, *Das deutsche Kaiserreich*, 152.

45. Schellack, "Sedan- und Kaisergeburtstagsfeste," 284–85.

46. *Beob.*, 20.8.1876.

47. *Beob.*, 2.9.1876.

48. *Beob.*, 4.9.1890.

49. *Beob.*, 1.9.1881.

50. Anderson, *Imagined Communities*, 16.

51. Elben, *Lebenserinnerungen*, 209. Similar conclusions were expressed by the *Beobachter* (11.9.1894). And see Hermann, *Geschichte der Stadt Bietigheim*, 221.

52. Geislingen, *Sch.Kr.*, 4.9.1887; Ulm, *Sch.Kr.*, 4.9.1886.

53. The decline of the holiday was also expressed in *Chronik der Kgl. Haupt- und Residenzstadt Stuttgart*, an annual publication of the Stuttgart city council about the events, achievements, and life in the city in the previous year. Every year throughout 1901 the holiday was mentioned in the section about cultural events and national celebrations in the city. *Chronik* of 1901 reported that the celebration in Stuttgart was one of the few in the land. This was the last time *Chronik* reported about Sedan Day in Stuttgart, proof that the holiday had become irrelevant to the city and its inhabitants. See *Chronik der Kgl. Haupt- und Residenzstadt Stuttgart*, 1901, 225–26. Similarly, in the 1890s reports about the holiday in the *Schwäbische Kronik* dwindled and after 1895 amounted to only two or three reports a year—a sharp contrast to the entire pages of reportage in the 1870s and 1880s.

54. See Baker, *Inventing the French Revolution*; Furet, *Interpreting the French Revolution*; Agulhon, *Marianne into Battle: Republican Imagery and Symbolism in France, 1789–1880*; Ozouf, *Festivals and the French Revolution*; and Hunt, *Politics, Culture, and Class in the French Revolution*.

55. One of the few exceptions is Jonathan Sperber's thoughtful discussion of the festivals in the 1848–49 Revolution in light of the symbolic and linguistic approach. See "Festivals of National Unity." The study of German political festivals is, again in contrast to France, itself relatively new. See note 6 in chapter 2.

56. See Hardtwig, "Nationsbildung und politische Mentalität," 301. See also "Erinnerung, Wissenschaft, Mythos."

57. Hardtwig, "Bürgertum, Staatssymbolik und Staatsbewußtsein," 289, 293.

58. The fact that most monuments presented Bismarck and the emperor in military outfit is in itself an insufficient proof for militarism and antidemocratic beliefs. The promoters of the monument might have had a host of other reasons, some quite banal, for choosing its form: for example, shortage of funds. Furthermore, in Central and Eastern Europe emperors have always been displayed in military outfit; it might reveal little but a routine of social bon ton. A typology of these monuments should take into account the dominant taste in Germany as well as Europe. Moreover, monument activists had, besides the monument, other affiliations and loyalties that were as important to their perceptions of society and politics. To infer a whole set of attitudes out of a monument is questionable.

59. To be sure, our investigation considered Sedan Day only in Württemberg, and doubtless regional experiences varied. It should be emphasized, however, that a small but increasing number of studies on the national symbolic representation created by the bourgeoisie reached similar conclusions. See the valuable volume of Hettling and Nolte, *Bürgerliche Feste*, and in particular the articles by Wienfort, "Kaisergeburtstagsfeiern," and Tacke, "Die 1900-Jahrfeier der Schlacht im Teutoburger Wald 1909."

60. Hardtwig, "Bürgertum, Staatssymbolik und Staatsbewußtsein," 293. Hardtwig does not subscribe wholesale to the *Sonderweg* thesis, although he argues that "a 'core' of the *Sonderweg* thesis survives" and "to this core belongs also the considerable deformation of the bourgeoisie's notion of and way of thinking about the state [*Staatsbewußtsein* and *Staatsgesinnung*]. These perceptions are of special consequence for the *Sonderweg* thesis" because the German bourgeoisie should be primarily understood in terms of "history of culture, mentality, and ideas." See ibid., 285–86. Students of Germany should take the contention that the bourgeoisie escaped from reality with more than a grain of salt. There seems always someone in German society who was out of step with reality: liberals, critics of modernity, Heimatlers (as we shall see), and the Nazis. One wonders whether this reality, from which Germans wished to escape, was real or an imaginary construct of historians? Is it not an ideal world, constructed in the wake of the barbarism of the Nazi regime, where one expects Germans to embrace modernity and democracy and behave in a politically progressive way, or else be defined as escapists? Let us assume for the sake of the argument that the liberals "avoided" (although, significantly, the right word should be "rejected") political compromise with the Catholic and labor movements, a compromise that was necessary for the development of democracy. On what grounds can this rejection be labeled escapism? The Italian Christian Democrats have avoided a political compromise with the Communist Party since 1948. Was this a flight from reality or a defense of one's political power and ideological stance? Let us assume further that the liberals did avoid "the conditions and possibilities of practical politics" and did work against their best interests by caving in to the authoritarian state. Is this enough to label them escapees from reality? Did their life not include a circle of friends, family life, professional activity, voluntary work in the community? Are all these not part of "reality"? The escape-from-reality argument is based on false logic and a theoretical pitfall: the bourgeoisie created the Bismarck cult; the cult "articulated the desire for a powerful and authoritative imperial chancellor"; therefore "the Bismarck cult stands for the progressive tendency of the German bourgeoisie to escape from reality." Thus an uncomplicated reading of a symbol leads to sweeping conclusions about the political mentality of the bourgeoisie. See Hardtwig, "Bürgertum, Staatssymbolik und Staatsbewußtsein," 293.

61. The catalyst for the rethinking of the liberal bourgeoisie's political mentality was Blackbourn and Eley, *The Peculiarities of German History*. For two excellent discussions of recent trends in the historiography of the bourgeoisie and of the liberals, see Blackbourn, "The German Bourgeoisie: An Introduction," and Jarausch and Jones, "German Liberalism Reconsidered."

62. Blackbourn, *Class, Religion, and Local Politics*, 74–75.

63. *Sch.Kr.*, 20.1.1896.

64. Elben, *Lebenserinnerungen*, 168.

65. Kittler, *Aus dem dritten württembergischen Reichstags-Wahlkreis*, 102.

66. For a discussion of the sociopolitical transformation in the 1890s, see Eley, "Notable Politics, the Crisis of German Liberalism, and the Electoral Transition of the 1890s."

67. The classic text of this approach is the highly influential study of Furet, *Interpreting the French Revolution*. The approach has been further elaborated by Hunt, *Politics, Culture, and Class in the French Revolution*, and Baker, *Inventing the French Revolution*. It symbolically displayed its historiographical authority in the publication of the revolutionary bicentennial multivolume study: Baker, *The French Revolution and the Creation of Modern Political Culture*.

68. Baker, *Inventing the French Revolution*, 5, 9.

69. Furet has been the most extreme in excluding the social realm from the meaning of the French Revolution. He attacked the idea that "circumstances"—that is, a whole range of social and political relations and conflicts—can explain anything in the progressive radicalization of the revolution, which he interpreted in terms of internal developments within a revolutionary political discourse that, once set in motion, had a logic of its own. By making "circumstances" exterior to the meaning of the revolution, Furet argued in fact that, as Steven Kaplan has argued, "the Terror had no further need of historicization" and that its kernel existed already in 1789. For an overview of the origins of and controversies around this approach and its relations to the revolutionary bicentennial, see Kaplan, *Farewell Revolution: The Historians' Feud*, esp. chaps. 3–4, here, 83. Lynn Hunt, whose study on the French Revolution was in great measure influenced by Furet, took a different approach. She acknowledged that "If revolutionary politics cannot be deduced from the social identity of revolutionaries, then neither can it be divorced from it" (Hunt, *Politics, Culture, and Class in the French Revolution*, 13). But her book fails to integrate successfully the symbolic representation and the social identity. Comprised of two parts—"The Poetics of Power" and "The Sociology of Politics"—the book includes in effect two separate essays that only with difficulty illuminate each other.

70. For a thoughtful discussion of both the strengths and weaknesses of the symbolic-linguistic approach, see Maza, "Politics, Culture, and the Origins of the French Revolution."

71. See the good critical discussion of Sperber, "Festivals of National Unity," 114–16.

72. Maza, "Politics, Culture, and the Origins of the French Revolution," 720–21.

73. Although Hunt and Furet emphasize different factors within the symbolic-linguistic interpretation, it is significant that their studies share this criticism. Kaplan recently observed that Furet "is interested in the people-as-concept for the role they play in legitimizing the Revolution and filling the political vacuum. But he is indifferent to the people-as-people" (Kaplan, *Farewell Revolution: The Historians' Feud*, 103). About Hunt, Robert Darnton argued that "None of the revolutionaries would have recognized [her revolution]. . . . Rather than attempt to interpret the revolutionaries' understanding of what they experienced, she turns to twentieth-century theoreticians." Darnton, "Revolution sans Revolutionaries," 23.

1. For studies of the Heimat idea as a primary human condition of loyalty, security, and social orientation, see Greverus, *Der territoriale Mensch*, and Weigelt, "Heimat—Der Ort personaler Identitätsfindung und sozio-politischer Orientierung."

2. Applegate, *A Nation of Provincials*.

3. Ibid., 6.

4. Cited in Lowenthal, *The Past Is a Foreign Country*, 97.

5. On invented traditions in Europe between 1871 and 1914, see Hobsbawm, "Mass-Producing Traditions." About England see Lowenthal, *The Past Is a Foreign Country*, 96–105. About the United States see Kammen, *Mystic Chords of Memory*.

6. This development in Württemberg is illustrated very clearly in Dehlinger, *Württembergs Staatswesen*, 2:701–11, which describes the expansion of rail lines after the first construction in 1843. The best account of the way in which the railway nationalized local perceptions is Eugen Weber's about France, where "the conjunction of secondary lines and of the roads built to serve them resulted in a crash program of national integration of unparalleled scope and effectiveness" (*Peasants into Frenchmen*, 206).

7. Blackbourn, "The Politics of Demagogy," 223–24.

8. For an introduction to the general argument, see Eley, "The Wilhelmine Right," and Blackbourn, "Politics of Demagogy." Blackbourn provides the best succinct description of this transformation in ibid., 222–23, upon which the following discussion is based.

9. Only in 1898 the turnout was less than 70 percent, 68 percent. On the politicization in the German Empire between 1890 and 1914 we have the fine study of Suval, *Electoral Politics in Wilhelmine Germany*. Suval observed about the change from local to national perceptions: "The Wilhelmine voter was genuinely engaged in a process that went beyond his parochial boundaries and was nationwide" (8).

10. For the entry of the peasantry into politics in the 1890s, see Blackbourn, "Peasants and Politics in Germany." For the Agrarian League in Southwest Germany, see Hunt, "The 'Egalitarianism' of the Right." For the Bavarian Peasant League, see Farr, "Populism in the Countryside."

11. Blackbourn, "The *Mittelstand* in German Society and Politics."

12. Gellately, *The Politics of Economic Despair*; Volkov, *The Rise of Popular Antimodernism*.

13. Chickering, *We Men Who Feel Most German*; Eley, *Reshaping the German Right*.

14. See Chickering, *Imperial Germany and a World without War*, and Evans, *The Feminist Movement in Germany*.

15. A list of *Ortsgeschichte* between 1819 and 1908, compiled by the teacher Fähnle in Flein, appeared in *Schwäbische Heimat* (February 1910): 92–98. The list is suggestive though incomplete. Fähnle included old local histories and Heimat books without discussing the changing meanings of local identity. We should not accept 1819 as a conclusive date for the publication of the first *Ortsgeschichte*; the history-nature-folklore formula to describe local identity was familiar in the eighteenth century and perhaps even before. On the content and meaning of Heimat history see also ibid. (November 1909): 67–72, 78–79.

16. On the bureau see Hartmann, "Zur Geschichte der württembergischen Landeskunde," 66–67; Dehlinger, *Württembergs Staatswesen*, 1:564–70. The institutionalization and governmental use of anthropology in Germany in the nineteenth century is illustrated by Linke, "Folklore, Anthropology, and the Government of Social Life."

17. Cited in Dehlinger, *Württembergs Staatswesen*, 1:582.

18. *Ellwanger Jahrbuch* (1910): iii–iv.

19. Seytter, *Unser Stuttgart*, 4–5.

20. This is not to argue that historians do not cultivate emotional attachment to their study. Of course they do. The most celebrated example in recent decades is perhaps the opening line of Fernand Braudel's *The Mediterranean and the Mediterranean World in the Age of Philip II*: "I have loved the Mediterranean with passion." But *The Mediterranean* is an exception. How many history books begin with such a personal statement? Historians customarily conceal their fondness for a topic for fear of being viewed as unprofessional, although it shines through the prose even when they are not as outspoken about it as Braudel. Historians are expected, according to the norms of the discipline, to present their research as equitably as possible without personal bias. The contrast between the personable Heimat history and the "objective" professional history is especially apt because the historians of the Second Empire believed in the capacity of professional history to represent the past scientifically, as it really was.

21. *Unsere Heimat in alter und neuer Zeit* [of Heidenheim district], 85.

22. Mayer, *Heimat-Buch für Kirchheim u. Teck und Umgebung*, 5. The first edition was published before 1914.

23. *Ellwanger Jahrbuch* (1910): iii.

24. *Staats-Anzeiger für Württemberg*, 13.3.1909, in HStA, E 150/07, no. 570.

25. *Arbeitsplan des Württembergischen Landesausschußes für Natur- und Heimatschutz*, 5, in HStA, E 150/07, no. 570. The booklet was published in 1911.

26. *Tü.Ch.*, 28.2.1884.

27. *Württembergischer Altertumsverein. Rechenschafts Bericht*, 1894, 125.

28. *150 Jahre Rottweiler Geschichts und Altertumsvereine e.V. Festschrift; Erster Rechenschaftsbericht des Württembergischen Altertums-Verein für das Jahr 1844*; Greiner, *Der Verein für Kunst und Altertum in Ulm und Oberschwaben*; Sülchgauer Altertumsverein; Häring, "100 Jahre württembergischer Geschichts- und Altertumsverein"; Dehlinger, *Württembergs Staatswesen*, 1:596–97.

29. Schneider, *Die "Württembergischen Vierteljahreshefte für Landesgeschichte,"* 6.

30. One exception was Schwäbisch Hall's Franconian Historical Association in Württemberg. The limited range of historical topics and periods explored by the associations comes into sharper focus when *Altertum* is translated as "antiquity."

31. *Schwäbisches Heimatbuch* (1913): 4–5. Schuster, "40 Jahre Bund für Heimatschutz in Württemberg und Hohenzollern." The Regional Committee for Nature Conservation and Heimat Protection comprised similar occupations (see *Staats-Anzeiger für Württemberg*, 13.3.1909, 428–29, in HStA, E 150/07, no. 570).

32. See Ottnad, "75 Jahre Historischer Verein Ludwigsburg," 10. For new Heimat publications see, for example, *Aus dem Arbeitsgebiet des "Württembergischen Landesausschusses für Natur- und Heimatschutz,"* the journal of the Committee for Nature Conservation and Heimat Protection (in HStA, E 150/07, no. 570).

33. Eppinger, *Beschreibung, Geschichte und Führer von Fellbach*.

34. See the title page of Wagner, *Heimatkunde für Stadt und Oberamt Hall*.

35. Members in the Bund für Heimatschutz came from Catholic and Protestant communities. See the list of members' provenance in *Bund für Heimatschutz in Württemberg und Hohenzollern. Mitglieder-Verzeichnis 1909–1929*, 39–40.

36. See the discussion on school textbooks at the end of this section.

37. A Heimat book for a religiously mixed district was, for example, *Neckarsulm. Heimatkunde des Oberamtsbezirks für Schule und Haus*; for a Catholic town, Kaißer, *Aus der Vergangenheit Gmünds*; for a Protestant town, Eisele and Köhle, *Geschichtliche Heimatkunde für den Oberamtsbezirk Göppingen*.

38. On the religiously and socially diverse Heimat movement in the Palatinate at the same

period and on the popularization of Palatinate history, see Applegate, *A Nation of Provincials*, chap. 3.

39. For Backnang, see "Vom Altertumsverein zum Heimat- und Kunstverein." For Heidenheim, *75 Jahre Heimat- und Altertumsverein Heidenheim e.V.*

40. *Bund für Heimatschutz in Württemberg und Hohenzollern. Mitglieder-Verzeichnis 1909–1929*, 39–40.

41. *Der Geschichts- und Altertumsverein Rottweil von 1832–1913*, 15.

42. For the Regional Committee for Nature Conservation and Heimat Protection, see *Arbeitsplan des Württembergischen Landesausschusses für Natur- und Heimatschutz*, 11–19, and *Staats-Anzeiger für Württemberg*, 3.3.1908, in HStA, E 150/07, no. 570. Professor Eugen Gradmann, the head of the state's preservation activities (*Der Landeskonservator*), wrote for the Ministry of Education and Religious Affairs an introductory booklet about monument care (*Denkmalpflege*) and Heimat care (*Heimatpflege*). Gradmann, *Anweisungen zur Denkmalpflege*.

43. On the inculcation of history to schoolchildren, see Ferro, *Comment on raconte l'histoire aux enfants*; Berghahn and Schissler, *Perceptions of History*.

44. *Lesebuch für die evangelischen Volksschulen Württembergs* (Stuttgart, 1874), 224–439. A chronology of world history appeared at the end of the book: 4000 B.C.—Adam, 2000 B.C.—Noah, and so on until A.D. 1871—the unification of Germany.

45. *Lesebuch für die katholischen Volksschulen Württembergs*, new ed. (Horb, 1895).

46. *Lesebuch für die katholischen Volksschulen Württembergs*, vol. 2: *Viertes bis siebtes (achtes) Schuljahr* (Stuttgart, 1910).

47. Translating *Völkerkunde* as "anthropology" would give the term a professional meaning that was inappropriate for a school textbook.

48. *Lesebuch für die katholischen Volksschulen Württembergs*, vol. 2: *Viertes bis siebtes (achtes) Schuljahr* (Stuttgart, 1910).

49. *Lesebuch für die evangelischen Volksschulen Württembergs*, vol. 2: *Viertes und fünftes Schuljahr* (Stuttgart, 1909), 292.

50. Applegate, *A Nation of Provincials*, 63. For an excellent study on Heimat environmentalism from the perspective of the national organization Deutscher Bund Heimatschutz, see Rollins, "Aesthetic Environmentalism."

51. Hagel, "Zur Geschichte der Verschönerungsvereine." On the occasion of the 125th anniversary of Stuttgart's Society, in 1986, Hagel sent localities in Württemberg a questionnaire about beautification societies. The material is in HStA, J 2, no. 624.

52. *Geschichtliches vom Verschönerungsverein Tuttlingen*, 3.

53. *Bericht über die Entwickelung und Thätigkeit des Verschönerungsvereins der Stadt Stuttgart*, 44. The social composition of the society is shown in table 3. The *Bericht* divides the occupational data into seventeen categories, which I reduced to eight categories to achieve a more comprehensive view of the society's social composition. Thus I joined the categories "civil servants" and "retired civil servants" and, in order to understand the full weight of the economic bourgeoisie, I included under commerce and manufacture entrepreneurs and manufacturers (*Fabrikant*), merchants and shopkeepers (*Kaufmann*), bankers and bank employees, innkeepers and restaurateurs, and wine growers. I created a new category comprising some of the classic bourgeois professions, most of which required university education: physicians, lawyers, architects, engineers, artists, journalists, booksellers, shopkeepers of musical instruments, and publishers. The categories of artisans, women, rentiers (*Privatiers*), education and religion, and miscellaneous existed in the original document.

In condensing seventeen occupation categories into eight, my choices were also determined by the available information. While bankers belonged under the commerce and

Table 3. Occupation of Stuttgart Beautification Society Members, 1885

Occupation	N	%
Civil service and military	350	23.6
Education and religion	80	5.4
Artists, journalists, booksellers, shopkeepers selling musical instruments, publishers, physicians, lawyers, architects, and engineers	177	12.0
Commerce and manufacture	448	30.3
Artisans	99	6.7
Rentiers	181	12.2
Women	112	7.5
Miscellaneous	28	1.8

Table 4. Occupation of Schramberg Beautification Society Members, 1881

Occupation	N	%
Civil service (including mayor)	5	5.3
Education and religion	7	7.5
Physicians, editors, photographers, architects, and artists	7	7.5
Commerce and manufacture[a]	27	29.0
Artisans	22	23.6
Women[b]	3	3.2
Miscellaneous and unidentified	22	23.6

a. This category includes members who listed their occupation as *Fabrikant* (an entrepreneur or manufacturer), *Kaufmann* (a shopkeeper), beer brewer, and restaurateur.

b. Not included in this category is one woman who listed her occupation as restaurateur.

manufacture category, bank employees may have been better represented under a white collar employees category. This differentiation was not possible because the *Bericht* provided one figure for the two occupations together. A differentiation between booksellers, shopkeepers of musical instruments, and publishers was not possible on similar grounds.

54. *Statuten des Verschönerungs-Verein Schramberg*, 6–8. Table 4 shows the society's social composition at the time of its founding.

55. Ibid., 5. *Bericht über die Entwickelung und Thätigkeit des Verschönerungsvereins der Stadt Stuttgart*, 42–43.

56. Hagel's emphasis on the role of the notables in the societies, while not totally inaccurate, ignores the societies' diverse social composition and oversimplifies their social dynamics (Hagel, "Zur Geschichte der Verschönerungsvereine," 357). It is more precise to argue that even in societies whose social composition was diverse the steering committee was usually manned by the leading local bourgeoisie. Even under these circumstances, however, the steering committee reflected the social and professional diversity of the Heimat movement, including growing numbers of bourgeois professionals (editors, artists, architects, and others) alongside more traditional occupations (teachers and clergymen, for example). Thus the board of the Alt-Wimpfen, Kur- und Verkehrs-Verein in Wimpfen (Old Wimpfen, The Association for Care and Transportation that acted as a multifunctional historical, beautification, and tourist association), for instance, included in 1905 a painter, a

publisher, a company director, a minister, the town accountant, two teachers, four merchants and entrepreneurs, and two city councillors (see *Wimpfener Zeitung*, 1.3.1905, in HStA, J 2, no. 624).

57. See the information on Württemberg societies in HStA, J 2, no. 624. See also *Geschichtliches vom Verschönerungsverein Tuttlingen*, 4–5.

58. The information about beautification societies in Württemberg is from Hagel, "Zur Geschichte der Verschönerungsvereine."

59. At times societies were responsible for the entire district, as in Kirchheim unter Teck.

60. Hagel, "Zur Geschichte der Verschönerungsvereine," 356; *100 Jahre Verschönerungsverein Metzingen*, 6–7; *100 Jahre Schwäbischer Albverein (1888–1988)*, in HStA, J 2, no. 624.

61. *Festschrift zum 25Jährigen Jubiläums des Schillergaues 1903–1928*, 13, in WDS: 325.

62. Weischedel, Weischedel, and Greb, *Geschichte des deutschen Naturkundevereins*, 1–3.

63. The net proceeds of Eppinger, *Beschreibung, Geschichte und Führer von Fellbach*, were assigned for the local beautification society.

64. See Applegate's discussion on the contemporaneity of the Heimat idea and its connection to modern life-styles, tourism, and division between work and leisure. *A Nation of Provincials*, 70–72.

65. *100 Jahre Verschönerungsverein Kirchheim unter Teck*, 13–14.

66. *Satzungen des württembergischen Schwarzwald-vereins*, in WDS: 325. It remained unchanged in the statutes of 1902 and 1908.

67. HStA, J 2, no. 624, Eningen.

68. Wagner, *Heimatkunde für Stadt und Oberamt Hall*; *Neckarsulm. Heimatkunde des Oberamtsbezirks für Schule und Haus*; Mönch, *Heimatkunde vom Oberamt Calw*.

69. See, for example, the publications of the Bund für Heimatschutz and the Regional Committee for Nature Conservation and Heimat Protection: *Arbeitsplan des Württembergischen Landesausschusses für Natur- und Heimatschutz*, 2; "Geschichte der Gründung des Bundes für Heimatschutz," 10.

70. "Geschichte der Gründung des Bundes für Heimatschutz," 9–10. Emphasis added.

71. See the discussion on Heimat iconography in chapter 7.

72. *Unsere Heimat in alter und neuer Zeit*, 85.

73. See the reprint, Bohnenberger, *Volkstümliche Überlieferungen in Württemberg*.

74. On the invention of *Tracht* and of traditions in the Palatinate, see Applegate, *A Nation of Provincials*, 80–83.

75. By the turn of the century traditional clothes in village communities became rare. See Mutschler, *Ländliche Kindheit in Lebenserinnerungen*, 60.

76. Bischoff-Luithlen, *Von Amtsstuben, Backhäusern, und Jahrmärkten*, 255–56.

77. *Trautes Heim*, 58–60. Betzingen had 2,217 inhabitants in 1890.

78. Minister report, Landeskirchliches Archiv Stuttgart, A 29/427, p. 2, cited in *Trautes Heim*, 60.

79. German, *Chronik von Schwäbisch Hall und Umgebung*, 300; Kaißer, *Aus der Vergangenheit Gmünds*, 165; Wagner, *Heimatkunde für Stadt und Oberamt Hall*, 33.

80. The association was one of the founding members of the Bund für Heimatschutz, "Geschichte der Gründung des Bundes für Heimatschutz," 10.

81. *Trautes Heim*, 57.

82. Freudenberger, *Schwabenreport 1900–1914*, 56.

83. Bischoff-Luithlen, *Von Amtsstuben, Backhäusern, und Jahrmärkten*, 256.

84. Bohnenberger, *Volkstümliche Überlieferungen in Württemberg*, ix.

85. *Unsere Heimat in alter und neuer Zeit*, 50–55.

86. Ibid., 50.

87. Fischer, *Schwäbisches Wörterbuch*, vii.

88. From the introduction in Rommel, *Reutlinger Heimatbuch*, 3. The introduction to the first edition, published in 1913, was reprinted in the 1929 edition.

89. *Unsere Heimat in alter und neuer Zeit*, 51. The same sentence, word by word, appeared in Kaißer, *Aus der Vergangenheit Gmünds*, 98. It proves that Heimatlers knew each other's works well and that although Heimat books hailed the distinctiveness of a locality, they did so in a similar language that formed unity of structure and meaning.

90. Seytter, *Unser Stuttgart*, 4.

91. In chapters 6 and 7 I discuss how, why, and whether bourgeois Heimatlers disregarded city life, industrialization, and the working class.

92. *Schwäbischer Merkur*, 3.4.1911, no. 156; 6.4.1911, no. 162.

93. *Schwäbischer Merkur*, 6.4.1911, no. 162, p. 1.

94. *Sch.Kr.*, 11.7.1912, no. 318, p. 5, and HStA, E 14 II, 1348. The catalog: *Bunte Blätter aus Württemberg und Hohenzollern*, 3.

95. Eppinger, *Beschreibung, Geschichte und Führer von Fellbach*, 50.

96. *Unsere Heimat in alter und neuer Zeit*, 59–60.

97. See, for instance, Bergmann, *Agrarromantik und Großstadtfeindschaft*; Glaser, *The Cultural Roots of National Socialism*; Kaes, *From "Hitler" to "Heimat,"* 163–66; Kramer, "Die politische und ökonomische Funktionalisierung von Heimat im deutschen Imperialismus und Faschismus"; Hartung, *Konservative Zivilisationskritik und regionale Identität*, 56–57; and Projektgruppe Deutscher Heimatfilm, *Der deutsche Heimatfilm*, 16, which is otherwise an excellent book, a result of a project guided by Wolfgang Kaschuba in the Ludwig-Uhland-Institute für Empirische Kulturwissenschaft at the University of Tübingen.

98. Applegate, *A Nation of Provincials*, 103–7. For a balanced view see also Rollins, "Aesthetic Environmentalism," 166–70, who convincingly shows the tendentiousness of the antimodern interpretation to the Deutscher Bund Heimatschutz's environmental activities, and Jefferies, *Politics and Culture in Wilhelmine Germany*, chap. 2.

99. *Arbeitsplan des Württembergischen Landesausschusses für Natur- und Heimatschutz*, 1–2.

100. Hesse, "Heimat. Calw," 121.

101. Berman, *All That Is Solid Melts into Air*, 13–14.

102. That the question—Was Heimat modern or antimodern?—misses the essence of the Heimat idea and of modernity itself can also be shown by the following conceptual consideration. The concept "antimodern" is a staple of historical analysis and historiographic discourse. As an analytical tool, this concept implies the existence of ideas that are pro-modern. But "promodern" has never been used because the concept "modern" actually substitutes for it, meaning "progressive and positive." The understanding of "modern" as progressive excludes from the concept a wide range of historical phenomena that fit modern conditions precisely because they represent people's attraction to and repulsion by modernity and its effects.

103. In one of the most original books in recent years about Germany's modernity project, Modris Eksteins has argued that "Germany more than any other state took us toward our 'postindustrial' or technological world . . . also in an experiential sense, in that she more intensively than any other 'developed' country has given evidence to the world of the psychic disorientation that rapid and wholesale environmental change may produce. The German experience lies at the heart of the 'modern experience.' Germans often used to refer to themselves as the *Herzvolk Europas*, the people at the heart of Europe. Germans are also the *Herzvolk* of modern sense and sensibility." Eksteins, *Rites of Spring*, 67–68. Eksteins focuses on Germany's forward-looking, modernist aestheticism in art and politics, but does

not discuss how Germans reconciled past sense and sensibility with the machine age or how they rethought the place of the environment in a technological world. The work of Peter Fritzsche, who explored German modernism as a "workshop of machine and masses," stands out in its imaginativeness. See *A Nation of Fliers* and "Landscape of Danger, Landscape of Design."

104. Berman, *All That Is Solid Melts into Air*, 24.

105. Foucault, *Discipline and Punish*, 301, 308, 304, 228.

CHAPTER SIX

1. See Walker, *German Home Towns*.

2. See Schivelbusch, *The Railway Journey*.

3. Eugen Weber described in *Peasants into Frenchmen* how the nation-state and modernization lifted peasants from a rather insulated local existence to a local existence inextricably connected to the forces of the modern world. Until the Third Republic peasants meant the next village when they said *je vais à l'étranger* (I go abroad).

4. Hobsbawm mentions that the process of imagining the nation as a community was a European phenomenon indicated, among others, in vocabulary changes. *Paese* in Italian and *pueblo* in Spanish mean both a village and national territory. *Patria* became identical with Spain only late in the nineteenth century; before it meant the locality where a person was born. See Hobsbawm, *The Age of Empire*, 148.

5. Eisele and Köhle, *Geschichtliche Heimatkunde für den Oberamtsbezirk Göppingen*.

6. In 1910 Reutlingen had 29,763 inhabitants, Fellbach 6,780.

7. During my research in Germany I inquired among many historians and laypersons about their concept of "Heimat." The responses are an interesting source about contemporary understanding of what Heimat meant and means. All those asked, without exception, identified Heimat with local territory, and many raised doubts and were perplexed about a research on the national Heimat.

8. Burckhardt, "Heimat," 19.

9. Grimm and Grimm, *Deutsches Wörterbuch*, 864–65.

10. It is difficult to ascertain whether this symbolic meaning influenced directly the evolution of the word "Heimat." A study about religious beliefs and the Heimat concept may illuminate this topic.

11. Greverus, *Der territoriale Mensch*, 28; Walker, *German Home Towns*, 347–53.

12. *Allgemeine deutsche Real-Encyklopädie für die gebildeten Stände*.

13. Götze, *Trübners Deutsches Wörterbuch*, v.

14. Ibid., 387.

15. Ibid., 388.

16. Greverus, *Auf der Suche nach Heimat*, 63.

17. Schmeller, *Bayerisches Wörterbuch*, 1108; Martin and Lienhart, *Wörterbuch der Elsässischen Mundarten*, 336; Koolman, *Wörterbuch der Ostfriesischen Sprache*, 61, 69.

18. Buurman, *Hochdeutsch-plattdeutsches Wörterbuch*, 303–4; Christmann and Krämer, *Pfälzisches Wörterbuch*, 772.

19. *Heimatschutz. Herausgegeben vom Geschäftsführenden Vorstand des Deutschen Bundes Heimatschutz* 10, no. 1 (1915): 2.

20. For detailed information about the regional associations and the Deutscher Bund Heimatschutz, see *50 Jahre deutscher Heimatbund. Deutscher Bund Heimatschutz*; *Der Deutsche Heimatschutz. Ein Rückblick und Ausblick*; and *75 Jahre Deutscher Heimatbund*. The

titles of the organizations were Niedersächsische Ausschuß für Heimatschutz, Heimatbund Mecklenburg, Rheinischer Verein für Denkmalpflege und Heimatschutz, Verein Heimatschutz in Brandenburg, Schleswig-Holsteinischer Landesverein für Heimatschutz, Landesverein Pommern des Bundes Heimatschutz, Schlesischer Bund für Heimatschutz, Hessischer Bund für Heimatschutz, Bayerischer Verein für Volkskunst und Volkskunde, Landesverein Sächsischer Heimatschutz, Bund für Heimatschutz in Württemberg und Hohenzollern, Badische Heimat, Verein Heimatschutz im Hamburger Staatsgebiet, and Bund Heimatschutz für das Eisenacher Land.

21. *Satzungen des Bundes "Heimatschutz,"* in HStA, E 151/07, no. 584. Emphasis added.

22. *Aufruf zur Gründung eines Bundes Heimatschutz*, in HStA, E 151/07, no. 584. Emphasis added.

23. Rollins studied 9,051 Heimatlers in nine Heimat organizations of seven German regions (Baden, Mecklenburg, Lower Saxony, Westphalia, Saxony, Schleswig-Holstein, and Thuringia). See Rollins, "Aesthetic Environmentalism," 244.

24. See Kocka, "Bildungsbürgertum—Gesellschaftliche Formation oder Historiker-konstrukt?"

25. The exact occupational breakdown among the 9,501 Heimatlers was as follows: civil service, law, and military—23.7 percent; education, religion, and culture—20.4 percent; commerce and manufacture—27.2 percent; artists and journalists—2.6 percent; health—4.7 percent; agriculture—5.4 percent; women—4.7 percent; miscellaneous and unidentified—11.4 percent.

26. Rollins estimates the participation of the nobility at less than 5 percent and of the agricultural sector at 5.4 percent. Artisans made up only 2.5 percent of the total membership and workers were virtually absent in the movement. Rollins, "Aesthetic Environmentalism," 173–74.

27. Hartung, *Konservative Zivilisationskritik und regionale Identität*, 83–85, here 84. We need additional regional studies of the Heimat movement to get a full picture of its social composition. Studies of the movement in agricultural regions, such as Eastern Prussia, may provide a corrective to the underrepresentation of peasants and the nobility in the movement. But given the information we have about the movement in the Palatinate, Lower Saxony, Württemberg, and the Deutscher Bund Heimatschutz in seven regions, it is im probable that the dominance of the bourgeoisie can be significantly challenged.

28. Rollins, "Aesthetic Environmentalism," 176.

29. Hartung, *Konservative Zivilisationskritik und regionale Identität*, 324, 93. See also 325.

30. This approach is evident also in Dieter Kramer's argument that the Heimat idea originated among the Junker aristocracy as an antimodern and antidemocratic ideology aimed to bolster its control of German society. See Kramer, "Die politische und ökonomische Funktionalisierung von Heimat im deutschen Imperialismus und Faschismus."

31. For Rollins's argument, see "Aesthetic Environmentalism," 141.

32. For the Pfälzerwald Verein, see Applegate, *A Nation of Provincials*, 65–67, here 65–66. For the beautification societies, see Applegate, "Localism and the German Bourgeoisie," 232. For the museum, Applegate, *A Nation of Provincials*, 93–101, here 93. When Applegate argues that the museum (and, by extension, the Heimat idea) was "a popular and inclusive conception of local culture," she presumably means among the German bourgeoisie, for she does not provide evidence about the reception of the idea among other social groups, notably the working class. The issue here is one of distinguishing between those who produced and those who received or rejected the Heimat idea. We know next to nothing about how the Heimat idea was or was not appropriated by, say, workers and the Social Democratic Party. My sense is that the common wisdom according to which the national

Table 5. Number of Heimat Museum Foundings, to 1918, by Region

Year of Founding	Württem-berg	Baden	Lower Saxony	Bavaria	Schleswig-Holstein	Westphalia	Hesse	Rhineland-Palatinate	Total
Before 1871	2	—	4	8	—	—	—	—	14
1871–80	3	1	1	1	3	1	3	2	15
1881–90	2	2	3	16	3	5	—	—	31
1891–1900	—	3	7	8	4	2	4	3	31
1901–10	6	3	9	31	9	6	4	7	75
1911–14	5	1	7	10	1	9	3	—	36
1915–18	1	—	1	2	—	1	1	—	6
Total	19	10	32	76	20	24	15	12	208

right wing in Germany was much more skillful than the labor movement in appropriating the Heimat idea is as subtle as the interpretation of the Heimat idea as antimodern and reactionary. I discuss the topic briefly in "The Nation as a Local Metaphor," 74–78.

33. We still do not have a comprehensive study of the Heimat museum phenomenon in imperial Germany. The figure here is from Karasek, *Die volkskundlich-kulturhistorischen Museen*, 225–26. Karasek, who provided a Marxist-Leninist interpretation of Heimat museums between 1890 and 1945, reached this figure by using the information available in *Jahrbuch der deutschen Museen* 8 (1938). In the overall period between 1890 and 1918, 76 new Heimat museums were founded between 1890 and 1899, 178 museums between 1900 and 1909, 103 museums between 1910 and 1914, and predictably only 14 during World War I.

34. I calculated the data from Hanswilhelm Haefs's *Die deutschen Heimat-museen*. The book, published before Germany's reunification in 1990, lists the operating Heimat museums in the former West Germany. Although the eastern regions of the German Empire were excluded from this survey, the general pattern that emerges is clear enough. The survey does not provide information about the total number of Heimat museums founded before 1918, only about the museums that have continued to exist until 1984. The number of Heimat museums does not indicate a number of communities, since some communities had more than one Heimat museum. The pattern of the foundation of Heimat museums in various German regions is shown in Table 5.

35. For example, Hamburg (founded in 1839 and 1863), Munich (1855), Fulda (1875), Frankfurt (1878).

36. The basic pattern of the foundation of Heimat museums between 1890 and 1914 inferred from Karasek's data is confirmed by Haef's partial survey. Compared with 31 new museums in the 1880s and again in the 1890s, the 1900s registered a qualitative jump with 75 new Heimat museums, a rise of 241 percent with respect to the previous decade. Moreover, in merely four years, 1911 to 1914, 36 new museums were established, more than in the entire decade of the 1880s or the 1890s. As a whole, 111 Heimat museums were added between 1901 and 1914, 53 percent of the total number of Heimat museums founded between 1871 and 1918 in the territories covered by Haefs. The only incongruity between Haefs and Karasek concerns the evidence about the 1890s, as Haefs indicates the establishment of 31 new museums, whereas Karasek indicates the establishment of 76 museums. This incongruity is easily explained as a result of Haefs's concentration on West German territories alone.

37. For a detailed information see Haefs's description of Heimat museums by community.

38. Göppingen, WDS: 54.

39. The Heimat museums phenomenon in the German Empire still awaits its historian. Anthropologists, museum professionals, and scholars of folklore and German studies have generally paid more attention in the past decades than historians to Heimat museums. They were prolific in the 1970s and 1980s during the wave of renewed interest in the public role of Heimat museums in West Germany. See the useful collections that focus primarily on the contemporary functions of Heimat museums: Bätz and Gößwald, *Experiment Heimatmuseum*; Kuhn and Schneider, *Geschichte lernen im Museum*; and Scharfe, *Museen in der Provinz*. For a study of German museums written during the Second Empire, see Scherer, *Deutsche Museen*. On Heimat museums in the Third Reich, see Crus-Ramirez, "The Heimatmuseum."

40. Roth, *Heimatmuseum*. Roth's study, though tendentious, offers a rich analysis of the theory, application, and function of Heimat museums.

41. Ibid., 36, 33.

42. Ibid., 250. For a recent similar interpretation, see Hochreiter, *Vom Musentempel zum Lernort*, 191–92.

43. Karasek, *Die volkskundlich-kulturhistorischen Museen*, 120, 46, 49, 36. Following the East German Marxist doctrine, Karasek draws a sharp distinction between the "objective" reality of social conditions and the "subjective" reality in the imagination. Thus the ruling classes, according to her, produced in the museums nationalistic Heimat feelings on the "subjective level," while disguising the "objective foundations of the Heimat idea," namely class domination, imperialism, and chauvinism (ibid., 36). Karasek's study is well researched, but filled with this kind of Marxist-Leninist jargon that was common among historical studies in East Germany.

44. Ringbeck, "Dorfsammlung—Haus der Heimat—Heimatmuseum," 289.

45. Applegate discusses with subtlety the social and cultural meanings of the historical museum in Speyer in the Pfalz, a site of cultural inclusiveness and conflict originated by popular and notable bourgeoisie (*A Nation of Provincials*, 48–50, 93–102). But her analysis is limited on two grounds: she focuses on the Speyer museum, the region's main historical museum, while neglecting the Heimat museums in small and more provincial localities, and she isolates the Speyer museum from the larger Heimat museum phenomenon in Germany, a methodological move that obscures some of its larger meanings.

46. To overcome the difficulty of conducting research in hundreds of Heimat museums, I sent a questionnaire to most of the museums established in the German Empire about their foundation, organization, social composition, and display of the past. The more than 100 valuable answers I received are the basis of the following analysis. In order not to encumber the text, I will provide only several telling examples to illustrate an argument. I indicate the region and foundation year, whenever available, of a Heimat museum the first time it is mentioned either in the text or in the footnotes.

47. Roth, *Heimatmuseum*, 42.

48. Cited in Bausinger, *Volkskunde*, 51.

49. Roth, *Heimatmuseum*, 44.

50. *Volkskunde* museums were a European phenomenon, with museums emerging in, for example, Copenhagen, Stockholm, Prague, and Vienna. Very influential in Germany was the Scandinavian open-air *Volkskunde* museum and, in particular, the work of Arthur Hazelius in Skansen, Sweden (founded in 1891). See Brückner, "Das Museumswesen und die Entwicklung der Volkskunde als Wissenschaft," 135.

51. Robert Mielke, *Museum und Sammlungen. Ein Beitrag zu ihrer weiteren Entwicklung* (Berlin, 1903), 36, as cited in Ringbeck, "Dorfsammlung—Haus der Heimat—Heimatmuseum," 289.

52. For Weinheim (Baden, founded in 1906), see *Weinheimer Anzeiger*, 9.3.1906.

53. For example, Schleswig (Schleswig, founded in 1879): Holger, "Das Städtische Museum," 143–44; Kaufbeuren (Bavaria, founded in 1879): Frank, *Die unmittelbare Stadt*, 5, and a letter from Stadtarchiv Kaufbeuren (7 July 1990) in my possession; Kempten (Bavaria, founded in 1883): Strauß, *Führer durch das Allgäuer Heimatmuseum*, 3; Rosenheim (Bavaria, founded in 1894): Brand, *Heimatmuseum Rosenheim*, 5; Wolfenbüttel (Lower Saxony, founded in 1894): a letter from Stadt- und Kreis-Heimatmuseum (17 July 1990) in my possession; Ludwigsburg (Württemberg, founded in 1901): Manke, "Das Ludwigsburger Heimatmuseum," 166–67. See also Eisel, "Geschichts- und Altertumsvereine."

54. In Weinheim, a watchmaker, two bakers, and two innkeepers signed the statement calling for the foundation of a Heimat museum together with such leaders of the community as the mayor, the local priest, merchants, and a professor (*Weinheimer Anzeiger*, 9.3.1906). For some examples of the distinguished membership of museum committees, see for Celle (Lower Saxony, founded in 1905): Roth, *Heimatmuseum*, 75; for Weißenhorn (Bavaria, founded in 1908): Heinle, "Das Heimatmuseum," 16–17; for Vilsbiburg (Bavaria, founded in 1910): Barteit, "Heimatverein Vilsbiburg," 3.

55. For Chiemsee (founded in 1913): *75 Jahre Heimatmuseum in Prien am Chiemsee*, n.p.; Schwandorf (founded in 1912): Hofbauer, "Das Schwandorfer Orts- und Heimatmuseum."

56. The short period passed between planning and realizing a Heimat museum was often a source of pride for the community. See Weinheim: *Weinheimer Anzeiger*, 16.3.1907.

57. Vilsbiburg: Barteit, "Heimatverein Vilsbiburg," 2; Ramsdorf (Westphalia, founded in 1899): *Heimatverein Ramsdorf*, 12; Miesbach (Bavaria, founded in 1907): *Miesbacher Anzeiger*, 23.5.1907; Weißenhorn: Heinle, "Das Heimatmuseum," 16–17.

58. Rottweil (Württemberg, founded in 1884): Goessler, *Arae Flaviae*, iii–iv. Manke, "Das Ludwigsburger Heimatmuseum," 167–68.

59. Applegate, *A Nation of Provincials*, 93–96.

60. Herborn (Hessen, founded in 1887): Holler, "Aus der über 100jährigen Geschichte des Herborner Museums," 116; Barteit, "Heimatverein Vilsbiburg," 5; *Weinheimer Anzeiger*, 10.11.1913.

61. *Weinheimer Anzeiger*, 16.3.1907; Mutschler, *Ländliche Kindheit in Lebenserinnerungen*, 106.

62. Holler, "Aus der über 100jährigen Geschichte des Herborner Museums," 116. See also *Mitteilungsblatt des Geschichtsvereins Herborn*, 54–63.

63. "70 Jahre Heimatmuseum," *Westfalenspiegel* 10 (1969): 21.

64. Leer (Friesland, founded in 1912): Wiemann, "Der Verein für Heimatschutz," 13–14.

65. Oettingen (Bavaria, founded in 1908): *Oettinger Amts- und Wochenblatt*, 1.7.1908.

66. Ibid., 6.6.1908.

67. Documents in my possession sent by the Städtische Heimatmuseum in Reinfeld on 3 August 1990. See also *Weinheimer Anzeiger*, 9.3.1906.

68. This argument was raised by, for example, Ellwangen (Württemberg, founded in 1904): *Schloß Ellwangen*, 2; Lüneburg (Lower Saxony, founded in 1878): *Jubiläumsausstellung 1978*, 10; Barteit, "Heimatverein Vilsbiburg," 2; *Weinheimer Anzeiger*, 9.3.1906.

69. *Oettinger Amts- und Wochenblatt*, 1.7.1908.

70. For example, Hofbauer, "Das Schwandorfer Orts- und Heimatmuseum"; Holler, "Aus der über 100jährigen Geschichte des Herborner Museums," 116.

71. The centrality of everyday objects in the museum explains how activists established a Heimat museum in no time by simply going from house to house requesting contributions; people donated objects that would have been, otherwise, sooner or later disposed of.

72. Weber, "Einige grundsätzliche Gedanken zum Museumswesen," 25.

73. On Heimat museums and the concept of origins, see Reif, Heinze, and Ludwig, "Schwierigkeiten mit Tradition," 235.

74. Doering, "Bayerische Volkskunstmuseen," 207.

75. Cited in Ringbeck, "Dorfsammlung—Haus der Heimat—Heimatmuseum," 288.

76. Behn, "Das Heimatmuseum auf Föhr," 199.

77. Lübeck (Lower Saxony, founded in 1915): Jessen, "Das Museum für Kunst- und Kulturgeschichte," 53; Oberammergau: Doering, "Bayerische Volkskunstmuseen," 209.

78. *Weinheimer Anzeiger*, 9.3.1906.

79. It is worth noting that the word and the image depicted the past very differently. Heimatlers wrote that the museums were well organized; in fact, while museums were orderly, they lacked a historical order. The words of activists described one type of museum organization, the image quite another. See *75 Jahre Heimatmuseum in Prien am Chiemsee*, n.p.

80. See, for example, *Die Altertümersammlung auf dem Schloß Ellwangen*; *Weinheimer Anzeiger*, 15.3.1907; *Miesbacher Anzeiger*, 20.1.1907; Holler, "Aus der über 100jährigen Geschichte des Herborner Museums," 118.

81. *Weinheimer Anzeiger*, 15.3.1907.

82. Utitz, "Ein neues Museum," 196.

83. Jessen, "Das Museum für Kunst- und Kulturgeschichte in Lübeck," 59.

84. A document in my possession by Hanns Baum, "Das Altertums-Museum in Weinheim," from 1912.

85. Behn, "Das Heimatmuseum auf Föhr," 194–95.

86. Hofmeister, "Heimatverein, Heimatpflege und Heimatmuseum in Krumbach," 36.

87. On tourism and Heimat, see Rollins, "Aesthetic Environmentalism," 376–92. The citation is from Philipp Stauff, "Touristensinn—Photographensinn," *Sauerländischer Gebirgsbote* 17 (February 1909): 23–25, here 24 as quoted in Rollins, "Aesthetic Environmentalism," 389.

88. Document in my possession sent by the Sylter Heimatmuseum in Keitum on 25 August 1990.

89. *Miesbach Anzeiger*, 21.3.1906.

90. Doering, "Bayerische Volkskunstmuseen," 212. See also *75 Jahre Heimatmuseum in Prien am Chiemsee*, n.p.

91. Kempff, "Die Entwicklung des städtischen Museum zu Rheydt," 146.

92. Freyer, "Das Kreismuseum in Hadersleben"; Roch, "Das Stadtmuseum Bautzen, Provinzialmuseum der sächsischen Oberlausitz."

93. Kempff, "Die Entwicklung des städtischen Museum zu Rheydt," 147–48.

94. Freyer, "Das Kreismuseum in Hadersleben," 60.

95. For Brandt's ideas, see his "Über Kreis- und Ortsmuseen," 135; "Museen und Heimatschutz"; and "Provinzial- und Lokal-Museen."

96. Müller, "Das vaterländische Museum in Celle," 79.

97. The idea that the Heimat museum was expandable and that it represented local, regional, and national identities was common also in the Weimar Republic. In 1928, Hans Lehner, the director of the regional museum in Bonn, contributed an essay to a book about Heimat museums, in which he discussed the tasks and aims of the museums. It deserves to be cited at length. "The different types of Heimat museums are today extremely diverse. We have village museums, museums of small, medium, and large cities, county museums, district museums, province museums, regional and central museums. In order to clarify the concepts of these museums we can classify the different types under three headings: the local museums [*Ortsmuseen*], museums that represent larger territory [*Territorialmuseen*],

and the central museums [*Zentralmuseen*]. . . . [T]he task of these three categories is actually the same, namely to represent the native [*heimatlichen*] culture and nature." The local museum, including village and city museums, was responsible for representing the nature and culture of the immediate locality. The territorial museum referred to museums representing identities from the district to the regional level. And the central museum had to give a view of the nation as a whole as it "expands its collection activity to the entire empire." See Lehner, "Das Heimatmuseum," 7, 13. A few points are worth mentioning: Lehner's symbolism of Heimat museums was also identical to the symbolism of Heimat association; by viewing the task of the central Heimat museum as "to represent the native culture and nature," Lehner, in essence, defined the nation as Heimat.

98. Schwabmünchen (Bavaria, founded in 1913): Pfandzelter, "Vom Bezirksmuseum 1913 zu Museum und Galerie der Stadt Schwabmünchen 1984," 8. The text is a speech Pfandzelter, the mayor of Schwabmünchen, gave in 1984 on the festive occasion of reopening the Heimat museum. He cited the 1 August 1909 statement of the museum committee.

99. Heidelberg (Baden, founded in 1909): Peltzer, "Die Städtische Sammlung," 16.

100. Jever (Friesland, founded in 1887): Hohnholz, "Das Heimatmuseum im Schloß zu Jever," 115. See also Miesbach, *Miesbacher Anzeiger*, 23.5.1907.

101. Emmerich (Westphalia, founded in 1915): Goebel, "Das Emmericher 'Heimatmuseum,'" 23.

102. *Lesebuch für die katholischen Volksschulen Württembergs*, vol. 2 (Stuttgart, 1910), 405–6.

103. Eppinger, *Beschreibung, Geschichte und Führer von Fellbach*, 11. Emphasis added.

104. Applegate, *A Nation of Provincials*, 95–96.

105. Barteit, "Heimatverein Vilsbiburg," 4.

106. *80 Jahre Heimatverein "Niedersachsen,"* 6–7; *Hamburger Fremdenblatt*, 25.8.1913, 26.8.1913; *Zevener Zeitung*, 26.8.1913.

107. This image reached its epitome in Heimat iconography discussed in the next chapter.

108. Peltzer, "Die Städtische Sammlung," 17; Jessen, "Das Museum für Kunst- und Kulturgeschichte," 49–59.

109. Lehner, "Das Heimatmuseum," 4–5.

110. *Festschrift zur Feier des fünfzig-jährigen Bestehen der K. Altertümersammlung in Stuttgart 1912.*

111. Freyer, "Das Kreismuseum in Hadersleben," 60.

112. Documents in my possession sent by the Städtische Heimatmuseum in Reinfeld on 3 August 1990.

113. Rain (Bavaria, founded in 1905): *Rainer Wochenblatt*, 24.9.1904.

114. Brandt, "Über Kreis- und Ortsmuseen," 134. See also Brandt, "Provinzial- und Lokal-Museen," 4.

115. The current historiography of the changes German society underwent in the 1890s has emphasized the conflicts between bourgeois notables, on the one hand, and the petite bourgeoisie and middle classes, on the other. Especially important in this regard have been the studies of Eley and Blackbourn, who have argued that the pressure from below by the popular middle classes on the privileges of bourgeois notables played a significant role in Wilhelmine Germany's political culture. While this argument is no doubt correct, it should not obscure the fact that symbolic common denominators also existed between the notables and the popular middle classes. See Blackbourn, *Populists and Patricians*, and Eley, *Reshaping the German Right*.

116. Applegate, *A Nation of Provincials*, 101.

117. Documents in my possession sent by the Städtische Heimatmuseum, Reinfeld on 3 August 1990.

118. Halbwachs, *The Collective Memory*, 78–87, 105–7.

119. *Treitschke's Origins of Prussianism*, 18.

120. Ibid., 18–19.

121. Funkenstein, "Collective Memory and Historical Consciousness," 21.

122. See ibid., 19.

123. The first professional use of oral history was by American historians in the 1930s. German historians began only much later in the 1960s.

124. David Lowenthal's study *The Past Is a Foreign Country* is dedicated to the manifestations and meanings of the obsession with the past in modern society.

125. Nora, "Entre mémoire et histoire," xvii.

126. *Weinheimer Anzeiger*, 15.3.1907.

127. Hagen, *Museum und Galerie der Stadt Schwabmünchen*, 65–67; Jahn, *Schwabmünchen*, 202–3.

128. Nora, "Entre mémoire et histoire," xvii, xx–xxx.

CHAPTER SEVEN

1. Seytter, *Unser Stuttgart*, 2.

2. *Schwäbisches Heimatbuch* (1949): 38–39. Underlined in the original.

3. Ibid., 21, 24.

4. Ibid., 29. A similar appreciation of the importance of images was expressed by the Landesausschuss für Natur- und Heimatschutz. See *Arbeitsplan des Württembergischen Landesausschusses für Natur- und Heimatschutz*, 17.

5. Vovelle, *Immagini e immaginario nella storia*. Simon Schama has been very successful in using images in *The Embarrassment of Riches* and *Landscape and Memory*. Rotberg and Rabb's *Art and History* is a book by historians that examines the common ground and different sets of assumptions of both disciplines. Carlo Ginzburg has been perhaps the most important historian lately to deal with art history. His contribution has gone beyond elucidation of the relations between history and art history, and has made a substantial impact on the method of art history itself, notably in *Indagini su Piero*. His article "From Aby Warburg to E. H. Gombrich" is an excellent introduction for historians to the pitfalls and advantages of using images.

6. Ginzburg, "From Aby Warburg to E. H. Gombrich," 35. Emphasis in the original.

7. On Panofsky and landscape, see Cosgrove and Daniels, "Introduction: Iconography and Landscape."

8. Panofsky, *Studies in Iconology*, 7.

9. Ibid., 16.

10. *Schwäbische Heimat* (August 1911): 42–43. Emphasis added. The Verein recommended other Heimat images painted by Strich-Chapell, such as *Lieb' Heimatland ade* (Farewell beloved Heimat land), glowingly described by the journal of the association, the *Schwäbische Heimat*: "The landscape, how marvelous is this morning atmosphere. . . . The man at the top looks with palpable nostalgia to the Heimat valley below" (September 1911, 60).

11. The Verein did not recommend only Heimat images, but above all religious images.

12. Nipperdey, *Deutsche Geschichte, 1866–1918*, 1:729.

13. On the German Werkbund and its relations to the Heimat movement, see Jefferies,

Politics and Culture in Wilhelmine Germany, chap. 3. In the Weimar Republic Schultze-Naumburg became an anti-Semite and an advocate of the race theory; this took place following the war, defeat, and revolution, and it is beyond the scope of this study to analyze the relationships between Schultze-Naumburg's worldview before and after World War I. In any event, it is anachronistic to project automatically Schultze-Naumburg's ideas after 1918 to the previous period.

14. Schultze-Naumburg, *Die Entstellung unseres Landes*, 9.

15. Ibid.

16. Furthermore, it is possible to establish that Heimat images in the *Heimatgruß* series were chosen consciously and not by happenstance. *Heimatgruß von Steinheim* began to appear in March 1906 without an image near its logo. The addition of an image a month later, perhaps in response to similar images in other *Heimatgruß* newspapers, demonstrated the awareness of the editors that a Heimat image was a powerful means to represent the community.

17. *Schwäbisches Heimatbuch* (1949): 23.

18. Ibid.

19. "Der Feind im Land!," in HStA, J 150, no. 232/8.

20. "Die Engländer," in HStA, J 150, no. 232/15.

21. For example, "In the Heimat—In the Heimat—There will be a Reunion" (In der Heimat—In der Heimat—da gibt's ein Wiedersehen) presents a soldier bidding farewell to his family with the Heimat locality visible in the background. Binder, *Mit Glanz und Gloria in die Niederlage*, 59. A postcard from "Der feldgraue Weihnachtsmann" series for the 1916–17 Christmas and New Year holidays displayed two soldiers guarding the distant homeland, represented as a Heimat locality. See *Glückwünsche auf Postkarte*, no. 118.

22. My discussion here relies on the well-illustrated book of Weill, *The Poster*, which is an excellent guide for the topic.

23. Ibid., 130.

24. Bernhard painted other, and more political, Heimat images as well. Two 1919 posters that called volunteers to fight Bolshevism in Eastern Prussia in Lüttwitz's Free Corps were entitled "Protect the Heimat," presenting a menacing hand over a classic Heimat locality. See *Plakate. Jörg Weigelt Auktionen*, 31, no. 122, and Malhotra, *Politische Plakate 1914–1945*, 80, no. 91.

The production of the Heimat war-loan posters shows the use by the state of the popular Heimat idea. The war-loan poster competitions were organized by the state while the Reichsbank purchased and diffused the winning posters all over Germany, also as postcards and small images. (See Lebeck and Schütte, *Propagandapostkarten*, 11.) The people responsible for German propaganda after 1914 used the Heimat image to further the aim of funding the war because the image had already been popular among Germans. Nevertheless, although institutions of the state ordered the war-loan posters, the activity around their creation was by no means controlled by them; the Verein der Plakatfreunde (Association for the Poster's Promoters), for instance, organized competitions of the war-loan posters.

25. *Die Heimat. Neue Kriegsgedichte.*

26. *Um die Heimat. Bilder aus dem Weltkrieg 1914*, collected by J. Kammerer, nine booklets published in Stuttgart between 1915 and 1917. *Die Heimat. Neue Kriegsgedichte*. The booklets cost 60 pfennigs.

27. *Die Heimat. Neue Kriegsgedichte*, 48.

28. Ibid., 35, 48, 50; Kammerer, *Um die Heimat*, vol. 2: *Der westliche Kriegsschauplatz*, 131.

29. "Ein Stuttgarter Plakat-Wettbewerb für die 7. Kriegsanleihe," *Das Plakat* 9 (January 1918): 37.

30. On Sigrist see Pazaurek, "Karl Sigrist." Sigrist produced yet another Heimat image in a war-loan poster that showed a man's face in front of the defended Heimat: a hometown, a child playing, and a mother breastfeeding a baby. See Missenharter, "Die württembergischen Gebrauchs-Graphiker," 72.

31. I am grateful to John Gillis for sharing with me his insights on the connection between the concepts of home and Heimat. See his *A World of Their Own Making*.

32. Kammerer, *Um die Heimat*, 7:119; *Die Heimat. Neue Kriegsgedichte*, 69.

33. *Die Heimat. Neue Kriegsgedichte*, 49.

34. *Der Kampf. Neue Gedichte aus dem Heiligen Krieg*, 44.

35. Schefold, *Das alte Württemberg*, 7.

36. Ulshöfer, *Bilder einer alten Stadt*, 103.

37. Schefold, *Alte Ansichten aus Württemberg*, 10–11.

38. For traditional *veduta* images that resembled Heimat images, see, for example, DaCosta Kaufmann, *Central European Drawings*, 254–55, 268–69; Andersson and Talbot, *From a Mighty Fortress*, frontispiece; Rowlands, *German Drawings*, 57–58, 60.

39. Bernhard, *Reisehandbuch durch Württemberg*, v.

40. For example, Kramer, "Die politische und ökonomische Funktionalisierung von Heimat im deutschen Imperialismus und Faschismus."

41. Similarly, Denis Cosgrove, attempting to explain the idea of landscape in the West since the Renaissance, has located it "as a way of seeing the world . . . within the materialist framework of the capitalist transition." Cosgrove, *Social Formation and Symbolic Landscape*, 55. Cosgrove has since substantially modified his Marxist approach to art history and turned to Warburg and Panofsky. See the fine volume, Cosgrove and Daniels, *The Iconography of Landscape*.

42. Bermingham, *Landscape and Ideology*.

43. *Die Stadt. Bild-Gestalt-Vision*, 16.

44. See also the observations about Friedrich by Paulson, "Types of Demarcation," 348–54.

45. *Die Heimat. Neue Kriegsgedichte*, 35, 49.

46. Ibid., 35.

47. I based my discussion of the postcard on the beautifully illustrated studies of Staff, *The Picture Postcard and Its Origins* and *Picture Postcards and Travel*, which are still excellent sources about the subject.

48. Braungart, "Künstlerische Ansichtspostkarten," 360.

49. Cited in Staff, *Picture Postcards and Travel*, 37.

50. Cited in ibid., 81.

51. On the social functions of the postcard, see Ripert and Frère, *La carte postal*.

52. See the picture postcards in *Calw, 1850–1925*, 84; Besch, *Alte Stadtansichten von Marbach*, 50; Knöpfle, *Alte Horb*, 114.

53. Staff, *Picture Postcards and Travel*, 44–52.

54. Ibid., 46.

55. This behavior has not been peculiar to bourgeois tourists in imperial Germany, but has generally characterized the phenomenon of tourism. Today, when tourism is a mass phenomenon that cuts across social divisions, lower-class tourists also prefer Tuscany's art treasures over the poverty of India or Sicily. It should be added, however, that a different kind of tourism has simultaneously developed that takes the modern traveler to poor and miserable places that are often considered exotic. Behind this phenomenon is the most often unspoken curiosity to observe the Other. This topic is beyond the scope of this discussion.

56. The hometown iconography of the Heimat idea was also established by *Heimat und Welt*, the journal of the Vereinigung Heimat und Welt (Union of Heimat and World), whose interests embraced Heimat history, geography, and folklore in Germany and the world. In spite of a turn to the right, when the Vereinigung began to cooperate with the Verein für das Deutschtum im Ausland (Union for the Germanism Abroad), the symbol of the journal remained unchanged, showing the German Heimat as a small town on a hill and the world around it. *Heimat und Welt. Monatshefte der "Vereinigung Heimat und Welt"* 1 (October 1910–September 1911): 9.

57. Messing, *Heilbronn in alten Ansichtskarten*, 26.

58. See also *Kirchheim unter Teck. Ansichten*, 16.

59. Jünger, "Der Kampf als inneres Erlebnis," 87. I am grateful to Elliot Neaman for bringing this passage to my attention.

60. Heimat and peace were also linked by the jury of the Seventh War Loan competition won by Sigrist.

61. The interpretation that Heimat equals fatherland has been advanced by scholars who argued for the nationalistic, manipulative, antimodern characteristics of Heimat. For example, Projektgruppe Deutscher Heimatfilm, *Der deutsche Heimatfilm*, 16.

62. Rilke, *The Notebooks of Malte Laurids Brigge*, 23.

63. See Blackbourn, "The German Bourgeoisie: An Introduction," 18; Langewiesche, "Deutscher Liberalismus," 13.

64. Blackbourn, "The Discreet Charm of the Bourgeoisie."

65. *Heimatschutz* 10, no. 1 (1915): 18. Underlined in the original.

66. Anderson, *Imagined Communities*, 15.

67. Applegate, "Localism and the German Bourgeoisie," 225. She similarly argued in her book that the "Heimat as a movement and as an object of civic organization, had represented the political unit's attempt to root itself firmly in local life while at the same time claiming membership in the nation. The local civic context of Heimat activities emerges from this perspective as not only the most important context in which to understand the Heimat movement, but perhaps the only one." Applegate, *A Nation of Provincials*, 106–7.

68. Applegate, *A Nation of Provincials*, 13.

AFTERWORD

1. Hobsbawm, "Mass-Producing Traditions"; Dodd and Colls, *Englishness*; Nora, *Les lieux de mémoire*.

2. Dodd, "Englishness and the National Culture," 22.

3. See, for example, Hellerstein, Hume, and Offen, *Victorian Women*, esp. part II.

4. Mackay and Thane, "The Englishwomen," esp. 191–93, 223–24.

5. See Evans, *Comrades and Sisters: Feminism, Socialism and Pacifism in Europe, 1870–1945*, 121–56, and *The Feminist Movement in Germany*; Kruse and Sowerwine, "Feminism and Pacifism: 'Women's Sphere' in Peace and War"; Stites, *The Women's Liberation Movement in Russia*.

6. HStA, E 151/07, 584.

7. *Aufruf zur Gründung eines Bundes Heimatschutz*, in HStA, E 151/07, no. 584, and *75 Jahre Deutscher Heimatbund*, 59.

8. See, for example, Dûval and Monahan, *Collecting Postcards*, nos. 7–15; Mordente, *Catalogo delle cartoline illustrate italiane*, 35–36, 225–31.

9. Stanley, *What Did You Do in the War Daddy?*, 41.

10. Howard, *Landscape: The Artists' Vision*, 137. Howard has observed that the use of patriotic landscapes in World War I was not common and that "the appointment of Official War Artists, in both wars, did not directly lead to much landscape work."

11. I have consulted the following books to compare Heimat iconography with national iconography of European countries in posters and postcards. Posters: Crawford, *Posters of World War I and World War II*; Stanley, *What Did You Do in the War Daddy?*; Weill, *The Poster*; Baker, "Describing Images of the National Self"; Darracott, *The First World War in Posters: From the Imperial War Museum, London*. Postcards: Dûval and Monahan, *Collecting Postcards*; Mordente, *Catalogo delle cartoline illustrate italiane*; Holt and Holt, *Picture Postcard Artists*; Laffin, *World War I in Post-Cards*.

12. Bloch, *The Historian's Craft*, 32.

13. "Jede Nation spottet über die andere, und alle haben Recht." Cited in Marías, *Understanding Spain*, 155.

14. Huizinga, "Patriotism and Nationalism in European History," 154–55.

Bibliography

PRIMARY SOURCES

Archival Sources

Stuttgart, Hauptstaatsarchiv: E 14 II, no. 1348; E 150/07, no. 570; E 151/07, no. 584; E 151a, no. 2932; J 2, no. 624; J 150, no. 232.
Württembergische Drucksachen: 400 boxes of printed material from the nineteenth and twentieth centuries (such as pamphlets and associations' publications directed to their members) in the Landesbibliothek Stuttgart.

Newspapers

In Württemberg
Der Beobachter.
Besondere Beilage des Staats-Anzeiger für Württemberg.
Chronik der Kgl. Haupt- und Residenzstadt Stuttgart, 1871–1918.
Schwäbische Kronik.
Schwäbischer Merkur.
Staats-Anzeiger für Württemberg.
Tübinger Chronik.
Wimpfener Zeitung.

In Germany
Hamburger Fremdenblatt (Hamburg).
Miesbacher Anzeiger (Miesbach, Bavaria).
Oettinger Amts- und Wochenblatt (Oettingen, Bavaria).
Rainer Wochenblatt (Rain, Bavaria).
Schwandorfer Tagblatt (Schwandorf, Bavaria).
Weinheimer Anzeiger (Weinheim, Baden).
Zevener Zeitung (Zeven, Lower Saxony).

Periodical Literature

Aus dem Arbeitsgebiet des "Württembergischen Landesausschusses für Natur- und Heimatschutz."

Ellwanger Jahrbuch. Ein Volksbuch der Heimatpflege für den Virngrund und das Ries. Edited by Geschichts- und Altertumsverein Ellwangen.
Heimatschutz. Edited by the Deutscher Bund Heimatschutz.
Heimat und Welt. Monatshefte der "Vereinigung Heimat und Welt."
Mitteilungsblatt des Geschichtsvereins Herborn.
Museumskunde.
Das Plakat.
Schwäbische Heimat. Blätter für Volkswohlfahrt und Heimatpflege.
Schwäbisches Heimatbuch.
Statistisches Jahrbuch des Königreiches Württemberg.
Die Tide. Monatsschrift für Nord-, Ost- und Westfriesland, Oldenburg, Friesische Inseln und Helgoland.
Westfalenspiegel.

Contemporary Printed Sources

Allgemeine deutsche Real-Encyklopädie für die gebildeten Stände. Leipzig, 1852.
Die Altertümersammlung auf dem Schloß Ellwangen. Ellwangen, 1912.
Arbeitsplan des Württembergischen Landesausschusses für Natur- und Heimatschutz. Stuttgart, n.d.
Behn, Fr. "Das Heimatmuseum auf Föhr." *Museumskunde* 4 (1908): 194–99.
Bericht über die Entwickelung und Thätigkeit des Verschönerungsvereins der Stadt Stuttgart in den ersten 25 Jahren seines Bestehens 1861–1886. Stuttgart, 1886.
Bernhard, Julius. *Reisehandbuch durch Württemberg und die angrenzenden Länderstriche der Nachbarstaaten. Historisch, pittoresk, statistisch-topographisch und industriell.* 2d ed. Stuttgart, 1864.
Bohnenberger, Karl. *Volkstümliche Überlieferungen in Württemberg.* Stuttgart, 1980.
Brandt, Gustav. "Museen und Heimatschutz." *Museumskunde* 5 (1909): 30–34.
——. "Provinzial- und Lokal-Museen." *Museumskunde* 2 (1906): 1–7.
——. "Über Kreis- und Ortsmuseen." *Museumskunde* 9 (1913): 133–38.
Bund für Heimatschutz in Württemberg und Hohenzollern. Mitglieder-Verzeichnis 1909–1929. N.p., 1929.
Bunte Blätter aus Württemberg und Hohenzollern. Ausstellung-Katalog. Edited by the Württembergisch-Hohenzollerischen Vereinigung für Fremdenverkehr. Stuttgart, 1912.
Buurman, Otto. *Hochdeutsch-plattdeutsches Wörterbuch. Auf der Grundlage ostfriesischer Mundart.* Vol. 1. Neumünster, 1962.
Christmann, Ernst, and Julius Krämer. *Pfälzisches Wörterbuch.* Vol. 3. Wiesbaden, 1980.
Doering, O. "Bayerische Volkskunstmuseen." *Museumskunde* 7 (1911): 207–14.
Egelhaaf, Gottlob. *Lebens-Erinnerungen.* Edited by Adolf Raap. Stuttgart, 1960.
Eichendorff, Joseph von. "Die Heimat." In *Heimat. Ein deutsches Lesebuch,* edited by Manfred Kluge, 72. Munich, 1989.
Eisele and Köhle. *Geschichtliche Heimatkunde für den Oberamtsbezirk Göppingen und seine Umgebung.* Göppingen, 1908.
Elben, Otto. *Lebenserinnerungen 1823–1899.* Stuttgart, 1931.
Eppinger, G. *Beschreibung, Geschichte und Führer von Fellbach.* Fellbach, 1908.
Erster Rechenschaftsbericht des Württembergischen Altertums-Vereins für das Jahr 1844. N.p., n.d.
Fest-Ordnung für die Feierliche Enthüllung des Kaiser Wilhelm-Denkmals in Heilbronn a.N. am Sedanstag, 2.September 1893.
Festschrift zum 25Jährigen Jubiläums des Schillergaues 1903–1928. N.p., n.d.

Festschrift zur Feier des fünfzig-jährigen Bestehen der K. Altertümersammlung in Stuttgart 1912. Stuttgart, 1912.

Fischer, Hermann. *Schwäbisches Wörterbuch.* Vol. 1. Tübingen, 1904.

Fontana, Theodor. "Anhang: Die Denkmäler." In *Der deutsche Krieg von 1866.* Vol. 2: *Der Feldzug in West- und Mitteldeutschland.* Berlin, 1871.

Frank, C. *Die unmittelbare Stadt und das kgl. Bezirksamt Kaufbeuren.* Kaufbeuren, 1899.

Freyer, Kurt. "Das Kreismuseum in Hadersleben." *Museumskunde* 12 (1916): 59–68.

German, Wilhelm. *Chronik von Schwäbisch Hall und Umgebung. Haus- und Familienbuch.* Hall, 1902.

"Geschichte der Gründung des Bundes für Heimatschutz in Württemberg und Hohenzollern." *Schwäbisches Heimatbuch* (1919): 8–19.

Geschichtliches vom Verschönerungsverein Tuttlingen. Tuttlingen, 1909.

Der Geschichts- und Altertumsverein Rottweil von 1832–1913. Rottweil, 1914.

Goebel, Ferdinand. "Das Emmericher 'Heimatmuseum.'" *Museumskunde* 13 (1917): 16–23.

Goessler, Peter. *Arae Flaviae. Führer durch die Altertumshalle der Stadt Rottweil.* Rottweil, 1928.

Götze, Alfred. *Trübners Deutsches Wörterbuch. Im Auftrag der Arbeitsgemeinschaft für deutsche Wortforschung.* Vol. 1. Berlin, 1939.

Gradmann, Eugen. *Anweisungen zur Denkmalpflege.* Stuttgart, 1912.

———. "Kriegerdenkmäler." *Schwäbisches Heimatbuch* (1916): 10–37.

Greiner, J. *Der Verein für Kunst und Altertum in Ulm und Oberschwaben. Ein Rückblick.* Stuttgart, 1922.

Grimm, Jacob, and Wilhelm Grimm. *Deutsches Wörterbuch.* Vol. 4, pt. 2. Leipzig, 1877.

Große, C., and C. Raith. *Beiträge zur Geschichte und Statistik der Reichstags- und Landtagswahlen in Württemberg seit 1871.* Stuttgart, 1912.

Hartmann, I. "Zur Geschichte der württembergischen Landeskunde." *Besondere Beilage des Staats-Anzeiger für Württemberg,* nos. 5–6 (16 June 1893): 66–67.

Die Heimat. Neue Kriegsgedichte. Jena, 1915.

Hesse, Hermann. "Heimat. Calw." In *Heimat. Ein deutsches Lesebuch,* edited by Manfred Kluge, 121–22. Munich, 1989.

Holmholz, D. "Das Heimatmuseum im Schloß zu Jever." *Die Tide. Monatsschrift für Nord-, Ost- und Westfriesland, Oldenburg, Friesische Inseln und Helgoland* (1921): 115–22.

Jessen, Peter. "Das Museum für Kunst- und Kulturgeschichte in Lübeck." *Museumskunde* 12 (1916): 49–59.

Kaißer, B. *Aus der Vergangenheit Gmünds und seiner Umgebung. Landschaftliche und Kulturhistorische Schilderungen in Eizelbildern.* Gmünd, 1911.

Kammerer J., ed. *Um die Heimat. Bilder aus dem Weltkrieg 1914.* 9 Vols. Stuttgart, 1915–17.

Der Kampf. Neue Gedichte aus dem Heiligen Krieg. Jena, 1914.

Kempff, Otto. "Die Entwicklung des städtischen Museum zu Rheydt." *Museumskunde* 13 (1917): 140–49.

Kittler, Gustav. *Aus dem dritten württembergischen Reichstags-Wahlkreis.* Heilbronn, 1910.

Kleiner Führer durch Tuttlingen und Umgebung. Tuttlingen, 1910.

Koolman, J. Ten Doornkaat. *Wörterbuch der Ostfriesischen Sprache.* Norden, 1879.

Lehner, Hans. "Das Heimatmuseum, seine Aufgaben und Ziele, Formen und Organisation." In *Heimatmuseen. Wesen und Gestaltung,* edited by Walther Schoenichen, 1–24. Berlin, 1928.

Lesebuch für die evangelischen Volksschulen Württembergs. Stuttgart, 1874.

Lesebuch für die evangelischen Volksschulen Württembergs. Vol. 2: *Viertes und fünftes Schuljahr.* Stuttgart, 1909.

Lesebuch für die katholischen Volksschulen Württembergs. New ed. Horb, 1895.

Lesebuch für die katholischen Volksschulen Württembergs. Vol. 2. Stuttgart, 1910.

Lesebuch für die katholischen Volksschulen Württembergs. Vol. 2: *Viertes bis siebtes (achtes) Schuljahr.* Stuttgart, 1910.

Martin, E., and H. Lienhart. *Wörterbuch der Elsässischen Mundarten.* Vol. 1. Strasbourg, 1899.

Mayer, Karl. *Heimat-Buch für Kirchheim u. Teck und Umgebung.* 3d ed. Kirchheim unter Teck, 1920.

Mielke, Robert. *Museum und Sammlungen. Ein Beitrag zu ihrer weiteren Entwicklung.* Berlin, 1903.

Mönch, Wilhelm. *Heimatkunde vom Oberamt Calw.* Calw, 1925.

Müller, Bernard. "Das vaterländische Museum in Celle." *Museumskunde* 6 (1910): 79–92.

Neckarsulm. Heimatkunde des Oberamtsbezirks für Schule und Haus. Heilbronn, 1913.

Peltzer, A. "Die Städtische Sammlung zu Heidelberg." *Museumskunde* 5 (1909): 13–23.

Roch, Wolfgang. "Das Stadtmuseum Bautzen, Provinzialmuseum der sächsischen Oberlausitz." *Museumskunde* 9 (1913): 69–85.

Rommel, Karl. *Reutlinger Heimatbuch. Bilder, Sagen und Geschichten aus Stadt und Amt.* Reutlingen, 1929.

Satzungen des württembergischen Schwarzwald-vereins. Stuttgart, 1884.

Scherer, Valentin. *Deutsche Museen. Entstehung und Kulturgeschichtliche Bedeutung unserer öffentlichen Kunstsammlungen.* Jena, 1913.

Schloß Ellwangen. Ausstellung für Heimatkunst. Edited by Geschichts- und Altertumsverein. Ellwangen, 1913.

Schmeller, Johann Andreas. *Bayerisches Wörterbuch.* Vol. 1. Aalen, 1872.

Schultze-Naumburg, Paul. *Die Entstellung unseres Landes.* 2d ed. Munich, 1907.

Seytter, Wilhelm. *Unser Stuttgart. Geschichte, Sage und Kultur der Stadt und ihrer Umgebung.* Stuttgart, 1904.

Sieg oder Tod. Neue Kriegsgedichte. Jena, 1915.

Statuten des Verschönerungs-Vereins Schramberg. Beschlossen in der konstituirenden Versammlung vom 25. Mai 1881. Anhang: Das Mitglieder-verzeichnis. Schramberg, 1881.

Stauff, Philipp. "Touristensinn—Photographensinn." *Sauerländischer Gebirgsbote* 17 (February 1909): 23–25.

Stuttgart. Führer durch die Stadt und ihre Bauten. Festschrift zur sechsten Generalversammlung des Verbandes deutscher Architekten- und Ingenieur-Verein. Edited by the württemb. Verein für Baukunde. Stuttgart, 1884.

Unsere Heimat in alter und neuer Zeit. Heimatkunde für Schule und Haus. Giengen an der Brenz, 1914.

Utitz, Emil. "Ein neues Museum." *Museumskunde* 6 (1910): 191–98.

Wagner, Friedrich, ed. *Heimatkunde für Stadt und Oberamt Hall.* Schwäbisch Hall, 1912.

Weber, Paul. "Einige grundsätzliche Gedanken zum Museumswesen, angeknüpft an das vaterländische Museum in Celle." *Museumskunde* 10 (1914): 24–29.

Weißer, Rudolf, ed. *Denkmale der Filder.* Stuttgart, 1929.

Württembergischer Altertumsverein. Rechenschafts-Bericht für die Jahre 1891 bis 1893, insbesondere Beschreibung der Jubiläumsfeier vom 22.–25. September 1893. Stuttgart, 1894.

SECONDARY SOURCES

50 Jahre deutscher Heimatbund. Deutscher Bund Heimatschutz. Edited by the Deutscher Heimatschutz. Neuß am Rhine, 1954.

75 Jahre Deutscher Heimatbund. Siegburg, 1979.
75 Jahre Heimat- und Altertumsverein Heidenheim e.V. 1901–1976. Heidenheim, 1976.
75 Jahre Heimatmuseum in Prien am Chiemsee. Prien am Chiemsee, 1988.
80 Jahre Heimatverein "Niedersachsen" e.V. Scheeßel, 1905–1985. Scheeßel, 1985.
"Ein Stuttgarter Plakat-Wettbewerb für die 7. Kriegsanleihe." *Das Plakat* 9 (January 1918): 37.
100 Jahre Verschönerungsverein Kirchheim unter Teck, 1864–1964. Kirchheim unter Teck, n.d.
100 Jahre Verschönerungsverein Metzingen, 1880–1980. Metzingen, 1980.
150 Jahre Rottweiler Geschichts- und Altertumsvereine e.V. Festschrift. Rottweil, 1981.
Agulhon, Maurice. "Imagerie civique et decor urbain." In *Histoire Vagabonde.* Vol. 1, 101–37. Paris, 1986.
———. *Marianne into Battle: Republican Imagery and Symbolism in France, 1789–1880.* Cambridge, 1981.
———. *The Republic in the Village: The People of the Var from the French Revolution to the Second Republic.* Cambridge, 1982.
———. "La 'statuomanie' et l'histoire." In *Histoire Vagabonde.* Vol. 1, 138–85. Paris, 1986.
Anderson, Benedict. *Imagined Communities: Reflections on the Origin and Spread of Nationalism.* London, 1990.
Andersson, Christiane, and Charles Talbot. *From a Mighty Fortress: Prints, Drawings, and Books in the Age of Luther, 1483–1546.* Detroit, 1983.
Applegate, Celia. "Localism and the German Bourgeoisie: The 'Heimat' Movement in the Rhenish Palatinate before 1914." In *The German Bourgeoisie,* edited by David Blackbourn and Richard Evans, 224–54. London, 1991.
———. *A Nation of Provincials: The German Idea of Heimat.* Berkeley, Calif., 1990.
Bachem, Karl. *Vorgeschichte, Geschichte und Politik der deutschen Zentrumspartei.* Vol. 4. Cologne, 1928.
Baeumer, Max. "Imperial Germany as Reflected in Its Mass Festivals." In *Imperial Germany,* edited by Volker Dürr, Kathy Harms, and Peter Hayes, 62–74. London, 1985.
Baker, Keith, ed. *The French Revolution and the Creation of Modern Political Culture.* 3 vols. Oxford, 1987–89.
———. *Inventing the French Revolution: Essays on French Political Culture in the Eighteenth Century.* Cambridge, 1990.
Baker, Steve. "Describing Images of the National Self: Popular Accounts of the Construction of Pictorial Identity in the First World War Poster." *Oxford Art Journal* 13, no. 2 (1990): 24–30.
Barteit, Peter. "Heimatverein Vilsbiburg 1928–1978." In *50 Jahre Heimatverein Vilsbiburg 1928–1978,* edited by Fritz Markmiller, 2–24. Sonderheft 2, *Der Storchenturm: Geschichtsblätter für die Landkreise um Dingolfing, Landau und Vilsbiburg.* Dingolfing, 1978.
Bastide, Roger. "Mémoire collective et sociologie du bricolage." *L'année sociologique* 21 (1970): 65–108.
Bätz, Oliver, and Udo Gößwald, eds. *Experiment Heimatmuseum. Zur Theorie und Praxis regionaler Museumsarbeit.* Marburg, 1988.
Bausinger, Hermann. *Volkskunde. Von der Altertumsforschung zur Kulturanalyse.* Darmstadt, 1971.
———. "Volkskundliche Anmerkungen zum Thema 'Bildungsbürger.'" In *Bildungsbürgertum im 19. Jahrhundert.* Vol. 4: *Politischer Einfluß und gesellschaftliche Formation,* edited by Jürgen Kocka, 206–14. Stuttgart, 1989.

Berdahl, Robert. "New Thoughts on German Nationalism." *American Historical Review* 77 (1972): 65–80.

Berghahn, Volker, and Hanna Schissler, eds. *Perceptions of History: An Analysis of School Textbooks*. Oxford, 1987.

Bergmann, Klaus. *Agrarromantik und Großstadtfeindschaft*. Meisenheim am Glan, 1970.

Bergson, Henri. *Matter and Memory*. New York, 1988.

Berman, Marshall. *All That Is Solid Melts into Air: The Experience of Modernity*. New York, 1982.

Bermingham, Ann. *Landscape and Ideology: The English Rustic Tradition, 1740–1860*. Berkeley, Calif., 1986.

Besch, Hans. *Alte Stadtansichten von Marbach am Neckar*. Marbach, 1980.

Binder, Gerhart. *Mit Glanz und Gloria in die Niederlage. Der Erst Weltkrieg in alten Ansichtskarten*. Stuttgart, 1983.

Binder, Hans-Otto. *Reich und Einzelstaaten während der Kanzlerschaft Bismarcks 1871–1890*. Tübingen, 1971.

Bischoff-Luithlen, Angelika. *Von Amtsstuben, Backhäusern, und Jahrmärkten. Ein Lese- und Nachschlagebuch zum Dorfalltag im alten Württemberg und Baden*. Stuttgart, 1979.

Blackbourn, David. "Catholics and Politics in Imperial Germany: The Centre Party and Its Constituency." In *Populists and Patricians: Essays in Modern German History*, 188–214. London, 1987.

———. *Class, Religion, and Local Politics in Wilhelmine Germany: The Center Party in Württemberg before 1914*. New Haven, Conn., 1980.

———. "The Discreet Charm of the Bourgeoisie: Reappraising German History in the Nineteenth Century." In *The Peculiarities of German History: Bourgeois Society and Politics in Nineteenth-Century Germany*, edited by David Blackbourn and Geoff Eley, 159–292. Oxford, 1984.

———. "The German Bourgeoisie: An Introduction." In *The German Bourgeoisie: Essays on the Social History of the German Middle Class from the Late Eighteenth to the Early Twentieth Century*, edited by David Blackbourn and Richard Evans, 1–45. London, 1991.

———. *Marpingen: Apparitions of the Virgin Mary in a Nineteenth-Century German Village*. New York, 1995.

———. "The *Mittelstand* in German Society and Politics, 1871–1914." *Social History* 4 (1977): 409–33.

———. "Peasants and Politics in Germany, 1871–1914." *European History Quarterly* 14 (1984): 47–75.

———. "The Politics of Demagogy in Imperial Germany." In *Populists and Patricians: Essays in Modern German History*, 217–45. London, 1987.

———. *Populists and Patricians: Essays in Modern German History*. London, 1987.

———. "Progress and Piety: Liberals, Catholics and the State in Bismarck's Germany." In *Populists and Patricians: Essays in Modern German History*, 143–67. London, 1987.

Blackbourn, David, and Geoff Eley. *The Peculiarities of German History: Bourgeois Society and Politics in Nineteenth-Century Germany*. Oxford, 1984.

Blessing, Werner. "The Cult of the Monarchy, Political Loyalty and the Workers' Movement in Imperial Germany." *Journal of Contemporary History* 13, no. 2 (1978): 357–75.

Bloch, Marc. *The Historian's Craft*. New York, 1953.

Böhme, Helmut. *Deutschlands Weg zur Grossmacht*. Berlin, 1966.

Borst, Arno. "Barbarossa Erwachen—zur Geschichte der deutschen Identität." In *Identität*, edited by Odo Marquard and Karlheinz Stierle, 17–60. Munich, 1979.

Bosl, Karl. "Die Verhandlungen über den Eintritt der süddeutschen Staaten in den Norddeutschen Bund und die Entstehung der Reichsverfassung." In *Reichsgründung 1870/71*, edited by Theodor Schieder and Ernst Deuerlein, 148–63. Stuttgart, 1970.

Brackenheim. Heimatbuch der Stadt Brackenheim und ihrer Stadtteile. Brackenheim, 1980.

Brand, Marinus. *Heimatmuseum Rosenheim.* Rosenheim, 1982.

Brandt, Peter. "Das studentische Wartburgfest vom 18./19. Oktober 1817." In *Öffentliche Festkultur. Politische Feste in Deutschland von der Aufklärung bis zum Ersten Weltkrieg*, edited by Dieter Düding, Peter Friedemann, and Paul Münch, 89–112. Hamburg, 1988.

Braudel, Fernand. *The Mediterranean and the Mediterranean World in the Age of Philip II.* London, 1972.

Braungart, Richard. "Künstlerische Ansichtspostkarten." *Das Plakat* 8 (August 1920): 360–72.

Brückner, Wolfgang. "Das Museumswesen und die Entwicklung der Volkskunde als Wissenschaft um die Jahre 1902/1904." In *Das kunst- und kulturgeschichtliche Museum im 19. Jahrhundert*, edited by Bernward Deneke and Rainer Kahsnitz, 133–42. Munich, 1977.

Burckhardt, Carl Jacob. "Heimat." In *Heimat. Erinnerung deutscher Autoren*, edited by Günter Birkenfeld, 19–27. Herrenalb/Schwarzwald, 1965.

Burke, Peter. "History as Social Memory." In *Memory: History, Culture and the Mind*, edited by Thomas Butler, 97–113. New York, 1989.

Calw, 1850–1925. Bilder aus einer württembergischen Oberamtsstadt. Horb, 1983.

Chickering, Roger. *Imperial Germany and a World without War: The Peace Movement and German Society, 1892–1914.* Princeton, N.J., 1975.

———. *We Men Who Feel Most German: A Cultural Study of the Pan-German League, 1886–1914.* London, 1984.

Colley, Linda. *Britons: Forging the Nation, 1707–1837.* New Haven, Conn., 1992.

Confino, Alon. "The Nation as a Local Metaphor: Heimat, National Memory and the German Empire, 1871–1918." *History and Memory* 5, no. 1 (1993): 42–86.

Conze, Werner, and Dieter Groh. *Die Arbeiterbewegung in der nationalen Bewegung.* Stuttgart, 1966.

Cosgrove, Denis. *Social Formation and Symbolic Landscape.* London, 1984.

Cosgrove, Denis, and Stephen Daniels. "Introduction: Iconography and Landscape." In *The Iconography of Landscape: Essays on the Symbolic Representation, Design and Use of Past Environments*, 1–10. Cambridge, 1988.

———, eds. *The Iconography of Landscape: Essays on the Symbolic Representation, Design and Use of Past Environments.* Cambridge, 1988.

Craig, Gordon. *The Politics of the Prussian Army, 1640–1945.* Oxford, 1955.

Crane, Susan. "(Not) Writing History: Rethinking the Intersections of Personal History and Collective Memory with Hans von Aufsess." *History and Memory* 8, no. 1 (1996): 5–29.

Crawford, Anthony, ed. *Posters of World War I and World War II in the George C. Marshall Research Foundation.* Charlottesville, Va., 1979.

Crus-Ramirez, Alfredo. "The Heimatmuseum: A Perverted Forerunner." *Museum* 148 (1985): 242–44.

DaCosta Kaufmann, Thomas. *Central European Drawings, 1680–1800: A Selection from American Collections.* Princeton, N.J., 1989.

Dahrendorf, Ralf. *Society and Democracy in Germany.* London, 1968.

Darnton, Robert. "Revolution sans Revolutionaries." *New York Review of Books*, January 31, 1985, 21–23.

Darracott, Joseph, ed. *The First World War in Posters: From the Imperial War Museum, London.* New York, 1974.

Dehlinger, Alfred. *Württembergs Staatswesen.* Vol. 1. Stuttgart, 1951.
——. *Württembergs Staatswesen.* Vol. 2. Stuttgart, 1953.
Deutsch, Karl. *Nationalism and Social Communication.* Cambridge, Mass., 1966.
Der Deutsche Heimatschutz. Ein Rückblick und Ausblick. Edited by Der Gesellschaft der Freunde des deutschen Heimatschutzes. Munich, 1930.
Die Stadt. Bild-Gestalt-Vision. Europäische Stadtbilder im 19. und 20. Jahrhundert. Ausstellung Kunsthalle Bremen. Bremen, 1973.
Dodd, Philip. "Englishness and the National Culture." In *Englishness: Politics and Culture, 1880–1920,* edited by Philip Dodd and Robert Colls, 1–28. London, 1986.
Dodd, Philip, and Robert Colls, eds. *Englishness: Politics and Culutre, 1880–1920.* London, 1986.
Düding, Dieter. "Das deutsche Nationalfest von 1814: Matrix der deutschen Nationalfeste im 19. Jahrhundert." In *Öffentliche Festkultur. Politische Feste in Deutschland von der Aufklärung bis zum Ersten Weltkrieg,* edited by Dieter Düding, Peter Friedemann, and Paul Münch, 67–88. Hamburg, 1988.
——. "Die Kriegervereine im wilhelminischen Reich und ihr Beitrag zur Militarisierung der deutschen Gesellschaft." In *Bereit zum Krieg. Kriegsmentalität im wilhelminischen Deutschland 1890–1914,* edited by Jost Dülffer and Karl Holl, 99–121. Göttingen, 1986.
——. "Nationale Oppositionsfeste der Turner, Sänger und Schützen im 19. Jahrhundert." In *Öffentliche Festkultur. Politische Feste in Deutschland von der Aufklärung bis zum Ersten Weltkrieg,* edited by Dieter Düding, Peter Friedemann, and Paul Münch, 166–90. Hamburg, 1988.
Düding, Dieter, Peter Friedemann, and Paul Münch, eds. *Öffentliche Festkultur. Politische Feste in Deutschland von der Aufklärung bis zum Ersten Weltkrieg.* Hamburg, 1988.
Durkheim, Émile. *The Elementary Forms of the Religious Life.* New York, 1915.
Dûval, William, and Valerie Monahan. *Collecting Postcards in Colors, 1894–1914.* Poole, Britain, 1978.
Eisel, Franz. "Geschichts- und Altertumsvereine als Keimzellen und Wegbereiter der Heimatmuseen." *Neue Museumskunde* 27 (1984): 173–82.
Eksteins, Modris. *Rites of Spring: The Great War and the Birth of the Modern Age.* New York, 1989.
Eley, Geoff. "Army, State and Civil Society: Revisiting the Problem of German Militarism." In *From Unification to Nazism: Reinterpreting the German Past,* 85–109. Boston, 1986.
——. "Defining Social Imperialism: Use and Abuse of an Idea." *Social History* 3 (1976): 265–90.
——. "Labor History, Social History, *Alltagsgeschichte*: Experience, Culture, and the Politics of the Everyday—A New Direction for German Social History?" *Journal of Modern History* 61 (June 1989): 297–343.
——. "Nationalism and Social History." *Social History* 6 (1981): 83–107.
——. "Notable Politics, the Crisis of German Liberalism, and the Electoral Transition of the 1890s." In *In Search of a Liberal Germany: Studies in the History of German Liberalism from 1789 to the Present,* edited by Konrad Jarausch and Larry Eugene Jones, 187–216. New York, 1990.
——. "Politica dei notabili e crisi del liberalismo nella transizione degli anni '90 in Germania." *Quaderni Storici* 71 (August 1989): 463–92.
——. *Reshaping the German Right: Radical Nationalism and Political Change after Bismarck.* New Haven, Conn., 1980.
——. "The Wilhelmine Right: How It Changed." In *Society and Politics in Wilhelmine Germany,* edited by Richard Evans, 112–35. London, 1978.

Elias, Norbert. *The Germans: Power Struggles and the Development of Habitus in the Nineteenth and Twentieth Centuries*. New York, 1996.

Englund, Steven. "The Ghost of Nation Past." *Journal of Modern History* 64 (June 1992): 299–320.

Evans, Richard. *Comrades and Sisters: Feminism, Socialism and Pacifism in Europe, 1870–1945*. Brighton, Sussex, 1987.

———. *Death in Hamburg: Society and Politics in the Cholera Years, 1830–1910*. Oxford, 1987.

———. *The Feminist Movement in Germany, 1894–1933*. London, 1976.

———. *The Feminists*. London, 1977.

———. "The Myth of Germany's Missing Revolution." *New Left Review* 185 (1985): 67–94.

Evans Richard, and W. R. Lee, eds. *The German Family*. London, 1981.

———. *The German Peasantry*. London, 1986.

Farr, Ian. "Populism in the Countryside: The Peasant Leagues in Bavaria in the 1890s." In *Society and Politics in Wilhelmine Germany*, edited by Richard Evans, 136–59. London, 1978.

Ferro, Marc. *Comment on raconte l'histoire aux enfants à travers le monde entier*. Paris, 1981.

Fletcher, Roger. "Recent Developments in West German Historiography: The Bielefeld School and Its Critics." *German Studies Review* 7 (1984): 451–81.

Foerster, Cornelia. "Das Hambacher Fest 1832: Volksfest und Nationalfest einer oppositionellen Massenbewegung." In *Öffentliche Festkultur. Politische Feste in Deutschland von der Aufklärung bis zum Ersten Weltkrieg*, edited by Dieter Düding, Peter Friedemann, and Paul Münch, 113–31. Hamburg, 1988.

Forstmeier, Friedrich, and Hans Meier-Welcker. *Handbuch zur deutschen Militärgeschichte, 1648–1939*. Vol. 4, pts. 1–2. Munich, 1976.

Foucault, Michel. *Discipline and Punish: The Birth of the Prison*. New York, 1979.

Fout, John, ed. *German Women in the Nineteenth Century: A Social History*. New York, 1984.

Freudenberger, Hermann. *Schwabenreport 1900–1914*. Stuttgart, 1975.

Friedländer, Saul. *Memory, History, and the Extermination of the Jews in Europe*. Bloomington, Ind., 1993.

———. "Die Shoah als Element in der Konstruktion israelischer Erinnerung." *Babylon*, no. 2 (1987): 10–22.

———. *When Memory Comes*. New York, 1979.

Fritzsche, Peter. "Landscape of Danger, Landscape of Design: Crisis and Modernism in Weimar Germany." In *Dancing on the Volcano: Essays on the Culture of the Weimar Republic*, edited by Thomas Kniesche and Stephen Brockmann, 29–46. Columbia, S.C., 1994.

———. *A Nation of Fliers: German Aviation and the Popular Imagination*. Cambridge, Mass., 1992.

Funkenstein, Amos. "Collective Memory and Historical Consciousness." *History and Memory* 1, no. 1 (1989): 5–26.

Furet, François. *Interpreting the French Revolution*. Cambridge, 1981.

Fussell, Paul. *The Great War and Modern Memory*. London, 1975.

Gellately, Robert. *The Politics of Economic Despair: Shopkeepers and German Politics, 1890–1914*. Beverly Hills, Calif., 1974.

Gellner, Ernest. *Nations and Nationalism*. Ithaca, N.Y., 1983.

Gillis, John. "Memory and Identity: The History of a Relationship." In *Commemorations: The Politics of National Identity*, edited by John Gillis, 3–24. Princeton, N.J., 1994.

———. *A World of Their Own Making: Myth, Ritual, and the Quest for Family Values*. New York, 1996.

Ginzburg, Carlo. "From Aby Warburg to E. H. Gombrich: A Problem of Method." In *Clues, Myths, and the Historical Method*, 17–59. Baltimore, 1989.

———. *Indagini su Piero*. Turin, 1981.

Glaser, Hermann. *The Cultural Roots of National Socialism [Spießer-Ideologie]*. London, 1978.

Gleich, G. von. *Die alte Armee und ihre Verirrungen*. Leipzig, 1919.

Glückwünsche auf Postkarte. Altonaer Museum in Hamburg Norddeutsches Landesmuseum. Hamburg, 1977.

Goody, Jack. *The Domestication of the Savage Mind*. London, 1977.

———. "Mémoire et apprentissage dans les sociétés avec et sans écriture: La transmission du Barge." *L'homme* 17 (1977): 29–52.

Graevenitz, Fritz von. *Die Entwicklung des württembergischen Heerwesens*. Stuttgart, 1921.

Gregory, Adrian. *The Silence of Memory: Armistice Day, 1919–1946*. Oxford, 1994.

Greverus, Ina-Maria. *Auf der Suche nach Heimat*. Munich, 1979.

———. *Der territoriale Mensch. Ein literatur-anthropologischer Versuch zum Heimatphänomen*. Frankfurt am Main, 1972.

Grimm, Reinhold, and Jost Hermand, eds. *Deutsche Feiern*. Wiesbaden, 1977.

Haefs, Hanswilhelm. *Die deutschen Heimat-museen*. Frankfurt am Main, 1984.

Hagel, Jürgen. "Zur Geschichte der Verschönerungsvereine in Südwestdeutschland." *Zeitschrift für württembergische Landesgeschichte* 46 (1987): 351–67.

Hagen, Bernt von. *Museum und Galerie der Stadt Schwabmünchen*. Munich, 1988.

Halbwachs, Maurice. *Les cadres sociaux de la mémoire*. Paris, 1925.

———. *The Collective Memory*. New York, 1980.

———. *La mémoire collective*. Paris, 1950.

———. *On Collective Memory*. Edited, translated, and with an introduction by Lewis Coser. Chicago, 1992.

———. *La topographie légendaire des Évangiles en Terre sainte. Étude de mémoire collective*. Paris, 1941.

Haltern, Utz. "Architektur und Politik. Zur Baugeschichte des Berliner Reichstags." In *Kunstverwaltung, Bau- und Denkmal-Politik im Kaiserreich*, edited by Ekkehard Mai und Stephan Waetzoldt, 75–102. Berlin, 1981.

Hardtwig, Wolfgang. "Bürgertum, Staatssymbolik und Staatsbewußtsein 1871–1914." *Geschichte und Gesellschaft* 16 (1990): 269–95.

———. "Erinnerung, Wissenschaft, Mythos. Nationale Geschichtsbilder und politische Symbole in der Reichsgründungszeit und im Kaiserreich." In *Geschichtskultur und Wissenschaft*, 224–63. Munich, 1990.

———. "Geschichtsinteresse, Geschichtsbilder und politische Symbole in der Reichsgründungsära und im Kaiserreich." In *Kunstverwaltung, Bau- und Denkmal-Politik im Kaiserreich*, edited by Ekkehard Mai und Stephan Waetzoldt, 47–74. Berlin, 1981.

———. "Nationsbildung und politische Mentalität. Denkmal und Fest im Kaiserreich." In *Geschichtskultur und Wissenschaft*, 264–301. Munich, 1990.

———. "Soziale Räume und politische Herrschaft. Leistungsverwaltung, Stadterweiterung und Architektur im München 1870 bis 1914." In *Soziale Räume in der Urbanisierung*, edited by Wolfgang Hardtwig and Klaus Tenfelde, 59–153. Munich, 1990.

Häring, Hermann. "100 Jahre württembergischer Geschichts- und Altertumsverein (1843–1943)." *Zeitschrift für württembergische Landesgeschichte* 7 (1943): 1–6.

Hartman, Geoffrey, ed. *Holocaust Remembrance: The Shapes of Memory*. Oxford, 1994.

Hartung, Werner. *Konservative Zivilisationskritik und regionale Identität. Am Beispiel der niedersächsischen Heimatbewegung 1895 bis 1919*. Hannover, 1991.

Heimatverein Ramsdorf e.V. Festschrift zum 90jährigen Jubiläum. Ramsdorf, 1989.

Heinle, Albert. "Das Heimatmuseum—ein Abbild der Heimat." *Achthundertjähriges Wissenhorn. Sonderausgabe der Zeitschrift "Bayerland,"* 16–19. Munich, 1960.

Hellerstein, Erna, Leslie Hume, and Karen Offen, eds. *Victorian Women: A Documentary Account of Women's Lives in Nineteenth-Century England, France, and the United States.* Stanford, Calif., 1981.

Henning, Friedrich. "Liberalismus und Demokratie im Königreich Württemberg." In *Die F.D.P./DVP in Baden-Württemberg und ihre Geschichte. Liberalismus als politische Gestaltungskraft im deutschen Südwesten,* edited by Paul Rothmund and Erhard Wiehn, 59–76. Stuttgart, 1979.

Hermann, Roemer. *Geschichte der Stadt Bietigheim an der Enz.* Bietigheim, 1956.

Hettling, Manfred, and Paul Nolte, eds. *Bürgerliche Feste. Symbolische Formen politischen Handelns im 19. Jahrhundert.* Göttingen, 1993.

Hobsbawm, Eric. *The Age of Empire, 1875–1914.* New York, 1989.

———. "Introduction: Inventing Traditions." In *The Invention of Tradition,* edited by Eric Hobsbawm and Terence Ranger, 1–14. Cambridge, 1983.

———. "Mass-Producing Traditions: Europe, 1870–1914." In *The Invention of Tradition,* edited by Eric Hobsbawm and Terence Ranger, 263–307. Cambridge, 1983.

Hobsbawm, Eric, and Terence Ranger, eds. *The Invention of Tradition.* Cambridge, 1983.

Hochreiter, Walter. *Vom Musentempel zum Lernort. Zur Sozialgeschichte deutscher Museen 1800–1914.* Darmstadt, 1994.

Hofbauer, Ludwig. "Das Schwandorfer Orts- und Heimatmuseum." *Schwandorfer Tagblatt,* 14 November 1955.

Hofmeister, Gottfried. "Heimatverein, Heimatpflege und Heimatmuseum in Krumbach. Ein Rückblick." *Krumbacher Heimatblätter* 7 (1989): 36–49.

Hohorst, G., J. Kocka, and G. A. Ritter, eds. *Sozialgeschichtliches Arbeitsbuch. Materialen zur Statistik des Kaiserreich, 1870–1914.* Munich, 1975.

Holger, Rüdel. "Das Städtische Museum—eines der ältesten Museen in Schleswig-Holstein." *Beiträge zur Schleswiger Stadtgeschichte* 34 (1989): 143–48.

Holler, Siegfried. "Aus der über 100jährigen Geschichte des Herborner Museums." *Hessische Heimat* (Sonderheft Herborn) 36, no. 3 (1986): 116–19.

Holt, Tonie, and Valmai Holt. *Picture Postcard Artists: Landscapes, Animals and Characters.* London, 1984.

Howard, Peter. *Landscape: The Artists' Vision.* London, 1991.

Huizinga, Johan. "Patriotism and Nationalism in European History." In *Men and Ideas: History, the Middle Ages, the Renaissance,* 97–155. New York, 1959.

Hull, Isabel. "The Bourgeoisie and Its Discontent: Reflections on 'Nationalism and Respectability.'" *Journal of Contemporary History* 17 (1982): 247–68.

Hunt, J. C. "The 'Egalitarianism' of the Right: The Agrarian League in Southwest Germany, 1893–1914." *Journal of Contemporary History* 3 (1975): 513–30.

Hunt, Lynn. *Politics, Culture, and Class in the French Revolution.* Berkeley, Calif., 1984.

———. "The Sacred and the French Revolution." In *Durkheimian Sociology: Cultural Studies,* edited by Jeffrey Alexander, 25–43. Cambridge, 1988.

Hutton, Patrick. "Collective Memory and Collective Mentalities: The Halbwachs-Ariès Connection." *Historical Reflections* 15 (1988): 311–22.

———. *History as an Art of Memory.* Hanover, N.H., 1993.

Imhof, Eugen, ed. *Blaubeurer Heimatbuch.* Blaubeuren, 1950.

Jacobi, Uwe. *Heilbronn: So wie es war.* Düsseldorf, 1987.

Jaeger, Karl. *Die deutschen Reichsmünzen seit 1871.* Basel, 1959.

Jahn, Joachim. *Schwabmünchen. Geschichte einer schwäbischen Stadt.* Schwabmünchen, 1984.

James, Harold. *A German Identity, 1770–1990.* London, 1989.

Jarausch, Konrad, and Larry Eugene Jones. "German Liberalism Reconsidered: Inevitable Decline, Bourgeois Hegemony, or Partial Achievement?" In *In Search of a Liberal Germany: Studies in the History of German Liberalism from 1789 to the Present,* edited by Konrad Jarausch and Larry Eugene Jones, 1–24. New York, 1990.

———, eds. *In Search of a Liberal Germany: Studies in the History of German Liberalism from 1789 to the Present.* New York, 1990.

Jefferies, Matthew. *Politics and Culture in Wilhelmine Germany: The Case of Industrial Architecture.* Oxford, 1995.

Joutard, Philippe. "Mémoire collective." In *Dictionnaire des sciences historiques,* edited by André Burguière, 447–49. Paris, 1986.

Jubiläumsausstellung 1978. Museumsverein für das Fürstentum Lüneburg. Lüneburg, 1978.

Jünger, Ernst. "Der Kampf als inneres Erlebnis." In *Werke.* Vol. 5. Stuttgart, 1960.

Kaes, Anton. *From "Hitler" to "Heimat": The Return of History as Film.* Cambridge, Mass., 1989.

———. "History and Film: Public Memory in the Age of Electronic Dissemination." *History and Memory* 2, no. 1 (1990): 111–29.

Kammen, Michael. *Mystic Chords of Memory: The Transformation of Tradition in American Culture.* New York, 1991.

Kantorovitz, Ernst. "*Pro Patria Mori* in Medieval Political Thought." *American Historical Review* 56 (1951): 472–92.

Kaplan, Steven. *Farewell Revolution: The Historians' Feud: France, 1789/1989.* Ithaca, N.Y., 1995.

Karasek, Erika. *Die volkskundlich-kulturhistorischen Museen in Deutschland. Zur Rolle der Volkskunde in der bürgerlich-imperialistischen Gesellschaft.* Berlin (East), 1984.

Kearney, Hugh. *The British Isles: A History of Four Nations.* Cambridge, 1995.

Kennedy, Katharine. "Regionalism and Nationalism in South German History Lessons, 1871–1914." *German Studies Review* 12 (February 1989): 11–33.

Kindheit und Jugend vor Neunzehnhundert. Hermann Hesse in Briefen und Lebenszeugnissen 1877–1895. Vol. 1. Frankfurt am Main, 1966.

Kindheit und Jugend vor Neunzehnhundert. Hermann Hesse in Briefen und Lebenszeugnissen 1895–1900. Vol. 2. Frankfurt am Main, 1978.

Kirchheim unter Teck. Ansichten von gestern und heute. Horb, 1988.

Kleine, Georg. *Der württembergische Minister-Präsident Frhr. Hermann von Mittnacht (1825–1909).* Stuttgart, 1969.

Kluge, Manfred, ed. *Heimat. Ein deutsches Lesebuch.* Munich, 1989.

Knöpfle, Fridiolin. *Alte Horb: Wie's die Großeltern kannten; Historische Photographien ab 1890 aus Horb und seinen jetzigen Stadtteile.* Horb, 1982.

Kocka, Jürgen. "Bildungsbürgertum—Gesellschaftliche Formation oder Historiker-konstrukt?" In *Bildungsbürgertum im 19. Jahrhundert.* Vol. 4: *Politischer Einfluß und gesellschaftliche Formation,* edited by Jürgen Kocka, 9–20. Stuttgart, 1989.

Kohn, Hans. *The Idea of Nationalism.* New York, 1967.

Koselleck, Reinhart. "Kriegerdenkmale als Identitätsstiftungen der Überlebenden." In *Identität,* edited by Odo Marquard and Karlheinz Stierle, 255–76. Munich, 1979.

Kramer, Dieter. "Die politische und ökonomische Funktionalisierung von Heimat im deutschen Imperialismus und Faschismus." *Diskurs* 6–7, nos. 3–4 (1973): 3–22.

Kruse, Darryn, and Charles Sowerwine. "Feminism and Pacifism: 'Women's Sphere' in

Peace and War." In *Australian Women: New Feminist Perspective*, edited by Ailsa Burns and Norma Grieve, 42–58. Melbourne, 1986.

Kuhn, Annette, and Gerhard Schneider, eds. *Geschichte lernen im Museum*. Düsseldorf, 1978.

Laffin, John. *World War I in Post-Cards*. Gloucester, 1988.

Langer, Lawrence. *Holocaust Testimonies: The Ruins of Memory*. New Haven, Conn., 1991.

Langewiesche, Dieter. "Deutscher Liberalismus im europäischen Vergleich: Konzeption und Ergebnisse." In *Liberalismus im 19. Jahrhundert: Deutschland im europäischen Vergleich*, edited by Dieter Langewiesche. Göttingen, 1988.

———. "Julius Hölder (1819–1887). Zur Geschichte des württembergischen und deutschen Liberalismus im 19. Jahrhundert." *Zeitschrift für Württembergische Landesgeschichte* 46 (1987): 151–66.

———. *Liberalismus in Deutschland*. Frankfurt, 1988.

———. *Liberalismus und Demokratie in Württemberg zwischen Revolution und Reichsgründung*. Düsseldorf, 1974.

———, ed. *Das Tagebuch Julius Hölders 1877–1880*. Stuttgart, 1977.

Lebeck, Robert, and Manfred Schütte, eds. *Propagandapostkarten I. 80 Bildpostkarten aus den Jahren 1898–1929*. Dortmund, 1980.

Le Goff, Jacques. *La naissance du purgatoire*. Paris, 1981.

Lehmann, Hartmut. "Friedrich von Bodelschwingh und das Sedanfest." *Historische Zeitschrift* 202 (1966): 542–73.

Lehnert, Detlef, and Klaus Megerle, eds. *Politische Identität und nationale Gedenktage. Zur politischen Kultur in der Weimarer Republik*. Opladen, 1989.

Linke, Uli. "Folklore, Anthropology, and the Government of Social Life." *Comparative Studies in Society and History* 32 (January 1990): 117–47.

Lowenthal, David. *The Past Is a Foreign Country*. Cambridge, 1985.

Lüdtke, Alf, ed. *The History of Everyday Life: Reconstructing Historical Experiences and Ways of Life*. Princeton, N.J., 1995.

McDannell, Colleen, and Bernhard Lang. *Heaven: A History*. New Haven, Conn., 1988.

Mackay, Jane, and Pat Thane. "The Englishwomen." In *Englishness. Politics and Culture, 1880–1920*, edited by Philip Dodd and Robert Colls, 191–229. London, 1986.

Maier, Charles. *The Unmasterable Past: History, Holocaust, and German National Identity*. Cambridge, Mass., 1988.

Malhotra, Ruth. *Politische Plakate 1914–1945. Museum für Kunst und Gewerbe Hamburg*. Hamburg, 1988.

Manke, Ilse. "Das Ludwigsburger Heimatmuseum." *Ludwigsburger Geschichtsblätter* 17 (1965): 165–75.

Marías, Julián. *Understanding Spain*. Ann Arbor, Mich., 1992.

Maza, Sarah. "Politics, Culture, and the Origins of the French Revolution." *Journal of Modern History* 61 (December 1989): 704–23.

Messing, Ursula, ed. *Heilbronn in alten Ansichtskarten*. Frankfurt, 1980.

Missenharter, Hermann. "Die württembergischen Gebrauchs-Graphiker." *Das Plakat* 11 (February 1920): 69–89.

Mit Gott für Kaiser, König und Vaterland. Krieg und Kriegsbild Tübingen 1870/71. Eine Ausstellung im Frühjahr 1986. Edited by Kulturamt der Stadt Tübingen (No. 26). Tübingen, 1986.

Moeller, Robert. "The Kaiserreich Recast? Continuity and Change in Modern German Historiography." *Journal of Social History* 17 (1984): 655–83.

———, ed. *Peasants and Lords in Modern Germany*. Boston, 1986.

Mommsen, Hans. "History and National Identity: The Case of Germany." *German Studies Review* 6 (October 1983): 559–82.

———. "Nation und Nationalismus in sozialgeschichtlicher Perspektive." In *Sozialgeschichte in Deutschland*, edited by Wolfgang Schieder and Volker Sellin, 162–85. Göttingen, 1986.

Mordente, Mario. *Catalogo delle cartoline illustrate italiane*. Rome, 1980.

Mosse, George. *Fallen Soldiers: Reshaping the Memory of the World Wars*. New York, 1990.

———. *The Nationalization of the Masses: Political Symbolism and Mass Movements in Germany from the Napoleonic Wars through the Third Reich*. New York, 1975.

Müller, Georg. "Friedrich von Bodelschwingh und das Sedanfest." *Geschichte in Wissenschaft und Unterricht* 14 (1963): 77–90.

Müller, H. "Die Deutsche Arbeiterklasse und die Sedanfeiern." *Zeitschrift für Geschichtswissenschaft* 17 (1969): 1554–64.

Mutschler, Susanne. *Ländliche Kindheit in Lebenserinnerungen. Familien- und Kinderleben in einem württembergischen Arbeiterbauerndorf an der Wende vom 19. zum 20. Jahrhundert*. Tübingen, 1985.

Niethammer, Lutz. *"Hinterher merkt man, daß es richtig war, daß es schief gegangen ist." Nachkriegserfahrungen im Ruhrgebiet*. Berlin, 1983.

———. *"Die Jahre weiß man nicht, wo man die heute hinsetzen soll." Faschismuserfahrungen im Ruhrgebiet*. Berlin, 1983.

———. *Lebenserfahrung und kollektives Gedächtnis. Die Praxis der "Oral History."* Frankfurt, 1980.

———. " 'Normalisierung' im Westen: Erinnerungsspuren in die 50er Jahre." In *Ist der Nationalsozialismus Geschichte? Zu Historisierung und Historikerstreit*, edited by Dan Diner. Frankfurt am Main, 1987.

Nipperdey, Thomas. *Deutsche Geschichte, 1866–1918*. Vol. 1: *Arbeitswelt und Bürgergeist*. 2d ed. Munich, 1991.

———. *Deutsche Geschichte 1866–1918*. Vol. 2: *Machtstaat vor dem Demokratie*. Munich, 1992.

———. "Nationalidee und Nationaldenkmal in Deutschland im 19. Jahrhundert." *Historische Zeitschrift* 206 (1968): 529–85.

———. "Verein als soziale Struktur in Deutschland im späten 18. und frühen 19. Jahrhundert." In *Gesellschaft, Kultur, Theorie. Gesammelte Aufsätze zur neueren Geschichte*, 174–205. Göttingen, 1976.

———. "Wehlers 'Kaiserreich.' Eine kritische Auseinandersetzung." In *Gesellschaft, Kultur, Theorie. Gesammelte Aufsätze zur neueren Geschichte*, 360–89. Göttingen, 1976.

Noltenius, Rainer. "Schiller als Führer und Heiland: Das Schillerfest 1859 als nationaler Traum von der Geburt des zweiten deutschen Kaiserreich." In *Öffentliche Festkultur. Politische Feste in Deutschland von der Aufklärung bis zum Ersten Weltkrieg*, edited by Dieter Düding, Peter Friedemann, and Paul Münch, 237–58. Hamburg, 1988.

Nora, Pierre. "Between Memory and History: *Les lieux de mémoire.*" *Representations* 26 (1989): 7–25.

———. "Entre mémoire et histoire." In *Les lieux de mémoire*. Vol. 1: *La République*, edited by Pierre Nora, xvii–xlii. Paris, 1984.

———. "Mémoire collective." In *La nouvelle histoire*, edited by Jacques Le Goff, Roger Chartier, and Jacques Revel, 398–401. Paris, 1978.

———, ed. *Les lieux de mémoire*. Vol. 1: *La République*. Vols. 2–4: *La nation*. Vols. 5–7: *Les France*. Paris, 1984–92.

Ottnad, Bernd. "75 Jahre Historischer Verein Ludwigsburg (Kreis und Stadt) e.V." *Sonderdruck aus Ludwigsburger Geschichtsblätter* 24 (1972): 8–22.

Ozouf, Mona. *Festivals and the French Revolution*. Cambridge, Mass., 1988.

Panofsky, Erwin. *Studies in Iconology.* New York, 1967.

Paulson, Ronald. "Types of Demarcation: Townscape and Landscape Painting." *Eighteenth-Century Studies* 8, no. 3 (1975): 337–54.

Pazaurek, E. "Karl Sigrist." *Das Plakat* 11 (February 1920): 65–67.

Petzoldt, Leander. *Volkstümliche Feste. Ein Führer zu Volksfesten, Märkten und Messen in Deutschland.* Munich, 1983.

Peukert, Detlev. "Ruhr Miners under Nazi Repression, 1933–45." *International Journal of Oral History* 1 (1980): 111–27.

Pfandzelter, Elmar. "Vom Bezirksmuseum 1913 zu Museum und Galerie der Stadt Schwabmünchen 1984 (anläßlich der museumseröffnung 30.3.1984)." In *Eröffnung von Museum und Galerie der Stadt Schwabmünchen,* 8–22. Heftchen: Sog. Weiße Reihe. Schwabmünchen, 1984.

Plakate. Jörg Weigelt Auktionen 14. Hannover, 1990.

"Politiques de l'oubli." *Le genre humain.* October 1988.

Projektgruppe Deutscher Heimatfilm. *Der deutsche Heimatfilm. Bildwelten und Weltbilder: Bilder, Texte, Analysen zu 70 Jahren deutscher Filmgeschichte.* Tübingen, 1989.

Proust, Marcel. *Remembrance of Things Past.* London, 1983.

Reif, Heinz, Sigrid Heinze, and Andreas Ludwig. "Schwierigkeiten mit Tradition. Zur kulturellen Praxis städtischer Heimatmuseen." In *Das historische Museum. Labor, Schaubühne, Identitätsfabrik,* edited by Gottfried Korff and Martin Roth, 231–47. Frankfurt am Main, 1990.

Renan, Ernest. "What Is a Nation?" In *Nation and Narration,* edited by Homi Bhabha, 8–22. London, 1990.

Retallack, James. "Social History with a Vengeance? Some Reactions to H.-U. Wehler's 'Das Deutsche Kaiserreich.'" *German Studies Review* 7 (1984): 423–50.

Rieber, Christof. *Das Sozialistengesetz und die Sozialdemokratie in Württemberg, 1878–1890.* Darmstadt, 1984.

Rieth, Adolph. *Denkmal ohne Pathos. Totenmale des zweiten Weltkrieges in Südwürttemberg-Hohenzollern.* Tübingen, 1967.

Rilke, Rainer Maria. *The Notebooks of Malte Laurids Brigge.* Translated by Stephen Mitchell. New York, 1990.

Ringbeck, Birgitta. "Dorfsammlung—Haus der Heimat—Heimatmuseum. Aspekte zur Geschichte einer Institution seit der Jahrhundertwende." In *Antimodernismus und Reform,* edited by Edeltraud Kleuting, 288–319. Darmstadt, 1991.

Ripert, Aline, and Claude Frère. *La carte postal: Son histoire, sa fonction sociale.* Lyon, 1983.

Robbins, Kieth. *Nineteenth-Century Britain: Integration and Diversity.* Oxford, 1988.

Rohlfes, Joachim. "Geschichte im Gedicht." *Geschichte in Wissenschaft und Unterricht* 40 (1989): 750–71.

Rollins, William. "Aesthetic Environmentalism: The Heimatschutz Movement in Germany, 1904–1918." Ph.D. diss., University of Wisconsin at Madison, 1994.

Rotberg, Robert, and Theodor Rabb, eds. *Art and History: Images and Their Meaning.* Cambridge, 1986.

Roth, Martin. *Heimatmuseum. Zur Geschichte einer deutschen Institution.* Berlin, 1990.

Rowlands, John. *German Drawings from a Private Collection.* London, 1984.

Santner, Eric. *Stranded Objects: Mourning, Memory, and Film in Postwar Germany.* Ithaca, N.Y., 1990.

Sauer, Paul. *Napoleons Adler über Württemberg, Baden und Hohenzollern. Südwestdeutschland in der Rheinbundzeit.* Stuttgart, 1987.

——. *Der schwäbische Zar. Friedrich: Württembergs erster König.* Stuttgart, 1984.

——. *Das württembergische Heer in der Zeit des Deutschen und des Norddeutschen Bundes.* Stuttgart, 1958.

Schama, Simon. *The Embarrassment of Riches: An Interpretation of Dutch Culture.* Berkeley, Calif., 1987.

——. *Landscape and Memory.* New York, 1995.

Scharfe, Martin, ed. *Museen in der Provinz. Strukturen, Probleme, Tendenzen, Chancen.* Tübingen, 1982.

Schefold, Max. *Alte Ansichten aus Württemberg.* Vol. 1. Stuttgart, 1956.

——. *Das alte Württemberg. 30 Stahlstiche und Lithographien des 19. Jahrhunderts.* Frankfurt am Main, 1969.

Schellack, Fritz. *Nationalfeiertage in Deutschland von 1871 bis 1945.* Frankfurt am Main, 1990.

——. "Sedan- und Kaisergeburtstagsfeste." In *Öffentliche Festkultur. Politische Feste in Deutschland von der Aufklärung bis zum Ersten Weltkrieg,* edited by Dieter Düding, Peter Friedemann, and Paul Münch, 286–92. Hamburg, 1988.

Schieder, Theodor. *Das deutsche Kaiserreich.* Cologne, 1961.

Schivelbusch, Wolfgang. *The Railway Journey: The Industrialization of Time and Space in the 19th Century.* Berkeley, Calif., 1986.

Schmahl and Spemann. *Geschichte des 2. Württembergischen Feldartillerie-Regiment. Nr. 29 Prinzregent Luitpold von Bayern.* Stuttgart, n.d.

Schmierer, Wolfgang. *Von der Arbeiterbildung zur Arbeiterpolitik.* Hannover, 1970.

Schmitt, Hans. "From Sovereign States to Prussian Provinces: Hanover and Hesse-Nassau, 1866–1871." *Journal of Modern History* 57 (March 1985): 24–56.

Schneider, Birgit. *Die "Württembergischen Vierteljahreshefte für Landesgeschichte," 1878–1936.* Cologne, 1987.

Schönhagen, Benigna, " 'Ich wüßte keinen besseren Wegweiser als den Sedanssieg.' " In *Mit Gott für Kaiser, König und Vaterland. Krieg und Kriegsbild Tübingen 1870/71. Eine Ausstellung im Frühjahr 1986,* 25–43. Edited by Kulturamt der Stadt Tübingen (No. 26). Tübingen, 1986.

Schuster, Felix. "40 Jahre Bund für Heimatschutz in Württemberg und Hohenzollern." *Schwäbisches Heimatbuch* (1949): 13–55.

Schweier, Gerhard. "Die Geschichte des Heidenheimer Kinderfests." In *75 Jahre Heimat- und Altertumsverein Heidenheim 1901–1976,* 232–38. Heidenheim, 1976.

Sheehan, James. *German History, 1770–1866.* Oxford, 1989.

——. *German Liberalism in the 19th Century.* Chicago, 1978.

——. "What Is German History? Reflections on the Role of the *Nation* in German History and Historiography." *Journal of Modern History* 53 (March 1981): 1–23.

Simon, Klaus. *Die württembergischen Demokraten.* Stuttgart, 1969.

Sivan, Emmanuel. "To Remember Is to Forget: Israel's 1948 War." *Journal of Contemporary History* 28 (1993): 341–59.

——. *The 1948 Generation: Myth, Profile and Memory.* In Hebrew. Tel Aviv, 1991.

Smith, Anthony. *The Ethnic Origins of Nations.* Oxford, 1986.

Smith, Helmut. *German Nationalism and Religious Conflict: Culture, Ideology, Politics, 1870–1914.* Princeton, N.J., 1995.

Soldoni, Simonetta, and Gabriele Turi, eds. *Fare gli Italiani. Scuola e cultura nell'Italia contemporanea.* Vol. 1: *La nascita dello stato nazionale.* Vol. 2: *Una società di massa.* Bologna, 1993.

Sperber, Jonathan. "Festivals of National Unity in the German Revolution of 1848/49." *Past and Present* 136 (1992): 114–38.

——. *Popular Catholicism in Nineteenth Century Germany.* Princeton, N.J., 1984.

Staff, Frank. *The Picture Postcard and Its Origins*. London, 1966.

——. *Picture Postcards and Travel: A Collector's Guide*. London, 1979.

Stanley, Peter. *What Did You Do in the War Daddy? A Visual History of Propaganda Posters*. Oxford, 1983.

Stites, Richard. *The Women's Liberation Movement in Russia: Feminism, Nihilism and Bolshevism, 1860–1930*. Princeton, N.J., 1978.

Strauß, Max. *Führer durch das Allgäuer Heimatmuseum*. Kempten, 1957.

Sülchgauer Altertumsverein Rottenburg a.N. Jubiläums-Schrift 1952. Tübingen, 1953.

Suval, Stanley. *Electoral Politics in Wilhelmine Germany*. Chapel Hill, N.C., 1985.

Tacke, Charlotte. "Die 1900-Jahrfeier der Schlacht im Teutoburger Wald 1909. Von der 'klassenlosen Bürgerschaft' zur 'klassenlosen Volksgemeinschaft'?" In *Bürgerliche Feste. Symbolische Formen politischen Handelns im 19. Jahrhundert*, edited by Manfred Hettling and Paul Nolte, 192–230. Göttingen, 1993.

Tittel, Lutz. "Monumentaldenkmäler von 1871 bis 1918 in Deutschland. Ein Beitrag zum Thema Denkmal und Landschaft " In *Kunstverwaltung, Bau und Denkmal-Politik im Kaiserreich*, edited by Ekkehard Mai und Stephan Waetzoldt, 215–76. Berlin, 1981.

Trautes Heim. Heitere Gefühle bei der Ankunft auf dem Lande. Bilder schwäbischen Land lebens im 19. Jahrhundert. Katalog zur gleichnamigen Ausstellung im Württembergischen Landesmuseum, Stuttgart 1983. Tübingen, 1983.

Treitschke's Origins of Prussianism (The Teutonic Knights). London, 1942.

Ulshöfer, Kuno. *Bilder einer alten Stadt Schwäbisch Hall*. Schwäbisch Hall, 1971.

Valensi, Lucette. "Silence, dénégation, affabulation: Le souvenir d'une grand défaite dans la culture portugaise." *Annales ESC* (1991): 3–24.

Vann, James Allen. *The Making of a State: Württemberg, 1593–1793*. Ithaca, N.Y., 1984.

Volkov, Shulamit. *The Rise of Popular Antimodernism: The Urban Master Artisans, 1873–1896*. Princeton, N.J., 1976.

"Vom Altertumsverein zum Heimat- und Kunstverein: 100 Jahre Heimat und Kunstverein Backnang." *Schriftenreihe des Heimat- und Kunstverein Backnang* 4 (1984): 9–23.

Vovelle, Michel. *Immagini e immaginario nella storia. Fantasmi e certezze nelle mentalità dal medioevo al Novecento*. Rome, 1989.

Wachtel, Nathan. "Memory and History: An Introduction." *History and Anthropology* 2 (1986): 207–24.

Walker, Mack. *German Home Towns: Community, State, and General Estate, 1648–1871*. Ithaca, N.Y., 1971.

Weber, Eugen. *Peasants into Frenchmen: The Modernization of Rural France, 1870–1914*. Stanford, Calif., 1976.

Wehler, Hans-Ulrich. *The German Empire, 1871–1918*. Leamington Spa, 1985.

Wehling, Hans-Georg. "Barock—bäuerliches Oberschwaben." In *Regionale politische Kultur*, edited by Hans-Georg Wehling, 130–45. Stuttgart, 1985.

Weigelt, Klaus. "Heimat—Der Ort personaler Identitätsfindung und sozio-politischer Orientierung." In *Heimat und Nation. Zur Geschichte und Identität der deutschen*, edited by Klaus Weigelt, 15–25. Mainz, 1984.

Weill, Alain. *The Poster: A Worldwide Survey and History*. London, 1985.

Weischedel, Inge, Waltraut Weischedel, and Helmut Greb. *Geschichte des deutschen Naturkundevereins (1887–1987)*. Sonderheft der Schriftenreihe des Deutschen Naturkundevereins e.V., 1987.

Wiemann, Johann Bernhard. "Der Verein für Heimatschutz und Heimatgeschichte e.V. von seiner Gründung bis zum Ausbruch des Ersten Weltkrieges." In *75 Jahre Verein für Heimatschutz und Heimatgeschichte Leer/Ostfriesland*, 10–15. Leer, 1984.

Wienfort, Monika. "Kaisergeburtstagsfeiern am 27. Januar 1907. Bürgerliche Feste in den Städten des Deutschen Kaiserreichs." In *Bürgerliche Feste. Symbolische Formen politischen Handelns im 19. Jahrhundert*, edited by Manfred Hettling and Paul Nolte, 157–91. Göttingen, 1993.

Wilson, Peter. *War, State, and Society in Württemberg, 1677–1793*. Cambridge, 1995.

Winter, Jay. *Sites of Memory, Sites of Mourning: The Great War in European Cultural History*. Cambridge, 1995.

Yerushalmi, Yosef Hayim. *Zakhor: Jewish History and Jewish Memory*. New York, 1989.

Yerushalmi, Yosef Hayim, Nicole Loraux, et al. *Usages de l'oubli. Actes du colloque de Royaumont (1987)*. Paris, 1988.

Young, James. *The Texture of Memory: Holocaust Memorials and Meaning*. New Haven, Conn., 1993.

Zerubavel, Yael. *Recovered Roots: Collective Memory and the Making of Israeli National Tradition*. Chicago, 1995.

Index

German Association for Agrarian Welfare
and Heimat Care (Deutscher Verein
für ländliche Wohlfahrts- und Heimat-
pflege), 122, 162
German nationalism. *See* Nationalism—in
Germany
German National Museum (Germanisches
Nationalmuseum), 137, 139, 151
German Peace Movement, 99
German unification (1871): and national
memory, 13–15; and Württemberg,
20–23; in school textbooks, 107; sym-
bolic meaning of, 125–26
Gerok, Friedrich Karl von, 17
Giengen an der Brenz, 36–38, 101, 120
Ginzburg, Carlo, 161
Goebel, Ferdinand, 147
Goethe, Wolfgang, 16, 44
Goody, Jack, 8
Göppingen, 49, 67, 134, 181, 207
Gradmann, Eugen, 160
Grimm, Jakob and Wilhelm, 104, 127, 137,
150

Hadersleben, 145–46
Halbwachs, Maurice, 8, 10, 12, 154
Hall, 105
Hambach, 41
Hamburg, 130, 138
Hannover, 132, 148
Hardtwig, Wolfgang, 84–85
Hartung, Werner, 131–32
Haußmann, J., 57
Haußmann, Konrad, 90
Hegel, G. W. F., 17
Heidelberg, 147, 149
Heidenheim, 105, 109, 111, 118, 120
Heilbronn, 17, 27, 37, 44, 74, 80, 90, 111,
181–83, 207
Heimat iconography: sources and method,
159–62; representation of generic com-
munity, 162–69; representation of Ger-
mans, 169–72; representation of time,
172–73; artistic precursor of, 174–77;
representation of nature, 177–79; and
postcards, 179–81; and modernity,
182–83; and European iconography,
212–13
Heimat idea: and tourism, 10, 113–14,

119–20, 145, 179–82; historiography of,
97; conditions for, 98–100; and new
political culture, 98–100, 104–7, 109–11,
150–53; social carriers of, 104–6, 109–11,
131–33; and school textbooks, 107–8;
origins of, 109–11, 150–53; commercialization of, 113–14, 119–20, 145, 179–82;
changes in meaning of, 126–29; regional
and national organizations of, 129–31;
and gender, 170–71, 185, 211–12; and
European national identities, 211–14
—associations of: Ellwangen's Historical
and Archaeological Association, 102;
Bund für Heimatschutz in Württemberg
und Hohenzollern (League for Heimat
Protection in Württemberg and Hohenzollern), 103, 105–7, 114–15, 126, 129, 160,
162, 164–65, 193; Regional Committee
for Nature Conservation and Heimat
Protection (Landesausschuss für Natur
und Heimatschutz), 103, 106, 121;
Archaeological Association of Germany
(Deutscher Altertumsverein), 104;
Archaeological Association of Württemberg (Württembergischer Altertumsverein), 104; Society for Ancient Ger-
man History (Gesellschaft für ältere
deutsche Geschichtskunde), 104, 150;
Swabian Jura Association (Schwäbischer
Albverein), 111; Black Forest Association
of Württemberg (Württembergischer
Schwarzwaldverein), 111, 129; Teachers
Association for Natural Science in
Württemberg (Lehrerverein für Natur-
kunde in Württemberg), 112; Associa-
tion for the Preservation of Popular
Folk Costume (Verein zur Erhaltung
der Volkstrachten), 115; Württemberg
Folklore Association (Württemberg
Vereinigung für Volkskunde), 115–16;
German Association for Agrarian Wel-
fare and Heimat Care (Deutscher Verein
für ländliche Wohlfahrts- und Heimat-
pflege), 122, 162; Deutscher Bund
Heimatschutz (German League for
Heimat Protection), 126, 129–32, 136, 138,
153, 163, 188, 212–13; Pfälzerwald Verein
(Palatinate Forest Association), 133;
Schwabmünchen Historical Association,

147; Association for Agrarian Welfare in Württemberg and Hohenzollern (Verein für ländliche Wohlfahrtspflege in Württemberg und Hohenzollern), 162–63, 183
— and modernity: 131–32, 188, 212; in Heimat history, 103; in Heimat nature, 112–15; in Heimat ethnography, 118–19; attitudes toward, 120–24; in Heimat museums, 135–37, 149–50; and perceptions of the past, 156–57; in Heimat images, 177–79, 182–84

Heimatkunde, 106

Heimatkunst, 122

Heimat museums: proliferation of, 134; interpretations of, 135–37; and representation of everyday life, 137, 140–41, 148–49; social origins of, 138–39; and local identity, 139; conception of the past in, 140–44; and representation of origins, 141–44, 148–49; meaning of, 144–48; and representation of the nation, 145–48; and tradition of historical museums, 150–51; and social trends, 151–53. *See also* Heimat idea; Museums

Herborn, 139

Hermann the Cheruskian, 148, 155

Herrenalb, 105

Herrenberg, 181, 205

Hesse, Hermann, 28, 40, 121

Hessen-Nassau, 130

Heuss, Theodor, 163

Historikerstreit, 11

Hobsbawm, Eric, 3, 13, 50

Hoheneck, 49

Hohenstaufen, 17, 49, 65, 67

Hohlwein, Ludwig, 166

Hölder, Julius, 20, 39, 54, 109

Hölderlin, Friedrich, 17

Holocaust memory, 11

Holstein, 140

Huizinga, Johan, 215

Hungary, 104

Hunt, Lynn, 84

Isny, 43–44

Italy, 14–15, 211, 213

Jahn, Friedrich Ludwig (Father Jahn), 65

Jena, battle of, 47

Jever, 147

Jünger, Ernst, 185

Kammen, Michael, 10

Karasek, Erika, 134–36

Karl I (king of Württemberg), 17, 21, 57, 66, 76, 78

Karl the Great (Charlemagne), 64

Karlsruhe, 32

Kaufbeuren, 140

Ketteler (bishop), 75, 82

Kirchheim unter Teck, 36, 38, 74, 103–4, 111, 113, 149

Kittler, Gustav, 90

Kohn, Hans, 5

Königgrätz, battle of, 66, 177

Krumbach, 145

Kulturkampf, 35–36, 81, 86, 88, 91. *See also* Sedan Day; Württemberg

Lake Constance, 16, 108

Landespartei, 22, 56, 91. *See also* Sedan Day

Langenau, 27

Leer, 139

Leipzig, 30

Leonberg, 111, 164

Liberals: confident after 1871, 34–36, 52–54; originate Sedan Day, 34–37, 50; political influence in Württemberg, 54–55; appropriate Sedan Day, 58–60, 79; perceptions of localness and nationhood, 70–72; anti-Catholic sentiments in Sedan Day, 75–77; and failure of Sedan Day, 79–80, 83–91, 186–87; political culture of, 80–84, 86–88; and national symbols, 84–86. *See also* Bourgeoisie; Past, representations of; Sedan Day

Lippe, 130

List, Friedrich, 17

Lorraine, Claude, 177

Lower Saxony, 130–32, 148

Lübeck, 141, 144, 149

Ludwig I (king of Bavaria), 151

Ludwigsburg, 105, 111

Lutz, Karl Gottlob, 112

Mainz, 75, 146, 151

Marbach, 43, 111

17, 57–58, 77–78, 86, 88–89; and 1871 unification, 20–23; and *Kulturkampf*, 22,
56, 75–77; local politics and Sedan Day,
52–58; 1890s political changes, 88–90.
See also Heimat idea; Sedan Day

Württemberg Folklore Association (Württemberg Vereinigung für Volkskunde),
115–16

Zollverein, 5, 20